I HAVE NOT YET BEGUN TO FIGHT

I Have Not Yet Begun to Fight

A Life of
John Paul Jones

James Mackay

MAINSTREAM
PUBLISHING

EDINBURGH AND LONDON

For Norma and John

First published in 1998 by
MAINSTREAM PUBLISHING COMPANY (EDINBURGH) LTD
7 Albany Street
Edinburgh EH1 3UG

ISBN 1 84018 057 9

A catalogue record for this book is available from the British Library

Typeset in Monotype Perpetua
Printed and bound in Great Britain by Butler & Tanner Ltd

Contents

Map 1 – The Coast of Britain

Map 2 – The Second Battle of the Liman, 1788

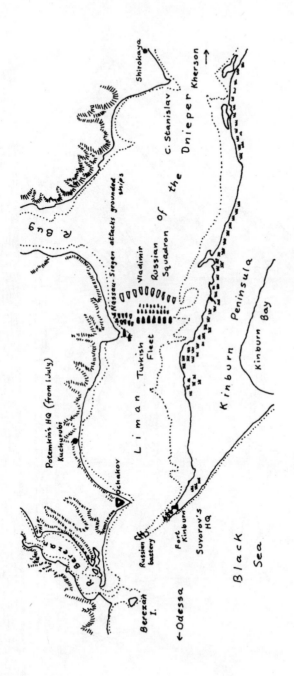

Diagram of Frigate

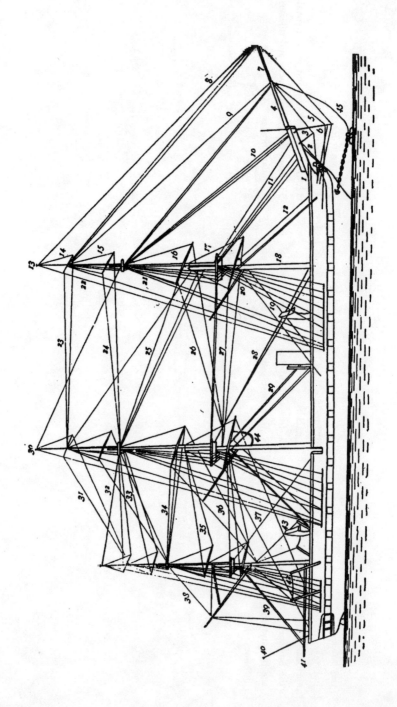

The spars and rigging of a frigate

1. the bowsprit
2. bobstays, three pairs
3. sprit-sail-gaffs, projecting on each side of the bowsprit – the ropes at the extremities are jib-guys and flying-jib-guys
4. jib-boom
5. martingale-stay and below it the flying-jib-martingale
6. back-ropes
7. flying-jib-boom
8. fore-royal-stay, flying-jib-stay and halyards
9. fore-top-gallant-stay, jib-stay and halyards
10. two fore-top-mast-stays and fore-top-mast stay-sail halyards
11. the fore-top-bowlines, stopped into the top and two fore-stays
12. two fore-tacks
13. fore-truck
14. fore-royal-mast, yard and lift
15. top-gallant-mast, yard and lift
16. fore-top-mast, top-sail-yard, lift and reef-tackle
17. fore-top, fore-lift and top-sail sheet
18. fore-mast and fore-shrouds, nine pairs
19. fore-sheets
20. fore-gaff
21. fore-top-mast back-stays and top-sail-tye
22. royal and top-gallant back-stays
23. fore-royal-braces and main-royal-stay
24. fore-top-gallant-braces and main-top-gallant-stay
25. standing parts or fore-top-sail-braces and main-top-mast-stays
26. hauling parts of fore-top-sail-braces and main-top-bowlines
27. four parts of fore-braces
28. main-stays
29. main-tacks
30. main-truck
31. main-royal-braces
32. mizzen-royal-stay and mizzen-royal-braces
33. main-top-gallant-braces and mizzen-top-gallant-braces
34. standing parts of main-top-sail-braces and mizzen-top-mast-stay
35. mizzen-top-sail-braces
36. hauling parts of main-top-sail-braces and mizzen-top-bowlines and cross-jack-braces
37. main-braces and mizzen-stay
38. standing part of peak halyards
39. vangs, similar on each gaff
40. ensign staff
41. spanker-boom
42. quarter-boats davits
43. one of the davit topping-lifts and wind-sail
44. main-yard-tackle
45. a bull-rope

Introduction

My late father was a sailor *manqué* whose opportunity to get away to sea finally came in 1939 when, on the outbreak of the Second World War, he joined the Royal Naval Volunteer Reserve as an engineer officer. Seven years and seven seas later he returned home with a chestful of medals and never went near the sea again. Steeped in the traditions of the Clan Mackay, however, he was inordinately proud of the fact that septs (branches) of the clan, the Pauls and the Nelsons, had produced the world's two greatest seamen. I have always been extremely dubious regarding my father's extravagant claims concerning the English admiral, but in the case of the subject of this biography he may well have been on surer ground, for the Pauls probably migrated from Sutherland to Fife, and thence to Edinburgh where the father of John Paul Jones was born in 1700.

Certainly there were many parallels in the lives of the men who are widely regarded as the fathers of the modern Royal and United States navies. Nelson was nine years younger than Jones but their careers overlapped, and Nelson may well have been one of the young Royal Navy officers with whom Jones consorted in the West Indies before moving to Virginia. Both had their own ships by the age of twenty-one and both had achieved immortality by their early thirties. Both were small of stature but possessed of immense charisma and extraordinary powers of leadership.

In one respect they differed: Jones never had the opportunity to develop, far less demonstrate, his genius as a strategist, but as a naval tactician he was without peer, defeating swifter and more powerful opponents by a combination of superior seamanship, skill, daring and the ability to turn every opportunity to his own advantage.

Like Nelson, Jones has been the subject of endless speculation, controversy and romance. A legend in his own lifetime, he was the subject of numerous popular ballads and over forty chapbooks. Later on, such eminent writers as Alexandre Dumas, Herman Melville, Fenimore Cooper, Thomas Carlyle, Rudyard Kipling and William

Makepeace Thackeray based novels, plays and poems on his life and exploits. One of Benjamin Disraeli's earliest literary efforts was a life of Jones, while Franklin Delano Roosevelt began writing a biography, but shelved the project when he became President of the United States. Jones has been the object of uncritical hagiography and the victim of denigration and character assassination. It is also regrettable that a two-volume biography published in 1900 is almost entirely a work of fiction. This has not only muddied the water but, as the basis of a popular film of the 1950s, has perpetuated many myths and distortions of the truth.

From the cradle to the grave and even beyond, the life of John Paul Jones (1747–92) was beset with mystery. From the rumours of illegitimacy and speculation as to his true parentage, to the search for his coffin more than a century after his death, the story of the gardener's son who became the founder of the United States Navy is an epic of spectacular exploits and outstanding achievements punctuated by disappointments and disasters that would have crushed a lesser man. Twice accused of murder and once of raping a minor, he was pilloried by the British press as a pirate; yet he was also lionised by Louis XVI of France and Catherine the Great.

The man of action, whose bravery and skills of seamanship earned him a knighthood and a sword of honour from the French and a unique gold medal from Congress, was at the same time the most literate of America's sea captains, a one-time Shakespearean actor and a poet of considerable merit. He was also a notorious lothario who changed partners so often that the British, whom he defeated at sea, took their revenge by naming a dance in derisive allusion to his womanising.

Of all the exploits of this outstanding figure of the naval campaign in the American Revolution, none surpassed his encounter off Flamborough Head with HMS *Serapis*, a larger, faster and much more powerfully armed ship than his own, an action which has been likened to a light cruiser taking on a battleship in the Second World War. The story of how Jones, by sheer guts, indomitable will and a refusal to admit the possibility of defeat, emerged victorious from the most desperate circumstances, has been an inspiration to sailors everywhere; and none more so than in the United States Navy itself, in the dark days that followed Pearl Harbor, when the immortal words of that dour little Scotsman – 'I have not yet begun to fight' – were in the mind of every American seaman.

This is the first major biography of John Paul Jones in forty years.

If it missed the 250th anniversary of John Paul's birth, in July 1997, it is, I hope, a fitting tribute to the United States Navy which celebrates its bicentenary in 1998. Jones, of course, did not live to see the great navy of which he dreamed and for which he campaigned so indefatigably. The United States Navy dates its birth to the launching of the USS *Constitution* – 'Old Ironsides' which, four times reconstructed, is the oldest ship in commission and occupying a position in the American Navy comparable to HMS *Victory*, Nelson's flagship, in the Royal Navy. The forerunners of the United States Navy, Washington's Army's Navy of 1775–76, the Continental Navy of Esek Hopkins and the later ships of the American Revolution, were to a large extent makeshifts, paid off and decommissioned as soon as hostilities ended. Congress, strapped for cash, turned a deaf ear to the entreaties of Jones to the necessity of maintaining a permanent navy. Two years after Jones's untimely death in 1792, Congress belatedly took action and authorised the construction of two frigates which were launched in 1797 and commissioned a year later, in nice time to do battle with the Napoleonic privateers which were playing havoc with American shipping. A few years later, the infant navy finally brought an end to the Barbary pirates, the scourge of Atlantic and Mediterranean mercantile traffic, and a project that had been very dear to Jones's heart.

Alone of the captains of the Revolutionary War period, Jones was far-sighted enough to advocate the systematic training of naval officers, though it was not until sixty years after his death that his dream was realised in the establishment of the Naval Academy at Annapolis. It is particularly fitting that the mortal remains of John Paul Jones should be interred in the crypt of the chapel at the Naval Academy.

During the period 1972–90 when I lived in and around Dumfries, I was introduced quite forcibly to the memory of John Paul Jones by the late James Urquhart who enlisted my help, such as it was, in his campaign to do justice to the memory of a local hero whom he regarded quite rightly as a bonnie fechter for freedom. On one memorable occasion Jimmy introduced me to Rear-Admiral Samuel Eliot Morison USN, whose biography of Jones (published in 1958) had come too late to prevent Warner Brothers from perpetrating a cinematic travesty, released the following year with Robert Stack playing the title role. The old sea-dog's pithy comments on this silly biopic are, alas, not suitable for reproduction.

Jimmy Urquhart, in his capacity as a local historian and a district councillor, cherished the ambition to see the cottage in which John Paul had been born restored and opened to the public as a museum to the great seaman. As long ago as 1831 Lieutenant A.B. Pinckham USN visited Arbigland and was shocked to find the gardener's cottage in which Jones had been born in a semi-derelict condition. Pinckham left a sum of money for the reroofing of the cottage and his generosity was rewarded by Jones's niece, Janette Taylor, who presented him with the Lowendahl miniature of her celebrated uncle. This miniature, one of the few authentic likenesses of Jones, is now in the National Portrait Gallery at the Smithsonian Institution, Washington, DC. Pinckham's timely intervention merely saved the cottage from total destruction, and a century and a half would elapse before his dream of an international shrine to one of the world's greatest seamen was realised.

This, I might add, was a campaign waged over many years, which became for Jimmy Urquhart something of a personal crusade, with many a setback that would have daunted a less persistent man. I must also pay tribute to Captain J.B. Blackett of Arbigland who unstintingly backed Urquhart in his dream and was instrumental in converting the cottage, then being used as a farmworker's dwelling, into the museum it has since become. Sadly, Rear-Admiral Morison died in May 1976 before permission for the renovation and conversion of the cottage was granted. The celebrations (on both sides of the Atlantic) of the bicentenary of American Independence in that year, however, stimulated renewed interest in the restoration project, and it was largely due to Jimmy's efforts that J. William Middendorf II, then Secretary of the United States Navy, paid a visit to Arbigland. The realisation of the museum project was almost as protracted as Urquhart's ambition to produce a book about John Paul Jones; in gestation in the early 1970s (as long as I had known him, in fact), it was not eventually published till 1982, and its production, at the printing works of the *Dumfries and Galloway Standard*, was almost as complex and as protracted as the plans for the museum itself.

Unlike that other local hero, Robert Burns, John Paul Jones left no direct descendants that we know of (the claims of a William Paul who died at Annan in 1844 to have been a son of Jones were fraudulent). Conversely, while no relatives of the Scottish national poet are now to be found in or around Dumfries, the descendants of Jones's sister Mary Ann continue to reside in the district. Jane Young, daughter of Mary Ann by her first husband Robert Young, married David Williamson who gained dubious immortality as that 'rascally haberdasher' whom Robert Burns on his deathbed imagined was about to have him thrown into a debtors' prison. With money inherited from her uncle, Jane Young established the Commercial Hotel (later the County Hotel), demolished in the 1970s to make way for Marks and Spencer's department store in the High Street. By Mary Ann's second marriage, to Mark Lowden, were descended the families of Louden or Lowden and Richardson who generously donated the heirlooms and relics of their illustrious ancestor to the birthplace museum. In particular I should like to single out the late Commander Louden Richardson RNR, great-great-great-grand-nephew of John Paul Jones, whose family continue to reside in Maxwelltown, Dumfries.

As we were going to press, my good friend Hamish MacLeod drew my attention to a number of references in books about the Isle of Skye concerning the repulse of John Paul Jones off Dunvegan in August 1779 by a funeral party which he mistook for a military force. I first heard this tale forty years ago and it has lost nothing in the telling. Sadly there is not a word of truth in it, the log of the *Bonhomme Richard* indicating that the ship sailed northwards well to the west of the Outer Hebrides, via St Kilda and the Flannan Isles. As it is probable that the ship was observed by the St Kildans, they would have reported it to the factor of MacLeod of MacLeod (who owned the island), and thus the sighting was transposed to Skye itself and has since become so deeply entrenched in MacLeod folklore that I am almost ashamed to debunk it.

I should like to thank my old friends, the journalist Frank Ryan and David Lockwood of Dumfries Museum, as well as the staff of the Kirkcudbright Museum and the trustees and curator of the Birthplace Museum. Farther afield, Anne Cook, Barbara Robinson and Sue Palmer of The Beacon, White-haven, were most helpful in my researches in that seaport with which Jones had so many connections. I am also grateful to the staff of the Naval Academy Museum and Library, Annapolis; the Library of Congress, Washington; the American Philosophical Society, Philadelphia; the National Archives, Paris; the Mitchell Library and University Library, Glasgow; and the British Library and the Public Record Office, London.

James Mackay
Glasgow
November 1997

1. Arbigland

1747–61

. . . the noblest prospect which a Scotchman ever sees, is
the high road that leads him to England!
— SAMUEL JOHNSON, IN BOSWELL'S *Life*, 6 JULY 1763

Kirkbean, the most easterly parish in the Stewartry of Kirkcudbright,
is bounded on the east by the estuary of the Nith and on the south
by the Solway Firth. It is a district of rolling hills and fertile plains;
its southerly aspect and the warm waters of the North Atlantic Drift,
a branch of the Gulf Stream, ensure a mild, equable climate. Not far
from Southerness, the low-lying promontory that juts into the firth,
lies the estate of Arbigland. To the north rears the impressive granite
hill known as Criffel from whose summit, on a clear day, one can
get a glimpse of five kingdoms – Scotland, England, Ireland, Man
and the kingdom of God (the heavens above). Even at ground level,
the view from Arbigland to the south is a panorama of the Cumbrian
coast beyond the expanse of the Solway, to the bustling ports of
Maryport, Workington and Whitehaven. The landscape behind
Arbigland, on the other hand, is characterised by a patchwork quilt
of fields and dense woodland. To a small boy growing up in a
cottage no more than four hundred yards from the beach, the sea
with its ever-changing moods would be the chief attraction.

To this quiet backwater, thirteen miles from Dumfries, the nearest
town of any consequence, came John Paul in the early 1730s. He
had been born at Leith, the port of Edinburgh, thirty years earlier,
his father William having migrated from Fife a few years previously.
John Paul trained as a gardener and, like William Burnes (the father
of the future national poet Robert Burns), he was employed in the
landscaping of Edinburgh when that city began to escape from the
confines of the castle hill and expand towards the south. Like Burnes
a few years later, Paul had the good fortune to make the acquaintance of a landed gentleman who was beginning to take an interest
in the newfangled notions of estate management and agricultural

improvement. William Craik's family had held land in the Stewartry for two generations, his grandfather having purchased Arbigland from the Earl of Selkirk in 1690. In the 1730s Craik began the development of Arbigland, in particular laying out its gardens which remain a showpiece to this day. In this project he was ably assisted by John Paul. The erection of the twelve-foot stone wall enclosing the garden was accomplished in 1745, at about the time that the Young Pretender's army was briefly occupying Dumfries.

As head gardener on the estate, John Paul was given the use of a single-storey cottage with adjoining outbuildings, about a quarter of a mile west of the big house. The cottage was sturdily built of local stone and consisted of three rooms with a flagstone floor. By the standards of the time it was quite commodious and would eventually house a family of seven: the parents slept in a box-bed in one room, the three girls in another and the two boys occupied the loft, to which access was gained by means of a step-ladder. The house was thatched, but it had several windows with small panes of glass. Thither John Paul brought his bride Jean Duff, formerly housekeeper to Mr Craik. She was the daughter of John Duff, a small tenant-farmer from New Abbey, six miles north of Arbigland.[1] Every writer on the subject of John Paul Jones, right down to the present time, has rendered her maiden surname as McDuff or MacDuff; and several have gone so far as to make much of the Highland blood that ran in the veins of the future naval hero. Robert Sands, who edited the Janette Taylor Collection of Jones papers, published at New York in 1830, commented that 'The MacDuffs were a respectable rural race in their own district; and some of them had been small landed proprietors in the Parish of Kirkbean for an immemorial period'; Edward Hamilton, author of a biography of Jones published at Aberdeen, went further and asserted that Jeanne MacDuff [sic] was the daughter of Ian MacDuff, a gunsmith who had migrated from Inveraray in Argyll to Dumfries in search of a wider market for his skills. 'Jeanne was a little girl when her father descended to the Lowlands; but she was born a Hieland lassie', and he added the claptrap, 'Little John Paul was clearly his mother's boy; at heart a Hielander!' From this nonsense Augustus C. Buell concocted a fanciful farago of his own:

> Apart from any such racial predilection, it is not to be denied
> that there were qualities in the character of Paul Jones and
> instincts exhibited in his career that bespoke the fierce blood

of the Gael rather than the placid strain of the Briton. The suddenness of temper, the swiftness of hand that he restrained with difficulty – if at all; the exultant valor, the scorn of peril, and the deathless grit that made him the conqueror where others might have succumbed, were perhaps the heritage, not of the peaceful farmer and fisher folk from whom his father sprung, but of his mother's ferocious ancestors in the Grampian Hills. It might be an interesting study in comparative ethnology to trace the savage instinct of foray that mastered him more than once, back to those 'plaided clans'.[2]

The plain fact is that Duff is an ancient but very common name throughout Dumfries and Galloway, and while undoubtedly Celtic in origin (from *dubh*, 'black' or 'dark'), it is entirely Gallovidian and not Highland in any sense at all. The Gallovidians were primarily of ancient British or Cymric stock, ethnically similar to the inhabitants of Cumbria across the Solway and the people of Wales; but they also contained elements of the Scots from Ulster and Dalriada as well as the Saxons and the Danes.

John Paul and Jean Duff were married on 29 November 1733 and some time early in 1735 their elder son William, named after his father's father, was born. Strangely enough, there is no record of his baptism in the Kirkbean parish registers. Janet was christened on 22 April 1739 and then Mary Ann on 8 March 1741. The youngest daughter Jean was christened on 28 April 1749. As these were the only children of John and Jean Paul to be recorded in the parish registers, details of the remaining offspring are derived solely from oral tradition. Between Mary Ann and Jean apparently came two children, sex unknown, who died in infancy; Augustus Buell is the highly unreliable source of the story that their names were Robert and Adam (in real life the names of the architect who redesigned Arbigland in 1755, though Buell did not make this connection). Then came John, who would later add Jones to his surname and whose birth is invariably given as 6 July 1747. William emigrated to Virginia as a young man and became a tailor at Fredericksburg where he died in 1774. Janet wed a local shopkeeper named William Taylor and died in 1817, while Jean never married. Mary Ann married Robert Young, a sailor from Whitehaven; after his death she married Mark Lowden in March 1777 and with him emigrated to Charleston, South Carolina. It is from the Young and Lowden offspring of Mary Ann Paul (who died in 1825) that the present-day kinfolk of John Paul Jones are descended.[3]

Perhaps the fact that the birth of baby John in 1747 was not recorded gave rise to the canard that the future sailor was illegitimate. Certainly such tales were commonplace in the early nineteenth century, when his fame was assured but he himself was not around to refute them. In rebutting these assertions we can only examine the known facts.

The myth that John Paul was, in fact, the illegitimate son of the Earl of Selkirk gained credence in the 1820s[4] and was most fully developed in Mrs Reginald De Koven's biography, published in 1913. As the octogenarian Third Earl died in 1744, three years before John Paul was born, Mrs De Koven asserted that the boy must have been born several years earlier, and that he spent his early boyhood at the Earl's residence, St Mary's Isle, on the outskirts of Kirkcudbright, where his uncle George Paul was head gardener. There was, indeed, a gardener named George Paul at Kirkcudbright (dead by October 1753), but he was no relation to John Paul of Arbigland and he was never employed by the Earl of Selkirk. The Fourth Earl of Selkirk, whom John Paul Jones tried to kidnap in 1778, was great-nephew to the Third Earl and was living abroad when he inherited the title and estate, and did not settle at St Mary's Isle till 1748. Significantly, in all the correspondence arising out of the Jones raid on St Mary's Isle, it was stated that the perpetrator was the son of the gardener at Arbigland whom the Selkirk family had never heard of prior to the raid. John Paul Jones himself, when asked if he were under any obligations to Lord Selkirk, replied quite categorically, 'I never had any obligation to Lord Selkirk, except for his good opinion, nor does he know me or mine, except by *character*.'[5]

The alternative allegation, that John was an illegitimate son of William Craik, is more plausible but equally untrue. Credence was lent to this by the fact that Craik had a bastard son named James, born in 1730. But he freely acknowledged this boy, who bore his surname and was raised by him at Arbigland. In due course, James Craik trained in medicine and emigrated to America where he became personal physician to George Washington and first Surgeon-General of the United States.[6] Jean Duff was already housekeeper to William Craik when John Paul senior was installed as head gardener. She married John Paul only three days after her employer married a neighbouring lady, Elizabeth Stewart of Shambellie, a circumstance which was later somehow regarded as proof that Miss Duff had been Craik's mistress. That may well have been the case – it would not have been the first time that the master of the house made free with his female staff – but it would be highly improbable that Mrs Paul would continue to bestow such favours on the laird years after she had quit his service. Other myths named the Duke of Queensberry as the father of John Paul. Apart from the fact that 'Old Q' (as the Third Duke was commonly known) never married but sired many a bastard, there is nothing whatsoever to connect him with the subject of this biography. In any event, the Duke would only have been seventeen at the time John Paul was born. If the Third Earl of Selkirk were too old, then the Third Duke of Queensberry was probably far too young to fit the role.

On the other hand, John was a dutiful son and it was he, rather than his elder brother or any of his sisters, who saw to it that his father had a decent burial, and erected the red sandstone slab over his grave which recorded it as the last resting place of 'John Paul senior who died at Arbigland the 24 October 1767 Universally Esteemed'. At the foot of the tombstone he added, 'Erected by John Paul junior'. The only anecdote concerning father and son illustrates the pawky humour of the elder Paul. The architect Robert Adam, who supervised the erection of Craik's new mansion-house in 1755, had a passion for symmetry which infected his client so much so that Craik decided to have not one, but two, summer-houses in the garden, much to his head-gardener's annoyance, in order to preserve this symmetry. John Paul got his own back one day when he caught a man scrumping apples from the orchard and locked him in one of the summer-houses. He then clapped John Paul junior into the other and sent for Mr Craik. The laird, astonished at the sight of wee John's anxious face at the window, enquired what he was doing there, whereupon the gardener, with a straight face, informed him, 'I just put him there for the sake of symmetry!'

Details of young John's early life are very scanty, and mostly the stuff with which the writers of chapbooks fleshed out their narrative. The oft-repeated tale of the little commodore on the cliff-top mar-shalling his school-fellows in rowing-boats as they engaged in a mock battle under his command smacks of hindsight. James Craik, how-ever, later recalled that John loved to tramp across the fields to Carsethorn. Today, it is a sleepy little hamlet on the Nith estuary, but at one time it was an important harbour in the Solway coastal trade and even vessels bound for the American colonies put in there.

It is likely, therefore, that the boy had his imagination fired by tales of America and the Indies from the sailors he encountered there. Such formal education as he had, he obtained at the parish school conducted by the minister, the Revd James Hogg, a graduate of King's College, Aberdeen, and respected as an old-fashioned parish dominie. Evidently John was well schooled in the rudiments. His handwriting was neat and his voluminous correspondence, reports and journals indicate a good grasp of grammar (if not spelling) as well as a literary turn of mind, developed by voracious reading. The parish school was attended not only by the sons and daughters of farmers and fisher-folk but the children of the country lairds. At a slightly later period Robert Burns would describe just such a school in Ayrshire where youngsters of different classes and social backgrounds mixed freely:

> I formed many connections with other Youngkers who possessed superiour advantages; the youngling Actors who were busy with the rehearsal of PARTS in which they were shortly to appear on that STAGE where, Alas! I was destined to druge behind the SCENES. It is not commonly at these green years that the young Noblesse and gentry have a just sense of the immense distance between them and their ragged Playfellows. It takes a few dashes into the world to give the young Great man that proper, decent, unnoticing disregard for the poor, insignificant, stupid devils, the mechanics and peasantry around him; who were perhaps born in the same village.[7]

Burns went on to add, however, that 'My young Superiours never insulted the clouterly appearance of my ploughboy carcase'; and young Paul in his hand-me-down homespuns, going barefoot most of the year, would probably have had nothing to complain about on that score either. And just as the young Burns admits that his 'young Superiours' often lent him books to feed his appetite for literature, so also we may imagine that young Paul benefited in many ways from close contact with the sons of the gentry at an early age. In later life John Paul Jones was an acute observer of men and manners, a habit he probably acquired in his youth. Young John was often employed of an evening up at the Big House when the Craiks were entertaining neighbours and visitors. He would lurk in the pantry and eavesdrop on the conversation of the great ones as they pushed the port round the table, and he would be on hand to help them as they tipsily mounted their horses to ride home in the wee small hours.

As well as imbibing a great deal of knowledge on a wide range of topics, he would have aped the manners and speech of his social superiors; certainly by the time he went to sea the rough Solway dialect had been eliminated, leaving only the slightest inflection to betray his Scottish origins. In playground fisticuffs he would have held his own against the school bully and shown those qualities of leadership and courage that were so outstanding throughout his turbulent career. At school he proved to be proficient in mathematics. Dominie Hogg would have started the brighter boys on Latin, to prepare them for possible admission to one of the universities. John Paul, however, was even then studying French, a language in which he would become fluent. Later he would also acquire a reasonable command of Spanish and even a smattering of Russian.

In making the most of his opportunities, John Paul was not unique. The parish school system ensured that Scotland not only had the most literate peasantry of any country but also that those who had ability could win a bursary that would take them to the universities of St Andrews, Glasgow, Edinburgh or Aberdeen. If they survived the rigours of the three-year course and graduated, they could become a teacher, minister or physician, or obtain a senior post in the rapidly expanding civil service. Many able boys instead chose to enter the armed forces or the service of the Honourable East India Company or the Hudson's Bay Company. A very high proportion of the soldiers and administrators of the developing British Empire were just such young Scots.

Still others chose the sea. The chapbooks contain many unsubstantiated anecdotes about John Paul's early seafaring days. Ignoring the preposterous suggestion made by some biographers that his father was a fisherman whose second son accompanied him from an early age, there is probably some substance in the notion that, in the school holidays at any rate, he would learn how to handle a sailing dinghy. Buell devotes an entire page to an apocryphal tale of a visit to Arbigland in the summer of 1759 of James Younger, a native of Caerlaverock on the Dumfriesshire side of the Nith, who was by that time a prosperous shipowner at Whitehaven. Prospecting for seamen to crew his ships, he notes a small fishing yawl beating up the firth against a stiff north-east squall to gain the shelter of the small tidal creek forming the boat-harbour of the hamlet. Younger doubts that the boat will make it, but he is proved wrong when the vessel is skilfully brought to the landing-place. At this point he realises that the crew consists of an old man trimming the boat by sitting on the weather-rail, while the boy steers, handles the sheets and gives commands. Among those watching the performance is old John Paul, unperturbed by the situation. 'That is my boy John conning the boat, Mr Younger. He will fetch her in. This isn't much of a squall for him!'[8]

It makes a colourful story, but it seems to be one of the many figments of Buell's fertile imagination. Buell has Younger signing up the boy as an apprentice on the spot. The truth is more prosaic. When John was twelve Britain was at the zenith of her naval might. The Seven Years' War (1756–63) was raging, but the turning point in that long struggle between Britain and France came in 1759 when Wolfe decisively defeated the French on the Heights of Abraham and Clive won a major victory at Plassey, ensuring that Canada and India would henceforward be British rather than French. These great victories, so far from the homeland, were only made possible by the Royal Navy. It was John's ambition to enter the Senior Service as a midshipman, but such a course required both money and connections. The Pauls had neither, so the next best thing was for the boy to enter the merchant navy.

At the age of thirteen John closed his schoolbooks and took the first step on his career. Someone as bright and self-possessed as young John Paul was must have stood out in a little community such as Kirkbean. Certainly, as the son of his head-gardener, the boy must have come to the notice of William Craik and it would not be surprising that that gentleman should take some interest in his advancement. The biographer Robert Sands, quoting from a letter in the Taylor Collection, says that John assured the laird, 'I shall take no step whatever without your knowledge and approbation'.[9] William Craik secured an introduction to John (not James) Younger who had a berth on one of his trading vessels for a stout lad.

There are neither portraits nor eye-witness accounts of John Paul's appearance in boyhood; but from portrait miniatures and locks of hair preserved in adulthood we may form an impression of a wiry youngster with reddish sandy hair, a freckled complexion, piercing hazel eyes and an aquiline nose which gave him a sharp, inquisitive look. He was small for his age, with small hands and feet. Even when fully grown he was slight of build and no more than five foot four inches tall. What he lacked in stature, however, he would make up for in his commanding presence. Indeed, it would be fair to say that his overweening self-confidence and a tendency towards arrogance in later life probably stemmed from the need to compensate for his lack of height. The best of his portraits was that painted by Charles Willson Peale at Philadelphia and this definitely shows him with light-brown hair and a fair complexion, contrary to the posthumous description in the penny chapbooks in which he was invariably described as swarthy, for no other reason than that pirates were supposed to be swarthy.

It was early in 1761 (not late 1759 as stated by his early biographers) that John, still not fourteen years of age, packed a sea chest, took a fond farewell of his parents and sisters and a handshake from William Craik, and trudged across to Carsethorn where he boarded the coastal sloop bound for Whitehaven, a seaport that would one day acquire immense significance in one of his naval exploits.

2. Ship's Boy to Sailing Master
1761–73

They that go down to the sea in ships: and occupy their
business in great waters.
— PSALM CVII, 23

Compared with Carsethorn, Whitehaven, twenty-five miles due
south, was a veritable metropolis. With the development of the
trade to and from the West Indies and the American colonies, it had
been transformed in a single generation from a small fishing port into
a mighty trading centre, the equal of Bristol, Liverpool and Glasgow
in the volume of shipping it handled each year. John Younger was
not only one of the most prominent merchants in the American trade
but also a member of the Board of Trustees of the Town and
Harbour. John Paul junior signed articles of apprenticeship, binding
him to serve Younger for seven years. He would receive a pittance,
but would gain invaluable experience in seamanship. On 5 April
1761 John embarked as ship's boy on the brig *Friendship* of 179 tons,
Robert Benson master, outward bound to Barbados and Virginia.[1]
　　The brig carried a crew of twenty-eight and was well armed with
eighteen guns, a match for French privateers. The voyage was
leisurely but uneventful and no French warships were encountered.
The ship called at Barbados and loaded 270 hogsheads of rum and
189 barrels of sugar, this cargo being entered at the customs office
of Hampton, Virginia, on 7 May. From there the *Friendship* sailed up
Chesapeake Bay and the Rappahannock River where, in the bustling
port of Fredericksburg, John was reunited with his brother William
whom he had not seen for several years. The elder Paul was by that
time well established as a tailor and gentlemen's outfitter in the
town. He was in his mid-twenties, unmarried and in a fair way of
business, but a far cry from the picture painted by Buell who created
the myth of 'William Paul Jones, then a man of thirty, married, and
managing the plantation, flour mill and trade of his adopted father,
William Jones'.[2] Furthermore, asserted Buell, 'the old Scottish-

American planter took a great fancy to little John Paul, and wished to adopt him also, offering to get him released from his indentures to Mr Younger'. To be sure, there *was* a William Jones, who figures spuriously in a much later episode, but that Jones lived in North Carolina, not Virginia.

John Paul did not record his first impressions of America, but later in life he would declare that it was 'my favorite country from the age of thirteen when I first saw it'.[3] In the early 1760s Virginia was still very much a frontier territory; civilisation did not extend far from the coastal towns, and the hinterland, inhabited by savage Indians, was still little explored or developed. But there was a vibrancy and pioneer spirit about Fredericksburg and Williamsburg that had a heady effect on an impetuous, adventurous youth like John.

The *Friendship* made annual trips between Whitehaven and Virginia via Barbados for three further years. She cleared the Rappahannock for Whitehaven on 7 August 1761 with 424 hogsheads of tobacco, 28 tons of pig iron and several thousand barrel staves. By late September she was back in her home port where she would be laid up for the winter. Young Paul spent the autumn and winter at Arbigland, doubtless regaling his family and friends with stories of his voyages and tales of Virginia. In the spring of 1762 he returned to Whitehaven and boarded the *Friendship* which entered the Rappahannock on 8 July with 163 hogsheads of rum and 138 barrels of muscovado sugar from Barbados. On this and subsequent trips to Virginia, Captain Benson allowed his apprentice to stay with his brother in Fredericksburg. There is still extant a receipt for £23 0s 3d paid by William Fisher in respect of sixteen barrels of flour and a cask, dated 22 September 1762 and signed 'Jno. Paul'. Benson found that he had contracted for more return cargo than the brig could carry, and significantly it was to his fifteen-year-old apprentice that he entrusted the responsibility of selling the surplus and collecting the cash.

The *Friendship* did not clear from the Rappahannock for Whitehaven until 5 October that year, so John Paul spent almost three months in Virginia on that trip. On 6 August 1763 she was back in Virginian waters heavily laden with 100 tons of salt from the Turks Islands. The war with France was now at an end, and the brig no longer carried guns, but she was in great need of an overhaul and repairs so that it was not until 30 November that she weighed anchor for home. On this voyage the master was William Benson, son of

Robert, and her cargo comprised 406 hogsheads tobacco, 16 tons pig iron, 5,000 barrel staves, 200 feet of planking and 'two Caskes Snakeroot', the juice of the plant *Aristolochia serpentaria* which was used in cases of snakebite.

In the aftermath of war there was a glut of merchant shipping and trade was depressed. Some early biographers claim that Younger went bankrupt, but there is no record of this. It is more probable that he decided to retire from business and sold the brig to A. Bacon and Company who despatched her, under the same master but with a reduced crew, to Bordeaux in 1764. With Younger's retirement, however, John Paul was released from his articles of apprenticeship. It is likely that he was one of the crew laid off when the ship was sold to Bacon for he makes no mention of the voyage to Bordeaux. Instead, he went straight into the slave trade, signing on as third mate aboard the *King George*, a notorious blackbirder. Documentary evidence, provided by the payment of £40 'on account' to John Paul by Thomas Riche on 6 June 1764 in respect of slaves delivered in a West Indian port,[4] gives the lie to the persistent canard that, on leaving the brig *Friendship*, John Paul entered the Royal Navy.

According to the 'Letter of a Fellow Lodger', published in 1825, the story goes that the Duke of Queensberry, seeing little John running about St Mary's Isle as a Selkirk bastard (or one of his own numerous illegitimate progeny) patted him on the head and promised his patronage. The biographer Lincoln Lorenz gives credence to this story: 'Perhaps it was the good will of the Duke of Queensbury [sic] which led to his appointment as acting midshipman in the British Navy; possibly it was the influence of Mr Craik, Mr Younger or Captain Benson.'[5] By way of supporting this notion, Lorenz quotes John Paul Jones himself when he wrote of his 'intimacy with many officers of note in the British Navy'[6] or his assertion that, prior to the American Revolution, he 'had sailed in armed ships and frigates'.[7] At Whitehaven and other ports on both sides of the Atlantic he would have had ample opportunity to meet officers of the Royal Navy socially rather than professionally, and a statement about service aboard armed vessels was true enough, if a trifle exaggerated. Neither of these statements, however, was tantamount to a claim to have actually served in the Royal Navy. It should be noted that Robert Morris wrote to him on 5 February 1776, 'I cannot doubt your being acquainted with these things [naval matters], knowing as I do that you have been a commander in the West India trade'. Had Jones served in the Royal Navy Morris would surely have mentioned the fact in this letter.

More significantly, later in life, when he was seeking a command in the US Navy, Jones never mentioned service in the Royal Navy in any of his numerous letters to members of the Continental Congress, for this would undoubtedly have qualified him for higher rank. Jones was acutely aware of the fact that his rivals, Captains Biddle, Manley and Nicholson, had served in the Royal Navy. Nor is there any reference to Jones deserting the Senior Service, in the petition by the Royal Navy officers in the service of Catherine the Great who objected to his appointment in the Russian Navy. Samuel Morison makes the shrewd observation that, in view of Jones's character and ambition, it is improbable that if he had once got into the British Navy he would have left it.[8] Lorenz explains away John Paul's brief and unhappy service aboard a British man o' war by saying that he found that the British Navy was almost as autocratic as the French 'which required as a feudal tradition that an officer should inherit the blood of four generations of the nobility'.[9] In view of the number of British officers of flag rank who had risen from the lower deck this notion is quite ludicrous. Captain James Cook would have been promoted to rear-admiral had he lived, yet he had started his career aboard a Whitby collier. John Paul had the shining example of John Campbell, born at the manse of Kirkbean in 1719, who entered the Royal Navy as a ship's boy and rose to the rank of admiral. The eighteenth-century Royal Navy was a profession open to talent. While influence could assist promotion, the lack of it could not hold back a man of real ability. Horatio Nelson, the son of a country parson, had very little advantage over John Paul, the son of a country gardener.

The myth that John served for a period as a junior officer in the Royal Navy, however, is sometimes used in order to minimise the time he spent in the slave trade, several writers claiming, for example, that he gave it up after only one or two voyages. In fact, he served for two years aboard the *King George* before he was engaged as chief mate aboard the slaver *Two Friends* of Kingston, Jamaica. The records show that this 30-ton brig arrived at Kingston on 18 April 1767 under the command of James Woodhouse, that she was constructed at Philadelphia in 1763 and was British-owned. She had a crew of six officers and men and carried '77 Negros from Africa'.[10] The conditions aboard such a tiny vessel, barely fifty feet in length, must have been dreadful and one cannot help wondering how many unfortunate Africans perished *en route*. This brig cleared from Kingston for the windward coast of Africa on 13 June that year, with a cargo of rum and naval stores as well as an augmented crew. It is not known when she was next in Kingston, but on that occasion John Paul obtained his discharge, utterly repelled by 'that abominable trade' as he called it. The wonder is that he stuck it out as long as he did. It not only outraged his basic sense of humanity and common decency but offended his senses. The Negroes, forced to wallow in their own excrement between decks, created such a foul stench that other ships could detect a slaver many miles to windward.

On 30 July 1768 the 60-ton brig *John* of Liverpool, newly constructed at New York, entered Kingston from Cork, bringing pickled beef and Irish butter. In Harbour Street John Paul ran into her master and part-owner, Samuel McAdam, a well-known native of Kirkcudbright. McAdam offered his young fellow-countryman a free passage home, which was eagerly accepted. Paul had spent the intervening year in Jamaica. Nothing definite is known about those twelve months, though inevitably myth abhors a vacuum and there are numerous tales of the youthful opportunist engaging in smuggling and piracy, not one of which merits serious consideration.

More intriguing is the story that during this period he was employed as a Shakespearean actor with a theatrical company run by John Moody. In view of John Paul's ability to quote Shakespeare from memory, both in conversation and correspondence, this is an attractive notion. It derives from a manuscript note by the celebrated actor John Philip Kemble, inserted in one of the books in his library.[11] It was supposed that Kemble got this information from Moody himself but doubt has been cast on the accuracy of the statement due to the fact that Moody, who was noted for his lapses of memory, left Jamaica in 1759 and from that date till 1796 was a member of the Drury Lane Company in London. Richardson Wright, in *Revels in Jamaica* (1937), states that after Moody left the island there were no theatrical performances in Kingston till 1775. This, of course, does not rule out the possibility of unofficial or amateur productions, but an exhaustive search of the records still extant in the Institute of Jamaica yields no trace of John Paul, as an actor or otherwise. Another biographer, Phillips Russell, however, turned up a theatrical playbill for a company touring the West Indies in 1768 in which John Paul was listed as playing the part of the younger Bevil in *Conscious Lovers* by Richard Steele. Unfortunately the document does not give the name of the island where this performance took place. It is probable that the same playbill was distributed wherever the actors were touring at the time.[12] On the other hand, Sands merely states that Paul filled in his time as mate aboard a coastal vessel.

The *John* left Kingston in August 1768. During the voyage home both master and mate, as well as several other members of the crew, were struck down by yellow fever and died. Command of the stricken ship devolved on John Paul who, with the surviving seven crew members, safely brought the ship back to Kirkcudbright. The owners, Donald Currie, Beck and Company, gave Paul and his crew a 10 per cent share of the cargo as summary salvage and appointed him master of the ship for her next voyage to America. In this capacity he made at least two round voyages to the West Indies.

At twenty-one John Paul was master of a merchant ship in the West Indies trade. While it was not unknown in New England for a young man scarcely out of his teens to get the command of such a vessel if he happened to be the son of the shipowner, it was quite unusual in the British Isles, and even more exceptional when it is remembered that young Paul had no family influence or patronage to assist him. Both then and all through his subsequent career, he only accomplished what he did through dogged tenacity, persistence and sheer pushiness when the occasion demanded; but above all on merit and force of character. Whatever else was said about John Paul Jones, nothing was more true than that he never suffered fools lightly. Laziness and incompetence would be punished swiftly and in person. Indeed, when one remembers that life at sea in the small craft of the period was perpetually hazardous, constant alertness and efficiency were essential to the well-being of ship and crew alike.

At twenty-one John Paul had achieved what most seafaring men might only attain in a lifetime. It would be over-simplifying matters to suggest that his new position turned his head, but certainly the overweening egotism which many would later find so unattractive in him became manifest at this time. He would not be the first martinet to pace the quarter-deck, nor was he as severe in the punishments he meted out as many of his contemporaries. But he was extremely prickly at the best of times and prone to sudden outbursts of temper. Nathaniel Fanning, who served as a midshipman aboard the *Bonhomme Richard*, recorded that one day:

> Commodore Jones had a dispute with one of his lieutenants and ordered him below under confinement to his cabin, and as he was descending the ladder, kicked him on the breach

several times; in half an hour afterwards he sent his servant
to invite the lieutenant to come and dine with him. Thus it
was with Jones, passionate to the highest degree one minute,
and the next, ready to make a reconciliation.[13]

What Fanning omitted to mention was that he himself was the
lieutenant who was kicked, as recorded in the deck log of the ship
Ariel. Even as the youthful commander of the brig *John*, John Paul
detested slackness and disobedience; but he was at all times a fair
man, much respected and generally well liked by superiors and subordinates for his competence and integrity. His fatal flaw, however,
was his quick temper, and this embroiled him in several tragic
incidents which a less touchy individual might easily have averted or
avoided.

Although he undoubtedly possessed a mercurial temperament,
John could also be urbane and charming when occasion demanded.
In his late teens he had given his manners a polish and acquired a
veneer of culture. He was perfectly at ease in any company, and in
Bridgetown, Barbados or Kingston, he was a welcome addition to
the best salons. Even at an early age he eschewed the company of
his fellow seamen whose principal recreations ashore were whoring
and excessive drinking. Morison hints that 'if he was a normal young
chap and followed the example of other sailors, he also became
initiated into venery'.[14] Whether or not he frequented the 'Cyprian
hotel-keepers', as the madames of Bridgetown were euphemistically
termed, is a matter than cannot be resolved; but later, when he was
no stranger to polite society in America and France, he was very
much a ladies' man with a string of amatory successes that easily
outnumbered his naval exploits. He possessed a vitality and personal
magnetism that completely captivated Abigail Adams, for example, a
lady who was never easily impressed. One of his sailors put it
succinctly when he said that he could be 'sweet like a vine when he
wished, but, when necessary, like a rock'.

As master of a small ship like the *John*, the burden of command
was a heavy one. Captain Paul was entirely responsible for the
rigging, the navigation and the discipline of the crew – no easy task,
especially when there was a cargo of rum in the hold, always a
temptation to thirsty sailors. He had to take one watch himself, as
the only other officers were the two master's mates. Ashore he had
the responsibility of getting the best price for his cargo and also for
securing a profitable cargo for the return voyage. He was quick to

learn from the experience of others and always ready to take advice from friendly merchants in the Indies, but ultimately the decision on buying and selling was his alone. Thus at an early age he acquired invaluable expertise in commerce as well as navigation. Horatio Nelson (eleven years younger than John Paul) made a voyage to the West Indies aboard a merchantman at the age of fourteen and later declared that it was a far better school of seamanship than the Royal Navy.

It is interesting to speculate whether Nelson was among those officers of the Royal Navy that John Paul cultivated while ashore in West Indian ports, as they were both in the Caribbean in 1772. They had a lot in common. Both were small of stature and slight of build, with sensitive features and charismatic qualities. Both were fastidious in their dress, with a predilection for smart uniforms and a pre-occupation with decorations. Both possessed unlimited ambition, backed by immense professional pride and that quality of dash and daring which the French call *panache*. They were not averse to taking tremendous risks, but these were always calculated risks, and their achievements were all the more spectacular as a result.

At twenty-one John Paul looked younger than his years. Now fully grown, he was barely five foot four inches tall, and his slight, wiry build and fresh complexion gave him a boyish appearance. His outstanding features were a sharp, wedge-shaped nose, high cheek-bones and a strong, cleft chin. His expression showed pride, eager-ness, sagacity and intellectual alertness. Both ashore and afloat he dressed well, more like a naval officer than a master mariner, and wore a sword at all times. This emblem of his rank would be the means of saving his life on at least one occasion.

What he lacked in formal education he made up for in the voracity of his reading and self-improvement. He read and re-read the plays and poetry of Shakespeare as well as Macpherson's *Ossian*. He was a devotee of Thomson, Shenstone and Young and was a prolific composer of sentimental verses in the same genre. In one respect he was at odds with the romantic writers of his generation: he seems to have had little or no appreciation of the beauties of nature. In the course of his career he visited some of the most beautiful parts of the world – the Caribbean islands, Nova Scotia, Galicia, the Baltic and the Black Sea as well as the eastern seaboard of America and the coasts of Britain – yet nowhere in his vast correspondence does he betray any appreciation of them. In only one letter, written in October 1780 in the aftermath of a great storm, does he allude to the majesty of the sea. It is not known whether he was acquainted with the poetry of Burns, the first American edition of whose works was published at Philadelphia in 1788, but it would be surprising if he was not. Interestingly, Burns, though one of the greatest poets of the sentimental era, shared Paul's lack of interest in scenery as such; it was the people in the scene that interested them both. Unlike Burns, however, John Paul had little or no interest in religion. Burns agonised frequently and at length on religious matters in his correspondence, but we search the letters of John Paul Jones in vain for any evidence of religious feeling or even those perfunctory references to 'the Deity' which were so fashionable in his day. Exceptionally, he peppered his love letters with pious platitudes and high-flown sentiments, a trait which he shared with Burns – and Nelson.

From the extant shipping records we can piece together a fairly accurate picture of Paul's movements over the ensuing four years. His first voyage in command of the *John* was to Jamaica, for he was at Kingston on 12 April 1769 when he gave bond to observe the Navigation Acts, undertaking to abide by the laws that stipulated that trade with the colonies must be confined to British ships. On 23 June he cleared Kingston for Kirkcudbright with a cargo of rum, sugar, pimento, cotton, mahogany and dyewood. Sailing north by the Old Bahama Channel along the north coast of Cuba, he passed through the Strait of Florida and went as far as Bermuda before turning to take full advantage of the westerlies. He was back in Kirkcudbright by the end of August, too late to start another voyage to the West Indies, and spent the winter at Arbigland with his widowed mother. In 1770 he made a leisurely trip to the Windward Islands and did not return to Kirkcudbright till very late in the year, with a cargo of rum, sugar, ginger and cotton-wool from Grenada.

It was on this voyage that Paul's violent temper got the better of him. In the autumn of 1769 Samuel McAdam senior, father of the late master and himself a partner in the shipping company, hired Mungo Maxwell, son of a prominent local figure, Robert Maxwell of Clonyard, as ship's carpenter. During the outward voyage Mungo's inefficiency, insolence and disobedience were so flagrant that Captain Paul, in a fury, ordered him to be triced up in the rigging and flogged with the cat-o'-nine-tails. When the *John* arrived at Tobago in May 1770, Maxwell lodged a complaint against his captain in the Vice-Admiralty Court and exposed his scarred back as evidence. Captain Paul declared that Mungo Maxwell had not only been incompetent but disobedient; and Judge-Surrogate James Simpson, after examining

Mungo's back and shoulders, declared that the stripes were 'neither mortal nor dangerous' and dismissed the complaint as frivolous.

Unfortunately, the matter did not end there. Maxwell shipped home on the *Barcelona Packet* but, a few days out from Tobago bound for Antigua, he contracted a fever and died. The packet berthed at London long before *John* reached Kirkcudbright, and even before John Paul got home disturbing rumours were reaching Arbigland about his responsibility for the death of a crew member. Robert Maxwell at Clonyard (about eight miles west of Arbigland) was so incensed when news of his son's death reached him that he immediately sent a petition to the Vice-Admiral of Scotland, with a copy to Commissary John Goldie at Dumfries, deponing that:

> On board the said vessel he was most unmercifully flogged, by the said John Paul, with a cudgel or baton, bled, and bruised, and wounded upon his back and other parts of his body, and of which wounds and bruises he soon afterwards died on board the *Barcelona Packet* of London, then in the West Indies, and lying near to the place where the said other vessel was. That the informer cannot learn the particular time or place when and where his said son received the aforesaid wounds, nor the particular time or place when and where he died, but he is well satisfied that the men and other sailors on board the said brigantine, upon examination before your lordships, will clear up the matter.[15]

Captain Paul had no sooner tied up at the jetty in Kirkcudbright than he was arrested by the sheriff's officer and lodged in the town's tolbooth without bail. A few days later, on 15 November, he entered a counter-petition in which he stated: 'There is not the least evidence or presumption that Mungo Maxwell died of any abuse received from the petititoner, nor was there any proof brought of his actually being dead.' He asked to be freed on bail to stand trial for the alleged crime; and this was granted on the consent of Robert Maxwell, provided that Paul agreed to appear in answer to any indictment in Scotland within six months under the penalty of one thousand merks Scots. In due course Paul made a voyage to Tobago in the spring of 1772 to obtain the affidavits from the Vice-Admiralty Court as well as James Eastment, master of the *Barcelona Packet*, that cleared him of the Maxwell murder charge. Back in London on 24 September 1772 he forwarded the precious documents to his mother at Arbigland. Characteristically, this bundle was accompanied by a letter in which he informed his mother: 'You will see with how little reason my life has been thirsted after, and, which is much dearer to me, my honor, by maliciously loading my fair character with obloquy and vile aspersions.' Paul even went to the trouble of sending certified copies of the affidavits to William Craik, whose 'nice feelings', he further wrote to his mother, 'will not perhaps be otherwise satisfied. His ungracious conduct to me before I left Scotland I have not yet been able to get the better of.' It rankled with him that the laird who had known him since he was a boy should have entertained some doubts over the affair, but it should be remembered that Robert Maxwell was a neighbouring laird whose views on the matter would have weighed heavily with him. At any rate, Craik's apparent coolness towards him, real or imaginary, was one of the reasons that gradually alienated John Paul from the place of his birth and upbringing.

While this grave matter was hanging over him, John Paul within days of his release on bail applied for membership of the St Bernard Lodge of Kirkcudbright and, on the recommendation of James Smith, a burgess of that town, he was 'initiated into the mysteries and privileges of Ancient Freemasonry' on 27 November 1770. Socially this was a mark of approval and acceptance, and indicates how little the solid citizens of Kirkcudbright regarded the charge which had been brought by a country laird. The importance of the masonic movement in the late eighteenth century cannot be overstated. It was the one organisation in which the nobility and gentry rubbed shoulders with professional men, tradespeople and even their tenantry on an equal footing. A mason in good standing in his home lodge could attend meetings of any other lodge throughout the Empire. A few years later Robert Burns would gain entrée to the highest levels of Edinburgh society through his masonic connections; and John Paul would find that freemasonry would open many doors to him in America, and later in France. His membership of the St Bernard Lodge would enable him to establish himself at Fredericksburg, Boston, Portsmouth (New Hampshire) and even Paris.

Early in 1771 the owners of the *John* sold the vessel and gave its master an honourable discharge dated 1 April, stating that, on two round voyages to the West Indies, 'he approved himself every way qualified as a navigator and supercargo'. A supercargo was the officer who took responsibility for the buying and selling of cargoes, and in the smaller vessels this function was usually handled by the captain.

This document, in effect, certified Paul's competence as a merchant as well as a seaman. Some of the early chapbooks state that Paul's next employment was as master of a coastal packet that traded between Kirkcudbright and the Isle of Man but no trace of this can be found in Scottish or Manx records. Following his return from Tobago in the autumn of 1772 he obtained the command of a large, square-rigged vessel, the *Betsy* of London, which plied between England, Ireland, Madeira and Tobago. From the meagre surviving documents it seems likely that he was also part-owner of this ship. These include letters from Thomas Scott of London concerning the replenishment of ships' stores and equipment, and the insurance of cargoes – matters which the ship's master would not in the normal course have been involved with.

Intriguingly, there are passing references in these, as well as in later letters to Alexander Smith of London, to John Paul's favourite sport while he resided briefly in the metropolis. Reminiscing about this period to Smith, in a letter of 1779 when the War of Independence was at its height, Jones (as he had become by this time) added that if he were not 'an old Man' (he was only thirty-two when he wrote these words) he 'would ask many Questions concerning the fair Ladies', among whom 'Miss Drew is still held in Remembrance', as well as the 'hospitality in P. Street'. It should be noted that the appellation 'Miss' was at that time only applied to very young girls or women of ill fame, and that Poland Street, Soho, was notorious as the preferred location of the 'Covent Garden Ladies' (prostitutes of the better class), it is more than likely that, at this stage in his career, Captain Paul preferred to pay for sex rather than risk any long-term commitment.

At Tobago he formed a partnership with Archibald Stuart, a young Scotsman of his own age who had established a lucrative business as a merchant and planter. Stuart imported wine from Madeira and dairy products from Ireland, and these formed the principal cargoes conveyed by the *Betsy*. Stuart was one of the most enterprising and energetic young merchants on the island, and John Paul, himself regarded as one of the coming men in the West Indian trade, was at the age of twenty-six well on the way to making his fortune. This was not an end in itself, for he had a hankering to purchase an estate in Virginia and settle down to the life of the country gentleman.

At this juncture fate stepped in and dealt him a cruel blow, though it has to be said that his troubles were partly of his own making. In January 1773 the *Betsy* left Plymouth, Devon, but, as John Paul wrote to John Leacock, his consignee at Madeira, on 15 April, 'The ship proved so very Leakey that it was with the greatest Difficulty that we could keep her free with both Pumps.' He had managed to put in at Cork, discharge his cargo and have the ship surveyed. This revealed a very disturbing situation: no fewer than thirty of her futtocks (the curved timbers forming the ribs of her mid-section) were broken. To make matters worse, Captain Paul went down with 'a severe fever' while waiting for instructions from the underwriters in London to go ahead with repairs, and this illness confined him to 'a bed of sickness' for sixteen days and left him in a much debilitated condition. While he recuperated at Cork the ship underwent extensive repairs, and it was not until the middle of June that the ship was fit to get under way.

By that time, the season of light summer winds had arrived, making a voyage all the way to Tobago, via Madeira, impracticable until the autumn. Thus it was not until October that John Paul anchored at Scarborough, Tobago, sold his wines and provisions and negotiated a cargo for the homeward voyage. It was here that there occurred the incident that he would later describe as 'the greatest misfortune of my life', putting to an end all hopes of early retirement to a Virginian plantation. His own version of the affair is the only one in existence, and was set out in a letter to Benjamin Franklin more than five years later.[16]

The trouble began at Scarborough when Paul refused to give his crew an advance on their wages. Prudently he wished to conserve his cash from the sale of his cargo in order to purchase the return cargo. It was not uncommon for seamen to receive their wages at the end of the return voyage, but in this instance it was the wrong decision. Many of the ship's complement were natives of Tobago and wanted money to spend ashore or give to their families. One seaman, whom Paul referred to only as 'the Ringleader', had behaved insolently on the outward voyage and was clearly a troublemaker. Now he egged on his shipmates to demand cash up front. John Paul tried to mollify them with gifts of clothing out of his own slop-chest, but the Ringleader insisted on lowering the ship's boat and attempting to go ashore without leave. When Captain Paul tried to prevent this the Ringleader (whom Paul described as 'a prodigious brute of thrice my strength') set upon him and forced him to take shelter in the master's cabin under the poop deck. Infuriated and humiliated in equal measure, Captain Paul grabbed his sword from the cabin table and rushed outside, hoping to intimidate the man.

Instead, this had the opposite effect. The Ringleader, who was then stepping into the jolly-boat with his cronies, turned about, seized a belaying-pin and rushed at the master, bawling threats and imprecations. John Paul, retreating before this onslaught, caught the heel of his shoe on the coaming of an open hatchway and came sharply to a halt, otherwise he would have toppled backwards into the hold. The Ringleader, then in the act of swinging his bludgeon to strike a lethal blow to the head, could not halt his headlong rush and was neatly skewered by the captain's blade. It must have pierced his heart, for he was killed instantly and fell to the deck.

The crew, now cowed and sullen, silently rowed their captain ashore. John made straightaway for a justice of the peace and offered up his sword in surrender. The justice said that that was not necessary until he was about to stand trial. Once the heat of the moment had passed John had second thoughts, apparently counselled by his friends who said that there was no authority in Tobago to try an admiralty case and that his life would be in danger if he stood a jury trial in a local court. The upshot was that he was advised to flee at once. Taking horse, he rode across the island to a bay on the other side where, by good luck, a vessel was about to weigh anchor. In this precipitate manner, abandoning all his business matters and property to Archibald Stuart and his agent Stuart Mawey, apart from fifty guineas which he had about his person at the time of the fracas, John Paul impetuously departed from Tobago.

It is regrettable that no corroborative evidence is now extant, for there are several aspects of this narrative which are very puzzling. In the first place, it was quite untrue to state that there was no authority in Tobago competent to deal with an admiralty case. Judge-Surrogate James Simpson and Lieutenant-Governor William Young (who held a vice-admiralty commission) were just the men to deal with such a matter. Not only had they handled the complaint of Mungo Maxwell and subsequently granted the affidavits Paul sorely required, but they were both personal friends of the ship's captain. Young was also Governor of Grenada, the Grenadines and St Vincent and it might have been that, at the time of the brawl, he was absent in one of those islands. But in his letter to Franklin Paul says that Young was one of those very friends who advised him to run.

Why he should have fled so precipitately is another mystery. The Ringleader's behaviour was a clearcut example of mutiny, a crime so heinous that he would have received short shrift in any court. By the same token, any ship's master who took extreme action to quell a mutinous act would have automatically been exonerated. John Paul had both legal and moral force on his side. His headlong flight, leaving his business affairs in disarray and abandoning his command, was totally out of character. Paul, who often asserted that he feared no man, and who often went out of his way in search of danger, had shown reckless irresponsibility on this occasion, for the command of the *Betsy* now passed to a first mate who had already shown himself to be unreliable and insubordinate. The letter to Franklin ended lamely with the admission that he had had 'to retire Incog. to the continent of America and remain there until an Admiralty Commission should arrive in the Island, then return'. On the face of it, Paul's actions were those of a coward, and the only mitigating circumstance may have been that the violent death of the Ringleader, a local man, had so whipped up local feelings that John Paul's friends were helpless to prevent the mob taking the law into their own hands.

3. *Virginia*
1773–75

I am not a Virginian, but an American.
— PATRICK HENRY, IN THE VIRGINIA CONVENTION, 1774

Between October 1773 and October 1775 (when he received a letter at Philadelphia, still extant), John Paul's movements are almost a complete mystery. In a letter of 4 May 1777 to Stuart Mawey, his agent in Tobago,[1] John stated that he had to live for twenty months on the fifty pounds he carried away from Tobago. Yet, from other sources, it appears that he must have had access to funds held on his behalf by a banker named Ferguson at Orange Valley, Tobago, to the amount of £909, but whether this sum was entirely his or whether part at least belonged to the owners of the *Betsy* is not clear. He also had an account in London with yet another Scottish merchant, Robert Young, to the sum of £281, and he had other assets in Tobago and elsewhere.

Had he gone straight to the American continent, there would have been no need for him to change his name; no system for the extradition of wanted men from the American colonies to the West Indies then existed. The fact that John Paul changed his name not once but twice, seems to imply that he remained in the Caribbean islands for some time after he fled from Tobago. This is borne out by the fact that there was no direct link between Tobago and the American mainland. The fugitive would have gone from Tobago to Barbados in the first instance. Shipping records indicate that there were five arrivals of sloops and schooners at Bridgetown, Barbados, from Tobago between 5 October 1773 and 17 January 1774. From Courland Bay, across Tobago from Scarborough, it is most likely that John Paul left the island aboard a packet vessel operated by the British Post Office from its base in Falmouth, Cornwall. The small, swift vessels used by the Post Office were only of 45 tons, comfort being sacrificed to speed which helped them outrun any French warship or privateer. From Tobago the packet boat went to

41

Grenada, St Vincent, Dominica, Antigua and Jamaica; at any one of these points John could have gone ashore and remained for an indefinite period. If he went all the way to Kingston, Jamaica, he could then have easily got a berth on a ship bound for the American mainland.

By the time he arrived in Virginia he was already travelling incognito. Lorenz,[2] influenced by the plethora of nineteenth-century chapbooks, naïvely assumed that during this mystery period the fugitive, having taken the name of John Paul Jones, had served aboard a Spanish privateer, and he repeated the tale that on one occasion he visited Martha's Vineyard off the coast of Massachusetts in order to give a shipmate a decent Christian burial. The sole source of this story was Thomas Chase who later served under Jones on the *Bonhomme Richard* and whose memoirs were unreliably cobbled together by his grandson.[3] The story goes that the *Black Buccaneer* (the unlikely name of the vessel) had encountered a British warship near Long Island and in the ensuing exchange of shots the captain of the privateer was mortally wounded. Captain Jones assumed command, put ashore at Martha's Vineyard, and got Chase to make a rough coffin. 'For a few days the inhabitants satisfied their curiosity in regard to the bronzed, hardy young captain, his motley crew, and his strange vessel.' Some of the chapbooks on which Chase's grandson based his account go much further in indulging their flights of fancy. One has the runaway captain in command of 'a set of Spanish and Portuguese desperadoes' making their forays against defenceless merchant ships from their lair in Corunna. That these stories are without foundation is hard to prove, but the fact that John was in a state of utter penury when he did emerge in America gives the lie to tales of piracy. The one thing he clung to was his honour, and it is extremely unlikely that he would have done anything against his principles. He was in a big enough mess as it was, but the considerable money he had at stake in Tobago and Britain ought to have been sufficient guarantee that he would return to face the music some day.

There has been a great deal of speculation over the aliases which John Paul adopted. By the time he reached Virginia in 1774 he was already calling himself John Jones. It may well be that he selected that surname merely because it meant 'son of John' and, being a very common surname, like Smith or Brown, it would not attract undue attention. Inevitably, however, the myth-makers concocted a tale that John Paul somehow travelled from Tobago to Halifax,

North Carolina, where he was picked up on the shore, destitute and in distress, by Willie Jones of The Grove, and in gratitude adopted the surname of his benefactor. Consequently, the 'tradition' that North Carolina was the fugitive's landfall has become hallowed by the passage of time, and is constantly repeated in reference works in that state. But there was no such place as The Grove near Halifax, whether the residence of Willie Jones and his brother Allen or otherwise. Among the voluminous correspondence of John Paul Jones there is not a single letter, or copy of a letter, to the Jones brothers, or from them to him, and there is not a single reference to them in his letters to men such as Joseph Hewes who knew them well.

In later years, when John had twenty casts of the bust by Houdon made for distribution to his friends, he sent none to Willie or Allen Jones who, if they had been the good Samaritans of North Carolinan tradition, would certainly have been recipients. One of the outstanding features of John's character was his steadfast gratitude towards people who helped him at various stages of his career. It would have been quite inconsistent with this for him to have neglected to thank Willie Jones had he helped him in the manner suggested. Furthermore, when he adopted a coat-of-arms in 1777, our hero did not take the heraldic device of the North Carolina Joneses but the stag of the Welsh Joneses, quartered with the arms of a Paul family of Gloucestershire.[4] Similarly there is no substance to the myth that he received a benefaction from a certain Cadwallader Jones of Virginia on condition that he adopted his surname.

On the other hand there is the curious account given in Purdie and Dixon's *Virginia Gazette*, published at Williamsburg on 17 March 1774:

> Some time last December a Sloop of about 100 Hogsheadsburthen stood in for Machotick Creek, on Potowmack, and ran aground on a Mud Bank, a little Way up the Creek. Soon after, a decent well looking Man, dressed in Black, and with a Gold laced Hat, came on Shore from the Sloop, and calling at a Gentlewoman's House in the Neighbourhood, told her he was bound for Alexandria, to purchase a Load of Wheat, but that his Hands had left him, and he wanted the Loan of a Horse to carry him to Leeds Town, to engage others. Being disappointed in getting a Horse, he went to a Planter's House a few Miles distant, where he lodged all Night, went off in the Morning, and has never been seen since. On his Way he

stopped at a petty Ordinary, where he left three ruffled Shirts, a neat Fowling Piece, and a great Coat; but carried with him a Pair of Saddle Bags, which the Landlord concluded, from their Weight, contained a considerable Sum of Money. After the Vessel had continued near a Fortnight in the Creek, with her Sails standing, some of the Gentlemen in the Neighbourhood went on Board; and upon searching her, found neither Provisions, Water, Chests, Papers, or any other Effects, than one Feather Bed, a Gold laced Hat, a Sailor's Jacket, a Pair of Trousers, some Cooking Utensils, and two Sea Compasses made in Salem. She is a long sharp built Vessel, with only a Cabin, containing five Births, and Hold. On her Stern is painted, in white Letters, *Falmouth Packet*; and the same Words, in Letters made of Cloth, are on her Pendant.

Unfortunately subsequent editions of this newspaper make no further reference to 'so mysterious an Occurance' as the editor termed it. The description of the ship's master and the ruffled shirts and gold-laced hats, unusually fine apparel for the captain of a small sloop, together with the tale of the crew having deserted *en masse*, tally with what one might have expected from John Paul. Moreover, Leedstown on the Rappahannock, a short distance overland from Machadoc Creek, was not far from Fredericksburg, where William Paul was living.

Lloyd's *Register of Shipping* for the period shows that there was only one sloop named *Falmouth Packet*, of 25 tons burden, owned by J. McClure of Cork where she had been built. No *Register* for 1774 is extant, but that for 1775 gives two masters for this vessel: 'Js Jones' which is crossed out and 'A. Cosgrave' substituted. In the 1779 and 1781–83 *Registers* 'J. Jones' is again shown as master. She was, in fact, the mailboat normally employed on the run from the packet station at Falmouth in Cornwall to the Channel Islands and Cork, her home port, but it is not inconceivable that this vessel should have been diverted to one of the West Indian routes in 1773; and her tonnage answers the quaint description given in the *Virginia Gazette*. Morison concluded that John Paul obtained temporary command of this sloop in Barbados, Grenada or St Vincent after he fled from Tobago, because her master James Jones had fallen ill of a fever.[5] John now assumed the name of Jones, if he had not already done so, beause it enabled him to sign entrance and clearance papers as 'J. Jones', simulating the name of the packet's regular skipper. Jones had the further merit from the incognito viewpoint of being a very common surname in the merchant navy. On the passage to Virginia, however, he worked the crew of the sloop so hard, or so exasperated them by outbursts of temper, that they ran the vessel aground at Machadoc Creek and jumped ship. Captain Jones decided to go to Alexandria to hire another crew and return a few days later, but never did.

So what then happened to upset the temporary captain's good intentions? On the way to Alexandria he stopped off at Fredericksburg to visit his brother William whom he had not seen for nine years, and found him dead or dying. In the hope of obtaining some of his brother's property, he decided to remain in Virginia. He secured the services of a new master for the sloop, the A. Cosgrave mentioned in the 1775 *Register*. Cosgrave, an Irishman, was glad of the opportunity to work his passage home and, with a fresh crew, took the packet back to Cork in the spring of 1774. Meanwhile, James Jones, the regular captain, had recovered from his illness, sailed in another vessel to Cork, and resumed command of the packet, as the 1779–83 records reveal. Morison cheerfully admitted that this was conjecture; but in default of any evidence to the contrary it remains the most plausible explanation of John Paul's movements in this period.

William Paul's tombstone, a red sandstone slab in the burial ground of St George's Episcopal Church in Fredericksburg, is merely inscribed 'Wm. Paul, 1774'. No death register for the period has survived, but other evidence, admittedly very slight, suggests that William died late in 1773. The tombstone was evidently provided by John and the date may merely record when the stone was erected; but the fact that his will (executed on 22 March 1772) was proved on 16 December 1774 suggests that William actually died in the latter year. None of the executors named in the will agreed to undertake that responsibility, because William had left all his property to his sister Mary Ann, and nothing at all to his wife, from whom he had been estranged for some time. Nothing was left to his brother either, but although he was not invited by the probate court to take over the executorship it is probable that, as the nearest relative, he was allowed to occupy William's house pending the settlement of the estate. The actual administration of the estate was ultimately entrusted to John Atkinson, who had witnessed the will.

By the time the estate was wound up, however, war was brewing and the Virginia ports were closed by the blockade of the Royal Navy and the proceeds from the sale of William's property could not be remitted to Mary Ann in Scotland. Presumably this legacy eventually reached her after the War of Independence. By that time Mary Ann and her sister Janet were no longer on speaking terms which may explain the fact that the latter's daughter Janette Taylor assumed, fifty years later, that her uncle had died intestate and that, as a result, his property amounting to some ten thousand dollars, passed automatically to his brother John. This erroneous assumption, in turn, would give rise to the myth that John inherited his brother's worldly goods, and from this the myth of John Paul Jones the Virginia planter and slave- owner arose. This could not have been further from the truth; John was given a brief respite in that he now had a roof over his head, but this was only a temporary dispensation until the property could be sold. John's fifty pounds had by now dwindled alarmingly and the only solution was to find employment. Fortunately, at Edenton, North Carolina, resided Robert Smith, brother of that James Smith of Kirkcudbright who had proposed John for membership of the St Bernard Lodge. Robert Smith was in partnership with Joseph Hewes, the most prominent shipowner, merchant and political figure in that part of North Carolina. It is possible that Jones, as we must now call him, travelled overland to Edenton via Richmond in the winter of 1774–75 in the hope of obtaining the command of one of the Hewes and Smith vessels. If he did so, he was disappointed; the political situation had now deteriorated so far that American vessels were bottled up in their ports and shipping was at a standstill.

Hewes would certainly have helped John Jones if he could have. The two men became firm friends, and their association continued until Hewes died in 1779. The only other staunch supporter who dates from the mystery period of 1774–75 was Dr John K. Read. Benjamin Franklin's wife was Read's Aunt Debby; through his uncle by marriage, Read was very well connected and in the forefront of revolutionary circles. He received his medical training at Philadelphia before practising in Charleston, South Carolina, and Hanover County, Virginia, then settling in nearby Goochland County in 1774. He was a rather Micawberish individual who only prospered after he married a wealthy widow. More importantly, he was a prominent freemason and subsequently Grand Master of the Order in Virginia. It is probable that Read and Jones met at the Fredericksburg lodge. The easy-going physician, a year older than the erstwhile sea-captain, was very different in temperament, but the two men seem to have hit it off immediately. It is the letter from Read addressed to 'Mr John Jones, to the care of Mr David Sproat, mercht., Philadelphia' dated 13 October 1775 that enables us to determine the point at which John was definitely using the first of his aliases.

This letter also proves that John Jones went to Philadelphia in September 1775, if not earlier. Through Dr Read, Jones made important friends there, notably Thomas Jefferson who was a friend of Read and the bearer of one of his letters to Jones. The letter of October 1775 alludes to two earlier letters from Read which Jones had apparently not answered. The next letter from Read to Jones which is still extant is dated 28 February 1778 and from this we can glean a few more scraps about John's movements in the mystery period. One sentence in particular is of interest: '. . . those fears were momentary & gave place to other feelings when I reflected on the many sentimental hours which (solitarily enough) passed between us at the Grove'. It will be remembered that this was the fictitious name of the estate where Willie Jones was supposed to have helped John Paul when he fled from Tobago. In reality, The Grove was (and still is) a small estate in Hanover County, not far, as the crow flies, from the Read residence in Goochland County.

The Grove was then the home of the Crenshaw family who were on intimate terms with Read and his wife. Three miles from The Grove was the home of Patrick Henry at Scotchtown; five miles distant in the opposite direction was the plantation of Nathaniel West Dandridge whose elder daughter Martha was named after her cousin, Martha Washington. Martha Dandridge was married to Archer Payne, brother to Mrs Read's first husband. Archer Payne's place was close to the Read farm in Goochland County, and it was probably there that John Jones first met Dorothea Dandridge. At that time the beautiful and spirited Dorothea was being courted by Patrick Henry, but that did not deter John Jones who had a three-mile start when visiting the young lady's home. Had John succeeded in winning her hand, and had times been more propitious, he would undoubtedly have used his credit in Tobago and London to purchase a Virginia estate and settle down, at twenty-eight, to a life of 'calm contemplation and poetic ease', his favourite quotation from Thomson's *Seasons*. Jones himself never referred to his abortive courtship of Dorothea Dandridge, and the only authority for it is Read, who supplied information on the subject which appeared in the *Memoirs* of 1830: 'Their affection was mutual, but circumstances forbade their union; from this period he formed the resolution of never marrying.' How much of this was Read, and how much the interpolation of Janette Taylor, editor of the *Memoirs*, cannot be ascertained; but the later Jones correspondence is studded with thoughts of taking a wife and settling down. Even if there were some substance to the affair between Jones and Dorothea it is probable that her parents vetoed any talk of marriage. The Virginia gentry might be more liberal in their outlook than their British counterparts, and go so far as to invite an unemployed sea-captain, brother of the deceased local tailor, to dinner; but the notion of their daughter marrying such a man would have been abhorrent.

In 1777 Dorothea married Patrick Henry, by that time Governor of Virginia and one of the most prominent figures in the American Revolution. He was a prosperous landowner and a successful politician, but he was a widower with six children by his first marriage and, at forty-two, almost old enough to be Dorothea's father. It was regarded as a good match, but one cannot help thinking that Dorothea would have been happier as Mrs John Paul Jones than bearing nine children to Patrick Henry and listening to him rehearsing his interminable speeches. As for Jones, he seems to have been quite philosophical about it. Ever the hardheaded Scot, he put Dorothea out of his mind and concentrated on resuming his career. The chapbook fantasists made much of Dorothea as the love of his life, and how he never got over her rejection of him; but he was far too practical a man for that. If he learned any lesson from this episode it was that he still had a long way to go before he became as eligible as he might. If he could find no short-cut to social advancement through marriage, he must obtain it through his chosen profession. And the means to achieve this were just around the corner. Ironically, when he was at the height of his fame and could have any woman he wanted, he enjoyed the pleasures of their bodies as well as their minds but chose to remain single. Back to sea he would go, and through the sea he would achieve infinitely greater fame and immortality than he ever could as a country gentleman in Virginia.

Trouble had been brewing between Britain and her American colonies for more than a decade. Ironically, it stemmed from the conclusion of the Seven Years' War which added vast territories – Canada, the Floridas and Louisiana – to the British Empire. The defeat of the French, however, removed the sense of dependence on

Britain for military aid; at the same time the costs of administering this huge new territory tended to fall on the American colonists, who actually stood to gain most from the opportunity to expand westwards without a continuing threat from the French and their Indian allies. In 1764 the British parliament passed the Sugar Act, a tax on the American colonies to defray the additional costs of patrolling the Caribbean by the Royal Navy. To cover the costs of a greatly increased military presence in North America, the British introduced a Stamp Act the following year. Resistance to this measure gradually crystallised in the formal resolutions of protest in the various colonial assemblies and in the creation of various bodies, such as the Sons of Liberty, which expressed their opposition by riots and mob violence. This in turn led to increased imperial control which inevitably raised the temperature of the dispute considerably. Eventually the British backed down and repealed the hated Stamp Act, but by that time irretrievable damage had been done. Having shown weakness in this matter, the British compounded their folly by asserting their right to tax the Americans.

The passage of the Townshend Acts (1767) provoked the outcry in the colonies 'No taxation without representation'. Not that the Americans were looking for a voice at Westminster; they just had no wish to be taxed from there. Again the British backed down and repealed these measures on the grounds that they were uncommercial. To assert the principle that Britain could tax its colonies if it so desired, however, the duty on tea was retained. Meanwhile, the city of Boston was rapidly emerging as a hotbed of rebellion. When customs officers seized the sloop *Liberty* belonging to John Hancock, the townspeople went on the rampage. The authorities retaliated by despatching two regiments to Boston. When some of the rabble pelted the soldiers with snowballs and called them lobsters and bloody-backs (derisive terms alluding to their red coats and the practice of flogging), the troops discharged their muskets into the mob. Few people were actually killed or wounded in this affray, but the propagandists magnified the event into the Boston Massacre. Popular uprisings in the town culminated in the famous Tea-party (16 December 1773) when 340 chests of tea were seized and tipped into the harbour. The Quebec Act of 1774 extended that Canadian province south to the Ohio River and prevented the westward expansion of the Americans. After that, matters escalated at an alarming rate. A series of Coercive Acts was met by Committees of Correspondence and other secret societies which culminated in the

First Continental Congress. The British had retaliated against rebellious Boston by closing its port and dismissing its elected council. These draconian measures were soon extended to the whole of Massachusetts and then, as the trouble spread, to the ports along the entire American seaboard. The colonies, with the exception of New York, North Carolina and Georgia, were excluded from the Grand Banks fisheries. The situation was now polarised and both parties drifted inexorably towards war.

Hostilities began in Massachusetts on 19 April 1775, when a military detachment was sent overland from Boston to seize or destroy the military stores which the colonists had amassed in the village of Concord. The minutemen, as the local militia were called, were tipped off about the advancing redcoats, and ambushed the column at Lexington. The running battle at Lexington and Concord was little more than a skirmish but it was soon overtaken by bloodier events, namely the American capture of Fort Ticonderoga in May and the battle of Bunker Hill in June. In August Britain retaliated by prohibiting trade between the rebellious colonies and the West Indies and despatched the Royal Navy to blockade the American ports and intercept ships that were foolhardy enough to run the blockade. At a personal level, this effectively froze John's assets in London and Tobago. He was powerless to return to Tobago to stand trial, even if he had felt so inclined. His money running out and reliant on the hospitality of his new-found friends, he chafed at the embarrassing and frustrating situation in which he thus found himself.

Just when his prospects seemed at their bleakest, something turned up to transform him. From the middle of 1774 onwards royal government gradually collapsed throughout the American colonies and the various colonial legislatures ceased to function by June 1775. In their place there emerged the Continental Congress which consisted of delegates from all the colonies and met at Philadelphia. After Concord and Bunker Hill a state of war existed between Britain and the colonies. In July 1775 Congress empowered George Washington to take command of the colonial militias and establish some degree of order and discipline among them. In August the British made their counter-move, planning to seize New York and Rhode Island as naval bases from which to tighten the blockade which, it was hoped, would be enough to bring the rebels to their knees without committing the military forces to an expensive land campaign. Congress braced itself for the great naval and military expedition expected from Britain in the spring of 1776 and laid its plans accordingly. While George Washington was appointed commander-in-chief of the Continental Army, Esek Hopkins was commissioned to head the proposed Continental Navy and soon began recruiting officers of the right calibre to command its warships.

In July or August 1775, therefore, John Jones went to Philadelphia in search of a naval commission. In that city he ran into David Sproat from Kirkcudbright, now a prosperous Pennsylvania merchant, and lodged with him. John took time out from canvassing the embryonic naval authorities to pay court to a local lady, unnamed but a close friend of the wife of Captain John Young whom he met in Philadelphia. In the City of Brotherly Love, however, John discovered that the name he had assumed was confusingly common, and at this juncture he decided on a compromise by resuming his original surname while retaining the alias of Jones. This neatly circumvented the embarrassing problem of dropping the name of John Jones by which he was now known to many, while enabling him to assert his individuality. Thereafter he would be known as John Paul Jones, though this was often shortened to Paul Jones. He was still known as John Jones as late as September that year, but within three months he would officially style himself 'John Paul Jones Esq.', the form of address that appeared on his commission as a first-lieutenant in the Continental Navy.

In Philadelphia, Jones cultivated the friendship of Joseph Hewes, whose partner, Robert Smith, was the brother of John's masonic sponsor at Kirkcudbright. Hewes not only represented North Carolina in the Second Continental Congress but was the chairman of the influential Marine Committee which set up the Navy and selected its senior personnel. It seems probable that Hewes and Jones met under the roof of David Sproat who was a close friend of Robert Smith. Jones later wrote to Hewes, care of Sproat. The clannishness of the Scots ensured that Smith and Sproat would naturally be inclined to help a fellow from the Stewartry, but Jones was a personable young man anyway and the first impression that Hewes formed of him was very favourable. It is possible that the friendship begun in Philadelphia was strengthened in August 1775 when Jones stayed with Hewes at Edenton. No record of what transpired at these meetings has survived, nor of any deliberations within the Marine Committee, but it was duly noted on 7 December 1775 that John Paul Jones (who received his lieutenant's commission on that date) had four days previously hoisted his flag in the armed vessel *Alfred*. From this it is inferred that Jones had already been informally in the naval service for several weeks, supervising the fitting out of his ship.

7 December – a date which sadly has tragic overtones in American naval history in another context and another era – marks John's crossing of his personal Rubicon. With the benefit of hindsight, this seems more dramatic, more drastic, than it really was at the time. Few Americans, even among the bitterest enemies of King George III, regarded their actions as a complete break with Britain. John's later correspondence often reverts to a favourite theme, that he drew his sword not for riches but from pure love of liberty and universal philanthropy. He did not regard himself as an American but as a 'Citizen of the World'. In this he echoed the sentiments of Thomas Jefferson, Samuel Adams and other founders of the United States. Similar sentiments of global patriotism stud the writings of James Otis, Thomas Paine and even the English historian Edward Gibbon. When John Paul Jones accepted his commission in December 1775 he sincerely believed that he was fighting not for anything so narrow as American independence but for the principle of Liberty – the right of a free people to determine their destiny without the coercion of a misguided monarch and a corrupt ministry. Significantly, the flag which he raised aboard the *Alfred* on 3 December 1775 was not the Stars and Stripes of an independent American republic but the Grand Union Flag, composed of the Union Jack and the red, white and blue stripes that represented the thirteen colonies, united in resisting tyranny but still nominally loyal to the British Crown.

4. Lieutenant John Paul Jones
1776

> This much is certain; that he that commands the sea is at
> great liberty, and may take as much and as little of the war
> as he will.
>
> — FRANCIS BACON, *Of the True Greatness of Kingdoms*

Just as the rebellious colonies drifted into conflict with the mother
country, with no clear idea of their future status, so too the
development of the armed services was haphazard and piecemeal.
The opening rounds of the conflict, not yet dignified by the term
war let alone revolution, were fundamentally defensive, and as the
situation crystallised the United Colonies continued for some time to
see their role as essentially defensive. For that reason more attention
was paid to building up land forces which would take on the redcoats
and German mercenaries on American soil. Only much later did the
notion of an offensive war develop, involving action which would
take the fighting to the enemy's doorstep. For such a role, of course,
a navy was vital; but even before matters had reached that stage, the
need for some armed ships to defend American ports and shipping
was perceived.

In fact the first sea battle between the rebels and the Royal Navy
occurred in April 1775, only a few days after the running fights at
Lexington and Concord. The inhabitants of Martha's Vineyard off the
coast of Massachusetts recaptured two American sloops which had
been seized by HMS *Falcon* in Vineyard Sound. Then on 9 May an
armed mob at Falmouth (now Portland) gave Captain Henry Mowatt
RN a rough time when he came ashore to remonstrate with them
when they had prevented his crew loading his vessel with timber;
when he demanded that they surrender their arms and ammunition
he was jeered and pelted with rubbish. Then the Maine minutemen
(militia) arrived and ignominiously bundled the naval officer into the
town gaol and attacked his ship at anchor. As soon as he was
released, Mowatt went back to his ship and poured broadside after

broadside of red-hot cannonballs and incendiaries into the town, destroying most of it. The burning of Falmouth, more than any other incident, hardened the attitudes of the colonists. Insensitive to the resentment which this and similar incidents caused, the British government later issued a directive to the Royal Navy in October 'recommending that the rebels should be annoyed by sudden and unexpected attacks on their seaboard towns during the winter'.[1]

During the autumn of 1775 Massachusetts and other colonies began issuing letters of marque and reprisal to merchant ships, authorising them to seize certain types of British vessel. This system was widely practised throughout the eighteenth century when belligerent countries relied heavily on privateers, as unofficial war-ships, to harass enemy shipping. In the American conflict the scope for seizing and making a prize of British ships was rapidly widened, and by the time Congress itself got around to authorising them, these privateers had increased considerably in number. Indeed, they threat-ened the existence of the Continental Navy itself, for they attracted the best and most daring seamen, lured by the prospects of much greater prize money than was apportioned to naval ships. When the war was at its height, it was estimated that over two thousand of these free-enterprise destroyers of commerce on the high seas were preying on British ships; and anything remotely resembling a British ship, whether it was or not, was liable to be attacked and its precious cargo and stores impounded.

Prize money, in fact, would become the greatest bugbear with which the Continental Navy had to contend. This was a long-standing tradition in the Royal Navy which continues to this day, and gave sailors an important advantage over soldiers, especially as the latter could be severely punished for looting. The money accruing from the sale of a captured ship, her stores, equipment and cargo, was paid to officers and men on a sliding scale. In the Royal Navy ships' crews were granted the full cash value of their seizures, but the Marine Committee of Congress, in its folly, did not follow this example. Instead, it felt that the Navy should help to pay for the war and as a consequence the prize regulations drafted on 25 November 1775 decreed that half the value of a prize (if a warship) and two-thirds (if a merchantman) would be earmarked for the public treasury. This caused so much resentment among naval crews that Congress was forced to give up its right to any share in a captured warship, and thereafter took only half the value of mer-chant prizes seized by the Navy. But privateers were not affected by the prize regulations, and all of the proceeds from the disposal of their captures went to them. Furthermore, as naval ships had far less opportunity for predatory expeditions, recruitment was seriously hampered, as most seamen preferred the infinitely more lucrative prospects of privateering. John Paul Jones (whom British propaganda would attack as a pirate) was not alone in complaining to the Marine Committee, or Congress itself, about the inequity of this system, especially when privateers tempted naval seamen to desert.

Jones and other seafaring men were acutely aware, as the summer of 1775 wore on and war seemed imminent, that the colonies would have to have a proper navy, rather than rely on the buccaneering tactics of privateers; but the first man actually to do something about it was none other than the Commander-in-Chief himself. Soon after taking command of American land forces at Cambridge, Massachusetts, on 15 July, George Washington chartered, armed and manned with soldiers from the New England regiments several fishing schooners and small sloops. What later came to be known as the Army's Navy made its début on 5 September when the schooner *Hannah*, under Captain Nicholas Broughton, set out to cut off the supply lines of the British forces then besieged in Boston. These little ships patrolled the New England coast during the autumn and winter of 1775 and took a number of prizes, including the storeship *Nancy*, low in the water with a valuable cargo of arms and ammunition that included two thousand muskets, a 13-inch mortar and many tons of ammunition. The most successful commander in the Army's Navy was John Manley, a simple fisherman from Marblehead, Massachusetts, who captured the *Nancy* and presented the mortar to the troops at Cambridge. This big gun, 'the noblest piece of ordnance ever landed in America',[2] was promptly christened 'Congress'. Captain Manley's exploits aboard the *Lee* and later the *Hancock* were widely publicised that summer throughout the colonies, adding to John Paul's sense of frustration as he kicked his heels in Philadelphia. The Army's Navy continued to operate successfully right through 1776 when it was disbanded. Three of its most successful officers, Manley, Samuel Tucker and Hector McNeill, transferred to the Continental Navy. In addition, General Benedict Arnold, before he defected to the enemy, organised a flotilla on Lake Champlain which checked the advance of British forces from Canada into upper New York.

A week before Washington created the Army's Navy, however, the Colony of Rhode Island and Providence Plantations formally resolved that an 'American Fleet' should be created, and the Rhode Island delegation introduced a motion to that effect in Congress. Samuel Chase of Maryland dismissed the notion, saying, 'It is the maddest idea in the world to think of building an American fleet . . . We should mortgage the whole Continent.' George Wythe of Virginia retorted, 'Why should not America have a navy? No maritime power near the sea-coast can be safe without it.'[3] Wythe cited the example of the Romans who built a navy specifically to deal with the threat posed by Carthage, and he concluded by hoping that America would do as Rome had done – *inter nubila condit* – that she built in time of trouble. That, in fact, is what she did.

At the time, however, it seemed insane to take on the might of the Royal Navy. By midsummer 1775 Vice-Admiral Thomas Graves had three ships of the line and six smaller warships, with a total armament of more than three hundred guns and two thousand men, based at Boston and other ports in northern New England. In addition, there were two sloops of war with thirty-six guns and 230 men at Narragansett Bay, a ship of the line and two sloops (ninety-six guns and seven hundred men) at New York; three sloops (fifty-six guns and 360 men) in Chesapeake Bay, together with a number of smaller ships at Charleston, South Carolina, and various ports between Halifax, Nova Scotia, and Florida. Many other men-o'-war were stationed in the West Indies, within easy reach of the American coast, while others were cruising the open Atlantic, the Mediterranean and British home waters and could be pressed into service in the American blockade if need be.[4]

Congress eventually took the first step towards the creation of a navy when it appointed a Naval Committee of Seven on 30 October 1775. The committee was charged with the management of the maritime affairs of Congress and to that end it was authorised to purchase, arm and equip a few ships for the protection and defence of the United Colonies. This date is therefore regarded as the birthday of the Continental Navy. The committee comprised four New Englanders (John Adams, Silas Deane, Stephen Hopkins and John Langdon) and three Southerners (Henry Lee of Virginia and Christopher Gadsden and Joseph Hewes of the Carolinas). Their numbers were soon increased to eleven, and the body renamed the Marine Committee, a title which it enjoyed till the middle of 1779 when it was reduced to three members as the Board of Admiralty. On 10 November 1775 Congress created the Marine Corps, effectively the fighting men afloat while the sailors were primarily concerned with gunnery and seamanship. Fifteen days later the capture of British warships and fleet auxiliaries was authorised, but not merchant vessels; and on 28 November *Rules for the Regulation of the Navy of the United Colonies of North America* was published. The author of this pamphlet was John Adams who would later become the second President of the United States. Some of the regulations seem quaint by today's standards. Commanding officers were required to punish men 'Heard to swear, curse, or blaspheme the name of God'. Officers were fined a shilling for this offence, but ratings were obliged to wear a wooden collar 'or some other shameful badge of distinction'. In marked contrast to the Royal Navy where the lash was all too freely employed, the cat-o'-nine-tails was limited to a dozen lashes on the bare back. While not engaged on acts of war the crew were expected to fish for their supper, thereby reducing the costs of victualling to a bare minimum.[5] Simultaneously Congress published a pay scale, ranging from $32 a month for captains and $20 for lieutenants and master mariners, to $8 for able seamen and $6.66 for landsmen (ordinary seamen). Extremely detailed specifications for the feeding of a ship's company were also drawn up; these were based on age-old naval custom and included a daily rum ration and one meatless day each week.

Most important of all, during November 1775 the Naval Committee, having been given a grant of $100,000 by Congress for the purpose, purchased four ships for the Continental Navy and began to fit them out. 'The first beginning of our Navy,' Jones later recalled, 'was, as navies now rank, so singularly small that I am of the opinion it has no precedent in history.'[6] The nucleus of the fleet consisted of four small merchantmen. The largest, previously the *Black Prince* and now renamed (with unconscious irony) the *Alfred* after the founder of the Royal Navy, was about 350 tons burthen. She was converted for combat and equipped with twenty 9-pounder guns and ten 6-pounders. With a complement of 220 men, conditions must have been very cramped aboard ship.

Next came the *Columbus*, formerly the *Sally* and now named in honour of the great Genoese seaman. She was slightly smaller than the flagship, with a gross tonnage of 300, eighteen 9-pounders and ten 6-pounders manned by the same size of crew as the *Alfred*. The two smallest vessels were the *Cabot* and the *Andrew Doria*, likewise named after famous Italian seamen; they were equipped with fourteen and sixteen 6-pounders respectively and carried crews of 120 and 130. Before these ships were ready for sea, four sloops were added with the names *Providence*, *Hornet*, *Wasp* and *Fly*, formerly the *Katy*, *Falcon*, *Scorpion* and *Lizard* respectively. A further three small merchantmen, pressed into service as the brig *Lexington*, the ship *Reprisal* and the sloop *Independence*, were fitted out early in 1776. Though not ready to sail with the rest of the fleet, they are regarded among the original navy and their names have been perpetuated in the warships of the US Navy down to the present day.

At this period the chairman of the Naval Committee was Stephen Hopkins, many times Governor of Rhode Island and the prime mover in the creation of the navy. Hopkins was then about seventy years of age, and he conferred the appointment of Commodore of the infant navy on his brother Esek, aged fifty-seven. Esek Hopkins had spent forty years before the mast and had served aboard privateers in the French and Indian War. Esek appointed his son John B. Hopkins to the command of the *Cabot*, while Abraham Whipple of the *Columbus* was a close relative. Command of the flagship *Alfred* was given to Dudley Saltonstall, brother-in-law of Silas Deane, and that of the *Providence* went to John Hazard who was also closely connected with Deane. Four of the principal officers were from Rhode Island, the smallest of the United Colonies, and the fifth from Connecticut. As an obvious sop to the seat of government in Philadelphia, the command of the *Andrew Doria* was granted to Nicholas Biddle of Pennsylvania.

The captaincy of the *Alfred*, by rights, should have gone to the Irishman John Barry who had been her master in the merchant service, but at this stage of the conflict merit was of no account. Nepotism was flagrantly practised by all the principal figures of the Revolution, Washington alone being impervious to the blandishments of kith and kin. The worst practitioners were Henry Lee, Arthur Lee and Richard Henry Lee of Virginia. In fairness, it should be pointed out that, in those perilous times, it was more a question of giving responsible positions to people on whom you could rely, rather than merely ensuring that your friends and relatives got good jobs. It was all the more remarkable, therefore, that John Barry, a foreigner without family influence in Congress, should have been appointed captain of the *Lexington*.

The Scotsman Jones, like Barry, was a newcomer, and was handicapped by having less immediate experience afloat. Nevertheless, his talents were recognised by his friend Joseph Hewes and through him he secured his appointment at the next level of command, as one of the first lieutenants to be commissioned into the navy. Jones's precise movements in the late summer and autumn of 1775 are not known, other than that he was at Philadelphia most of the time. It seems likely that he was engaged in converting the former *Black Prince* into the *Alfred* and he acted as commanding officer until Captain Saltonstall reported for duty on 23 December. It was Jones who had the honour of raising the Grand Union Flag on the jackstaff of *Alfred* as she lay at her berth in Philadelphia on 3 December. Everyone remembers that Betsy Ross produced the first Stars and Stripes but no one remembers Margaret Manny, the Philadelphia milliner who, at Jones's request, ran up the first Grand Union Flag, using a Union Jack to which she sewed 49 yards of broad and 52 yards of narrow bunting (purchased from James Wharton) to form the seven red stripes and six intervening white stripes that made the first ensign.[7] A similar flag was hoisted by George Washington a month later, on Prospect Hill at the siege of Boston.

Esek Hopkins was present and it seems that Jones persuaded the elderly commodore to make a ceremony of it. The crew were drawn up at attention or manned the yards, while the Marine Corps fifes and drums struck up 'The British Grenadiers' to which the rebel colonists had supplied new lyrics entitled 'War and Washington'. A crowd of several thousands lined the banks of the Delaware to watch this historic moment. Jones's commission and formal appointment to the ship came through four days later. It seems strange that his lieutenant's commission should have been thus delayed, but it was, in fact, the earliest lieutenancy granted by Congress. It was duly confirmed, along with all the other captains' and lieutenants' commissions, by Congress on 22 December.

Esek Hopkins had sailed into Philadelphia aboard the sloop *Katy*, formerly of the Rhode Island Navy, handed her over to Congress, and converted her into a twelve-gun warship renamed *Providence* after her home port. Joseph Hewes offered Jones the command of this vessel with the rank of captain but the Scot refused on the grounds that he had never sailed a sloop and felt that he could be more useful, and learn more, as first-lieutenant under a flag-captain. It has been insinuated that Jones turned down this command because it was an insult, but there is no reason to doubt the explanation which he gave. *Providence* was a seventy-footer with a huge gaff-headed mainsail, a long boom overhanging the stern and a bowsprit almost as long as the deck. Sailors like Jones, used to handling square-rigged vessels, regarded these big sloops as dangerous and difficult to handle, which, indeed, they were. Jones's other reason was sensible in light of the fact that, in December 1775, few people dreamed of severing connections with the mother country. A determined show of resistance to King George III was one thing, but all-out rebellion was another matter altogether. At that stage Jones did not want to take any irrevocable steps that might prejudice his chances of returning to Tobago to get a fair hearing in the Admiralty Court. Later on, however, he regretted that he had not accepted the command of the *Providence* when it was offered to him. A captaincy at that early period would have enhanced his seniority in the Navy. Instead the command went to John Hazard, another of the commodore's cronies from Rhode Island, whom Captain Biddle dismissed (even before the fleet sailed) as 'A Stout Man very Vain and Ignorant – as much low cunning as capacity'.[8] Back in December 1775, however, when Congress was uncertain how far to go in tweaking the British lion's tail, and the Mecklenburg Resolves had not been developed into the Declaration of Independence, there were many able officers who refused commissions, according to Jones, because 'they did not choose to be hanged'.[9] In the same letter he recalled caustically that:

> Other respectable gentlemen accepted appointments of cap-
> tain and lieutenant of a provincial vessel for the protection
> of the river, after our fleet had sailed from it; and on board
> of which they had refused to embark, though I pretend not
> to know their reason.

Before the fleet got under way, Jones's main enemies were boredom and the temptation to desert. He countered the first by incessantly drilling his crew. 'I formed an exercise and trained the men so well to the great guns in the *Alfred* that they went through the motions of broadsides and rounds as exactly as soldiers generally perform the manual exercise.'[10] The second he dealt with by posting marines to guard the gangways and prevent sailors slipping ashore without authorisation. He chafed at inaction while Congress decided on a course of action. The commodore acted promptly when he received the directive of Congress, given on 5 January 1776, that:

> with the utmost diligence you proceed with the said Fleet to
> Sea and if the Winds and Weather will possibly admit of it
> to proceed directly for Chesapeak Bay in Virginia and when
> nearly arrived you will send forward a small swift sailing

Vessel to gain intelligence of the Enemie's Situation and
Strength. If by such Intelligence you find they are not greatly
superiour to your own you are immediately to Enter the said
bay, search and attack, take and destroy all the Naval force
of our Enemies that you find there."

This was a tall order, and rather vague withal, so as an afterthought
a clause was added which gave the commodore a way out:

Notwithstanding these particular Orders, which 'tis hoped
you will be able to execute, if bad Winds or Stormy Weather
or any other unforeseen accident or disaster disable you so
to do, You are then to follow such Courses as your best
Judgement shall Suggest to you as most useful to the
American Cause and to distress the Enemy by all means in
your power.

These orders betray the muddled thinking of Congress at the time.
The only clear objective was Chesapeake Bay for the Royal Navy had
several warships there, giving support to Lord Dunmore, Royal
Governor of Virginia, who had organised his own navy consisting of
Tory merchantmen augmented by captured rebel vessels. The combined naval might of Lord Dunmore and the Royal Navy posed a
constant threat to Maryland and Virginia and to communications
between the northern and southern colonies. If this threat could be
eliminated by determined naval action, it would have a tremendous
impact on the morale of the colonists.

On immediate receipt of the orders from Congress, the commodore's flotilla weighed anchor and drifted down the Delaware
towards the open Atlantic, but the weather had been unusually harsh
since Christmas and ice in the river impeded their progress, to such
extent that the four warships had only got as far as Reedy Island in
two weeks. There they remained icebound for a further month, at
which time they were joined by *Providence* and *Fly*. A number of men
jumped ship during this lull and it was all that Jones and the other
lieutenants could do to keep the rest from deserting in droves. On
14 February conditions had improved sufficiently for the ships to sail
as far as Whorekill Roadstead inside Cape Henlopen, and now they
were joined by the remaining two smaller vessels, *Hornet* and *Wasp*,
which had been fitted out at Baltimore. As *Providence* had no captain,
this appointment was offered to Jones, but again he declined on the

grounds that it was no more than a despatch boat, the proper command of a midshipman. Once again Jones's judgment (perhaps on this occasion clouded by temperament) let him down, for the command went to Hoystead Hacker, first-lieutenant on the *Cabot*, who thus obtained seniority over Jones.

Whether Commodore Hopkins had ever intended heading for Chesapeake is debatable; but certainly by 14 February he had changed his mind, for on that date he ordered his captains to head for Great Abaco in the Bahamas. On his own initiative Hopkins had decided to launch a surprise attack on New Providence which was reputed to have a considerable arsenal and powder magazine. To be sure, Congress was short of gunpowder and had voted that measures be taken to obtain supplies from the Bahamas where the inhabitants were thought to be sympathetic to the northern colonies, but there is no evidence that Hopkins had orders to implement this proposal, though the possibility of some secret verbal instructions cannot be ruled out. Jones would later assert that the New Providence expedition had been his masterplan, and that he had been responsible for the finer details. Again, there is nothing to support this claim, and the fact that Hopkins and Saltonstall were familiar with the islands and had fought in these waters during the French and Indian War casts doubt on Jones's version. One thing is certain, however, and that is that the commodore and the flag-captain would have no shortage of advice from such an assertive lieutenant.

When the fleet finally got into blue water the weather improved and, with a fair breeze filling their gleaming sails, the little armada must have made a splendid spectacle. The flagship had topsides newly painted bright yellow, and a figurehead of a knight holding a sword, the Black Prince now metamorphosed into King Alfred. *Cabot* likewise had yellow topsides, but the other vessels were painted black over all, the customary practice for smaller ships. On 1 March 1776 the fleet anchored off Hole-in-the-Wall near Great Abaco. Two island sloops were promptly taken and their skippers impressed as pilots. In those days Nassau, the island capital, was little more than a village high on a hill fronting the harbour protected by the long narrow spit of Hog Island, with Fort Nassau on the west and Fort Montague on the east. There was a good depth of water close to Fort Nassau so that large ships could come alongside, but off Fort Montague the water was much shallower so that only the smaller vessels could approach it. A company of the Fourteenth Regiment had been stationed in the forts, but the soldiers had inexplicably been withdrawn a short time previously. Similarly, the sloop-of-war *Savage* had been recalled from this station. It has been suggested that Hopkins was privy to this good news, but the arrival of the American fleet seems to have been quite fortuitous.

New Providence, therefore, was undefended apart from a handful of civilians, and they were unlikely to put up much of a fight, as the Bahamians were supposed to be very sympathetic to the American colonists. The capture of the island, together with its valuable arsenal, should have been a pushover, but the ensuing operation almost ended in farce. On 2 March the commodore crammed two hundred marines led by Captain Samuel Nicholas and fifty seamen led by Lieutenant Weaver below decks in the two captured sloops and sent them into Nassau harbour with the intention of taking the town by surprise; but, as the arrival of the American fleet was common knowledge, the landing was expected. Lieutenant-Governor Montford Browne had ordered his scratch militia into Fort Nassau when the American fleet hove in sight, and he seemed surprised when the Americans sailed right under Fort Montague and dis-embarked there. The gun batteries in Fort Nassau, manned by civilians, fired wildly in the direction of Fort Montague but no casualties were sustained. By nightfall the Continental flag was flying proudly from the ramparts. The following morning Nicholas and his marines advanced on the town itself. Governor Browne promptly surrendered the keys of Fort Nassau and, on the signal of the marine captain, the American fleet sailed into the harbour. Two weeks were spent in loading a rich booty which included eighty-eight cannon of various sizes up to 36-pounders, fifteen brass mortars, 5,458 shells and 11,077 cannonballs, together with assorted gun-carriages and ordnance equipment. Disappointingly only twenty-four casks of powder were discovered, as well as a cask of rum which was rapidly consumed by sailors and marines who, rendered paralytic as a result, were subsequently discharged from the navy as unfit through 'tropical fever', which seems to have been a convenient euphemism for alcoholic poisoning. It later transpired that Browne, with the assistance of a Scottish sea-captain named William Chambers, had spirited away 162 barrels of gunpowder. Chambers jettisoned his cargo of lumber to accommodate the precious powder and, in the dead of night, had slipped silently through the unguarded eastern channel for St Augustine to deliver it safely to Governor Tonyn.[12]

On 17 March the fleet weighed anchor and headed north towards Rhode Island. Aboard the flagship were three important prisoners,

Browne, his secretary and a Tory councillor from South Carolina. The homeward voyage was without incident, though the weather was very bad, with strong northerly winds and incessant rain. By 3 April the fleet was off Montauk Point, at the eastern extremity of Long Island, and two days later they anchored off Block Island, Rhode Island. The seal on their success was set by the capture the previous day of two small warships, the armed schooner *Hawk* and the bomb brig *Bolton* which formed part of the British squadron under Captain William Wallace, which was based at Newport. The British warships patrolling Narragansett Bay blockaded Providence, Warwick and Bristol but were increasingly ineffectual against the swarms of privateers. Quite small vessels approached the British warships under cover of night and discharged fusillades into them. The Rhode Island Assembly had decreed it a capital offence for anyone to give succour to the enemy and the ships were running out of provisions and fresh water, and whenever one of the vessels sought a quiet anchorage in one of the many creeks and inlets, in no time at all a party of colonists would appear with a cannon or two and pepper them with shot. Casualties were few, but British morale was low and desertion was rife.

Hopkins and his fleet were in high spirits when Block Island appeared on the horizon. The day was spent in sweeping the sea to the south in the hope of capturing other British ships, but without success. By nightfall the American fleet was offshore before a light north-west wind. At one o'clock on the morning of 6 April, when about twenty miles south-east of Block Island with wind from the north and a full moon riding high, the *Andrew Doria* sighted a ship to leeward, crossing the bows of the fleet. The strange vessel turned out to be HMS *Glasgow*, twenty guns, under Captain Tryingham Howe, a relative of General William Howe commanding British land forces and his brother Admiral Earl Howe, commanding the naval forces. Captain Howe was, in fact, carrying despatches from Newport to his kinsman the general in Charleston at the time his ship was intercepted. Word spread round the American fleet and each ship went to general quarters, but the commodore gave no orders to form line of battle, though he had ample time to do so before the enemy came within range. Nor, indeed, did he subsequently issue any orders; instead, it was left to each captain to engage the enemy as he thought best, with the result that chaos ensued.

The first fleet action of the Continental Navy, by a strange coincidence, occurred close to the last, off Block Island on 6 May

1945 when the USS *Moberley* and *Atherton* sank the German submarine *U-853*. Captain Howe spotted the fleet of 'seven or eight sail' at roughly the same time that Captain Biddle sighted *Glasgow*. Howe immediately brought his ship round and headed towards the ships to ascertain who they were. Within thirty minutes *Glasgow* was within pistol shot of *Cabot*. When the British ship hailed the American vessel and asked what ships were with her, Captain John B. Hopkins answered, 'The *Columbus* and the *Alfred*, a twenty-two-gun frigate', in the hope that this would frighten off the interrogator. At that moment, an over-zealous marine in *Cabot*'s main-top lobbed a grenade on to *Glasgow*'s deck, and this was the signal for all hell to break loose. The *Cabot* fired a rather ineffectual broadside from its main armament of 6-pounders, and *Glasgow* responded with two broadsides of 9-pounders which wounded Captain Hopkins, killed the master and several seamen, and temporarily disabled the ship. *Cabot* disengaged at this point, permitting *Alfred* to position herself broadside to the enemy.

With twenty 9-pounders and ten 6-pounders, the American flagship should have been more than a match for the *Glasgow*. Now Jones's incessant drilling of his gunners began to pay off, as he directed the fire of the 9-pounders on the lower gundeck; but a lucky shot from *Glasgow* smashed *Alfred*'s wheel-block and the lines controlling the tiller. Out of control, she drifted off broadside to the wind, presenting a perfect target for *Glasgow* which raked her fore and aft, holing her below the water-line, blasting chunks out of the mainmast and tearing her rigging to shreds. Precious minutes were lost while the crew rigged new steering gear and brought the ship under control. Now Biddle came to the rescue but he had to tack to avoid colliding with the helpless *Cabot*, then alter course to avoid *Alfred*. Eventually he succeeded in closing the enemy's port quarters and engaged him with rapid gunfire. *Columbus* was blanketed by the other ships so that her sails would not draw, and Whipple was tardy in getting her into action. *Providence* played absolutely no part in the fight. According to the commodore's report, the battle lasted for three glasses (an hour and a half), but Biddle commented pithily on reading this account in the newspapers, 'They must mean half-minute glasses!' *Columbus* eventually got within range on *Glasgow*'s starboard quarter and discharged her guns as she crossed the enemy's stern, but her gunners fired so wildly that no damage was done. Captain Howe, fearing that he was about to be boarded on all sides, extricated his ship and bore away for Newport 'with the whole fleet within Musket shot on our Quarters and Stern'. In fact, only three of the American ships were able to give pursuit. Subsequently, an American prisoner aboard *Glasgow* reported that the ship had been extensively damaged. Her hull pierced, her mainmast hit ten times and her sails in tatters, she should have been easy prey for the pursuing Americans, but they were severely hampered by the weight of the arms and ammunition seized in the Bahamas and were too low in the water to give effective chase. The action degenerated into a running fight, with *Glasgow*'s stern-chasers keeping the pursuers at a respectful distance. The sun was well up before Commodore Hopkins signalled the other ships to come about in order to aid the crippled *Cabot* and secure the two prizes. That was his only wise decision, for just over the horizon were several British men-o'-war, alerted by the sound of gunfire, who had now come out to cover *Glasgow*'s retreat.

Bearing in mind that most of the action took place at close quarters, there were remarkably few casualties on either side. *Glasgow* lost one man and had three wounded, all from shots fired by the American marines. A marine lieutenant and five men on *Alfred* were killed and six wounded. *Cabot* lost her master and three marines, with seven others wounded, and *Columbus* had one slight casualty. The first fleet action of the war was a draw, though the Americans came off rather better than the British. Commodore Hopkins completed his self-appointed mission satisfactorily and brought his entire fleet, including the prizes, into New London on 8 April. *Glasgow* was so badly damaged that she had to be sent back to England for repairs.

Congress ecstatically hailed Commodore Hopkins and congratulated him on 'the Spirit and Bravery shown by the men'. The New Providence expedition and the encounter with HMS *Glasgow* were hyped up in the American press. Newspapers ran special victory editions, and a Massachusetts poet was inspired to produce an instant ode to Hopkins ruling the waves, with Neptune resigning his crown and trident to Congress. Extravagant praise was followed, just as swiftly, by recrimination and condemnation once it was realised that the American fire-power was at least three times greater than the enemy. Even while the commodore was still being lauded to the skies, his captains were privately disgusted with his conduct. Biddle dismissed the battle off Block Island with the comment that 'a more imprudent, ill conducted Affair never happened'. Inevitably Jones had plenty to say on the subject, on 14 April writing to Joseph Hewes:

I have the pleasure in assuring you that the Commr. in Chief is respected thro' the Fleet and I verily believe that the Officers and men in general would go to any length to execute his orders. It is with pains that I confide this plaudit to an individual. I should be happy in extending it to any *Captain* and Officer in the service – praise is certainly due to some – but alas! there are Exceptions. It is certainly for the Interest of the Service that a Cordial interchange of Civilities should subsist between Superiour and Inferiour Officers – and therefore it is bad policy in Superiours to behave towards their inferiours indiscriminately as tho' they were of a lower Species. This is a Conduct too much in Fashion in our Infant Fleet – the ill Consequence of this is Obvious. Men of liberal Minds, who have long been Accustomed to Command, can Ill brook being thus set at nought by others not Posted to Claim to the monopoly of sense. The Rude ungentle treatment which they experience creates such heartburnings as are no wise consonant with that Chearful ardour and spirit which ought ever to be the Characteristick of an Officer. And therefore whoever thinks himself hearty in the service is widely mistaken when he adopts such a line of conduct in order to prove it – for to be well obeyed is necessarily to be Esteemed.[13]

Jones had Dudley Saltonstall in mind when he wrote these words. Ironically, Jones's subordinates in *Ranger* would make similar complaints about him later on.

When the commodore's conduct was questioned, the debate soon polarised along North–South lines, the New Englanders stoutly defending Hopkins and the delegates from Virginia and the Carolinas being loudest in denouncing him. The matter was resolved by Congress ordering the Marine Committee to hold an imformal enquiry into the conduct of Commodore Hopkins, Captain Saltonstall and Captain Whipple. The two captains and several junior officers (but not Jones) were duly summoned to Philadelphia where they were questioned by the Committee which subsequently reported back to Congress that the complaints against Saltonstall were not proven, but that 'the charge against Captain Whipple amounts to nothing more than a rough, indelicate mode of behaviour to his Marine officers'. Whipple demanded a court-martial in order to refute the allegation that he had shown cowardice in not getting

Columbus into the action earlier, and was duly acquitted. Hoysted Hacker of *Providence*, however, was also court-martialled, but his conduct during the battle was only the last straw. Charged with a string of offences including the embezzlement of his ship's stores, he was found guilty on several counts and dismissed from the service. Jones sat on both courts-martial, and it was to him that the commodore passed the command of the sloop *Providence* on 10 May 1776, with only the temporary rank of captain. This time there was no holding him back. By that date any hopes he may previously have entertained about the conflict being short-lived, and that soon he would be resuming his peacetime profession between Tobago and Scotland, had long since evaporated.

After offloading its booty at New London, the fleet sailed to Narragansett Bay. The sailors who had been discharged after consuming that huge quantity of rum at Nassau were replaced by two hundred volunteers out of Washington's land forces who were then on their way from Boston towards New York. By the time the fleet reached Narragansett Bay, however, Washington needed his men desperately, and Jones's first task on assuming command of *Providence* was to transport a hundred of them to New York.

While at New York on 19 May, Jones took the opportunity to write a very long letter to his friend Joseph Hewes. It was a remarkable performance by any standards, and is most revealing of Jones's character. Apart from the passage about the qualifications of a naval officer (which generations of US Navy midshipmen were required to learn by heart), it contains blunt criticism of his superior officers as well as a preoccupation with rank and seniority. Jones's concern, amounting almost to an obsession, on the latter topic reflected the fact that, unlike most of his contemporaries, he had no family position or influence other than with Hewes. His appointment to *Providence* was temporary and given verbally at that. Now he sought assurance of his position, knowing full well that Congress had undertaken to construct a fleet of frigates. The command of one of these fine new ships was now his dearest wish.

The letter to Hewes began with a reference to the previous letter which Jones had written to Hewes on 14 April, giving an account of the recent cruise to the Bahamas and the encounter with HMS *Glasgow*. That letter had also contained 'some free thoughts on Certain Characters in the Fleet' but by mischance the letter had fallen into 'hands not the most agreeable on its way to the Post

Office', for Jones now suspected that it had never reached its destination. The letter had been enclosed in a cover addressed to David Sproat (another native of Kirkcudbright), but Jones had just seen Sproat's nephew, Captain David Lenox, and he said that his uncle had not received any communication from Jones lately.

In the present letter Jones enclosed transcripts of the two courts-martial and gave a general account of his recent doings as well as his reflections on the battle:

> The Unfortunate Engagement with the *Glasgow* seems to be a general reflection on the Officers of the Fleet. But a little reflection will set the matter in a true light – for no Officer who acts under the Eye of a Superiour and who doth not stand charged by that Superiour for Cowardice or misconduct can be blamed on any Occassion whatever. For my own part I wish a General Enquiry might be made respecting the Abilities of Officers in all Stations and then the Country would not be Cheated.
>
> I may be wrong, but in my opinion a Captain of the Navy ought to be a man of Strong and well connected Sense with a tolerable Education, a Gentleman as well as a Seaman both in Theory and Practice – for want of learning and rude Ungentle Manners are by no means the Characteristick of an Officer. I have been led into this Subject on feeling myself hurt as an Individual by the Censures that have been indiscriminately thrown out – for altho' my station confined me to the *Alfred*'s lower Gun Deck where I commanded during the Action – and tho' the Commodores letter which hath been published says 'All the Officers in the *Alfred* behaved well' – Yet Still the Publick blames me among others for not taking the Enemy.
>
> I declined the Command of this Sloop at Philadelphia – nor should I now have accepted it had it not been for the Rude Unhappy Temper of my late Commander – I now reflect with Pleasure that I had Philosophy sufficient to avoid Quarreling with him – and that I even Obtained his blessing at Parting. May he soon become of an Affable even disposition, and may he find pleasure in Communicating Happiness around him.[14]

Further lengthy paragraphs agonised about his prospects of getting a substantive captaincy. In particular, Jones was appalled when the commodore, on appointing him to the command of *Providence*, told him that he would have to refer to Congress to get the appointment confirmed. Since then, there had been no word from Philadelphia, nor the coveted captain's commission. Jones also reminded Hewes that he had previously declined a captain's command in the hope of learning from men of greater experience. He had soon discovered, however, that the position was reversed, and it was he who taught them. He pointed out that *Providence* was badly needing a refit; but while that was being carried out he would be more than happy to proceed to Philadelphia 'to act under the more immediate direction of Congress especially in one of the new Ships'.

This letter was entrusted to the commodore's steward who had been given leave to travel to Philadelphia to visit his wife. He had instructions to deliver the letter, then call again on Hewes when his leave was up, in the hope of picking up a reply. It appears, however, that he returned to his ship empty-handed, for in due course Jones took the sloop back to her name port where she was careened on the banks of the river. Her hull was badly fouled with weed and barnacles after the cruise in southerly waters, and the task of heaving down was a very complicated one which necessitated the removal of all ballast, cannon and heavy stores and the lowering of the upper masts. The ship was then carefully run ashore near high tide and rolled over on her bilge so that half her bottom was exposed at low tide. When one side had been scraped, scoured and repainted, the laborious process was reversed and repeated. The ship was then reballasted, rearmed, rerigged and floated. Such a tedious operation could take several weeks. During this period Jones lived ashore, sampling the delights and amenities of Providence. A letter from Jones to Whipple some time later recalled the joys of this period: 'You have been very unkind in not telling me a Word about our agreeable Widow, or my little affair of the Heart at Providence.'[15] Neither lady was mentioned by name, and the amatory dalliance with them was apparently soon forgotten.

On 13 June Jones was ordered by Commodore Hopkins to escort *Fly* carrying some of the New Providence cannon to Washington's forces on Fishers Island at the mouth of Long Island Sound. Twice British cruisers intercepted the little American ships and chased them back to Narragansett Bay, but at the third attempt Jones managed to evade the blockade. He then picked up merchant ships at Stonington and convoyed them to Newport. On the way, he rescued a brigantine carrying military stores from Hispaniola, which was being pursued by HMS *Cerberus*. While *Providence* turned and engaged the British thirty-two-gun frigate, the brigantine made good her escape. The next mission was to proceed to Boston and escort a fleet of colliers to Philadelphia, where Jones arrived on 1 August, after successfully evading the fleet of Black Dick Howe which was escorting brother Billy's army from Halifax to New York.

His first independent command may not have been important, in terms of the size of his ship; but in a summer when the rest of the fleet was inactive, Jones's exploits were outstanding. After the worst of the summer heat, Congress had reconvened, and the Naval Committee was now renamed the Marine Committee. Hewes was still an influential figure, who presently introduced the intrepid young commander to John Hancock, the Committee's new chairman, and Robert Morris. Having secured the attention of these important figures, Jones subsequently got into the habit of sending confidential despatches direct to Morris. Hewes continued to be a good friend, but Jones felt that there was no harm in hedging his bets. Subsequently he wrote to Hewes asking him to explain to Morris about his 'very great misfortune' (the incident with the mutineer at Tobago) 'which brought me into North America'. All this string-pulling eventually paid off, when Jones was granted a regular captaincy by Congress, dated 8 August 1776, the first captain's commission to be issued after the Declaration of Independence. He was also offered the command of the brigantine he had rescued from the British, now impressed into the Continental Navy under the name of *Hampden*; but Jones, who had noted that she was a slow sailer, decided to stay where he was for the time being.

5. Captain Jones
1776–77

The long, long anchorage we leave,
The ship is clear at last, she leaps!
She swiftly courses from the shore,
Joy, shipmate, joy!

— WALT WHITMAN, *Joy, Shipmate, Joy*

Two days before his captain's commission was issued, Jones received his orders direct from the Marine Committee. Addressed to 'John Paul Jones Esqr, Commander of the Sloop *Providence*', the document was signed by nine of the Committee, beginning with the chairman, John Hancock, and including Robert Morris, Joseph Hewes and William Whipple of New Hampshire, a relative of Abraham Whipple. Jones was ordered to take his ship to sea and cruise around Bermuda. The directive concluded with instructions regarding which ships could be taken as prizes and an injunction to treat any prisoners with 'Humane kind Treatment'.[1]

The *Providence* was a fast and trim little ship, seventy feet overall, not counting a forty-foot bowsprit and flying-jib-boom. Her eighty-four-foot mast was rigged to carry a gaff-headed fore-and-aft mainsail. She carried twelve 4-pounders, eight of which were mounted on the open gundeck and the others on the quarterdeck, but she also had several small swivel-guns mounted on the bulwarks. She carried a complement of seventy; in retrospect Jones would regard them as the finest men he ever commanded, and certainly this cruise was the happiest and most rewarding of his naval career. His officers comprised two first-lieutenants, William Grinnell and John Peck Rathbun, master William Hopkins and surgeon Henry Tillinghast, all from Providence. The cruise commenced with only one midshipman, Joe Hardy, on board, but another, Barney Gallagher, was picked up from a prize. The ship's muster roll listed seven petty officers, ten seamen, three boys, thirteen marines under Captain Matthew Parke (with whom Jones had served aboard *Alfred*), and seventeen soldiers of the Rhode Island Brigade, a body recruited locally for combined operations. Shortly before she weighed anchor, her complement was made up by the transfer of six petty officers, three seamen and seven landsmen (ordinary seamen) from the sloop *Hornet*. Most of the crew were veterans of the cruise to New Providence under Commodore Hopkins but significantly they also included twenty-eight men, including a lieutenant and a midshipman, who had till recently served in the Royal Navy aboard *Hawk* and *Bolton* and had become prisoners-of-war when these prizes were taken. Jones seems to have been adept at persuading captive Britons to re-enlist under his command.

Providence cleared the Delaware Capes on 21 August 1776 and sailed eastward in the neighbourhood of Bermuda as Jones had been directed by the Committee. A few days later he took the whaling brigantine *Britannia*, placed a prize crew on board, and despatched her to Philadelphia. Close to Bermuda, on 1 September, he fell in with five sail, bound for New York from Jamaica, escorted by the 28-gun frigate *Solebay*. Lured by the prospect of rich pickings – one of the merchant ships appeared to be a large East Indiaman – the officers of the *Providence* persuaded Jones against his better judgement to close in on the convoy, and too late found themselves within range of a heavily armed British warship. In the nick of time Jones realised his mistake and veered off and made a run for it, close-hauled on the wind and in a heavy cross sea, with *Solebay* in hot pursuit. The chase lasted over ten hours, from seven in the morning till half past five in the afternoon. At the halfway point *Solebay* had got within musket range of the sloop and fired two 9-pounders on the *Providence*'s lee quarter. Jones now showed his colours, to which the frigate responded by running up an American flag and firing guns to leeward, the traditional signal for 'I am friendly'. This ploy failed because Jones knew only too well that the Continental Navy did not boast a ship of that class. Now his superlative seamanship came into its own. Having edged imperceptibly on the lee bow of *Solebay*, Jones suddenly put his helm up, set his steering sails and all his light canvas, and bore away across the forefront of the enemy, to leeward dead before the wind. The dexterity and unexpectedness of this manoeuvre were such that, before the frigate could counter, Jones 'was almost out of reach of grape and soon after out of reach of cannon shot. Our hairbreadth escape and the saucy manner of making it must have mortified him not a little.'[2] Captain Symonds was so astonished at such panache that he missed his chance to fire on the sloop when she lay athwart his bows, although she was then within pistol shot, and the 9-pounder balls he subsequently fired went wild. He was, indeed, mortified at the American's audacity and kept up the chase till nightfall.

On 3 September *Providence* took the Bermudan brigantine *Sea Nymph* bound from Barbados to London with a valuable cargo of rum, sugar, oil and Madeira wine. Sending this good prize off to Philadelphia, Jones took the opportunity to write to Robert Morris, complaining that his captain's commission of 8 August should have been backdated to 10 May. If this were not done, he feared he would have to yield seniority to men who had been his junior in 1775 and he would rather 'be fairly broke and dismissed the Service' than suffer such humiliation. Accompanying this letter was the gift of a turtle, but Morris did nothing about the commission. Three days later *Providence* took the brigantine *Favourite* bound from Antigua to Liverpool with a cargo of sugar. A prize crew went aboard and set sail for a Continental port, but were intercepted by HMS *Galatea* which recaptured the brigantine and ran her into Bermuda.

From 7 September *Providence* cruised for a week without sighting a single sail. Jones surmised that most of the British West Indiamen were now beyond his reach and, running short of food and water, he now headed north towards Nova Scotia where he hoped to recruit replacements for the men he had been compelled to send off as prize crews. On 16 and 17 September Jones rode out a severe gale which forced him to dismount his guns 'and stick everything I had in the hold'. Two days later, he sighted Sable Island, the notorious graveyard of the Atlantic, where many a fine ship had come to grief on treacherous reefs. By now the sloop was within a hundred miles of the Nova Scotian coast. The following day, while hove to for the purpose of catching fish as enjoined in the Navy Regulations, *Providence* sighted to windward a British frigate, HMS *Milford*, escorting a merchant ship. The frigate swooped on the American ship, but Jones coolly waited till she was within cannon range, then hoisted all sail and:

> gave him a wild goose chase, and tempted him to throw away powder and shot. Accordingly a curious mock engagement was maintained between us, for eight hours, until night, with her sable curtains, put an end to this famous exploit of English knight-errantry. He excited my contempt so much by his continued firing, at more than twice the

proper distance, that when he rounded to, to give his broadside, I ordered my marine officer to return the salute with only a single musket.[3]

At dawn the frigate was seen hull down heading for Halifax, so *Providence* turned towards Canso. On 22 September the sloop anchored in the harbour, took on water and provisions, and recruited several local fishermen to replenish his depleted crew. Jones also burned an English fishing schooner in the harbour, sank another and captured a third which he loaded with the dried fish cargoes of the other two and sent back to the nearest Continental port under Barney Gallagher. Jones also took a fast shallop which he subsequently used as a tender, or light support vessel.

At Canso he learned that there were several Jersey ships at anchor in the twin harbours of Île Madame, so he sent the shallop and his own ship's boat to reconnoitre. They found nine vessels at 'Narrow Shock and Peter the Great', Jones's phonetic rendering of Arichat and Petitdegrat, took them completely by surprise and bagged the lot. Jones had insufficient personnel to man these prizes so he struck a deal with the Jersey fishermen: they could keep the schooners *Betsy* and *Hope* to carry the fishermen back to the Channel Islands, and in return they helped him fit out and rig the others as prizes. No sooner was this task completed than a severe gale blew up on the night of 25 September. *Providence* and one of the prizes, the 250-ton vessel *Alexander*, managed to ride out the storm at the entrance to Arichat harbour, but the schooner *Sea Flower* ran ashore and had to be destroyed. The schooner *Ebenezer* likewise dragged her anchor and ran on to a reef where she broke up.

The following afternoon *Providence* and her surviving prizes, *Alexander*, *Kingston Packet* and *Success*, put to sea. A fourth vessel, the brigantine *Defiance*, had almost been driven ashore during the storm, but a boat's crew from *Providence* had cut her cable and taken her out to sea, and made for an American port independently of the others. By now Jones was so short-handed that he decided to head home, but on the way he took one more prize, the whaling sloop *Portland* off Louisburg. On 8 October 1776 he re-entered Narragansett Bay with four prizes, at the conclusion of a cruise lasting seven weeks, in which he had manned and sent in eight prizes, and burnt or sunk a similar number. His destruction of the British fisheries at Canso and Île Madame showed the enemy that the destruction of American ports like Falmouth and Norfolk would no longer be tolerated.

The three ships captured earlier had also reached port safely, but Barney Gallagher had a very bad experience that illustrates the vagaries of fortune in this war. The former British midshipman, who joined the crew of the *Providence*, had gone as prizemaster aboard the fishing schooner captured at Canso. This vessel, while on its way to an American port, was intercepted by a Salem privateer, *General Gates*, whose captain, finding that she had no papers, took Gallagher and his crew prisoner. A British warship then chased *General Gates* into Petitdegrat and ran her ashore, where her crew and prisoners fled into the woods. The British ship, assisted by the local inhabitants, rounded them up and took them to Halifax where they were confined in a prison hulk until October when they were sent to Marblehead, Massachusetts, in a prisoners' exchange ship under flag of truce.[4]

The triumphant return of Jones, the national hero, contrasts sharply with the shabby treatment he received at the hands of Congress. Only two days later, on 10 October 1776, Congress formally accepted a seniority list of captains, which had been drawn up by the Marine Committee. This list was not actually published till the following January so Jones was oblivious of the fact that he had been ranked eighteenth, below men who had joined the Navy much later than he; even below Hoystead Hacker who had been reinstated to the command of the brig *Hampden*. Jones was blissfully unaware of this, and as it did not come to his attention till early the following year the implications belong to the next chapter. For the moment, Jones was much more concerned about the prize money due to him and his crew. On 17 October he wrote to Robert Morris, complaining that it was virtually impossible to recruit seamen at Narragansett Bay for naval service because privateers offered them the full value, whereas the Navy only got one-third. He pointed out that:

> Unless this is corrected and the private Emoluments of individuals in our Navy is made superiour to that in Privateers it never can become respectable – it never will become formadable. And without a Respectable Navy – alas America! It is to the last degree distressing to contemplate the state and establishment of our Navy. The common class of mankind are actuated by no nobler principle than that of self-interest. If our Enemies, with the best established and most formadable Navy in the Universe, have found it expedient to

assign all Prizes to the Captors – how much more is such policy essential to our infant Fleet.[5]

Fortunately Morris heeded these words and conveyed their sentiments to Congress which responded on 30 October by increasing the captors' share of the net product of prize merchantmen, transports and storeships from a third to a half, and granted captors the entire value of a prize if it were a privateer or warship.

This certainly went some way towards improving the situation but it did not go far enough. Bickering with privateers and wrangling over prize money continued to preoccupy the Navy and Congress unduly throughout the war and for many years thereafter. The decision of 30 October merely touched the tip of a very contentious iceberg. By 6 January 1777 Congress had come to a practical decision, dividing the captors' share into twentieths. One-twentieth was to go to the commander-in-chief for prizes taken by ships 'under his orders and command', two-twentieths to the captain, if cruising alone, or divided among all the captains of a fleet; three-twentieths to be divided among captains of marines, masters and Navy lieutenants; two-and-a-half-twentieths to be shared equally by marine lieutenants, masters' mates, surgeons, chaplains, chief gunners and chief carpenters; three-twentieths to midshipmen, warrant officers and petty officers (such as stewards, cooks and coxswains) and marine sergeants; and the remaining eight-and-a-half-twentieths among the rest of the ship's company, or all the seamen and landsmen of ships' companies in the case of a fleet share-out.

This fell far short of the British system, where all the prize money went to the Navy and nothing to the Treasury. In the Royal Navy captains got 37.5 per cent, unless a flag-officer were present in which case he got 12.5 per cent. An eighth was divided among lieutenants and marine captains; an eighth among chaplains, chief petty officers and marine lieutenants; an eighth to midshipmen and petty officers; and a quarter to the remaining crew members. Comparing the American and British systems, therefore, the American captain would only get a fifth of what his British counterpart could expect to receive. Proportionally speaking, the ratings in the American service came off better in relation to the jack tars of the Royal Navy – 25 per cent compared with 21.25 per cent; but the officers and petty officers were decidedly worse off.

The distinction between prizes taken by ships on an independent cruise and those taken as a result of a fleet action ought to have been clear; but before setting out on the New Providence expedition all officers and men under Esek Hopkins had been obliged to sign an agreement that they would share equally the product of all prizes taken on the cruise, even those taken by a ship acting independently. This meant that the proceeds were shared out among all the ships of the fleet, regardless of size or fire-power, or indeed of individual participation in the appropriate action. To make matters worse, Congress ratified this system on 6 January 1776. By contrast, the Royal Navy established a rating for each ship by multiplying the number of her crew by the sum of the calibres of the cannon she carried. Thus a ship with 150 men armed with twenty 9-pounders would rate 150 x 180, or 27,000, while a ship in the same fleet with 200 men, twenty 9-pounders and ten 12-pounders would rate 200 x 300, or 60,000. If the total to be shared among the fleet added up to 270,000, the first ship would get 10 per cent and the second 45 per cent of the prize money.[6]

Apart from the general inequity of the American system, Jones strongly objected to Commodore Hopkins receiving 5 per cent of every prize taken by his fleet, while he remained ashore, or lived in comfort aboard his flagship *Warren* at anchor in Newport Harbour or Providence River. For this reason Jones had been at pains to secure direct orders from the Marine Committee for his *Providence* cruise; that way, he cut out the commodore and kept the 5 per cent for himself. Later on, while captain of the *Ranger*, he insisted on keeping 15 per cent of prize money, and was furious with a Continental agent who queried this. If this attitude seems unduly mercenary, it should be noted that prize money was of paramount importance in all navies. By August 1777 Jones admitted to having received just over three thousand dollars in prize money,[7] a handsome return for eighteen months' naval service. He used this money to live on and even make cash advances to his seamen, while allowing his pay to accumulate. This turned out to be a wise move, as his arrears of pay were eventually settled in gold, rather than the depreciating paper currency of the period. By comparison, it has been estimated that D'Estaing's fleet shared 2,423,535 livres ($484,707) in gold as prize money arising from the expedition to North America and the West Indies in 1778–79, while De Grasse's fleet in 1781–82 netted over three million livres. These French admirals amassed considerable fortunes as a result.

In some respects, American seamen were better off than their British counterparts, the rates of pay for non-commissioned ranks being noticeably higher. Commissioned officers, on the other hand, were much worse off in the Continental Navy, captains receiving little more than half of what their British opponents enjoyed; but compared with the prize money, pay was of little consequence. In November 1776 Congress was persuaded (principally by Jones) to increase the rates of pay. Captains now got $48 or $60 a month, depending on the size of ship they commanded, while lieutenants got $24 or $30. By this revision, the captain of one of the larger American ships was a shilling a day better off than the captain of a fifth-rate (thirty-two-gun) ship in the Royal Navy. After April 1777, however, the real value of American pay was eroded as the Continental currency was hit by inflation.

The terms of service in the opposing navies were very different. British seamen, both volunteers and impressed men, served for the duration of the war, whereas Americans enlisted for only twelve months at a time. Jones expressed his regrets on that score loud and long, but Congress remained obdurate. Indeed, it is very difficult to imagine how sailors could have been recruited on any other basis at that period.

On 5 September 1776, while Jones was on his epic cruise, Congress introduced dress regulations for the Navy. Captains were to wear a blue coat with red lapels, slash cuffs, stand-up collar, flat yellow buttons decorated with anchors, red waistcoat edged in gold lace, and blue breeches. Apart from a non-regulation buff waistcoat, this is the uniform which Jones was wearing when his portrait was painted by Charles Willson Peale. There was no prescribed form of headgear although officers usually wore a gentleman's three-cornered hat with a cockade affixed. Lieutenants and masters wore a similar uniform, but without gold lace on the waistcoat or slashed cuffs. Midshipmen, on the other hand, were distinguished by red facings on their cuffs and red stitching on buttonholes. All officers had a single epaulette of gold lace on the right shoulder. Marine officers had a green coat faced with white, and white breeches piped in green. The epaulette was a French naval fashion which was not adopted by the Royal Navy till 1795. Interestingly, both Jones and Nelson were early and enthusiastic wearers of elaborate epaulettes, a device which gave the illusion of greater stature.

On this subject it should also be noted that Jones chaired a meeting of naval officers at Boston in March 1777 at which changes in uniform were high on the agenda. Out of their deliberations came a paper entitled *Uniform dress for the Navy agreed to at Boston by the*

Major Part of the Captains, and bearing Jones's imprimatur. Jones recommended that the new dress uniform for captains should be a navy-blue coat with white linings and lapels and a stand-up collar, white waistcoat, breeches and stockings. This was, in fact, remarkably similar to the uniform of the Royal Navy, and would enable Jones to carry out one of his more audacious deceptions, during the descent on Leith in September 1779. Only a close look at the epaulette, with its rattlesnake inscribed 'Don't Tread on Me', or the gilt buttons similarly embellished, would have given the game away. Junior officers would now wear a short coatee jacket, and midshipmen and masters something similar but without lapels. Altogether, the 1777 ensemble was much smarter than its earlier counterpart. Congress never formally adopted this dress code, but such was Jones's influence throughout the Navy by that date that it was generally adhered to. No attempt was made to prescribe a uniform for enlisted men, although even here Jones had pronounced views. The clothing was comfortable rather than smart, with a brown jacket, round hat and long baggy trousers.

In his letter of 17 October 1776 to Robert Morris, Jones had also proposed a naval expedition to the west coast of Africa with a view to smashing Britain's African trade. As part of his elaborate plan, he recommended the seizure of the island of St Helena in the South Atlantic, a popular port of call for East Indiamen on both outward and inward voyages. The notion was quixotic, although, given Jones's determination and meticulous planning, it might well have succeeded; but Commodore Hopkins had more mundane objectives in mind. In August the Marine Committee had ordered the commodore to send *Alfred*, *Columbus*, *Cabot* and *Hampden* on a six-month expedition to Newfoundland and Canadian waters with the object of destroying British fisheries and capturing storeships bound for Quebec as well as the merchant fleet of the Hudson's Bay Company bound for Britain. The cruise was also partly a public-relations exercise: the Continental flag was to be displayed along the Canadian coast and the Declaration of Independence proclaimed in the British dominions, as well as in the tiny French islands of St Pierre and Miquelon off the south coast of Newfoundland.

So far, this directive from the Committee had been a dead letter, Hopkins being more preoccupied with maintaining his ships in Narragansett Bay and trying, ineffectually, to drum up recruits. Frustrated by the privateers, who offered seamen twice as much pay as the Navy, the commodore even tried to persuade the Rhode Island legislature to impose an embargo on privateers and merchantmen until his manpower quota was filled, but his plea fell on deaf ears. 'I thought I had some Influence in the State I have lived so Long in,' he complained to the Marine Committee,

> but now I find that Private Interest bears more sway. I wish I had your orders giving me leave, whenever I found any man on board the privateers, not only to take him out, but all the rest of the men. That might make them more cautious of taking the men out of the service of the States.[8]

Recognising Jones as the most energetic of his captains, Hopkins gave him orders to carry out the Committee's directive. He was re-assigned to the command of *Alfred*, Dudley Saltonstall having in the meantime been given command of a new frigate, and in company with *Hampden* to raid Cape Breton in Nova Scotia. Now Jones had the independent command of a square-rigged man-o'-war, and he repaid the trust and confidence of the commodore by taking along with him, as a volunteer, the commodore's son Esek Hopkins junior. The principal objective of the expedition was the release of American prisoners who were being compelled to work in the Sydney coal-mines. Having freed the prisoners, Jones was expected to seize the British coal fleet on which General Howe's army at New York was depending for fuel over the coming winter. Having achieved these objectives, Jones was at liberty to continue to Newfoundland and wreak havoc on the cod fisheries if time and weather permitted.

Jones's first act was to transfer all the men, tried and true, from the sloop *Providence* to *Alfred* whose complement was increased to 140 officers and men. Jones must have been less than happy at the prospects of Hoystead Hacker as his back-up. Since his reinstate-ment, Captain Hacker had not shown evidence of having mended his ways, and indeed, shortly before the expedition set sail, Jones had to preside over the court-martial of James Bryant, *Hampden*'s gunner, for having 'collard and otherwise abused' his skipper and challenged him to a duel. Bryant was found guilty and dismissed the service, with the forfeiture of his share of the prize money. Hacker's previous service afloat had been the command of a packet plying between Providence and Newport, and he was supposed to know Narragansett Bay like the back of his hand. But the expedition got off to a very bad start on 27 October 1776 when Hacker's ship hit a submerged rock and was damaged so badly that she had to turn back. Her officers and men, including the unrepentant Hacker, were transferred to Jones's old ship *Providence* and the expedition set off again on 1 November. Despite its inauspicious beginning, this cruise proved to be even more spectacular than the previous one.

The commodore and Jones were in accord regarding the unfair competition of the privateers, and consequently Jones's first action on putting to sea was to call in at Tarpaulin Cove in the Elizabeth Islands off Cape Cod. Here he found the privateer *Eagle* from Rhode Island which, he suspected, had enlisted Navy deserters. He boarded and searched this vessel, and found two fleet deserters and a couple from the Rhode Island Brigade hiding behind a false bulkhead. Having seized these four men he took a fine revenge on the privateer by impressing a score of others. This high-handed action had grave repercussions for Jones on his return from the cruise, when he found that *Eagle*'s owner had taken out a writ against him for £10,000 damages. Somehow Jones concluded that the commodore had repudiated his action and refused to back him up, on the grounds that his orders to impress deserters were purely verbal and not written. Jones was misinformed on that score, however, for Hopkins wrote to the Marine Committee as early as 8 November 1776 (within days of the actual incident), stoutly defending Jones. And, lest Jones should harbour any notions to the contrary, Hopkins informed him in December, following his return to port, that he had initiated a counter-suit against the captain of the *Eagle* for enlisting naval deserters. In the end the legal action by *Eagle*'s owner was thrown out by the court, and Hopkins subsequently advised Jones to let the impressed men share his prize money. But the damage was done; Jones formed the impression that, somehow, Hopkins had stabbed him in the back, and this remained an *idée fixe* till the end of his life. The majority of Jones's biographers took their cue from his correspondence and embellished this animosity after their own fashion.[9]

On 11 November, off Cape Breton, Jones took his first prize on this cruise, the brigantine *Active* bound for Halifax from Liverpool with a mixed cargo. With Midshipman Spooner as prizemaster, Jones sent her to Edenton, North Carolina, consigned to Robert Smith, the partner of Joseph Hewes. To send a prize on such a long voyage, when there were many Continental ports much closer to hand, can only be explained by Jones's desire to show favour to his patron on the Marine Committee as well as his old friend from Kirkcudbright.

Smith, as an accredited prize agent, was entitled to 10 per cent of the proceeds before the captors got a penny, and Jones reckoned that *Active*'s cargo alone was worth six thousand pounds. These best-laid schemes, however, went agley when Spooner, faced with bad weather, ran the prize into Rhode Island, depriving Jones's Edenton friends of their percentage.

The following morning *Alfred* fell upon a much more valuable vessel, the 350-ton armed transport *Mellish*, carrying a cargo of ten thousand winter uniforms for the forces under Generals Burgoyne and Carleton as well as heavy-duty clothing and other stores destined for the British troops at Quebec. 'This will make Burgoyne shake a cloth in the wind and check his progress on the Lakes,' wrote Jones exultantly to John Hancock the same day, and he promised the chairman of the Marine Committee that he would rather sink such a valuable cargo than let the transport be retaken by the enemy.[10] He later discovered that the uniforms reached Washington's thread-bare army in time for the battle of Trenton. *Mellish* also carried about sixty passengers, including the families of British officers. Jones decided not to risk sending this prize to North Carolina, but placed Lieutenant Philip Brown in command, with two dozen of *Alfred*'s picked men and ten guns, and gave orders that the vessel should stay within signalling distance at all times. On 16 November *Alfred* and *Providence* seized the *Kitty* of London, bound from Gaspé to Barbados with a cargo of fish and oil. Lieutenant Joseph Allen was appointed prizemaster and ordered to take this vessel into Rhode Island.

At this juncture, with more severe weather imminent, trouble flared up aboard *Providence*. The ship's officers signed a round robin to Captain Hacker, stating that she was leaking so badly after the foul weather previously encountered, and had lost so many men assigned to prizes, that it would be hazardous to sail farther north. Hacker not only endorsed this petition, but strongly recommended that the expedition be abandoned. Jones conferred with Hacker and his principal lieutenants, exhorting them 'to relieve our Captive, ill treated Brethren from the Coal Mines', but his entreaties fell on deaf ears. The following night, under cover of a snow shower, *Providence* quietly slunk off back to her home port. The desertion of *Providence* had a bad effect on the crew of *Alfred* – 'epidemicall discontent' was how Jones later described it – but in spite of their pleas their gallant skipper pressed on. By 22 November *Alfred* was off Canso again, and Jones sent in armed boats which burned a beached supply ship, destroyed an oil warehouse and seized a smart schooner, a letter-of-marque from Liverpool carrying sixteen guns, which he subsequently manned to replace *Providence*. His hopes of liberating the hundred-odd American prisoners from the coal-mines were dashed by frozen harbours which prevented him making an assault on Sydney.

Unable to carry out his main objective, Jones now learned that a squadron of British frigates was scouring northern waters for him. Commodore Sir George Collier had, in fact, sent the frigates *Juno* and *Milford* and two smaller warships *Lizard* and *Hope* to patrol the Gulf of Maine and the line between Cape Cod and Sable Island. Near Louisburg on 24 November *Alfred*'s lookout espied three strange ships. Fortunately it soon transpired that they were not Collier's squadron but three coal ships from Sydney, heading for New York as part of a convoy escorted by the British frigate *Flora* which was actually obscured by fog. Jones took all three colliers without difficulty, and from their crews he learned that his 'ill treated Brethren' had been released from the coal-mines and were now serving aboard ships of the Royal Navy. This resolved Jones's dilemma, so he now turned southwards. The following day *Alfred* seized the ten-gun letter of marque *John* bound for Halifax from England. With Midshipman Robert Sanders as prizemaster, Jones added this ship to his flotilla and headed for Boston. The weather was now deteriorating rapidly and the convoy made slow progress, some of the prize ships getting separated. While crossing the northern edge of St George's Bank east of Cape Cod, Jones ran into a British frigate which turned out to be his old adversary *Milford*. Much larger and stronger than *Alfred*, this ship had twenty-eight guns and a crew of two hundred under Captain Burr whose log reveals that at three o'clock on 8 December he sighted 'five strange sail ahead and to leeward, distant about twelve miles'. Burr cleared for action and closed range. Jones recognised *Milford* and, anxious to protect his prizes, made signals which convinced Burr that the 'strange sail' were the frigate *Flora* escorting some Sydney colliers bound for New York. Night fell before Burr realised his mistake.

As an added precaution Jones now hoisted a brightly lit lantern to his main truck and ordered his prizemasters (except Sanders in *John*) to hold their westerly course for Boston when they saw by the light that he had tacked and was standing north-easterly. By this ruse Jones hoped to lure the frigate into following him while the prizes made their escape, but in the event it was unnecessary as Burr continued to believe they were friendly. At midnight *Alfred* and *John* came about, heading in a north-easterly direction on the port tack.

Milford followed them, suddenly suspicious of the change of course, which a ship escorting a convoy to New York would not have taken. As dawn came up, *Milford* found *Alfred*, *John* and their tender about nine miles ahead on the weather bow. Uncertain of his opponent's armament but tempted to try a conclusion with a British frigate, Jones signalled Sanders to drop slowly astern 'until he could discover by a view of the Enemies side whether she was of Superiour or Inferiour Force and to make a Signal accordingly'. As the truth dawned on him, Burr suddenly shook the reefs out of *Milford*'s topsails, set topgallant sails and wore ship, standing south-west. Now *John* and *Alfred* turned and gave chase. At half past eleven *Milford* tacked ship to meet them and by midday Jones was close enough to loose off four cannon at the enemy. *Milford* tacked again in pursuit, and *John* fell astern of her. *Alfred* and her tender were now on the weather bow of *Milford* which cracked on all the sail she could carry in the circumstances of squally weather, tacked, and gave chase. *Alfred*, however, proved to be the faster vessel and was soon out of range. At three in the afternoon Burr gave up the chase but came about on the port tack and bore down on *John* which was no match for the frigate. In the middle of a hailstorm *Milford* forced the little merchantman to heave to, with a couple of shots across her bows, and sent across a boarding party. Sanders and his prize crew were taken prisoner and sent, with the ship, into Halifax.

The loss of this prize, together with a good officer, rather detracted from Jones's sense of satisfaction at the conclusion of this expedition, and his mood was not improved when he discovered that Sanders had managed to get word to Commodore Hopkins from his confinement in Halifax that Jones had let him down by not coming to his aid when he needed it. Jones's own version of the encounter with *Milford*, published three years later, accused Sanders of being too ready, through cowardice, foolishness or treachery, to surrender his ship.[11] Both Jones and Sanders were wrong, as the log of *Milford* fairly indicates. The heavily out-gunned *John* stood no chance against the frigate and had no option but to surrender or be blown out of the water; and Jones, twelve miles ahead, could not have turned back in time to help. The only question is why Jones did not signal Sanders to follow him instead of falling astern, after he had fired on *Milford*. That question was neither asked nor answered at the time.

Alfred and her tender made course for Boston and, after a great deal of beating to windward, entered Massachusetts Bay on 14 December with only two days' provisions and water remaining.

With safety in sight, however, *Alfred* nearly came to grief. A strong offshore wind got up suddenly, leaving Jones with the choice of either hauling off to eastward or squeezing into Plymouth on the starboard tack. Jones took the latter option, but while tacking during a snow squall he 'got in irons making sternway'. Any competent seaman can extricate a ship from such a predicament if he has plenty of sea-room; but *Alfred* had a dangerous reef close astern and presently drifted on to it. Many a skipper would have given up his ship at that point, but Jones with the help of his tender got anchors out to windward, which slowed the vessel down and prevented her from driving hard and fast aground. On the flood-tide the following morning *Alfred* floated off and Jones, keeping a cool head, sailed her into Boston with only minor damage.

His chief prize *Mellish*, along with *Active*, berthed at Dartmouth (New Bedford), *Kitty* reached Boston and the sloop *Providence* made her home port safely. Only one of the three colliers was saved. *Milford* recaptured one while a second was retaken by HMS *Chatham* of Sir Peter Parker's squadron off Newport. Unfortunately, that port had only just fallen into British hands again, unbeknown to the prizemaster. Nevertheless, the *Mellish* alone would have justified claims that this cruise had been a great success, and the sale of her cargo gave Jones and his crew very substantial prize money. Mindful of the trouble he had got into at Tobago, Jones paid out of his own pocket the crews of *Alfred* and *Providence* whose twelve-month enlistment had now expired. He was not reimbursed by Congress until the war ended seven years later.

Now Jones returned to Providence to face his accusers over the *Eagle* affair. The owners of the privateer enlisted the services of an elderly lawyer named Joseph Lawrence who accompanied the sheriff's officer to arrest Captain Jones in the street. Jones promptly drew his sword and threatened to 'clip' any man who touched him. Lawrence, in the heat of the moment, made the supreme gaffe that the sheriff's man was a King's officer and should not be opposed on that account. Jones riposted, 'Is he? By God, I have a commission then to take his head off!' The sheriff's officer beat a hasty retreat crying, 'He lies! He lies! I ain't no King's officer!' Lawrence remonstrated with the lawman, ordering him to do his duty and arrest Jones; but this minor functionary replied, 'The devil – don't you see his poker?' So Jones evaded arrest and was duly vindicated by the counter-suit of Commodore Hopkins.

As the momentous year drew to a close, John Paul Jones stood out as the undisputed hero of two highly successful cruises. On land, the war was going badly for the Americans. Howe's victories at Long Island in August and White Plains in October forced Washington on to the defensive and culminated in the British capture of Manhattan and the seizure of Fort Washington with three thousand prisoners, the greatest disaster of the war until that time. The British then swept down through New Jersey with designs on Philadelphia and the seat of the rebel government. Only Washington's brilliant rearguard action at Trenton on 26 December, when he turned on the Hessian mercenaries and captured almost a thousand of them, saved the situation. Against the background of military reverses and naval inaction in general, Jones's exploits alone put heart in the Americans and boosted their flagging morale at the most crucial time in the Revolution. But America's most distinguished sailor was about to be rewarded with the bitterest disappointments of his life.

6. Boston and Portsmouth
1777

All delays are dangerous in war
— JOHN DRYDEN, *Tyrannic Love*, I, i

John Paul Jones spent Christmas and the New Year at the London Tavern in Boston and, apart from a brief trip to Philadelphia, he remained there until late March 1777. During those three months Jones enjoyed convivial company and made many friends at all levels of society. Among them were Thomas Russell, one of the city's most prominent citizens, Abraham Livingston whose father Philip was a member of the all-important Marine Committee, the merchant William Turnbull and Major John Gizzard Frazer of Virginia. The three last seem to have also had lodgings at the tavern, and over the course of several weeks Jones habitually dined with them. They became his closest confidants; 'our Boston family' is how he described them. Not that Jones was idle during this time. There were the manifold tasks involved in the repair and refitting of *Alfred*, supervising the care and disposal of more than a hundred and fifty British prisoners taken during the recent cruise, paying off the ship's crew and the drawn-out litigation over the privateer *Eagle*; but this still left plenty of time for Jones to dash off long letters to Joseph Hewes, Robert Morris and the Marine Committee in general. Whatever his other talents and qualities, Jones certainly comes across as the most cerebral of the Navy's senior officers; there is no comparable volume of correspondence for all of the other captains and Commodore Hopkins combined.

On 12 January 1777 Jones wrote to Hewes recommending that Hoystead Hacker be court-martialled for deserting him in the sloop *Providence*. Before any response was forthcoming, however, Jones suffered the first in a series of humiliations when he received a letter from Hopkins (then bottled up in Providence River by the British blockade), informing him that by vote of Congress he was relieved of the command of *Alfred* which now passed to Captain Elisha

Hinman. Hopkins concluded lamely that all he could offer Jones was the sloop *Providence* or 'any other vessel that is in my power to give you'. This letter, written at Providence on 14 January, reached Jones six days later and his immediate response was to fire off an angry broadside to the Marine Committee, under cover of a personal letter to Robert Morris. The general tone of Jones's letter to the Committee was dignified, though he could not stop himself making some very pointed remarks about the commodore, and went so far as to declare that most of the officers at present serving in the Navy were incompetent. This was followed by the passage, previously quoted, in which Jones set out in memorable terms the qualities and characteristics of the ideal naval officer. He reasserted his claim to have entered the Navy 'as a free Citizen of the World in defense of the Violated rights of Mankind', but he would be 'a degenerate' were he not 'in the highest degree Tenacious' of his 'Rank and Seniority – as a Gentleman'.

Ironically, at the time he sent off this letter, Jones was not yet aware how bad his position really was, despite the hint conveyed in the commodore's letter of 14 January. Eight or nine days later, just after the furious letter was despatched to the Committee on 21 January, Jones was finally apprised of the seniority list which Congress had approved the previous October, but which, for some unaccountable reason, was not published till thirteen weeks later. The first fourteen captains on the list were assigned to the frigates of thirty-two or twenty-eight guns then under construction; the other ten were appointed to the existing but much smaller and less heavily armed vessels. Jones was placed eighteenth in the list – after all the other captains and lieutenants of Hopkins' original fleet, after officers whose commissions dated after Jones, including several who had refused to enter the Navy in the early stages of the Revolution for fear of being hanged as rebels, after even the incompetent and dissolute Hacker whose seamanship and general conduct had left so much to be desired.

At the time this crucial list was compiled, however, Joseph Hewes was absent from Philadelphia, while the delegates from Virginia – neither then nor subsequently – lifted a finger to help Jones. At first glance, the list seems ludicrous, with absolutely no consideration to merit. At the very time it was being compiled Jones was actually the one captain at sea, on convoy duties in *Providence*, so he was not in Philadelphia, as others were, to canvass Committee members and other Congress delegates. By the time of his return to base in

December he had actually achieved infinitely more, in *Providence* or later *Alfred*, than all the other captains put together, and it seems strange that in light of his achievements the opportunity was not taken to revise the list before it was actually made public. The reason for the seemingly irrational decision of Congress in the first place, and why it was never modified or rescinded, can be summed up in two words – provincial bias. Out of the twenty-four captains on the list, twenty-three hailed from the northern colonies, the only outsider being John Paul Jones of Virginia. Some writers, latching on to the famous outburst of John Adams in 1813 against 'emigrants' like Barry and Jones being called fathers and founders of the Navy, have made much of the American regional xenophobia of the period, drawing attention to the fact that if Scotsmen were disliked in Virginia they were positively detested in New England which had suffered more than most from the depredations of the Highland regiments of the British Army; but this ignores the fact that James Nicholson (who actually headed the list), Hector McNeill (third) and Thomas Read (eighth) were Scotsmen, while John Barry (seventh) was an Irishman. John Manley, who had been the commodore of Washington's Army's Navy and was now second on the list, was an Englishman born and bred. Nicholson and Manley were former officers of the Royal Navy, as were Nicholas Biddle (fifth) and Abraham Whipple (twelfth).

The real root of this seemingly illogical list lay in the fact that the construction of the ships, purpose-built for the Navy, had been parcelled out by Congress among Massachusetts, New Hampshire, Pennsylvania and Maryland. No contracts for the new frigates were awarded to shipyards in any of the southern states. This regional partiality was also reflected in the home states of the captains appointed to the new frigates: four hailed from Pennsylvania (Biddle, Barry, Alexander and Wickes), two from Massachusetts (Manley and McNeill), two from New York (Grinnell and Hodge), two from Rhode Island (Whipple and John B. Hopkins) and one each from Connecticut (Saltonstall), Maryland (Nicholson) and New Hampshire (Thompson). William Hallock of Maryland got command of the brig *Lexington*, Hoystead Hacker of Rhode Island got the brig *Hampden* and Isaiah Robinson of Pennsylvania was assigned to the brig *Andrew Doria*. Even officers below Jones in the list fared better, Elisha Hinman of Connecticut (twentieth) getting *Alfred* and Joseph Olney of Rhode Island (twenty-first) getting the brig *Cabot*. A more detailed analysis of the seventeen captains placed ahead of Jones reveals that they had close family ties with members of the Committee, New England delegates to Congress or the companies that won the ship-building contracts. Against them all, John Paul Jones, the incomer, the outsider, the maverick, the man with a shadowy past and no family influence, stood no chance. If Joseph Hewes, the one man on whom he could have counted back in September and early October 1776 when the list was being compiled, was unfortunately absent at the time, then Jones was ill-served by the other Southerners who were in a position, on grounds of state alone, to help him. But for some inexplicable reason Arthur and Richard Henry Lee of Virginia, both then and later, were ranked among Jones's principal detractors, and broke the normal North-South divide by aiding and abetting Sam Adams of Massachusetts in trying to undermine Jones in his subsequent career.

On the other hand, Jones belatedly had the confidence and support of a number of New Englanders, and their influence shaped his later career; but when the list was drawn up he was still virtually unknown to John Hancock, the all-powerful President of Congress. It should not be overlooked that it was a New Englander, Esek Hopkins, who gave Jones his first opportunities, and the rift that developed between them was to a large extent of Jones's own making. Jones's staunchest allies would eventually be Robert Morris and Benjamin Franklin, both of whom hailed from Pennsylvania and thus not adopting so extreme a position as was evident in the New England states. Within the Navy itself, while James Nicholson, for personal reasons of jealousy, would continue to try to pull Jones down, other senior officers recognised Jones's utter professionalism and remained firm friends to the end of his career. These included Hector McNeill of Boston, John Young of Philadelphia and Richard Dale of Virginia.

In fact, the vicissitudes of Jones's career can be largely explained as clashes of personality rather than the underlying factional, sectional or regional differences so evident in the infant United States. Other men were treated unfairly, and there is an interesting parallel between Jones and Barry, the man with whom he is most often linked in the annals of the United States Navy. John Barry, born at Tacumshane, County Wexford, in 1745 and thus two years Jones's senior, had become the captain of a Philadelphia merchantman at the age of twenty-one and had spent fifteen years in America before the Revolution, latterly as master of *Black Prince* before she was transformed into *Alfred*. By rights he should have got command of *Alfred*, but was passed over in favour of Saltonstall. Barry accepted the situation with good grace and contented himself with the brig *Lexington* which led to a better command later on.

By comparison, Jones never got over the humiliation of his supposed demotion, and he continued to write furious letters to Robert Morris, Joseph Hewes, the Committee and John Hancock, complaining about the injustice of his treatment and simultaneously attacking the character and conduct of some of those placed ahead of him, notably Manley, Hacker and Thompson. This querulousness became almost an addiction, and while these angry letters no doubt helped Jones to let off steam, they had a cumulative effect on those who received them. This episode left a bitter legacy on Jones's part, but it also goes some way towards explaining the shabby treatment which he suffered on various occasions until the end of his turbulent life.

Coupled with the whingeing complexion of Jones's letters was an unattractive trait of grabbing all the credit for himself. His despatches and reports are invariably couched in personal terms, and seldom refer to subordinates whose skill and courage must have played a major part in ensuring his success. Morison[1] rightly draws attention to John P. Rathbun, first-lieutenant on *Alfred* during the Nova Scotia expedition, of whom we might never have heard at all, had he not been singled out by Commodore Hopkins who wrote to John Hancock saying that most of Jones's success in that cruise was due to Rathbun's 'Valour and Conduct', a shrewd estimate borne out by Rathbun's later distinguished naval career. Benjamin Franklin, later one of Jones's most ardent supporters, was not blind to this defect in his character and chided him gently on that score:

> Hereafter, if you should observe an occasion to give your officers and friends a little more praise than is their due, and confess more fault than you can justly be charged with, you will only become the sooner for it, a great captain. Criticising and censuring almost every one you have to do with, will diminish friends, increase enemies, and thereby hurt your affairs.[2]

That this was the truth would speedily become apparent. Jones was the most efficient captain in the Navy, and fine he knew it. Had his professionalism been tempered by modesty and humility, he would have gone much farther in his new career, but his character was fatally flawed by his overweening egotism. Habits of pugnaciousness had been bred into him on the quarterdeck, doubtless compensating for a lack of stature in squaring up to insubordinate officers and mutinous seamen; but he carried this attitude over into his dealings with the Committee and Congress and later in his encounters with the American Commissioners in France and ultimately in his relationships with Prince Potemkin and the Empress Catherine. His prickliness and quickness of temper certainly did not diminish with the passage of years.

In the short term, however, Jones's persistent letters to the Committee, together with more considered appraisal of his most recent exploits, soon brought the Committee round. On 17 January 1777, even before Jones was made aware of the seniority list, Hancock wrote to Robert Morris:

> I admire the spirited conduct of little Jones; pray push him out again. I know he does not love to be idle, & I am as certain you wish him to be constantly active, he is a fine fellow & he shall meet with every notice of mine & I am confident you will join me.[3]

By this time the Committee were coming to the conclusion that Commodore Hopkins would have to make way for a younger and more energetic commander. Indeed, Hopkins himself had suggested that perhaps he ought to stand down. By now the fleet was either immobilised by the British blockade or unable to put to sea on account of the shortage of skilled manpower. On 21 January 1777 the commodore received orders to fit out his flagship *Warren* and the new frigate *Providence* 'with all possible expedition' and cruise against the enemy's warships which were wreaking so much havoc on American commerce off the coast of Virginia. Hopkins could not or would not take appropriate action and on 5 February Morris informed him that:

> By consent of the Honorable Congress, I have this day given instruction to John Paul Jones Esq., commander of the *Alfred*, to take upon him the conduct of an expedition wherein he will require the assistance of the *Columbus*, *Cabot*, *Hampden*, and sloop *Providence*, and you will please to order the commanders to join him and put themselves under his command.

I flatter myself with having your utmost exertions to get these vessels well and expeditiously manned and completely fitted that they may sail as soon as possible.[4]

A few days earlier Morris wrote at length to Jones, giving him direct orders to command the expedition which was aimed against the Caribbean island of St Christopher (St Kitts) and the north coast of Jamaica, and then on to Pensacola, then as now an important naval base on the Gulf coast of Florida. The purpose of this expedition was to disrupt British communications and create general mayhem rather than to seize enemy ships. As the prospects for taking prizes would consequently be slim, Jones was faced with a tall order indeed. Morris's letter emphasised the strategy to be adopted:

> Destroying their settlements, spreading alarms, showing and keeping up a spirit of enterprise that will oblige them to defend their extensive possessions at all points, is of infinitely more consequence to the United States than all the plunder that can be taken.[5]

Foolishly Commodore Hopkins ignored the orders and countered the Committee's intentions with orders of his own to Jones on 16 February, directing him 'to enlist as many men as you think sufficient to man the sloop *Providence*, as soon as possible, in order to go out on a cruise'. Not surprisingly, Jones swiftly informed his commodore that he had direct orders from the Committee and pointedly reminded Hopkins of their precise contents. The commodore ignored this and deliberately sent off *Hampden* and *Cabot* on independent cruises for up to six weeks. Left to their own devices, their skippers kept out of harm's way – and the reach of Captain Jones. On 28 February Jones wrote a third time to Hopkins requesting the ships in compliance with the Committee's orders. His letter, written in white heat, was a curious mixture of contempt and conciliation, accusing the commodore of leaving him 'in the Lurch', telling him his duty and reminding him that he, Jones, had stood by him when he 'needed friends' over the *Glasgow* affair. Having vented his spleen, Jones concluded on a calmer note:

> I did not think you capable of prevarication . . . However, waiving everything of a private nature, the best way is to co-operate cheerfully together that the public service may be

forwarded, and that scorn may yet forbear to point her finger
at a fleet under your command.

The commodore's response was terse: 'I do absolutely think that it
is impracticable to get those vessels fitted or manned for your
proposed expedition and shall acquaint the Honorable Marine Board
with my reasons.'[6] On 28 January (and therefore prior to the receipt
of Jones's angry letter), Hopkins wrote to Robert Morris saying that
he would do his best to comply with orders, but that *Hampden* had
already sailed, while *Columbus* and the sloop *Providence* were cooped
up in upper Narragansett Bay with no more than skeleton crews.
Alfred was being repaired at Boston and would not be ready to sail
for at least six or eight weeks, while *Cabot* was already under sailing
orders and would not be available for six weeks. And he reserved a
broadside of his own for the upstart Jones in the final pragraph of
his letter:

> On the whole it is Impossible to mann and get these Vessels
> together Soon for any Expedition and from the number of
> Complaints I have had from the Officers and people Late
> under Captn Jone's Command in Respect to his Conduct
> during the Last Cruize, and Since he came home in Regard
> to both their wages and prize money, I am well Convinced
> that it will be more difficult to mann Vessels under his
> Command than to do it under any Officer of the Fleet that
> I am acquainted with and Necessity will Oblige me to wait
> your further Orders Respecting the Expedition you have
> Order'd, And as Six Weeks' time will be soon enough for
> the *Alfred*, I have thought best to let Captn Olney range for
> Six Weeks to prevent his men from deserting.[7]

One of the 'Officers and people Late under Captn Jone's Command'
was the commodore's son. Esek Hopkins Junior complained to his
father that Jones had been 'unpardonably rude' to him during the
recent expedition. In addition, the commodore had received
numerous complaints from Jones's crew regarding his tardiness in
settling wages and prize money. In fact, Jones had deliberately
withheld payment to those seamen whose terms of enlistment had
come to an end, in a desperate bid to get these trained men to sign
on for a further twelve months. He also tried to get the men to
appoint him as their prize agent. In both respects, however, he acted

from the best possible motives. Continental prize agents were so inefficient, lazy or dishonest, if not all three, that they kept seamen waiting for months on end for their prize money and pay, a grievance that did nothing to counter the inducements of the privateers whose agents settled promptly. Jones, in effect, was having to advance pay to his men out of his own pocket.

Armed with such testimony, Hopkins appealed to Hancock for a court-martial to try Jones on the charge of having deserted the prize ship *John* as well as on a trumped-up charge of having stolen a quantity of gold from the prize ship *Mellish*. This hysterical plea, in fact, marked the effective end of the commodore's naval career. When the allegation was put to Jones he promptly rebutted it with the sworn testimony of the prize agents. Hancock saw through Hopkins and ignored his calls for a court-martial. Hancock and other members of the Committee were now tiring of the old buffer's feeble conduct. It was bad enough that he had let the British Navy blockade him, but when the British frigate *Diamond* ran aground on Warwick Neck, Hopkins failed lamentably to take advantage of the situation. Even his own crew were demoralised at the commodore's weakness and timidity; the entire wardroom and chief petty officers' mess of *Warren* thereupon petitioned the Committee to remove him as unfit for command, and despatched Captain John Grannis of the Marines to Philadelphia to present their complaints in person.

Ironically, the commodore's downfall was secured by a cabal of Rhode Island businessmen who had an important stake in the privateering business, and who had been irked by Hopkins defending Jones over the *Eagle* affair. They conspired with the Revd John Reed, a naval chaplain, who had remonstrated with the commodore over his profane language. Later, Reed would admit that he had been put up to this 'by some gentlemen of the town' but the damage was done, reinforced by the formal petition of Captain Grannis and nine other crew-members of the commodore's flagship. This was soon followed by similarly damning documents which blackened the commodore's character. Significantly, much was made of his 'most irreligious and impious example' and of Hopkins 'ridiculing virtue'. Others swore that the commodore had characterised Congress as 'a pack of damned rascals, the best of them lawyers' clerks, who knew nothing about their business'. This might well have been true, but when this savage judgment reached the ears of Congress, the commodore's career was in jeopardy. The Marine Committee, exasperated by the commodore's vacillation and ineffectiveness, finally took action. On 26 March 1777 he was suspended from his command and then, the following January, formally dismissed from the Navy.

It was a sad end to the career of the Navy's first commander, and while not entirely unjustified, in mitigation it should be emphasised that Hopkins was more sinned against than sinning, a victim of political circumstances. The greed and selfishness of his fellow Rhode Islanders were at the heart of his troubles. Quite apart from their general involvement in the privateering enterprise, these solid citizens were up to their armpits in corruption. When Hopkins discovered that the shipowners of Providence were siphoning off the funds voted by Congress for the construction of frigates to the repair and maintenance of their privateers, the old man exploded with wrath; but he was powerless to prevent them diverting construction workers and materials, and they combined to secure his removal. Earlier biographers made much of the rift between Hopkins and Jones, dismissing the former as being insanely jealous. But Hopkins had given Jones his first command and had been consistently friendly towards him, putting his own neck on the block by defending him against the privateer owners, and only rebuking him after repeated complaints. Morison alone put the relationship of Jones and Hopkins into proper perspective.[8]

Meanwhile, the new frigates, constructed with great enthusiasm and speed, were now ready for action, in theory at any rate. On 4 April 1777 the Marine Committee issued orders to Captains John B. Hopkins, Abraham Whipple and Dudley Saltonstall to take the frigates *Warren*, *Providence* and *Trumbull* to sea, but this was a dead letter owing to the British blockade. The first two remained at their moorings in Providence River for a year. In March 1778 Hopkins succeeded in taking *Warren* out of Narragansett Bay one moonless night under the very noses of the British, and after a short cruise got as far as Boston. Soon afterwards Whipple scraped together a short crew of 160 men for *Providence* and fought his way out of Narragansett Bay on 30 April 1778, eventually getting his ship safely to France. *Trumbull* remained idle in the Connecticut River for two years, then spent a further year at New London before she finally got into action, but was captured by the British.

The much-vaunted new frigates proved to be a dead loss. *Raleigh*, built in under two months, did not get to sea till eighteen months later (August 1777), due to a lack of cannon and the usual dire shortage of manpower. The rest were either boxed in at their shipyards by the blockade, destroyed on the stocks to avoid capture as the war ebbed and flowed, or were simply never completed at all. The few frigates that were completed proved to be unseaworthy on account of the unseasoned timber that was so hastily used in constructing their hulls. The fiasco of the frigates was an object lesson in how not to conduct a naval campaign. Things might have turned out differently had there been a strict control over the building programme, proper training for officers and men and the appointment of senior officers on merit rather than political considerations. But incompetence, corruption and self-interest all too often got in the way of the best intentions.

In the end, therefore, Congress had to rely to a great extent on the original Continental Navy, the motley collection of vessels under Esek Hopkins, when hostilities broke out. The fate of these ships, however, is a dismal litany of failure. *Cabot* was driven ashore in March 1777 but salvaged by the British; *Wasp* ran aground in Chesapeake Bay and was blown up to prevent her falling into British hands; *Lexington* was captured in September 1777; *Andrew Doria* was burned in Delaware Bay in November 1777 to avoid capture; *Alfred* was captured by the British on 9 March 1778; *Columbus*, driven ashore on 1 April 1778 when trying to evade the blockade, was burned by her crew; *Hampden* ran aground in Narragansett Bay and broke up; and the sloop *Providence*, last survivor of the original Navy, was blown up by her crew to prevent capture in the Penobscot in 1779.

Chagrined at being passed over for one of the fine new frigates, and grievously disappointed at being fobbed off with the little single-masted sloop *Providence*, Jones went to Philadelphia late in March 1777 to press his claims personally on the Committee. He spent a month there, frantically pulling strings and impressing upon the Committee, individually and collectively, the need for positive action. On 25 March Congress resolved to purchase three ships and convert them for war service. One was earmarked for 'Captain John Paul Jones, until better provisions be made for him'. Jones was partially mollified, but there was still the vexatious matter of his seniority. He broached the subject with John Hancock who fulsomely complimented 'little Jones' on his exploits and promised to put the matter right. Hancock asked him for his captain's commission of 8 August 1776, so that a new one, back-dated to 10 May (when Jones was appointed to the sloop *Providence*), could be made out. Later Hancock issued him with a commission bearing the ominous date of

10 October 1776 and added insult to injury by endorsing it 'Number 18'. So Jones's commission was now post-dated and the humiliating number was made permanent. His own account of this sorry episode describes his reaction when Hancock handed him this document.

> I told him that was not what I expected, and requested my former commission. He turned over various papers on the table, and at last told me he was sorry to have lost or mislaid it. I shall here make no remark on such conduct in a President of Congress. Perhaps it needs none.'

Hancock told him that the list of 10 October 1776 had been hurriedly drawn up, 'without well knowing the different merits and qualifications of the officers', but that Congress intended 'to render impartial justice, and always to honour, promote, and reward merit'. And Hancock concluded this interview by promising Jones that, until he was perfectly satisfied respecting his rank, he should have a command. What Hancock had in mind was bizarre in the extreme.

While Jones was in Philadelphia, the French armed merchantman *Amphitrite* of twenty guns, arrived at Portsmouth, New Hampshire, with a much-needed cargo of arms and ammunition from Roderique Hortalez and Company of Paris, a curious mercantile operation that was funded partly by France and partly by Spain and operated under the control of no less a personage than the playwright Beaumarchais. The ship was under orders from Paris to proceed to Charleston, South Carolina, to take on board a cargo of rice and then return to France. Some bright spark on the Marine Committee came up with the brilliant idea of sending Jones across the Atlantic aboard this vessel, in order to take command of one of the powerful warships which the American Commissioners were then in the process of procuring. This ploy had the added attraction that it got the querulous little captain out of everyone's hair, and also removed him from the sectional in-fighting going on in Philadelphia.

On 9 May Jones received the strangest orders ever given to a naval officer anywhere. He was to go aboard *Amphitrite* 'appearing or acting on suitable Occasions as Commander', and with as many extra seamen and petty officers as he deemed necessary to engage the ships in naval action. On the way to Charleston and thence to France, he was to take prizes and split the proceeds three ways: a third to Hortalez and the French crew, a third to Congress and a third to Jones and his Americans. On arrival at Paris Jones was to report to the American Commissioners and take command of the 'fine ship' which they had purchased for him. This he was to man and fit out 'with the utmost Expedition' and follow the Commissioners' orders for a cruise in the narrow seas – the English Channel and the Irish Sea – and eventually sail her to America. Jones would have agreed to anything at that juncture, just to get command again. On receipt of these orders at Boston on 21 May, he went off to Portsmouth to inspect *Amphitrite* and interview her French skipper, Fautrel. The latter, however, flatly refused to take Jones on board under the preposterous conditions laid down by Congress. Had he been foolish enough to give way to the wishes of Congress, one wonders what sort of expedition would have resulted. The notion of Jones and Fautrel in joint command, or jockeying for control of the ship, let alone subsequent action and the three-way split of the prize money, boggles the mind.

When the master of another French ship, *Le Mercure*, interceded with an offer to convey Jones across to France as a passenger, he turned this down on the grounds that the ship was too lightly armed for his comfort. He seriously considered fitting out his prize ship *Mellish* as a man-o'-war, but then Colonel John Langdon of Portsmouth solved the problem by offering Jones the command of a new twenty-gun sloop which had just been launched. Langdon, who had briefly been a member of the Marine Committee, had constructed this ship at the Committee's behest, and had provisionally appointed an elderly merchant skipper from Cork named John Roche. This Irishman had turned up at Portsmouth shortly before the war as master of a ship from Quebec carrying a valuable cargo of furs, which he alleged were his personal property. Having sold the furs and pocketed the proceeds, he set himself up as a merchant in partnership with Langdon, and had lately been employed as a consultant in the building of the sloop. His felonious activities came to light in June 1777 when an official complaint against him was lodged by the State of Massachusetts Bay, exposing him as 'a person of doubtful character and ought not to be entrusted with such a command'. As a consequence, on 14 June Congress resolved that Roche be suspended and that Captain John Paul Jones be appointed to command of the ship *Ranger*. These resolutions were printed in the Journals of Congress immediately after:

> *Resolved*, That the Flag of the thirteen United States be thirteen stripes, alternate red and white; that the union be

thirteen stars, white in a blue field, representing a new constellation.

Thus the most spectacular phase in Jones's career coincided with the birth of the Stars and Stripes. It will be remembered that Jones had had the honour of first hoisting the Grand Union flag aboard *Alfred* in December 1775. Now he would be one of the first to hoist the new flag aboard a ship of war.

Jones received his new orders at Boston on 1 July 1777 and ten days later he travelled to Portsmouth. In the interim he was gainfully occupied in drumming up recruits. At Danvers, north of Boston, he got a handbill printed by E. Russell that held out the promise of an opportunity to 'all gentlemen seamen and able-bodied landsmen' to distinguish themselves in the 'glorious cause of their Country, and make their Fortune'. The advertisement was cleverly worded by Jones himself and concluded with the reproduction of a resolution of Congress dated 29 March 1777 which promised under the name of John Hancock an advance of forty dollars to able seamen and twenty to ordinary seamen 'to be deducted from their future Prize-Money'. Jones himself was named in the main text, asking potential recruits 'to repair to the Ship's Rendezvous in Portsmouth, or at the sign of Commodore Manley in Salem, where they will be kindly entertained, and receive the greatest encouragement'.[10] The records show that Jones paid $713 out of his own pocket to seamen who enlisted under Hancock's terms, and many months passed before Congress reimbursed him. He also spent $542 on advertising and other expenses incurred in the recruiting drive (which presumably included the kind entertainment at the Commodore Manley, an unfortunate choice of tavern, in the circumstances). When some of the newly enlisted men deserted to privateers after getting their advances, Jones pursued them relentlessly, an effort that incurred a further expense of $82.66.

Other matters which occupied at least some of his time at Boston in the spring and summer of 1777 cast an interesting light on Jones's character. Captain John Paul Jones, the rising star of the United States Navy, now began to cut quite a dash in polite society. As well as kitting himself out with a fine new wardrobe, he devised a coat-of-arms for himself, and had an escutcheon painted to his precise specifications. The same device was simultaneously engraved for use as a seal. Jones's bogus arms prominently displayed the stag, used by several Jones families in Wales, quartered with the arms of a Paul family in Gloucestershire with whom he actually had no connection whatsoever. The Jones stag formed the crest, while the motto (the only original aspect of this heraldic achievement) was the Latin tag *Pro Republica*. Some biographers speculate that the fine clothes and the coat-of-arms were part of the trappings of a gentleman necessary to his courtship of Dorothea Dandridge that summer, ignoring the fact that the lady had already become the second Mrs Patrick Henry. Jones was not the man to retrace his steps where matters of the heart were concerned. His habit, both then and later on in France, seems to have been amatory dalliance with a rapid succession of lustful ladies, though there is no doubt that had a suitably prominent society belle come to his notice, Jones would have given serious consideration to her potential for his social advancement.

In Boston there were certainly plenty of ephemeral affairs but nothing serious. More cerebral delights, however, were to be had in the company of Phillis Wheatley, one of the most extraordinary intellects of her generation. A native of west Africa, she had been kidnapped and sold into slavery on the block at Boston at the age of eight. Fortunately, her owners recognised her superior intelligence and gave her a sound education; by the age of thirteen she was addressing her poetry to the University of Cambridge in New England, and later received acclaim for her amazing talents in London as well as Boston. In an age that believed in heaven-taught genius, Miss Wheatley's verses were highly regarded by Washington, Jefferson and others. Jones, who was no mean versifier himself, composed an ode which he sent via his friend Hector McNeill, to 'the Celebrated Phillis the African Favorite of the Nine and of Apollo'.[11] The poem, by a former mate on slaveships, reveals Jones to have been a passionate believer in the fundamental tenet that all mankind had the right to live free. The poem reveals an utter repugnance of slavery, a revulsion which developed as a result of seeing one of the most degrading aspects of slavery at close quarters. This, of course, makes a nonsense of sundry references in early biographies to Jones being the owner of slaves, particularly the fiction dreamed up by Buell concerning Cato and Scipio, Jones's slaves who served as cabin-boys aboard *Ranger*.[12]

During his extended sojourn at Boston in the spring and summer of 1777, Jones continued to enjoy the congenial company of his 'Boston family'. His boon companion in this period was Major John Gizzard Frazer, assistant quartermaster-general in Washington's army in the early stages of the war. By the spring of 1777, however,

Washington had seen fit to dispense with the gallant major's services and he was now living on his wits and half-pay while seeking some fresh appointment. Jones tried to secure a commission for him in the Marine Corps, but Robert Morris refused the petition. As a consolation, Jones invited Frazer to sail with him to France, in the hope that something suitable might arise there. Frazer readily assented, though only on condition that he could bring along his 'Girl'. Lest Jones, man of the world that he was, should be in any doubt as to the young lady's relationship with the major, Frazer asked Jones to find lodgings for her 'in some decent private house' in Portsmouth, prior to embarcation, and, as he wished 'to have as much of her Company as I can, let none of my acquaintances there know of it'. From Portsmouth in September Frazer wrote to Carter Braxton of King William County, Virginia, to get his help in buying on behalf of Captain Jones 'a small landed estate on the Mattapony called Foxes [*sic*] Ferry'. Jones, he added, was so impressed by his 'truly Elysian' description of Fox's Ferry that he wished to purchase it for the asking price of twelve hundred pounds. The deal never materialised, probably because Carter or Jones discovered that the estate was the subject of litigation between the Fox and Frazer families, neither of whom had clear title.

Jones himself reached Portsmouth on 12 July and immediately went aboard *Ranger* to check the arrangements for fitting her out. Originally named *Hampshire* at her launching, the sloop was soon afterwards renamed in honour of Rogers' Rangers, the celebrated forerunner of the modern-day Rangers and a unit in which many Portsmouth men had served, though ironically Major Rogers himself was now serving with the British Army. The name was singularly appropriate to a ship under Jones's independent command. Designed by William Hackett, she was constructed in Langdon's yard on Rising Castle (now Badger) Island in the Piscataqua opposite the town of Portsmouth. Portsmouth was then the shipbuilding centre of America, and from this same yard came the frigate *Raleigh* as well as the great ship of the line *America* towards the end of the war.

Ranger had a gross tonnage of 318.5 and was about 110 feet overall in length. She was twenty-five feet shorter than her namesake which defended the America's Cup in 1937 and was about the same length as the submarine-chasers of the Second World War. Unlike the single-masted sloop *Providence* which Jones had previously commanded, *Ranger* was rated as a sloop of war, square-rigged on all three masts, carrying royals as well as topgallants and studding sails.

Her bulwarks were originally designed for twenty guns, but Jones reduced her armament to eighteen 9-pounders, which he felt was the maximum consonant with speed and manoeuvrability. Her topsides were painted black with a broad yellow band, harmonising with a figurehead of the same colour. A British officer, Captain Gurley, who got a good look at *Ranger* in the Irish Sea, thought that she was Bermuda-built – which was quite a compliment as Bermuda was noted for its sharp, rakish vessels built for speed.

Jones had hoped to take his new ship to sea by the end of July, but he had not anticipated how many problems would arise, and a further three months elapsed before she was ready. Primarily there was a desperate shortage of manpower, and this grave matter gave Jones endless headaches. First he appealed to his old comrade-in-arms, Captain Matthew Parke of the Marines, then stationed at Providence, whom Jones asked to send round 'a Drum, Fife and Colours' to attract recruits. Parke eventually mustered twenty-two recruits for Jones, only to have them hijacked by John Hopkins for his frigate *Warren*. Marine Lieutenant Samuel Wallingford tried to enlist men in and around Boston but found himself up against stiff competition from the frigate *Raleigh* as well as the privateers. Significantly, Jones got no help from Colonel Langdon, who had his own reasons for hindering the enterprise, as William Whipple of the procurement committee explained to Josiah Bartlett of Portsmouth, shortly after *Ranger* set sail:

> There is at this time 5 Privateers fitting out here, which I suppose will take 400 men. These must be by far the greater part Countrymen, for the Seamen are chiefly gone, most of them in Hallifax Gaol. Besides all this, you may depend no public ship will ever be manned while there is a privateer fitting out. The reason is plain: Those people who have the most influence with Seamen think it their interest to discourage the Public service, because by that they promote their own interest, viz. Privateering. In order to do this effectually, every officer in the public service (I mean in the Navy) is treated with general contempt.[13]

He might have added that one of the chief culprits was John Langdon himself, owner of several of the privateers then fitting out, as well as a number of other ships engaged in the same lucrative business. Whipple concluded that unless Congress took action to remedy this disgraceful state of affairs the United States Navy would be 'officered by Tinkers, Shoemakers and Horse Jockeys, and no Gentleman worth employing will accept a Commission'. Jones had written innumerable letters to the Committee along similar if less colourful lines. Sadly, something approaching that situation was eventually the case, and the infant Navy was hampered by a singular lack of professionalism. By the end of August Jones was reduced to writing to the New Hampshire legislature seeking permission to enlist 'from the matross [gunnery] companies in the Batteries in the Piscataqua Harbour a number of men not exceeding twenty'.

Though he eventually made up the requisite numbers of seamen, Jones was also hampered by a lack of basic supplies. In this respect he clashed frequently with Langdon who felt, as the builder of the ship, that he had some say in the procurement of stores, for which he took a nice commission from ships' chandlers. On his own initiative the indefatigable Jones set about procuring the necessary materials for sails but by 20 September had only managed to obtain sufficient hessian (a cloth markedly inferior to the usual sail-canvas) to make up a single suit of sails. Out of this grew the charming myth, repeated in countless chapbooks and early biographies, that Jones had exercised his charm on the ladies of Portsmouth into giving up their best silk petticoats to fashion sails and a flag for *Ranger*. Three weeks later he crossed swords with Langdon over the yawl or cutter to be used as *Ranger*'s tender. This he regarded as part and parcel of the ship's equipment and when Langdon refused to comply, Jones reminded him forcibly that he had been authorised by Congress and expected his orders 'to be duly honored'. Langdon ignored this angry plea. On 30 October he wrote to Langdon again, howling with rage because Langdon had refused to honour his bank draft: 'Your refusing to pay my order is perhaps the first instance of the kind that hath happened in our navy, it is the first draft of mine that ever was dishonored.'

He went on to complain that he was about to weigh anchor with no more than thirty gallons of rum, which was sufficient only for medicinal purposes. Even something as trifling as a boatswain's whistle had not been supplied as ordered. What made matters worse was that Langdon, who had continually obstructed him, had had the nerve to complain to the Marine Committee of Jones's dilatoriness in getting the ship ready for sea. To counter this, Jones sent off the same day a letter to John Brown, the Secretary of the Marine Committee, complaining in detail of Langdon's shortcomings. The matter of the inadequate supply of rum was raised, Jones declaring 'This alone was enough to cause a mutiny!'[14]

The following day Jones made his will, naming Robert Morris and Joseph Hewes as his executors, each of whom was to have a mourning ring, worth £100, in his memory. The rest of his estate was to go to his mother and sisters in Scotland. At the same time he despatched letters to both of his executors, reiterating his complaint about the injustice of his low ranking in the seniority list and declaring that several captains senior to him were 'altogether illiterate and Utterly ignorant of Marine affairs' and hotly refuting 'the dirty and Ungrateful insinuations' which Esek Hopkins had made about him.

It was in a sombre, resentful mood that Captain Jones, on the morning of 1 November 1777, gave the order to weigh anchor. At nine o'clock precisely a gun was fired, the boatswains piped shrilly using the new silver calls provided belatedly at the captain's expense, and the Marines' fifes and drums played a lively tune as the men heaved on the capstan bars to break out the anchor. *Ranger*, whipped round under the fresh autumnal breeze from the White Mountains, with a strong ebb current under her keel, slipped her moorings and headed out into the channel. On the quarterdeck Captain John Paul Jones, USN, in his fine new blue uniform, and Major John Gizzard Frazer, USMC, in continentals, waved their cocked hats and bowed gallantly to the ladies lined up on the bank to watch the warship's departure. The sloop gathered speed as she squared away, glided round Fort Point, set lower courses, topgallants and stunsails as she passed Jaffray Point, hauled up sharp on the port tack to pass the Isles of Shoals and headed out to sea at last.

7. Paimboeuf to Whitehaven
1777–78

And the ships shall go abroad
To the Glory of the Lord
Who heard the silly sailor-folk and gave them back their sea!
— RUDYARD KIPLING, *The Last Chantey*

'The best crew I have ever seen, and, I believe, the best afloat' is how Jones described the ship's company in a letter to the Marine Committee dated 2 October 1777. There were about 150 men aboard. Jones shared his quarters with Frazer who, at the last moment, had left his girl behind and brought a Negro man-servant instead, together with a large stock of wines and spirits which he used liberally but which Jones barely touched. In hindsight, it would have been better had Jones messed with the other officers in the wardroom where, in an informal atmosphere, he might have fostered their goodwill and loyalty through his scintillating conversation and great personal charm. In fairness to Jones, it was not customary at that period for captains in the United States Navy to dine with their subordinate officers; and Jones himself would later be one of the first to break with this practice. The able seamen and landsmen were, for the most part, natives of the Piscataqua area or Essex County in Massachusetts, although they included a sprinkling of Irishmen, a French Canadian and a Swede, Edward Meyer, who proved to be more loyal to Jones than most of the American crew-members. There were also two New Hampshire free blacks, Cato Carlile and Scipio Africanus (the source of Buell's canard about Jones's cabin-boys).

Lieutenant Elijah Hall and Surgeon Ezra Green (a Harvard graduate) both kept journals of the cruise, but the most vivid account was that written by Jones himself to John Wendell, his closest friend in Portsmouth. Wendell's son David Wentworth Wendell served as a midshipman on the voyage. He was arguably the best-connected officer that Jones ever had under his immediate command, being the grandson of Colonel Wendell and Pascal Wentworth of Portsmouth, a nephew of Colonel Quincy of Braintree and a cousin of John Hancock and John Adams. In spite of these impressive connections, young Wendell was a modest, unassuming young man who never attempted to exploit the situation and sought no special treatment from his commanding officer. From Nantes on 11 December Jones wrote to the boy's father, and this letter is worth quoting in full, showing as it does his natural exuberance and the pleasure he took in his fine ship, a fair wind and an excellent crew.

My Dear Sir,

The *Ranger* was wafted by the Pinions of the gentlest, and most friendly Gales, along the Surface of the Blue profound of Neptune; and not the swelling bosom of a Friend's nor even of an *Enemi's Sail*, appeared within our placid Horizon, untill after we had passed the Everlasting Mountains in the Sea (called Azores) whose Tops are in the Clouds, and whoe's Foundations are in the Center. When lo! this Halcyon Season was interrupted! the 'gathering Fleets o'erspread the Sea' and Wars alarms began! Nor ceased day or night untill, aided by the mighty Boreus, we cast Anchor in this Asylum the 2d. Currt. but since I am not certain that my Poetry will be understood, it may not be amiss to add, *by way of marginal note*, that after leaving Portsmouth nothing remarkable happened untill I got to the Easterward of the Western Islands; and that from that time untill my arrival here, I fell in with Ships every day and sometimes every Hour; within Eighty Leagues of Ushant, I met with an Enemies fleet of Ten Sail bound up Channel, but not withstanding my best endeavours, I was unable to detach any of them from the strong Convoy under which they sailed. I met with and brought too a variety of other Ships none whereof proved British Property, except two Brigantines from Malaga with Fruit for London, which became Prizes, the one is arrived here, the other I am told in Quiberon Bay; as I have met with and brought too several Ships in the Night, I had the most agreeable Proof of the Active Spirit of my Officers and Men.

I have forwarded my dispatches to Paris, by Express, and determine not to go myself unless I am sent for. I understand that in Obedience to Orders from the Secret Committee, the Commissioners had, some time ago, provided One of the finest Frigates for me that can be imagined, calculated for Thirty two Twenty four Pounders, on one deck, and longer than any Ship in the Enemies Fleet; but that it has been found necessary to give her up, on account of some difficulties which they have met with at Court. My Heart glows with the most fervent Gratitude for this, and every unsolicited and unexpected instance of the favo'r and Approbation of Congress; and if a Life of Services devoted to the Intrests of America, can be made Instrumental in securing its Independence; I shall be that happiest of Men, and regard the continuance of such Approbation, as an Honor far superior to the empty Peagantry (*sic*), which Kings ever had Power to bestow.

I esteem your Son as a promising and deserving young Man, I have just now had some Conversation with him and am much Pleased with his diffidence and Modesty, he would not he says accept of a Commission untill he thinks himself equal to the duty of the Office of Lieutenant; there I think he shows a true Spirit; in the mean time, he tells me he is perfectly satisfy'd with his present Situation, any thing within my Power to render his Situation happy and Instructive, shall not be wanting.

I must rely on you to make my best Compliments acceptable to the fair Miss Wendell, and to the other agreeable Ladies of my acquaintance in Portsmouth. The Captain of the *Raleigh* I understand is well, and has lately been figuring it away at Paris, whereof please to acquaint my *Sister* Officer. I should be exceedingly happy to hear from you, but as my destination depends on what I am to hear from the Commissioners, I cannot at Present give you my Address, but will drop you another, How do you do, shortly.

I am with Sentiments of Respect & Regard,

My dear Sir,

Your Obliged, very Obedient, most humble Servant

Jno P. Jones[1]

The cryptic reference to 'my *Sister* Officer' alluded to Captain Thomas Thompson and his wife. Thompson wrote to Jones from Paris on 26 December 1777, thanking him for buying a pair of shoes for his wife and hoping that the Captain would soon enjoy the 'pleasure which Paris afourds'.

The ship's log for the first part of the voyage has not survived, but from the diary of Surgeon Green it is known that *Ranger* ran into a severe gale on 14 November which lasted three days, during which a tiller rope snapped with the result that the ship was in danger of broaching. Green also mentions the seizure of the brigs *Mary* and *George* and of shadowing a British convoy without success. The surviving log begins on 26 November when the ship again encountered a 'fresh gail'. Later entries laconically record 'fresh Breze and Dirty Weather' and 'ship'd a grate Deal of Water', followed (on 29 November) by 'hard Gaile and Dirty Weather from the SE'. Despite the mixed weather which belies Jones's own poetic account to Wendell, *Ranger* made the crossing in the excellent time of thirty-one days, of which two or three were spent in chasing prizes. Land was sighted at dawn on 2 December when the ship was off the coast of Brittany and by mid-morning *Ranger* was off St Nazaire, standing in towards the mouth of the Loire. A pilot came aboard at four-thirty in the afternoon and steered the ship into an anchorage off Paimboeuf at midnight. Jones was carrying historic despatches of Burgoyne's surrender at Saratoga on 17 October, and was anxious to get this good news to the American Commissioners at Paris as soon as possible. Consequently he wasted no time in getting the ship's cutter launched and he, accompanied by Dr Green and Major Frazer, were rowed several miles upriver in the dead of night to Nantes. Only later did he learn to his chagrin that the packet *Penet* had beaten him to it with the glad tidings which marked the turning-point of the war.

Green's journal endorses Jones's views about a willing crew. Their morale was very high when they reached the Loire, and the taking of the two prizes had not only kept their spirits up but provided excellent opportunities for Jones to put the men through their paces, especially during night operations. To William Whipple at Portsmouth Jones wrote jubilantly that the crew's behaviour throughout the voyage had been 'to my entire Satisfaction'. But Jones was blissfully unaware of discontent beginning to develop even before they reached France. The only man-management problem during this trip came from Major Frazer who passed the time drinking himself 'to intoxication' and staggered ashore at Nantes to sample the delights of the *estaminets* and whorehouses of the region.

Jones's first official despatch to the Marine Committee, however, painted a less rosy picture than he conveyed to Wendell. Although the French officers who inspected the ship pronounced *Ranger* 'un *parfait bijou'* (a perfect gem), she was 'crank', with a distressing tendency to heel over excessively in a moderate wind. Such dash might be all right in a racing yacht, but it was not desirable in a warship, because then her weather broadside fired up in the air while the lee gun-ports had to be kept shut to prevent sea-water rushing into the gun deck. Added to that, *Ranger's* bottom was foul, since she had not been careened since her launching, and her hessian sails suffered wear and tear. Jones reported to the Committee that he intended remedying all these defects at the soonest opportunity, by heaving her down for a good graving, obtaining new spars and sails and ballasting her with thirty tons of lead. To Robert Morris he wrote soon after reaching port, 'As America must become the first Marine Power in the world, the care and increase of our seamen is a consideration of the first magnitude, and claims the full attention of Congress.'[2] Jones practised what he preached, and there was no officer in the Navy more assiduous in looking after his crew. He was at great pains always to see that they were well fed and in excellent health; but in return he expected good discipline and subordination to his will at all times. Characteristically, his first task on reaching Paimboeuf was to advance cash to every crew-member out of his own pocket, Congress having apparently omitted to make any arrangements for the men to draw pay in France. Even before leaving for his midnight jaunt upriver to Nantes he gave instructions to Lieutenant Simpson to purchase fresh bread, meat, vegetables and a cask of brandy for the crew, and chartered a lighter for ship's service to and from the shore in order that the men be relieved of the tedium of constantly launching and hoisting in the ship's boats. Morison shrewdly observes that although there were many complaints against Captain Jones by his officers and men, not one of these was about the food. 'This I regard as significant, since food is the first thing that sailors growl about.'[3]

Soon Jones organised the necessary repairs and settled down to enjoy the social life of Paimboeuf. He was heartened to find his old friend, John Young of Philadelphia, now captain of the sloop *Providence* which was at Paimboeuf being upgraded to a brig. In Nantes Jones discovered quite a sizeable American community, including Joshua Johnson of Maryland whose daughter married John Quincy Adams; Franklin's nephew Jonathan Williams and his partner Thomas Morris, the half-brother of Robert Morris; and John Ross, a Scottish merchant who sympathised with the American cause. Jones also ran into Benjamin Hill who, as pilot on *Providence*, had been her navigator during the raid on Nova Scotia. Hill wished to ship again under his former commander and did so; but as *Ranger*'s muster of officers was complete he had to enlist as a volunteer midshipman without pay. Nevertheless, Ben Hill would prove to be one of Jones's most loyal and efficient officers.

The 'frigate' referred to in Jones's letter to Wendell was *L'Indien* of forty guns, 154 feet in length, which was being constructed in an Amsterdam shipyard at the behest of the American Commissioners in Paris. This had been promised to Jones before he left Portsmouth, but by the time he reached Nantes the Commissioners, who had run out of money and into problems with the Dutch, had sold the ship to the French government. The brief reference to this turnaround in the Wendell letter conceals the immense disappointment which Jones felt. In fact he moved heaven and earth to get the new arrangement revoked, even going over the head of Benjamin Franklin and appealing to the French Minister of Marine; but in diplomatic manoeuvring Jones was soon out of his depth. The British government, whose spies in Paris monitored the comings and goings of the American Commissioners as well as Captain Jones, leant on the Dutch authorities to prevent the ship falling into American hands.

Apart from the prospect of such a splendid ship, Jones had good reasons for pressing his claims. Thompson in *Raleigh* and Hinman in *Alfred* were already in France, taking on vital munitions and stores, and Jones was afraid that the Commissioners, having failed to get him *L'Indien*, might assign him with *Ranger* to a squadron under the command of Thompson, twelve numbers ahead of him in the seniority list. This fear had been with him ever since he discovered that Thompson was also bound for France. Jones liked Thompson well enough as a man, but he had no respect for him as a seaman and to Robert Morris he had sworn vehemently: 'I am determined never to draw my sword under the command of any man who was not in the Navy as early as myself, unless he has merited a preference by his superior services and abilities.' Fortunately, the Commissioners had other ideas. Before the year was out, they despatched *Raleigh* and *Alfred*. During the voyage, however, *Alfred* was captured in a running battle with HMS *Ariadne* and *Ceres*. *Raleigh* got away without making any effort to help her sister ship, and consequently Thompson was court-martialled and broken. There was more than a hint of *Schadenfreude* in Jones's reaction to this news.

Jones was back aboard *Ranger* on 9 December, and busy during the ensuing week supervising the careening and refit, which involved shortening the lower masts, moving the mainmast farther aft and adding ballast, all operations which were beyond the comprehension of both officers and men who began to grumble at what they regarded as quite unnecessary chores. On 17 December Jones received an urgent summons from Benjamin Franklin in Paris, but he delayed his departure for several days, sending a letter to the Commissioners explaining that he wished to leave his ship 'in such a situation as to expect to find her nearly ready for sea on my return, as I think it will be for the interest of the service that I should then proceed with her alone unless an additional force can be very soon procured'.[4] Jones compensated for his delay by going to Paris by French government post-chaise. By this means he reached the capital within forty-eight hours; the journey by ordinary stage-coach would have taken five days to travel the three hundred miles.

It is not known precisely when Jones reached Paris, nor where he lodged during this period. He probably arrived at the end of December or the beginning of January and went straightaway to the suburb of Passy where the American Commissioners had their *de facto* embassy in a pavilion attached to the Hôtel Valentinois. Here lived Benjamin Franklin, the most remarkable man of his generation and the most talked-of celebrity in Paris. Philosopher, scientist, publisher and postmaster-general turned diplomat, Franklin was in his seventies but retained the vigour, passion and alert mind of a much younger man. He and Jones (who was less than half his age) hit it off immediately. A deep and lasting friendship developed between them; Jones admired, revered and hero-worshipped the old man, and Franklin repaid the young naval officer with unswerving loyalty, often sticking out his neck to support him against rivals and detractors alike.

Jones also formed a close friendship with Dr Edward Bancroft, Fellow of both the Royal Society and the Royal College of Physicians, who was Franklin's confidential secretary. He was also a British spy, paid a thousand pounds a year to send to London transcripts of secret conversations and copies of all despatches to and from his American master. Bancroft had had a remarkable career; a Massachusetts apprentice who absconded with his master's property and ran away to sea, he later turned to medicine and rose to the top of his profession, but along the way he published a novel vilifying Christianity and, while posing as a respectable man of science, he was also engaging in insider-trading on the stock exchanges of Paris and London. One of his biggest coups was to profit from news of the British defeat at Saratoga; being privy to the despatches before they were made public, he made a considerable killing, not only in Paris but also in London through his agent Samuel Wharton. Jones was completely taken in by this real-life Jekyll and Hyde, and would later lay his own honour on the line in defending Bancroft when rumours of his double-dealing began to surface.

By contrast to the friendship of Franklin and Bancroft, Jones rapidly fell foul of the second Commissioner, Arthur Lee, largely on account of Lee's bitter hatred of Franklin. In background the two men could not have been more different; the patrician, Old Etonian Lee was poles apart from the self-made Pennsylvanian. Arthur Lee did everything in his power to undermine Franklin and even went so far as conspiring with his brother Richard Henry Lee and Samuel Adams in Congress in an attempt to have Franklin recalled in disgrace. In the interests of symmetry, however, Lee, too, had a confidential secretary, Major Thornton, who was in the pay of the British. The third Commissioner was Silas Deane of Connecticut, whom Jones had previously known as a member of the Marine Committee. Deane had taken that job seriously, and as a result Jones admired and respected him. In Paris the two men got on well. Deane's confidential secretary, William Carmichael, also became a close friend of Jones and, unlike Bancroft and Thornton, he served his master and his country faithfully. Deane himself, despite his many good qualities, was an unmitigated rascal and ultimately a traitor to his country, doomed to die an exile in England. Amid all this treachery and double-dealing there was the malevolent influence of the Lee family of Virginia. Four brothers – Arthur, Thomas, Richard Henry and William – among them held two seats in Congress, four foreign missions, the French commercial agency and even a London aldermanship; two cousins, Richard and Francis, were signatories of the Declaration of Independence, while a son of Richard Henry held the position of commercial agent at Nantes. Another cousin, 'Light Horse Harry' Lee, would later be governor of Virginia and father of General Robert E. Lee.

Not only was there bitter animosity among the American Commissioners which tended to undermine their effectiveness, there were also the intrigues of French officials and courtiers to contend with. France's attitude towards the infant United States was guarded and ambivalent. On the one hand, pursuing the traditional line that the enemy of my enemy is my friend, France was inclined to help the Americans in their struggle with Britain. On the other hand, the French establishment was suspicious and distrustful of the republican spirit with which the American Revolution was imbued. At a practical level, this ambivalence was reflected in the conflicting policies of officialdom, now helping, now hindering, the Americans in their quest for much-needed military supplies. News of Burgoyne's surrender, however, tipped the scales in America's favour, and the Comte de Vergennes, then French foreign minister, abandoned his previous vacillation and took the decision to align his country with America against Britain; and this resulted in the treaty of amity, alliance and commerce signed by the Commissioners and representatives of the French government on 6 February 1778. Undoubtedly, the successful outcome of this mission was due largely to the personality of Franklin who commanded immense respect in France. He had many close friends among the French, not to mention lady friends. Among the latter were Madame Helvetius to whom the septuagenarian diplomat proposed marriage, and Madame Brillon de Jouy who often sat on his lap and who played chess with him while she took a bath. Although she flirted outrageously with him it is doubtful whether the affair was ever consummated.

Jones does not appear to have made these ladies' acquaintance, for he never referred to them in his letters to Franklin. On the other hand, the gallant captain met Madame Le Ray de Chaumont, wife of the proprietor of the Valentinois. Jacques Donatien Le Ray made his money in the East India trade, and in addition to the luxurious Valentinois he bought the *château* of Chaumont on the Loire, adopting the title of Seigneur de Chaumont. He was honoured by Louis XV who appointed him a privy counsellor. He continued to have extensive interests in overseas trade and owned a fleet of merchantmen. Mercantile rivalry with the British drove Le Ray de Chaumont into the American camp, and, with Beaumarchais, was one of the chief conduits of French aid to the rebel colonies before the treaty of amity was signed. There was no aspect of Franco-American affairs in which he was not heavily involved, from the negotiation of major financial deals to hosting to the American mission. Jones was not slow in appreciating the importance of Le Ray, and in his efforts to get command of *L'Indien* he turned all his Scottish charm on Chaumont and, more importantly, his wife. Madame de Chaumont, born Thérèse Joguer, was much younger than her husband, but several years older than Jones. Attraction seems to have been mutual, for Thérèse could not resist the dashing young naval hero, while Jones, who invariably wore his heart on his sleeve, would probably have been susceptible to her charms even had he not been following Franklin's dictum that the best way to get things done in France was through the ladies. Besides, bedding her was a good way of brushing up his schoolboy French. As the Seigneur was frequently absent on business trips, Jones and his new mistress had ample opportunity to slake their passion.

Unfortunately Jones tired of the lady before she tired of him; his ardour diminished when all hopes of getting the new frigate evaporated, and he was later put in the embarrassing situation of having to depend heavily on Chaumont for selling his prizes and fitting out his fleet. Relations with Thérèse were still cordial when Jones left Passy on 25 January with Chaumont's draft for five hundred gold louis in his pocket, and returned to Paimboeuf.

In the intervening weeks the crew of *Ranger* had been hard at work carrying out their captain's orders. What with careening the ship and carrying out major structural alterations to masts and spars, the men should have been too busy to grumble but, sailors being sailors, they found plenty to complain about. Paimboeuf lacked the bright lights and the allure of Paris, where the skipper was obviously having a fine time. The ship was more or less ready for sea several days before Jones left Passy and idleness in the interim gave rise to restlessness and discontent. The crew felt, not unreasonably, that they could be at sea taking more lucrative prizes. Despite Jones's provision of good food and fine brandy, as well as advances of cash, he returned to Paimboeuf to find the men sullen and morose. At the heart of the problem was the first-lieutenant, James Simpson, who undermined his authority and led the crew to believe that Jones would soon be leaving *Ranger*. Instead, here was the captain back from Paris, working them harder than ever and planning crazy schemes for raids on the British coast that provided no scope for prize money. Several of the men had retained the recruiting handbill and muttered sarcastic comments in the captain's hearing or quoted from the leaflet about 'an agreeable Voyage in this pleasant Season of the Year' (Paimboeuf was now in the grip of winter, with ice and snow on the deck and the rigging). They had been promised that they would 'make their Fortunes' but so far they had taken only two lousy fruit-boats and had not seen a penny in prize money. They had been addressed as 'Gentlemen Seamen' but were now being worked like dogs, and by a 'furriner' at that. New Englanders almost to a man, they were used to local skippers who mixed freely with them, not aloof Scotsmen. As Christmas and New Year passed, the crew was assailed with 'the Epidemical malady of Homesickness' as Jones described it later.

Clearly, the antidote to sinking morale was to get the ship to sea as quickly as possible. Fortunately, Jones had received orders from the Commissioners on 16 January:

> After equipping the *Ranger* in the best manner for the cruise you propose, that you proceed with her in the manner you shall judge best for distressing the Enemies of the United States, by sea or otherwise, consistent with the laws of war, and the terms of your commission.

His instructions included the names of prize agents at Bilbao and Corunna in Spain as well as at Bordeaux and Lorient. As France was still nominally neutral when the orders were issued, he was advised that if he made 'an attempt on the coast of Great Britain' he ought not to return to France for the time being. Furthermore, he was warned not to give offence to the subjects of France, Spain or any other neutral country. The orders were signed by Franklin and Deane, but not Lee. Effectively they gave Jones *carte blanche*, the phrase 'by sea or otherwise' giving Jones a free hand to raid inland towns if the opportunity arose. And Jones was the sort of man to do just that, as his letter to the Marine Committee, soon after receipt of these orders, reveals:

> I have in contemplation several Enterprizes of some importance – the Commissioners do not even promise to Justify me should I fail in any bold attempt; I will not, however, under this discouragement, alter my designs. When an Enemy thinks a design against them is improbable, they can always be surprised and attacked with advantage.[5]

Prophetic words, indeed, when one remembers Pearl Harbor. Jones's 'scheem', as he called it in his correspondence, was a hit-and-run raid on a British port to destroy shipping. The Commissioners anticipated that this was what he had in mind, for they promised that his crew would get a cash bonus in lieu of prize money if the plan succeeded.

While he was completing his preparations to take *Ranger* to sea, the Franco-American treaty was signed on 6 February. Four days later, while Jones was as yet unaware that it had been signed, he wrote to the Commissioners outlining a bold plan for a French expedition against Lord Howe's fleet in Delaware Bay. Ten or twelve ships of the line, with some frigates, could capture the British squadron in the Delaware, then deal with the naval ships based at New York and finally intercept Admiral Byron's fleet then *en route* from England. An otherwise very sound and detailed plan was marred only by Jones's confident prediction that British seamen would be so tired of 'salt horse' that they would gladly desert to the French Navy to get better grub. In its boldness and imagination the plan shows Jones to have been as much of a strategic genius as Franklin was a diplomatic one. Sly Silas Deane palmed off the plan on Louis XVI as his own, and was rewarded with a diamond-encrusted miniature portrait of His Majesty. Louis dithered for some time, reluctant to make the first move against Britain; and when the fleet under the Comte d'Estaing eventually left Toulon on 18 April and reached the Delaware on 8 July, Earl Howe had moved his squadron to the comparative safety of New York. D'Estaing was thwarted when local pilots refused to guide his ships through the Narrows into the Upper Bay where the British lay at anchor. That Jones's plan, as transmitted by Deane, was used by d'Estaing is borne out by the fact that the French translation preserved in the naval records of the National Archives is annotated in contemporary handwriting, '*Cette insinuation a pu déterminer l'envoi de l'escadre du comte d'Estaing*' ('this suggestion probably decided the despatch of the Comte d'Estaing's squadron').

Jones spent two weeks at Paimboeuf, completing the fitting-out. In this period Thomas Morris died and Jones attended the funeral, during which *Ranger* fired thirteen minute-guns in his honour. The crew's morale soared again when Morris's successor, Jonathan Williams, came down from Nantes to distribute prize money from the sale of the two brigantines. Williams was invited on board for the cruise and, in company with the armed brig *Independence*, *Ranger* weighed anchor as the first grey streaks of dawn lit the sky on 13 February 1778. That evening *Ranger* anchored in Quiberon Bay and exchanged salutes with the squadron of frigates and ships of the line under Admiral La Motte Piquet. The manner in which this was done is well documented. Jones sent a note by the ship's cutter to William Carmichael, Deane's confidential secretary, who happened to be at Quiberon, asking him to present his respects 'to the French Admiral whom I mean to salute with thirteen guns under American

Colours – provided he will Accept the Compliment and Return Gun for Gun'. La Motte Piquet sent a brief reply to Jones in French saying that if *Ranger* and *Independence* saluted the royal ensign with thirteen guns, he would return nine guns. Jones was taken aback, and wrote to Carmichael the following morning, complaining that even 'the haughty English return Gun for Gun to foreign Officers of equal rank, and two less only to Captains by flag officers'. Thus *Ranger* should have at least eleven guns returned; a mere nine was unacceptable. Carmichael advised him not to hold out for more as nine guns was all that the American privateer *General Mifflin* had received from Admiral du Chauffault at Brest the previous summer, and even that was thrice the ordinary acknowledgment by a French rear-admiral to a thirteen-gun salute. Jones was stung to be compared with a privateer, but he gave in. That evening, as the American warships entered Quiberon Bay and passed the stern of the French flagship, *Ranger* fired thirteen guns and received nine. The following day, 15 February, Jones repeated the salute and again got nine in response. Perhaps he hoped that La Motte Piquet would relent and give him another couple of guns. Later Jones claimed that he had had the honour of the first salute to the American flag by a foreign ship. In fact that honour went to *Andrew Doria* which, flying the Grand Union flag, had exchanged salutes with the fort at St Eustatius in the Danish West Indies (now the American Virgin Islands) in November 1776. *General Mifflin* had likewise flown the Grand Union flag, but what Jones may have meant was the first salute to the Stars and Stripes.

Ranger spent the next ten days moored near the head of the bay while the elements raged outside. During this enforced delay Jones had time to socialise with officers of the French fleet, 'a very well Bred set of men' whom he entertained aboard ship while the crew manned the yards in their honour. In return, Jones and Carmichael were received by the admiral aboard his flagship and treated 'with every mark of respect and Gladness and saluted with a Feu de Joie', a volley fired by French marines. Clearly Jones revelled in that 'Peagantry' which he had earlier affected to despise. Jones had hoped to prevail upon La Motte Piquet to join in his 'scheem' and was bitterly disappointed to find, on the morning of 25 February, that the French squadron had left Quiberon without a word of goodbye. Immediately, Jones gave orders to weigh anchor and set sail in a stiff breeze that turned very squally as he made for Belle Île. Making no headway he wore ship and turned back for Quiberon Bay but, unable to negotiate the narrows between the mainland and the reefs, he was forced to ride out the storm outside the harbour. To make matters worse, a sudden squall blew up and the ship heeled over. Coals dislodged in the galley started a blaze but the fire was soon brought under control. As night fell, *Ranger* ran to leeward of Belle Île and darted back and forth under close-reefed sails till dawn when the ship managed to re-enter Quiberon Bay 'after a short but very tedious & unprofitable Cruize' as Dr Green drily recorded.

Through his impatience, Jones hazarded his ship; now he had to kick his heels at Quiberon Bay for another week, but as soon as the foul weather showed signs of abating he set off once more, this time heading for Brest where he hoped for French naval support. He weighed anchor on 3 March but two days later had only progressed along the dangerous coast of Brittany as far as Benodet where Green was sent ashore with a ship's boy, Joseph Ratcliff, who had contracted smallpox. After seeing the boy lodged as comfortably as possible, with a local doctor in attendance, Green returned to the ship, convoyed by fishing boats whose crews cried '*Vive le Congrès!*'

Early on 6 March the ship left Benodet and the following morning succeeded in rounding the treacherous Pointe du Raz, noting a French frigate astern which ran aground. Dreadful weather and treacherous shoals and reefs made the voyage to Brest painfully slow. The inner and outer harbours of the great naval base were crammed with the ships of the Comte d'Orvilliers and there was no berth for *Ranger* which anchored at Camaret eight miles away. Over the ensuing days Jones commuted to Brest in his cutter, presented his compliments to the French admiral and was promised a frigate and tender to accompany *Ranger*. During this further delay *Ranger*'s crew were kept gainfully occupied re-rigging the ship and shifting the ballast to improve her trim, much to the disgust of Lieutenant Hall (a shipbuilder in civilian life) who opined that these alterations were 'to little or no purpose', though in actual fact they did improve *Ranger*'s handling and speed quite considerably. Eight of the crew jumped ship, but the French police apprehended seven of them. Jones, Green and Lieutenant Simpson went into Brest on 14 March to see the sights; while the others returned to the ship, Jones tarried overnight as he hoped to discuss his plans with d'Orvilliers. While he was absent, Madame de Chaumont arrived unexpectedly with her two sisters, and Green had the congenial task of entertaining the ladies aboard ship, much to Jones's annoyance when he returned after their departure. *Les girls* came back three days later, and this time Jones was on hand in his dandiest uniform to play the charming host.

On 23 March *Ranger* entered Brest harbour and saluted the flagship *La Bretagne* with thirteen guns. D'Orvilliers returned the compliment, though Jones did not record how many guns he got. The sloop was allocated a naval mooring at last, and here she would remain for almost three weeks, waiting for some improvement in the weather. During this period Jones procured a vast quantity of red cloth to cover the ship's sides. From the Intendant de la Marine he learned of a convoy of twenty English merchantmen anchored in a nearby port, likewise waiting for a break in the weather before returning home. At this point Britain and France were not yet at war, though French sympathies were clearly with the Americans. Jones planned to disguise his ship, covering the telltale gunports and masquerading as a peaceful freighter, then mingle with the convoy and strike when the moment was right. D'Orvilliers, with whom Jones had struck up a firm friendship that would last for the rest of the Scotsman's life, promised a frigate to escort *Ranger* past the British warships standing out from Brest and keeping a watchful eye on French movements. Before leaving Brest, however, Jones let his old comrade in arms, Matthew Parke, go. His place as officer in charge of the marine detachment was taken by a Swedish lieutenant, Jan or Jean Meijer. After entrusting d'Orvilliers with a letter addressed to Sartine, the Minister of Marine (a last plea for *L'Indien*), Jones took his ship out of Brest on 2 April, saluting the French flagship as he did and getting eleven guns in return – two more than La Motte Piquet had accorded him. *Ranger* returned to Camaret to be careened once more, and finally got under way on 10 April, with the frigate *Fortunée* and a tender for company. After getting the Americans safely past the British blockade, *Fortunée* left *Ranger* on 14 April and returned to her home port.

Having missed the English convoy, Jones now turned to his original plan of raiding a British seaport, destroying shipping and perhaps kidnapping some important person in order to force the British authorities to release American seamen held in English prisons. In October 1777 General John Vaughan had burned the town of Esopus on the Hudson, and Jones now sought revenge. Through French military intelligence, he was apprised of the instructions of Lord George Germain to Sir Henry Clinton, dated 8 March 1778, to destroy ports and shipping all along the American coast, from New York to Nova Scotia, 'so as to incapacitate them from raising a Marine, or continuing their Depredations upon the Trade of this Kingdom'.[6] Jones's stated aims were the exchange of American prisoners and 'making a good fire in England of *Shipping*' to put an end to the burning of American ports. The first priority was a matter very dear to Jones's heart, partly out of humanity and partly because the continued incarceration of American seamen in Fortin Prison near Portsmouth and the Mill Prison, Plymouth, was a sore point. Soldiers captured on the field of battle were regularly exchanged, but the British regarded American seamen aboard armed ships as pirates, hence the very different treatment meted out to them.

Shortly after parting company with *Fortunée*, Jones fell in with the brigantine *Dolphin*, bound from Ostend to Wexford in Ireland with a cargo of flaxseed. The crew were taken prisoner but the ship itself was scuttled as being not worth the trouble of assigning a prize crew to take her into a friendly French port. On 16 March *Ranger* sighted Old Head of Kinsale and turned eastwards to run up St George's Channel. Off Wicklow she intercepted the 250-ton *Lord Chatham*, bound for Dublin (her home port) with a mixed cargo that included a hundred hogsheads of best English porter – a case of 'coals to Newcastle' since Arthur Guinness had been brewing his famous stout for nigh on twenty years. The ship was taken without a struggle and sent into Brest under a prize crew. By the time Jones got back to Brest most of the porter had vanished and he had great difficulty in salvaging some for himself and his friends. *Ranger* sailed due north across the Irish Sea, and by ten in the morning of 18 April was off the Point of Ayre, the most northerly headland of the Isle of Man. At this juncture she was challenged by the British revenue cutter *Hussar* whose skipper Gurley thought *Ranger* looked suspicious and decided to take a closer look at her. *Hussar* followed the sloop heading in a north-easterly direction and pulled level near the Big Scares ledges at the mouth of Luce Bay in Galloway. Later, Gurley reported that the skipper of the strange vessel was 'dressed in white with a large Hat Cocked'.[7] This is intriguing for white clothing was not worn in any navy or mercantile marine. No plausible explanation has ever been adduced, nor did Jones himself mention the subject. Morison[8] conjectured that Jones wore a white coat for sheer bravura, just as Nelson invited enemy sharpshooters to make him a target by wearing all his medals and orders at Trafalgar.

Gurley hailed the ship and observed that while the officers appeared like Frenchmen they spoke good English. On being challenged, the deck officer (Master David Cullam) said the ship was the *Molly* from Glasgow. When questioned about her movements, Jones replied, 'Bring to, or I'll sink you directly!' At that, Cullam fired a musket and the man in white cried, 'Up all ports!' at which the disguise was raised and the guns run out, but the cutter beat a hasty retreat before *Ranger* could deliver a broadside. *Ranger* tacked and fired at the cutter, hitting her stern and holing her mainsail twice, but Gurley dodged and weaved and by sheer dexterity slipped from *Ranger*'s grasp to take refuge in Luce Bay. The tide was ebbing fast and Jones dared not pursue the cutter into the shallow bay.

The following morning, off the Mull of Galloway, *Ranger* encountered a Scottish coaster bound for Irvine with oats and barley, sank her, and captured her crew. From them Jones learned of a merchant fleet in Loch Ryan and decided to wreak havoc on them, but was prevented by a change of wind. Instead, he chased an armed cutter as far as Ailsa Craig in the Firth of Clyde before turning back, then intercepted a sloop from Dublin in ballast and sank her to prevent her revealing his whereabouts. On 20 April, off Carrickfergus in northern Ireland, Jones detained a fishing-boat whose crew told him that a ship he had sighted at anchor in Belfast Lough was HMS *Drake*, a twenty-gun sloop of war. Jones wished to sail into the Lough and cut her out, but his crew absolutely refused. As a compromise, however, they agreed to surprise the British warship that night by anchoring just to windward in order to sweep her decks with gunfire, then grapple and board. This daring plan miscarried because *Ranger*'s anchor caught on the cathead and the anchor detail, under a drunken quartermaster, failed to free it until *Ranger* had shot past *Drake*. She came to on *Drake*'s port quarter, barely thirty metres away, but as *Drake*, taken in by the other ship's disguise, made no hostile move, Jones decided that discretion was the better part of valour and sheered off, intending to return the following night. Once more, he was dogged by foul weather; the following day *Ranger* barely managed to cross a very rough sea and shelter in the lee of the Scottish coast. Green recorded that the crew were 'very much fatigued' and doubtless muttering more mutinously than ever.

Dawn broke on 22 April, fair but frosty, and Jones observed a dusting of snow in three kingdoms – Scotland, Ireland and Man. He now headed in an easterly direction in pursuit of his original plan to descend on Whitehaven and burn the shipping. Jones had nothing against Whitehaven as such, but it was a port with which he was very familiar and into which he could sail without a pilot. Lambert

Wickes in *Reprisal* and Henry Johnson in *Lexington* had cruised round the British Isles the previous year, taking many prizes, but had never attempted a landing. No enemy had dared attack an English port since the Dutch Admiral de Ruyter had raided Sheerness in June 1667. In the intervening century the Royal Navy had become the most powerful in the world and British coastal defences were thought to be impregnable. Only John Paul Jones knew better. Just as Sir Francis Drake 'singed the king of Spain's beard' by burning upwards of 10,000 tons of shipping in Cadiz Harbour in 1587, Jones longed to perform a similar exploit that would make King George sit up and take notice.

Unfortunately, Jones's crew did not view the enterprise in the same light; they were only interested in the money accruing from prizes, and the burning of ships yielded no profit. The fiercely independent-minded Yankee crew felt that a shipboard 'town meeting' should have been called, so that they could take a vote on it. Surgeon Green tactfully put it to the captain that the plan was not only foolhardy but that 'Nothing could be got by burning poor people's property'. To be sure, the motley collection of coastal traders, colliers and fishing-boats lying in Whitehaven would have been poor pickings anyway; but no one aboard *Ranger*, apart from Jones himself, grasped the propaganda value of such a raid. Jones suspected that Lieutenant Simpson was the ringleader of the mutinous seamen; certainly he had encouraged the mutterings against the captain's authority. Ironically, it was seaman Edward Meyer who tipped off the Swedish volunteer Meijer about the imminent mutiny. Meijer, in turn, warned Jones who, when Master David Cullam rushed at him as a signal for the mutiny to begin, coolly drew a pistol and put it to Cullam's head. That was sufficient to calm things down and, reasserting his authority, Jones now explained his plan and called for volunteers. Lieutenants Simpson and Hall declined because they were 'overcome with fatigue' but Jones eventually mustered a force of forty officers and men, in two boats. He himself took command of one, with Meijer as his second-in-command. Lieutenant Wallingford of the Marines commanded the other boat, with Midshipman Hill as his assistant. At midnight the boats pulled away from the ship, now becalmed in the Solway Firth, and after three hours' hard rowing against the tide, reached Whitehaven Harbour as dawn broke.

Wallingford and his men landed at the Old Quay slip where they headed for the nearest tavern and 'made very free with the liquor'.

While they were boozing the rest of the night away, Jones and his party scaled the wall of the south battery by climbing on each other's shoulders, found the sentries asleep in the guardhouse and secured them. They spiked the guns and toppled them into the sea. (One of the cannon was salvaged in 1963 and, mounted on a trunnion, now stands on the South Beach, with a brass plate recording the event.)

Jones, accompanied only by Midshipman Joe Green, later spiked the guns in the north battery. Meijer, as a precaution, remained by the captain's boat to prevent the crew leaving Jones on the beach as they openly threatened they would. Apart from insubordination and mutiny, Jones had to contend with treachery. One of the crew, an Irishman named David Freeman, had enlisted under the false name of David Smith at Portsmouth in the hope of getting home. Now he rushed from house to house along the seafront, banging on doors and warning the townspeople that their houses and shipping would be burned by pirates. In no time at all the harbour was swarming with people. Before their eyes Jones posted sentries to keep them at bay while he coolly lit a wad of canvas dipped in brimstone and tossed it into the collier *Thompson*, followed by a tar-barrel which soon produced a tremendous conflagration. By now it was five o'clock and, as Jones noted in his report, echoing Young's *Night Thoughts,* 'the sun was a full hour above the horizon, and as sleep no longer ruled the world it was time to retire'. After releasing all but three of their captives, the two boats' crews re-embarked, Jones being the last to jump aboard. By six o'clock they were safely back on *Ranger*, out of range of the wild, ragged fire from some guns which Jones had inadvertently overlooked. The good folk of Whitehaven, assisted by a heavy downpour, managed to douse the flames and save *Thompson*.

No casualties were sustained on either side, though Jones was genuinely concerned at the loss of one man, the traitor Freeman, and it was not till much later that he learned the truth. Freeman swore an affidavit to the effect that *Ranger* was a privateer 'commanded by John Paul Jones, fitted out at Piscataqua, in New England'. Someone in the crowd by the harbour recognised the captain as John Paul who had served his apprenticeship in *Friendship* of Whitehaven 'and was well known by many people in this town'. This statement appeared in the local newspaper the following day and was reprinted in the *Morning Post* of London on 28 April. It was the first time that the name of John Paul Jones came before the British public; it would not be the last by any means.

Jones estimated that there were at least 150 large vessels, between two and four hundred tons burthen, in the North Harbour and a further seventy to a hundred aground in the South Harbour. At a conservative estimate, therefore, he might have destroyed four times as much shipping as Drake had at Cadiz. Instead, the combination of wind and tide, mutinous crew, drunken insubordination and actual treachery, combined to reduce the material effect of the raid (British estimates of damage sustained ranged between £250 and £1,250). But the moral impact was incalculable. The raid on Whitehaven threw the coastal towns and communities from Land's End to John o'Groats into a monumental panic, and the newspapers had a field day, thundering against the defenceless state of the coast and the inexcusable laxity of the government. Horace Walpole seems to have been alone in seeing the funny side of the affair, writing that he considered Jones ungrateful, since America owed her independence to the Scots – 'though, to be sure, in strictness it was not what the Scots intended for them'.[9]

With the passage of time Whitehaven's attitude towards the 'pirate Jones' has mellowed and he has become a major tourist attraction. The splendid Beacon Museum on the South Harbour (opened in 1996) devotes the whole of the third floor to the American connection, noting the visit of Benjamin Franklin to Whitehaven to inspect the coalmines, and the fact that George Washington's father Augustine was educated there and that his grandmother Mildred Warner is buried there. But attention is mostly focused on John Paul Jones, represented by a lifelike figure in American uniform with his sword drawn and a suitably pugnacious expression on his face.

8. St Mary's Isle and After

1778

Of this person's character, this parish cannot boast. His pillage of the house of the Earl of Selkirk; his attempts to burn the town of Whitehaven, out of whose harbour he had served his apprenticeship; and his conduct to his native country, during the American war, are instances of ingratitude and want of patriotism, generally known, and over which, for the honour of humanity, we would wish to draw a veil.

— REVD EDWARD NEILSON, KIRKBEAN, IN *Statistical Account*, c.1791

Unaware of Freeman's betrayal, Jones concluded that his plan had misfired because the raid began so late and lacked the support of the men. The latter, in particular, did not bode well for the rest of the cruise; but Jones, not a man to dwell on failure, took a positive line and began planning to strike again while the British public were still in shock after his attack on Whitehaven. For sheer bravado and originality this new plan would be hard to beat. He would strike at St Mary's Isle in Kirkcudbright Bay, only a short sail across the Solway, and kidnap the Earl of Selkirk. The noble Earl's ransom would be the release of all American prisoners in British hands. Like the Whitehaven raid, the descent on St Mary's Isle achieved very little in real terms, but its psychological effect was stupendous, and it marked the turning-point in Jones's career.

St Mary's Isle, named after a twelfth-century priory, is not an island but a peninsula jutting southwards into the bay. The 'castle' described so romantically by many early writers on John Paul Jones was, in fact, a country house, a mixture of late-Jacobean stone with early-Georgian brick extensions. It was the residence of Dunbar Hamilton, who succeeded to the earldom in 1744. Fourteen years later the Fourth Earl married Lady Helen Hamilton, granddaughter of the Earl of Haddington. The myth that John Paul was Selkirk's bastard son has already been discussed and disposed of, but the Earl was a close friend of William Craik and a frequent visitor to Arbigland. Both then, and later during his merchant service in Kirkcudbright, John Paul would have known of Selkirk and probably had an inflated idea of the Earl's importance; but, despite liberal leanings, he had no political significance whatsoever. He was the father of Lord Daer, the friend of Robert Burns (who composed the famous Selkirk Grace on a visit to St Mary's Isle in 1793), and of the Fifth Earl who founded the Red River Settlement in Canada, but his own sole claim to fame stems from the fact that he was a target for the *Ranger* expedition. Were it not for his indirect association with John Paul Jones, the Fourth Earl would probably not be remembered at all.

Jones's ship made the twenty-mile crossing from Whitehaven to Kirkcudbright in record time, and by ten o'clock the same morning she was abreast of the Little Ross, a rocky islet at the entrance to the bay. For a distance of two kilometres north of the Little Ross, the bay has a good depth of water at all states of the tide, enabling *Ranger* to manoeuvre under shortened sail. For a further two kilometres northwards, the bay is shallow, much of it exposed mud-flats at low tide, though the channel of the River Dee is navigable by small craft. The ship's cutter was launched and Jones, accompanied by David Cullam, the Marine lieutenant Wallingford and a dozen men set off to row upstream. By eleven o'clock the cutter had run ashore at the Point and, leaving a couple of men on guard, Jones and the rest of his party trudged up the path to the big house. Along the way they ran into the head gardener, whom Jones, in his best quarterdeck manner, informed that they were a Royal Navy press gang. The gardener scurried off to warn 'all the stout young fellows' of the household who promptly took to their heels into Kirkcudbright to avoid impressment. The gardener told the naval party that the Earl was not at home, having gone to Buxton, Derbyshire, to take the waters.

At this bad news Jones decided to abort the raid, but Cullam and Wallingford stood their ground, arguing that they would not return to the ship without first ransacking the mansion. They complained that the Whitehaven raid had netted them nothing, and they forcefully reminded their captain that the British had burned and looted the homes of their kith and kin in New England. Jones had the good sense to give way on this occasion. As a compromise, he agreed to them going up to the house and taking the family silver provided that they did not loot the house or molest the inhabitants,

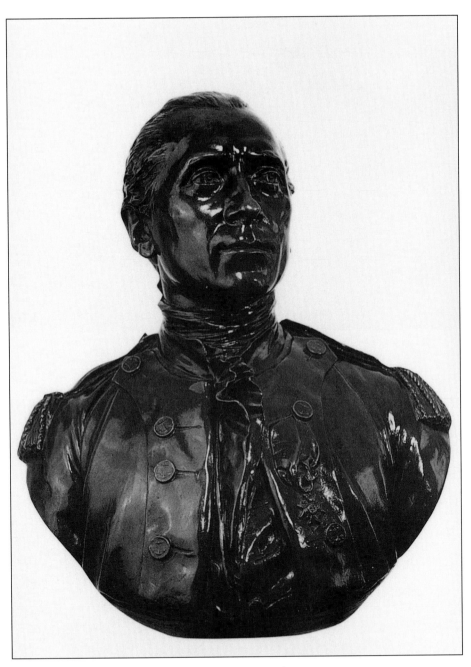

The bronze bust of John Paul Jones by Jean-Antoine Houdon, 1780

OPPOSITE PAGE: Arbigland House and the formal rose gardens originally laid out by the father of John Paul Jones

THIS PAGE: the John Paul Jones Birthplace Museum, Arbigland (TOP), and the Tolbooth in Kirkcudbright where Jones was imprisoned

G R E A T
ENCOURAGEMENT
F O R
SEAMEN.

A LL GENTLEMEN SEAMEN and able-bodied LANDSMEN who have a Mind to diftinguifh themfelves in the GLORIOUS CAUSE of their COUNTRY, and make their Fortunes, an Opportunity now offers on board the Ship RANGER, of Twenty Guns, (for FRANCE) now laying in PORTSMOUTH, in the State of NEW-HAMPSHIRE, commanded by JOHN PAUL JONES Efq; let them repair to the Ship's Rendezvous in PORTSMOUTH, or at the Sign of Commodore MANLEY, in SALEM, where they will be kindly entertained, and receive the greateft Encouragement.---The Ship RANGER, in the Opinion of every Perfon who has feen her is looked upon to be one of the beft Cruizers in AMERICA.---She will be always able to Fight her Guns under a moft excellent Cover ; and no Veffel yet built was ever calculated for failing fafter, and making good Weather.

Any GENTLEMEN VOLUNTEERS who have a Mind to take an agreable Voyage in this pleafant Seafon of the Year, may, by entering on board the above Ship RANGER, meet with every Civility they can poffibly expect, and for a further Encouragement depend on the firft Opportunity being embraced to reward each one agreable to his Merit.

All reafonable Travelling Expences will be allowed, and the Advance-Money be paid on their Appearance on Board.

In C O N G R E S S, MARCH 29, 1777.

RESOLVED,

THAT the MARINE COMMITTEE be authorifed to advance to every able Seaman, that enters into the CONTINENTAL SERVICE, any Sum not exceeding FORTY DOLLARS, and to every ordinary Seaman or Landfman, any Sum not exceeding TWENTY DOLLARS, to be deducted from their future Prize-Money.

By Order of CONGRESS,

JOHN-HANCOCK, PRESIDENT.

DANVERS: Printed by E. RUSSELL, at the Houfe late the Bell-Tavern.

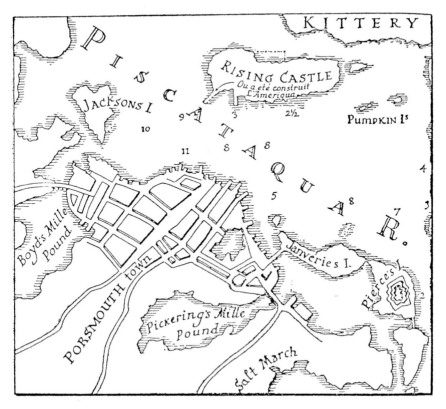

Recruiting poster published by John Paul Jones at Danvers, Massachusetts, in the hope of raising a crew for the *Ranger* (LEFT); and a map showing the town of Portsmouth, New Hampshire, and the Piscataqua River, where the *America* was built

ABOVE: A model of a French East Indiaman, contemporary with the *Bonhomme Richard*; OPPOSITE PAGE: a reconstruction at Arbigland of Jones's cabin on the *Bonhomme Richard* (TOP); and *Ranger* is saluted by a French squadron at Quiberon Bay, 14 February 1778, making this the first recognition of the American flag by a foreign government

Three very different views of John Paul Jones
(CLOCKWISE FROM ABOVE): the bloodthirsty pirate, as
seen by the British shortly after the battle off
Flamborough Head; the dignified and successful naval
commander, as seen by the French; and the sensitive
gentleman, as seen by one of his mistresses, the
Comtesse de Lowendahl

THIS PAGE: A wooden portrait of John Paul Jones
carved by Tim Jeffs, in the Selkirk Arms Hotel, Kirkcudbright
OPPOSITE PAGE: The specially commissioned gold medal
awarded to John Paul Jones by Congress in 1787 (TOP);
and the Dupre Medal illustrating the battle off
Flamborough Head

A study for the statue of John Paul Jones which stands in West
Potomac Park, Washington, close to where the Navy Day exercises
are held every year

who included Countess Helen, her youngest son (the future Fifth
Earl and Canadian pioneer), several daughters and their governess
Mary Elliot, as well as four guests, the widow of John Wood
(recently deceased Governor of the Isle of Man) and her three
grown-up daughters. There were also numerous domestic servants,
mostly women and elderly men. Just after eleven, the Countess
happened to glance out of the dining-room window and saw some
'horrid-looking wretches' armed to the teeth and wearing no
recognisable uniform. Thinking that they were pirates, Lady Selkirk
ordered her guests and maidservants to take her children to the top
floor and barricade themselves in, while she, Mrs Elliot and Daniel
the butler remained below to deal with the marauders. Cullam and
Wallingford entered the building and informed the Countess that
they were from the American frigate *Ranger*, 'Captain Paul Jones
Esquire commanding', and that acting under his orders they intended
to take the household silver. If she complied, she would not be
molested, nor the house searched. Lady Selkirk, realising that
resistance was hopeless, led them to the pantry where Daniel was
trying to hide some of the silver in a maid's apron. Her ladyship
ordered him to hand everything over. Later she described the senior
officer (Cullam), who was wearing a dark blue suit that did not
resemble a uniform, as having 'a vile blackguard look, still kept civil
as well he might'. On the other hand she described Sam Wallingford
as 'a civil young man in a green uniform, an anchor on his buttons
which were white' who seemed 'naturally well bred and not to like
his employment'.[1] Proof that loot had not been their primary
objective was the fact that the officers asked for sacks to carry away
the silver. When this was completed Cullam called for the inventory
of the silver, in order to check that nothing had been omitted.
Casting his eye over the list, he noted that the coffeepot and teapot
were missing from his haul. They were still on the dining table but
were handed over, containing the dregs from breakfast. The booty
amounted to 250 ounces of silver, but nothing else, neither watches
nor jewellery, was taken. Mrs Elliot was much impressed at this
punctiliousness and chatted with the raiders, asking them 'a thousand
questions' about America, to which they 'behaved with great
civility'.[2]

The raid lasted no more than a quarter of an hour, as the
Americans were anxious to be off before the people of Kirkcud-
bright, a mile to the north, were alerted and came to the rescue.
When the Countess coolly demanded a receipt for the silver, Wal-

lingford began writing 'This is to cert . . .' but Cullam impatiently brushed the paper aside. Before they left the house, however, Cullam and Wallingford accepted a parting glass of wine from the Countess, courteously took their leave, formed up their men in two ranks and marched them off smartly back to the cutter where Jones was waiting anxiously. They rowed at least four kilometres to rejoin *Ranger* drifting at the mouth of the bay with the Union Jack hoisted and her gunports shrouded to keep up the pretence of being a British freighter. They made sail in a south-westerly direction and rounded Burrow Head where they were sighted by a revenue cutter which pursued them the rest of the day till they made their escape under cover of night off the Mull of Galloway.

Lady Selkirk was the heroine of the hour. She had faced these ruffians courageously and behaved impeccably, neither provoking them with disparaging remarks or insults, nor giving way to a fit of the vapours. She and Mary Elliot (who was a distant kinswoman) showed immense fortitude, especially as they were uncertain whether they would be taken prisoner themselves or even subjected to that fate worse than death. They had barely time to compose themselves after the Americans marched off, before a band of townspeople armed with pikes and muskets surrounded the house. Somewhat later, a rusty cannon was manhandled from Kirkcudbright down to the Point where a few rounds were discharged at a rock in the bay which, in poor light, was thought to be the American ship. Suddenly the vulnerability of Scotland, deprived of her militia since the Jacobite Rebellion of 1745–46, was starkly apparent. Agitation to rescind the ban on local volunteer forces, in fact, began immediately after news of the raid on St Mary's Isle was published.

Within days Lady Selkirk had discovered that her attacker was a local man. Writing to William Craik on 25 April she told him the American officers had given her the name of their commanding officer:

> whom I understand you know better than me, being John Paul, who they say was born in your ground, and is a gardener's son of yours. Afterwards he had the command of a trading vessel in this place, and is understood to have deserved the gallows oftener than once. It seems it is known this is the name he takes, and he was seen in the Isle, though the tenderness of his heart, they said, would not allow him to come to the house.

This 'tenderness of his heart' was corroborated by Jones himself, in the long, rambling apologia which he penned shortly after leaving St Mary's Isle, but could not entrust to the post until the cruise ended. The letter, carefully and clearly written, was probably drafted and polished a number of times before reaching its final immaculate version. It was posted at Brest on 8 May under cover to Lord le Despencer, the British Postmaster-General. With considerable misgivings he forwarded it to the Countess who received it about a month later. It was a remarkable letter by any standards, and obviously caused Jones a great deal of soul-searching. It is also extremely self-revelatory, especially regarding Jones's sense of chivalry and his personal philosophy:

> Madam:
>
> It cannot be too much lamented that in the profession of Arms, the Officer of fine feelings, and of real Sensibility, should be under the necessity of winking at any action of Persons under his command, which his Heart cannot approve: — but the reflection is doubly severe when he finds himself Obliged, in appearance, to countenance such Action by his Authority.
>
> This hard case was mine when on the 23d of April last I landed on St Mary's Isle. Knowing Lord Selkirk's interest with his King, and esteeming *as I do* his private Character; I wished to make him the happy Instrument of alleviating the horrors of hopeless captivity, when the brave are overpowered and made Prisoners of War.
>
> It was perhaps fortunate for you Madam that he was from home; for it was my intention to have taken him on board the *Ranger*, and to have detained him till thro' his means, a general and fair Exchange of Prisoners, as well in Europe as in America, had been effected.
>
> When I was informed by some Men whom I met at landing that his Lordship was absent; I walked back to my Boat determining to leave the Island: by the way, however, some Officers who were with me could not forbear expressing their discontent; observing that in America no delicacy was shown by the English; who took away all sorts of movable Property, setting Fire not only to Towns and to Houses of the rich without distinction; but not even sparing the wretched hamlets and Milch Cows of the poor and helpless

at the approach of an inclement Winter. That party had been with me, as Volunteers, the same morning at White Haven; some complaisance therefore was their due. I had but a moment to think how I might gratify them, and at the same time do your Ladyship the least Injury. I charged the Two Officers to permit none of the Seamen to enter the House, or to hurt anything about it — To treat you, Madam, with the utmost Respect — to accept of the plate which was offered — and to come away without making a search or demanding anything else.

I am induced to believe that I was punctually Obeyed; since I am informed that the plate which they brought away is far short of the Inventory which accompanied it. I have gratified my Men; and when the plate is sold, I shall become the Purchaser, and I will gratify *my own feelings* by restoring it to you, by such conveyance as you shall be pleased to direct.

Had the Earl been on board the *Ranger* the following Evening he would have seen the awful Pomp and dreadful Carnage of a Sea Engagement, both affording ample subject for the Pencil, as well as melancholy reflection for the contemplative mind. Humanity starts back from such scenes of horror, and cannot but execrate the vile Promoters of this detested War.

> For *They*, 'twas THEY unsheath'd the ruthless blade,
> And Heav'n shall ask the Havock it has made.

The British Ship of War, *Drake*, mounting 20 guns, with more than her full complement of Officers and Men, besides a number of Volunteers, came out from Carrickfergus, in order to attack and take the American Continental Ship of War, *Ranger*, of 18 guns and short of her complement of Officers and Men. The Ships met, and the advantage was disputed with great fortitude on each side for an Hour and Five minutes, when the gallant Commander of the *Drake* fell, and Victory declared in favor of the *Ranger*. His amiable Lieutenant lay mortally wounded besides near forty of the inferior officers and crew killed and wounded. A melancholy demonstration of the uncertainty of human prospects, and of the sad reverse of fortune which an hour can produce. I buryed them in a spacious grave, with the Honors due to the memory of the brave.

Tho' I have drawn my Sword in the present generous Struggle for the rights of Men; yet I am not in Arms as an American, nor am I in pursuit of Riches. My Fortune is liberal enough, having no Wife nor Family, and having lived long enough to know that Riches cannot ensure Happiness. I profess myself a Citizen of the World, totally unfettered by the little mean distinctions of Climate or of Country, which diminish the benevolence of the Heart and set bounds to Philanthropy. Before this War began I had at an early time of Life, withdrawn from the Sea service, in favor of 'calm contemplation and Poetic ease'. I have sacrificed not only my favorite schemes of Life, but the *softer Affections of the Heart* and my prospects of Domestic Happiness: — And I am ready to sacrifice Life also with cheerfulness — if that forfeiture could restore Peace and Goodwill among mankind.

As the feelings of your gentle Bosom cannot but be congenial with mine — let me entreat you Madam to use your soft persuasive Arts with your Husband to endeavor to stop this Cruel and destructive War, in which Britain can never succeed. Heaven can never countenance the barbarous and unmanly Practices of the Britons in America, which Savages would Blush at; and which if not discontinued will soon be retaliated in Britain by a justly enraged People. — Should you fail in this, (for I am persuaded you will attempt it: and who can resist the power of such an Advocate?) Your endeavours to effect a general Exchange of Prisoners, will be an Act of Humanity, which will afford you Golden feelings on a Death bed.

I hope this cruel contest will soon be closed; but should it continue, I wage no War with the Fair. I acknowledge their Power, and bend before it with profound Submission; let not therefore the Amiable Countess of Selkirk regard me as an Enemy. I am ambitious of her esteem and Friendship, and would do anything consistent with my duty to merit it.

The honor of a Line from your hand in Answer to this will lay me under a very singular Obligation; and if I can render you any acceptable service in France or elsewhere, I hope you see into my character so far as to command me without the least grain of reserve.

I wish to know exactly the behavior of my People, as I
determine to punish them if they have exceeded their
Liberty.

I have the Honor to be with much Esteem and with
profound Respect,

Madam,

Your most Obedient and most humble Servant

Jno P. Jones

Incidentally, the couplet quoted in the middle of this letter has never
been attributed to any published poet, and the conclusion is that
Jones composed the verse himself.

This was, of course, the Sentimental Era, and no more ardent
proponent of 'sensibility' to use a buzz-word of the 1770s and
1780s, existed than John Paul Jones, who prided himself on his skills
and expertise when it came to handling women in all levels of
society. The high-flown sentiments and the poetic effusion were
worthy of Burns in his impassioned correspondence with Clarinda a
few years later. Here we see Jones marshalling all the weapons in
his arsenal to capture the female heart: his detestation of war and
violence, his tender feelings for the poor, his compassion for the
sufferings of prisoners-of-war, even the hint of being lovelorn and
all alone in the world, calculated to rouse sympathy, and his stern
promise to punish his men if they were found to have exceeded his
strict orders. This carefully composed letter was designed to strike
a pose of Jones as a gentleman of refinement and taste. By purchasing the family plate and returning it – presumably in person,
once this disagreeable war was over – Jones revealed a desire to
ingratiate himself with the Selkirks. There is an echo of this in his
Mémoire of 1786 to King Louis XVI, in which he stated that Lady
Selkirk was so anxious to meet him that she proposed accompanying
Cullam and Wallingford to the Point to invite Captain Jones to dine
at St Mary's Isle.

Jones was so inordinately proud of this epistle that he not only
sent the Countess three originals in his own hand, by different
intermediaries to ensure that she got the message, but had numerous
copies made to impress his friends. One went to Franklin, another
to Arthur Lee, a third to the Dutch politician and American
sympathiser, J.D. Van der Capellen, and a fourth to Robert Morris
for the Marine Committee. It also appeared in full, as an appendix
to his *Mémoire* to the King of France.

The Countess never answered Jones's letter, but her husband, on his return from Buxton, put pen to paper at Dumfries on 9 June. The wrapper was addressed in French to 'Monsieur J.P. Jones, Capitaine du Vaisseau Americain, *La Ranger*, à Brest'. Unlike the Jones letter, the Earl's was written on the spur of the moment, but it was a pretty cool and studied performance for all that. While appearing to agree with Jones on a number of points, he managed to put matters in a rather different light. Thus he agreed with Jones that it was fortunate for Lady Selkirk that he was not at home when the raid took place, but pointed out that her ladyship was well advanced in her pregnancy and he dreaded to think what might have happened to her if he had been taken prisoner. 'I own I do not understand how a man of *Sensibility to fine feelings* could reconcile this to what his heart approved,' he wrote, and went on to point out that he had absolutely no influence with the King or his ministers, of whose measures 'I have generally disapproved . . . and in particular of almost their whole conduct in the unhappy and ill-judged American War'. When it came to delivering a lecture on the Rights of Man, Lord Selkirk (who was on the liberal wing of the Whig party), could certainly outdo Jones, and administered a rebuke at the same time for the latter's impropriety in 'departing from the established and usual practice of Modern War'. Lord Selkirk confirmed that the Americans had behaved properly, and added his condolences on learning that Wallingford had been killed in the engagement with *Drake* 'for he in particular showed so much civility and so apparent dislike at the business he was then on, that it is surprising how he should have been one of the proposers of it'.

Jones's offer to return the silver plate was rebuffed: 'Your genteel offer, Sir, of returning the plate is very polite, but at the same time neither Lady Selkirk nor I can think of accepting it, as you must purchase it you say for that purpose.' Instead, the Earl suggested that Jones give his share of the proceeds to the seamen who had behaved so well during the raid, and concluded: 'You, Sir, are entitled to what is more honorable, viz: the Praise of having your men under good discipline, which on all occasions I take care to make known.' Jones never received this letter because the Postmaster-General refused to forward it 'to such a Rascal and Rebel as this Jones'. This was perhaps just as well, for had he read between the lines of this politely contemptuous letter, Jones might have realised what a fool he had made of himself in writing in such highfalutin vein to Lady Selkirk; but he remained blissfully ignorant of its effect and to the end of his days was convinced that he had shown himself to be the very epitome of sense and sensibility.

That Jones entertained the hope that some day he would return to Galloway, and settle there as a landed gentleman like William Craik, is evident in an interview which he gave to an anonymous journalist at Texel, Holland, on 1 November 1779 and which appeared in the London newspapers a month later under the heading of 'Extract of a Letter from Holland'.[3] In this he stated that he had ordered agents to purchase land for him on the Solway Firth where he intended to end his days. This provoked a furious response in the Scottish and English newspapers attacking him as a pirate and impugning his honour. Later on, the vitriolic reaction of British officers in the Russian service to his appointment would also have disabused him of any notions he might once have entertained about returning to his roots. That morning when he stood on the beach at St Mary's Isle would be the last time he set foot on Scottish soil.

Unaware of the Selkirks' refusal to take back their plate, Jones was as good as his word. At Brest he had the silver appraised by a dealer but was told that there was no market for old-fashioned English plate. As scrap, it was valued at three thousand livres, which translated into American money as $600. This was actually twice its bullion value, though well short of the ridiculous value placed on it by the Swiss merchant J.D. Schweighauser, reporting to Arthur Lee in December 1779. Fifteen per cent was Jones's share, but he paid the remaining $510 out of his own pocket. After the war he arranged for the silver to be crated up and returned to St Mary's Isle by way of Calais and Dover to the Countess of Morton in London (a close relative of Lady Selkirk). It proved to be intact – right down to the dried tea-leaves still adhering to the bottom of the teapot. Lord Selkirk, mellowed by the passage of time and mollified by this act, wrote a gracious acknowledgment to Jones. It should be added that, as a propaganda exercise, the return of the silver had beneficial results in restoring good relations between France and Britain, as well as in improving British attitudes towards the former colonies. The Comte d'Estaing no less, was effusive in his praise of Jones, while Calonne, the French minister of finance, not only waived customs duty on the consignment, but wrote to Jones: 'That action, Sir, is worthy of the reputation which you acquired by your conduct, and proves that true valour perfectly agrees with humanity and generosity.'[4]

There was a strange tailpiece to this story. Robert Burns so vividly recalled his first meeting face to face with a lord that he wrote a poem about it entitled 'Lines on meeting with Lord Daer', then a twenty-three-year-old student at Edinburgh University, staying with Professor Dugald Stewart at his country home in Catrine, Ayrshire. Basil, Lord Daer, had inherited his father's liberal outlook and following the outbreak of the French Revolution had gone to Paris as a delegate from the Friends of the People. It was in this context that he met John Paul Jones in 1791, both being guests at a dinner-party given by William Short, the American chargé d'affaires. Both men were in the same room for upwards of two hours before being introduced. Daer, who was fifteen at the time of the raid and absent at boarding-school in Edinburgh, chatted amiably with Jones about the raid in general and the silver in particular, expressing his father's gratitude at its safe return and for the exemplary conduct of his men. 'He seems a sensible little fellow,' wrote Daer to his father. 'He is not as dark as I had heard.'[5] Trapped in France by the outbreak of war with Britain in 1793, young Daer died there the following year, pre-deceasing his father who died in 1799.

St George's Day 1778 was not one that the people of Britain would readily forget. Within days the Admiralty in London was being inundated with letters and despatches from every part of the kingdom, reporting sightings of *Ranger*. The Admiralty ordered HMS *Stag* to go in pursuit of the American raider, while HMS *Doctor* was despatched to the Firth of Clyde. Correctly guessing that it would take the Royal Navy several days to react to his raids, Jones coolly remained in the area, determined to challenge HMS *Drake*. By dawn on 24 April *Ranger* was off Kilfoot Point near Carrickfergus, when *Drake* was sighted. Her elderly skipper, Captain Burden, had been warned about an American privateer in the vicinity but he was uncertain whether this strange ship now approaching might not be a peaceful merchantman. Burden sent off his gig to investigate, while many yachts and fishing-boats from both sides of Belfast Lough put out to watch the fun. If they were looking for a good scrap, they certainly got one. The ensuing battle, which Jones had described so pathetically to Lady Selkirk, was packed with drama.

It began with the approach of *Drake*'s gig. To the young lieutenant in command of the gig, studying the stranger through his telescope, she seemed innocent enough, so skilfully had Jones masked the gun-ports. *Ranger*'s crew were concealed below decks as the gig came alongside. The British officer clambered aboard and began questioning the deck officer (Jones) who, by way of response, informed him quietly that he was a prisoner of Captain John Paul Jones of the United States Navy. According to Jones, this 'tickled the caprice' of his surly crew who were at that moment taking the opportunity to hold a town-meeting below decks, presided over by Simpson, and were on the point of mutiny. 'Soothed again into good Humour', however, they decided to fight and with the prospect of a goodly fistful of prize dollars, they put up a 'truely Gallant' fight as their captain subsequently reported.

The pleasure craft, seeing the gig taken in tow, and observing that *Drake*'s frantic signals were ignored, drew back to a safe distance, and presently alarm beacons were lit along the shores of the Lough. Jones cleverly retreated into the open sea where he would have better room to manoeuvre, and *Drake* fell for the ploy. Jones let the enemy get within hailing distance, and noted with wry amusement that her figurehead of a man in armour was just like that on *Alfred*. Later he discovered that his adversary had been built at Philadelphia for the tobacco trade, had been captured by the British and converted to a twenty-gun sloop of war. *Drake* hoisted the Union Jack and *Ranger* the Stars and Stripes. A verbal challenge was issued and answered, and then the two warships squared up to each other. Action commenced about an hour before sunset, as *Ranger*, athwart *Drake*'s bow, raked her decks with grapeshot.

Ranger was the larger of the two vessels, and better armed, with eighteen 9-pounders to *Drake*'s twenty 6-pounders; but *Drake* was more heavily manned, so it was essential that Jones keep the enemy from getting close enough to grapple and board. He concentrated on keeping about thirty metres from the British ship, so as to direct accurate gunfire and musketry on her crew and rigging while doing as little damage as possible to her hull. After an hour or so, Captain Burden was killed by a musketball through the brain and the first-lieutenant, Dobbs, was mortally wounded. The ship's master, third in command, realising that the masts and spars had been so badly damaged as to make the ship unmanageable, called out: 'Quarters!' Firing ceased immediately and Jones sent over a boarding party in *Drake*'s own gig. The boarders found the decks awash with blood and rum; a cask of liquor, brought out prematurely to celebrate victory, had taken a direct hit from a Yankee cannonball. Casualties were relatively light on both sides. The Americans lost Sam Wallingford and two seamen, with five wounded, while the British sustained four dead and nineteen wounded. Burden and Dobbs were buried at sea with full naval honours. At Brest, Jones found a letter from a British firm at Bordeaux, addressed to Lieutenant Dobbs, and felt constrained to reply:

> It gives me real Pain to inform you that he is no more: he survived the Engagement only 36 hours. In the Course of that time I paid him two Visits on board the *Drake* and found him in such spirits that I had no apprehension of what so soon followed. I freely consented to land him among his Friends the day after the Engagement when we passed Belfast; but the Surgeons as well as himself thought the Risque was too great, after a loss of Blood. His Boy was therefore at his desire sent ashore. He was buried in the Ocean with the Honors due to the Brave and the respect due to his private Character. I would write to his Brother, but wish to avoid the too tender Subject. I am convinced that he was shewed all possible care and tenderness. Consequently his Hurt exceeded the Art of the Surgeon and the Skill of the Physician. You are at liberty to Communicate this Account to his Relations.[6]

This was a strange war, indeed, in which the niceties were observed between belligerents who spoke the same language.

No fewer than 133 prisoners were taken. After the dead had been buried at sea and the wounded patched up, *Ranger* took *Drake* in tow and headed south. On 25 April they anchored off Ballywater, County Down, where the prisoners, under the supervision of Elijah Hall, carried out repairs to *Drake* as well as armed and refitted the brigantine *Patience* of Whitehaven, bound for Norway, which had been easily taken. When the wind changed direction Jones's tiny flotilla turned about and headed north. At the entrance to Belfast Lough again that evening Jones liberated the fishermen he had captured the previous week, furnishing them with one of his own boats, a new sail and some ready cash. Green duly recorded that 'The grateful fishermen were in raptures; and expressed their joy in three huzzas as they passed the *Ranger*'s quarter'.[7]

This kind gesture went a long way towards establishing Jones's popularity in the British Isles, and helped to create the legend of him as a maritime Robin Hood. Typical of the fables that persist to this day is the story, endlessly retold in Islay, that Jones and his merry men took shelter at Lochindaal on 28 April, detained two fishermen whom he later let go, and planned to take the Campbell of Islay hostage. When told by the fishermen that the laird was not at home, but was expected shortly on a ship carrying treasure from the Far East, Jones intercepted the East Indiaman and relieved her of her cargo. Unfortunately this stirring tale is not supported by any facts recorded in *Ranger*'s log or Jones's own narrative of the cruise. Instead, the ships lay off the Mull of Kintyre on 27 April while repairs on *Drake* were completed. The following day, off Islay, Jones appointed Simpson prizemaster with orders to stick close to *Ranger*, about a cable's length on the starboard quarter. Should they be separated by bad weather, *Drake* was to make her way to a French port, preferably Brest.

This was by no means the first victory of an American Continental vessel over a British warship.[8] The sloop of war *Lynx* was taken by the privateer *Cromwell* in May 1776, while Manley and McNeill, in *Hancock* and *Boston*, captured the frigate *Fox* on 7 June 1777. *Fox* was later recaptured by the British, then seized by the French frigate *Junon* and taken into Brest in September 1778; Jones, who was there at the time, hoped he might get command of her. On the other hand, the battle between the closely matched ships *Ranger* and *Drake* was the longest and most ferocious to date and, taking place so close to shore, was witnessed by thousands of onlookers. The *Morning Chronicle* of 9 May, conducting a post mortem on the battle, concluded that *Drake* was beaten by her inferior gunfire and shoddy gunpowder. The first-lieutenant and boatswain had recently died and not been replaced; Captain Burden, who was overdue for retirement, was ill at the time; and the fatal injuries which he and Dobbs sustained meant that the ship was virtually leaderless. Normally, opined the newspaper, such handicaps would not have adversely affected the outcome if French or Spanish ships had been involved, 'but the case is different when we engage with our own countrymen; men who have the same spirit and bravery with ourselves'.

By the end of April a formidable taskforce was on the search for the American raider. *Stag* and *Doctor* were now joined by the thirty-six-gun frigate *Thetis* from Glasgow, the sloop of war *Heart of Oak* from Liverpool, the thirty-two-gun *Boston* from Waterford and a number of smaller warships. Jones and his ships, however, gave them all the slip and sailed round Donegal and down the west coast of Ireland. The weather was good and the ships made an uneventful passage until 4 May when they were approaching the French coast and re-entering the war zone. By now *Drake* was lagging behind under her jury rig, so Jones took her in tow again, but the following morning, off Ushant, a likely prize hove in sight. Jones released the tow and *Ranger* went off in pursuit, ordering *Drake* to follow as best she could. Simpson either ignored this order or claimed to have misunderstood it, for he continued on course for Brest. The strange vessel proved to be a neutral Swedish ship, so Jones turned about and resumed his southerly course, catching up with *Drake* on 6 May. Jones was now beside himself with rage at what he perceived to be Simpson's flagrant insubordination. After an unedifying spectacle as Jones and Simpson harangued each other by loud-hailer from their respective quarterdecks, Hall was sent aboard *Drake* to take over the prize, while Simpson was suspended from duty and placed under close arrest. It was an unpleasant conclusion to an otherwise successful cruise.

Jones had performed the most spectacularly daring exploit of the naval campaign so far, with a land raid, two merchantmen seized and others destroyed as well as a British warship taken. When the ships entered Brest at sunset on 8 May, *Drake* with two hundred prisoners on board flew 'English Colours inverted under the American Stars'. Despite the rank insubordination of most officers and men, arguably the most craven and disloyal crew Jones had ever sailed with, the captain had a sense of elation as he entered the harbour. He deserved a hero's welcome but, to his bitter disappointment, nobody but his friend d'Orvilliers took much notice of him. The studied indifference in France to his exploits was in marked contrast to the impact Jones had made in Britain. From this episode date the many ballads and sea-shanties and the countless broadsides and chapbooks out of which the myth of John Paul Jones was created.

Jones's euphoria on returning to Brest swiftly gave way to a feeling of crushing disappointment. At first, of course, he was too busy coping with the manifold problems arising out of the cruise, such as the disposal of the prisoners, the payment of wages and prize money to the crew and the court-martial of Simpson. France was still nominally at peace with Britain; although ambassadors had been withdrawn in mid-March, war did not break out till 17 June. If the British prisoners were handed over to the French authorities they would have no alternative but to release them, so d'Orvilliers advised Jones to ship them back to America. This was unsatisfactory, as Jones wished to have them close to Britain, the better to bargain for their exchange with the Americans then languishing in Fortin and

Mill prisons. D'Orvilliers compromised by consigning the prisoners to a hulk in Brest Harbour while Jones worked frantically through Franklin to undermine British intransigence, though it was not until February 1779 that an exchange of prisoners took place, 228 Americans being freed in return for the 164 taken prisoner by Jones and a further sixty captured by the French. This was a step in the right direction, but over a thousand American seamen continued to rot in British gaols till the spring of 1780.

Jones was anxious to sell *Drake*, *Lord Chatham* and *Patience* at Nantes or Bordeaux as he had done with the fruit brigantines, but the outbreak of war between France and Britain made this difficult, and he was at first advised to take them across the Atlantic and dispose of them in some American port. Fearing that they might be recaptured *en route*, he went to Paris and eventually persuaded the French Admiralty to let him sell his prizes in France. By that time, however, his friend Jonathan Williams had been superseded as agent at Nantes by the devious Swiss Schweighauser, a tool of Arthur Lee, who turned out to be extremely obstructive. It was Schweighauser who would not release to the thirsty Jones his share of the *Lord Chatham*'s porter, who set a value on the Selkirk silver many times its bullion worth and tried to claw back a percentage for himself, and who sold Jones and his men short on the disposal of the prize ships because the auction was not properly advertised. The problem was alleviated to some extent when Jonathan Williams, in his private capacity, bought the shares of *Ranger*'s crew in advance. That way the subordinate officers and seamen got a few louis d'or in their hands, and with that they were reasonably satisfied.

In the matter of back pay, Jones ran up against bureaucracy when he made out, and partly drew upon, a draft on the American Commissioners for a thousand louis ($4,800) in order to pay the men. His consideration for his crew landed him in trouble when his draft was dishonoured on a technicality, and in desperation he turned to a business friend at Brest for a loan against the value of the prizes, and also went cap in hand to the royal abattoir to obtain sufficient meat to feed his crew. To a proud and honourable man like Jones this was 'a Deplorable & disgraceful Situation in the sight of the French Fleet'.[9] Jones was unaware of the infighting that now had the Commissioners at loggerheads. Franklin wrote a palliative letter on 1 June, but even he was now being undermined by Arthur Lee and John Adams (who had replaced Silas Deane) who conspired to use the discomfiture of Jones in their campaign to strike at their adversary.

While these unseemly wrangles continued, and Jones bombarded the Commissioners with ever-more hysterical letters, the case of Lieutenant Simpson proceeded to a most unsatisfactory conclusion. Jones wanted a court-martial, but there were no American naval officers in France of sufficient seniority to handle such a matter. Simpson, even under arrest, proved to be a very troublesome fellow. Instead of being placed in irons, he had the use of his cabin and the run of the quarterdeck where he continued to undermine the crew. Jones had him transferred to a private cabin aboard the prison ship and there Simpson created so much trouble that d'Orvilliers clapped him in the naval prison ashore, described in a subsequent petition by *Ranger*'s crew as 'a Lousey, Dirtey French Gaol unfit for a Faithful, true & Fatherly Oficer, our First Lieutenant'. This round robin, subscribed by seventy-seven seamen as 'the Jovial Tars Now on board the Continental Sloop of war *Ranger*' was sent directly to Franklin, along with a similar petition signed by twenty-eight warrant and petty officers. Hall, Cullam and Green also wrote separately in similar vein. On the other hand, about thirty of the crew and all the midshipmen remained loyal to their captain.

As a result of these petitions, the Commissioners urged Jones to adopt a more conciliatory attitude. Bowing to this pressure, Jones released Simpson and appointed him to the command of *Ranger* for her passage back to America, saving face all round by claiming that he was the only navigator competent enough to take the ship home. Simpson was piped aboard his new command on 27 July, 'to the joy and Satisfaction of the whole Ship's Company' as Green smugly noted. Had Simpson left the matter at that, all would have been well; but over the ensuing weeks he strutted about the naval base, loudly claiming that Jones was discredited and out of a job. Jones thereupon renewed his demand for Simpson to be court-martialled. By mid-August, when Captains Whipple and Tucker arrived at Brest, Jones had the necessary senior officers for such an action; but Whipple refused to convene a court-martial, arguing that by releasing Simpson and appointing him to command, Jones had effectively wiped out the charges. Meanwhile the crew, from Hall and Green downwards, continued to back Simpson against Jones, Hall going so far as to maintain that Jones 'was the cause of the Disorder because his mode of Government is so far from ours that no American of spirit can ever serve with Cheerfulness under him'. Jones was no martinet in the tradition of William Bligh, but he differed fundamentally from this crew in trying to run *Ranger* like a warship and not a privateer, a distinction which he made clearly in a memorandum to the Commissioners:

> When *Gain* is the ruling principle of Officers in an Infant Navy – it is no wonder that they do not cultivate by their precepts nor enforce by their Example the principles of *Dutiful Subordination, Cheerful unrepining* Obedience in those who are under their command, nor is it strange that this principle should weaken the sacred bonds of order and Discipline, and introduce the Mistaken and baneful Idea of Licentiousness and Free Agency under the specious name of 'Liberty'.[10]

Putting this in perspective, it should be noted that Nicholas Biddle lost an entire ship's company through desertion when his frigate *Randolph* put in at Charleston, South Carolina, and a year passed before he could muster a replacement crew; Lambert Wickes suffered an actual mutiny while stationed on the French coast, and John Barry and Hector McNeill had continual problems with indiscipline. The only skippers who were untrammelled by such problems were those who never got to sea, or who lost their ships early on. To make matters worse, there was a complete lack of solidarity among the Continental captains who, when not coping with mutinous crews, quarrelled among themselves and denounced each other to the Marine Committee. While Jones denounced Hacker and Manley, Nicholson tried to block Jones's promotion, and Whipple and Thompson resorted to the newspapers to air their grievances and personal animosities.

Much to Jones's disgust, Simpson took *Ranger* back to Portsmouth, New Hampshire, without incident and was subsequently rewarded with a captain's commission. *Ranger* was later captured by the Royal Navy and renamed HMS *Halifax* but was sold off cheaply in 1781 on account of rotting timbers and ended her days as a merchant ship, a sorry conclusion to the one-time terror of the narrow seas. After a spell in a British prison hulk, Simpson was repatriated, got command of a privateer and was lost at sea. Hall and Jones were eventually reconciled, and the former was offered the first-lieutenancy of *America* which Jones hoped to command. Master David Cullam came off best of all, investing his prize money wisely and ending up as one of the most prosperous citizens of Portsmouth.

With the exception of the Marine lieutenant Sam Wallingford, the midshipmen Hill and Wendell, and the Swedish volunteer lieutenant Meijer, *Ranger*'s officers were a poor bunch – cowardly, insubordinate, ill-disciplined and self-seeking. With such a motley crew, it is miraculous that Jones achieved all that he did.

9. Bonhomme Richard

1778–79

I wish to have no Connection with any Ship that does not
sail fast, for I intend *to go in harm's way.*
— JOHN PAUL JONES AT BREST, NOVEMBER 1778

As spring turned to summer, the frustration of Captain John Paul
Jones increased steadily. He had the chagrin of seeing his *bête noire*,
Simpson, set off in triumph for America while rumours spread that
he, Jones, had been suspended from sea-duty. His efforts to get a
ship – any ship – were constantly thwarted. He tried to get command of the prize ship *Fox*, he addressed endless desperate appeals
to Sartine, the French Minister of Marine, and would even petition
King Louis himself in the forlorn hope of getting command of
L'Indien; but it was all to no avail. Desperate to get back to sea under
any circumstances, he prevailed upon his one true friend, Admiral
d'Orvilliers, to allow him to serve as a volunteer aboard his flagship
when it put to sea in search of Admiral Keppel's fleet. D'Orvilliers
was very agreeable to this, and accordingly sought approval from
Sartine, but unfortunately the minister did not get around to
granting this request until the fleet had sailed. Jones actually dined
aboard *Bretagne* on the very day the expedition set out, and even
remained aboard while the flagship manoeuvred into the roadstead,
but having waited as long as he dared for Sartine's permission, he
was reluctantly put ashore in a gig. He kicked his heels at Brest while
d'Orvilliers and Keppel brought their respective fleets to battle off
Ushant on 27 June. Four days of jockeying for position culminated
in an inconclusive exchange of broadsides, both fleets claiming
victory. The British and French governments thought otherwise;
Keppel was court-martialled but acquitted, while the reputation of
d'Orvilliers was severely dented. In addition, Rear-Admiral the Duc
de Chartres, scion of a cadet branch of the Bourbon family, had used
his royal connections to secure command of the blue squadron, but
he became the scapegoat for the French failure to destroy Keppel's

fleet and was deprived of his command, though Marie Antoinette subsequently intervened and secured his appointment as colonel-general of hussars.[1] Jones, who had assiduously cultivated the royal rear-admiral and his beautiful Duchess (whose father, the Duc de Penthièvre was Grand Admiral of France), suffered yet another setback when Chartres was disgraced.

Meanwhile Jones had been pulling strings to get command of *L'Indien*, now the property of the French government but still at her berth in Amsterdam. At first, his persistence seemed to have paid off when he heard from Franklin that it was settled that he should have command of her. On receipt of these glad tidings in mid-June, he had left Brest and gone to Passy where he stayed at the Hôtel Valentinois till 7 August, consoling himself in the arms of Madame de Chaumont while she persuaded her compliant husband to intercede with Sartine on her lover's behalf. All that came out of this episode was a letter from the minister to Franklin formally requesting that Jones remain in France for a ship and a mission as yet undetermined. To this end, Sartine despatched to Amsterdam the Prince de Nassau-Siegen, a high-class soldier of fortune who, being distantly related to the Dutch Stadholder, William of Orange, was believed to have some influence with the Dutch authorities. Nassau-Siegen, however, proved ineffectual and the Dutch, anxious to avoid confrontation with Britain, refused to release the warship. Ironically, the French subsequently sold the ship to the Duc de Montmorency who leased her to Alexander Gillon, commodore of the South Carolina Navy who had been hanging round the French ministry of marine for more than a year in the hope of getting a ship. Under the name of *South Carolina*, she eventually got to sea in the summer of 1781 but her career as the flagship of her name-state was brief and inglorious.

In mid-July Sartine offered Jones command of *L'Epervier*, a captured British corvette of sixteen guns, but Jones declined such an insignificant command, saying that he expected to return to America shortly to receive

> the Chief Command the first squadron destined for an Expedition . . . and when Congress see fit to appoint Admirals, I have Assurances that my Name will not be forgot. These are flattering prospects to a Man who has Drawn his Sword only upon principles of Philanthropy and in support of the Dignity of Human Nature. But as I prefer

a solid to a shining Reputation, a useful to a splendid
Command, I hold myself Ready, with the approbation of the
Commissioners, to be Governed by you in any Measures that
may tend to Distress and Humble the Common Enemy.[2]

The minister now asked Jones for his thoughts on any prospective
expedition, and this promptly brought forth a lengthy memorandum
in which he set out various proposals for raids on Glasgow, the west
coast of Africa, the Newfoundland fisheries, Hudson's Bay and
English merchant fleets in the Baltic trade. For any of these raids
Jones stipulated that he would require the command of a taskforce
of two or three French frigates with ancillary vessels. Sartine seems
to have been merely playing with the hyperactive little Scotsman, for
there is no evidence that he took any of these proposals seriously.
The nearest Sartine came to a positive decision was a suggestion that
Jones be given command of the frigate *Renommée* for the purpose of
a raiding cruise, but in the end this ship was assigned to a French
captain. Then he was invited to take part in a raid on the British
privateers based in Jersey but declined when he learned that overall command was to be given to Nassau-Siegen. His hopes of getting
HMS *Fox* were dashed when she was given to another Frenchman,
and when Sartine jokingly suggested that he might like to go back
to America in *une bonne voiture* (a good carriage), Jones's patience
finally ran out. He wrote immediately to Chaumont, complaining
that the minister had treated him 'like a Child five successive times
by leading me on from Great to little and from little to less'.[3] And
to a good friend at court, the Duc de la Rochefoucauld, he complained that Sartine's little joke was

> absolutely adding insult to injury, and it is the proposition of
> a man whose veracity I have not experienced in former cases
> . . . The Minister, to my infinite mortification, after
> possessing himself of my schemes and ideas has treated me
> like a Child five times . . . M. de Sartine may think as he
> pleases, but Congress will not thank him for having thus
> treated an officer who has always been honoured with their
> favour and friendship.[4]

When Chaumont tried to mollify Jones by offering him the
command of one of his privateers, *L'Union*, Jones replied stiffly that
'as a servant of the Imperial Republic of America' he could not serve

'either myself or even my friends, in any private line whatever, unless where the honor and interest of America is the premier object'.[5] To Sartine Jones also complained that 'I have already lost near five months of my time, the best season of the year, and such opportunities of serving my country, and *acquiring honor, as I cannot again expect this year*'. And he threatened that unless he now received a direct written apology, 'suitable to the injury which I have sustained', he would 'publish in the gazettes of Europe the conduct he has held towards me'.[6] Sartine's immediate reaction to this outburst was to suggest to Franklin that it might be best all round if Jones were sent home as soon as possible. When Lieutenant Peter Amiel, Jones's bilingual aide, conveyed this to him, Jones riposted, 'Perish that thought. It is impossible. I would now lay down my life rather than return to America before my honor is made perfectly whole.'

In desperation Jones now fired off letters to all three American commissioners *and* their private secretaries, to Joseph Hewes and Robert Morris, to John Ross and Jonathan Williams. If diplomats, merchants, commissioners, ministers, counts and dukes had failed him, Jones had only one recourse left, and this was a petition to King Louis himself. Two copies were made, one sent to the King via William Franklin (who was asked to get his grandfather to deliver it personally to His Majesty) and the other via the Duchesse de Chartres. This remarkable document speaks passionately of Jones being 'chained Down to shameful Inactivity for the space of Five Months'. Jones hoped that Franklin would accompany the Duchess for an audience with the King, in order to explain the situation more fully.

Something not unlike paranoia had overtaken Jones by this time, understandable in view of the fact that he seemed to be given the runaround by all concerned. His letters in this period reveal mounting distrust of the commissioners, even the 'good Doctor' Franklin coming under suspicion. His vituperation was mainly reserved for Arthur Lee ('the Wasp') and John Adams ('that wicked and conceited upstart' or 'Mr Roundface'). Someone as egocentric as Jones was bound to see the action or inaction of others in terms that affected him personally; but in fairness to the American pleni-potentiaries, the summer of 1778 was an exceedingly busy time for them, and they did have a great deal more on their minds than fulfilling the wishes of Captain Jones.

Paranoia gave way to deep depression with the final humiliation, the appointment of Simpson to the command of *Ranger* on 15 August. In hindsight, it can be seen that to waste the energies, resourcefulness and talents of John Paul Jones in that fateful summer was the height of stupidity, but who exactly was to blame cannot be ascertained. To be sure, there were plenty of French frigates lying idly at their moorings in Brest after the inconclusive action off Ushant, and d'Orvilliers could have spared two or three for Jones's expedition had Sartine a mind to permit it. And the American commissioners might have exerted themselves rather more in this matter, as well as in securing the release of *L'Indien* from the Dutch. If Montmorency could obtain the ship, why could not Franklin, or someone associated with him?

Such inactivity on the French side of the Atlantic contrasts starkly with the poor showing of the American Navy on the other. On 7 March 1778 the frigate *Randolph* blew up, killing Captain Biddle and all but four of her crew, during an engagement with HMS *Yarmouth* in the West Indies. Other ships had difficulty running the British blockade and were either bottled up in their home ports or ran aground. The only bright spot in an otherwise dismal year was the cruise of the French fleet under d'Estaing which effectively prevented Lord George Germain from carrying out his orders to burn every American port from Maine to the Carolinas. By the end of the year the American Navy had been reduced to five frigates stuck in Boston, the frigate *Alliance* in course of fitting out, *Ranger* and the sloop *Providence*. While the American press extolled Jones's exploits and gloated over British panic arising from the Whitehaven raid, Congress ignored its naval hero and the Marine Committee did not communicate with him for several months. The only crumb of comfort was a letter of 12 November 1778 which Jones received from Thomas Bell, commander of a privateer (belonging to Robert Morris no less) which docked at Lorient. Bell, an old comrade-in-arms from the Continental Navy, gave Jones a vivid if illiterate account of the state of affairs at Philadelphia. Many of the captains had been laid off by Congress for lack of ships, and had accepted the command of privateers. Bell added that, although some of the 'Northward Gentlemen' had spoken disparagingly of Jones, 'the publick to the Southward thinks you the finest fellow belonging to America'. Bell painted a sorry picture of Philadelphia – 'no Ships or Sailors nor nothing dowing but What Mr Morris dos. my Brig belongs to him She mounts 12 six pounders & the Onley Squar Rigd Vesell when I left it'.

Jones replied from Brest on 15 November, deploring the shocking state of Philadelphia and the Navy but urging Bell not to despair:

> Tho' I am no Prophet, the one will yet become the *first City*, and the other the *first Navy* within a much shorter space of time than is generally imagined. When the Enemies land force is once conquered and expelled the Continent, our Marine will rise as if by Enchantment, and become, within the memory of Persons now living, the wonder and Envy of the World . . .

Interestingly, the letter ended on a light-hearted note, Jones fearing that some rival had stolen the heart of 'my fair Mistress', though the lady in question was not named. 'I'm afraid this making Love by Proxy will not answer; and I shall Despair of its Success Unless I soon receive some Encouragement.'

Bell's letter was given to Jones personally by James Moylan, an Irish businessman in Lorient to whom Jones had previously written with a plea to find a French ship that might be suitable for outfitting as a warship. At the end of November Moylan wrote to say that he had found just such a vessel. She was a French East Indiaman of 900 tons named *Le Duc de Duras*. Jones delayed responding to this suggestion as he was at that moment toying with the idea of fitting out one of the British prizes which had recently been taken into Brest and of which Chaumont was now disposing. These prizes were a poor prospect and in rejecting them all Jones made his famous statement: 'I wish to have no Connection with any Ship that does not sail *fast*, for I intend *to go in harm's way.*' Sadly, this was a wish unfulfilled, and Jones would have to make do with what he was offered. By 7 December he was in Lorient, the base of the French Compagnie des Indes, and there he inspected the *Duc de Duras*, twelve years old but the best vessel available. Several letters to Chaumont over the ensuing days reveal Jones as increasingly enthusiastic about the prospect of obtaining this ship, and increasingly impatient that Chaumont should buy her and fit her out as a ship of war. The owner of the ship, one Bérard, was pressing for a decision. Given ten days to conclude the purchase, Jones wrote breathlessly to Chaumont urging him on. He spent an anxious and fretful Christmas and New Year with Moylan, daily afraid that this ship would elude him. Letters to Williams and Father John Mehegen, the Irish chaplain to d'Orvilliers, betray Jones's anxieties at this critical time. On 2

January 1779 word reached him at last that King Louis had allocated funds for the purchase of the ship, and had given Chaumont approval to go ahead. There were further anxious moments in January 1779, but by the first week of February Jones learned that he had, at last, got his long-awaited ship. Sartine himself wrote to Jones a letter delivered personally by M. Garnier, formerly French chargé d'affaires in London:

> In consequence of the distinguished manner in which you
> have served the United States and the complete confidence
> that your conduct has deserved on the part of Congress, His
> Majesty has thought proper to place at your disposition the
> ship *Le Duras* of 40 guns, now at Lorient.

Sartine went on to state that the proposed expedition would be under the American flag, the armaments at the cost of France, and the crew to consist of volunteers, not sailors in the French service. As for the expedition itself, Jones would have *carte blanche*. Jones replied immediately, a minor masterpiece of diplomatic writing:

> It shall be my duty to represent in the strongest terms to
> Congress the generous and voluntary resolution which their
> great ally, the protector of the rights of human nature, and
> the best of kings, has taken to promote the honor of their
> flag, and I beseech you to assure His Majesty that my heart
> is impressed with the deepest sense of the obligation which
> I owe his condescending favor and good opinion and which
> it shall be my highest ambition to merit, by rendering every
> service in my power to the common cause. I cannot insure
> success, but I will endeavor to deserve it.[7]

And Jones also expressed his gratitude to Benjamin Franklin in whose honour the ship was renamed in French *Bonhomme Richard* – or 'Good Man Richard' as her American crew often called her – in allusion to Franklin's famous book *Poor Richard's Almanac* which had recently appeared in a French edition under the title of *Les Maximes du Bonhomme Richard*.

Effusive thanks all round turned out to be a trifle premature for a further six months would elapse before Jones could take his new ship to sea, six months of frustration and exasperation, of bureaucratic muddle and bloody-minded obstruction. In the midst of this there was also an embarrassing situation which left Jones smarting. In February he paid a flying visit to Passy to pay his respects to Franklin and his devotions to Madame de Chaumont. During this brief sojourn there occurred an incident which later caused intense embarrassment to Jones, though doubtless his friends and acquaintances in Passy only found it hilarious.

Not long after he returned to Lorient, Jones received a letter of 24 February from Franklin which, after discussing various business matters, ended with a jocular postscript about the mystery in Jones's life now being cleared up. Franklin assumed that this matter had already been imparted to him by Madame Thérèse. In fact, Jones had not the faintest idea what Franklin was on about, and wrongly assumed that he was alluding to that unfortunate affair in Tobago which had brought him so precipitately to the American colonies. He decided to make a clean breast of it, and on 6 March wrote a long autobiographical letter which gave his version of the Tobago mutiny. Franklin, in turn, was mystified by this confession, as he had no previous inkling of the affair. In due course he wrote back to Jones, stating that the mystery to which he had referred was 'a carnival prank' perpetrated by one of the Valentinois chambermaids.

Shortly after Jones had left Passy, the Abbé Rochon, curé of Passy, called on Franklin to tell him that the gardener at the Valentinois alleged that Jones had tried to rape his wife the previous evening. The good priest was relieved that Jones had departed, for the gardener's three sons had sworn to kill him. According to Franklin, this tale

> occasioned some Laughing; for the old Woman being one of the grossest, coarsest, dirtiest & ugliest that we may find in a thousand, Madame Chaumont said it gave a high Idea of the Strength of Appetite and Courage of the Americans!
>
> A day or two after I learned that it was the *femme de chambre* of Mademoiselle de Chaumont who had disguised herself in a suit, I think, of your clothes, to divert herself under that masquerade, as is customary the last evening of carnival; and that meeting the old woman in the garden, she took it into her head to try her chastity, which it seems was found proof.[8]

Everyone had a good laugh over the prank – everyone, that is, except Jones who was not noted for seeing the funny side of things.

He had been the indirect butt of a chambermaid's silly joke, which was bad enough; but this had led him unwittingly into confessing about an incident in his past life which he would far rather have concealed, and he was angry that he had blurted out facts which someone, less well disposed towards him than Franklin, might somehow use against him.

On board *Bonhomme Richard* on 13 June 1779, while he was preparing for the greatest exploit of his career, Jones wrote to Madame de Chaumont. Significantly, it was the first of any letters to the women in his life of which he retained a draft, and it is only in this form that the letter apparently survives. One cannot help speculating whether Thérèse was enraged at its impertinent pomposity and immediately consigned it to the flames; or whether she merely shrugged off the insolent fellow's barbs and cast around for some fresh amatory diversion; probably the latter, for Le Ray de Chaumont divorced her as soon as the French Revolution made such a termination of an unsatisfactory marriage feasible. While the letter professed 'affectionate friendship', Jones let her know in no uncertain terms that 'To Support the Cause of Human Nature, I sacrifice all the soft emotions of the Heart at a time of Life, too, when Love is my Duty'. Although he ended 'with Sentiments of real Esteem Affection and Respect', he was effectively letting her know that the affair was at an end.[9]

Long before he wrote this sailor's farewell, Jones was committed body and soul to the forthcoming enterprise. Converting and fitting out the former East Indiaman, arming her and recruiting a crew took up all of his time. His new command was at least twice the size of any of his previous ships. Built for the China trade in 1766, she had made two round trips for the Compagnie des Indes before being sold to the Crown for 100,000 livres in 1771. Under royal control, she had made two further round trips to the Far East and then been sold to a private merchant. Several trips and changes of ownership later, she had been bought by Bérard who originally planned to fit her out as a privateer, but then sold her to the ministry of marine for 220,000 livres. King Louis personally incurred the expense of fitting her out and paying the wages of her crew.

Though Bérard had managed to wangle six 18-pounders out of the French Navy for his proposed privateer, Jones needed considerably more guns before *Bonhomme Richard* was ready for his expedition. March and April were largely spent in touring the ordnance factories and arsenals of Nantes, Périgueux, Angoulême and Bordeaux, looking for suitable cannon. In the end he obtained sixteen of the latest type of 12-pounders from the French Navy. Bérard's guns were mounted in the gunroom, the junior officers' wardroom under the after part of the gun-deck. Six 9-pounders were mounted on the forecastle and quarterdeck, and sixteen new and twelve old 12-pounders formed the main battery on the covered gun-deck. The manifold tasks of fitting out his ship put new zest into Jones. Next to fighting (and making love) there was nothing he enjoyed more than preparing a new vessel for war. Late in April he received word from Franklin that the young Marquis de Lafayette, now a major-general in the United States Army, had just returned to France and would be given the command of the land forces in Jones's proposed expedition. Anticipating that the general and his staff would require accommodation, Jones had a round-house erected on the deck.

As the scope of the proposed raid on the British coast was enlarged, so also the size of Jones's command increased. Lafayette planned nothing less than a full-scale amphibious assault on Liverpool or Bristol. Informing Jones of this proposal, Franklin wrote: 'There is honor enough to be got for both of you if the expedition is conducted with a prudent unanimity,' adding that Lafayette, being a major-general, would command the landing operations. Lafayette himself wrote to Jones saying that he would be happy to divide with him 'whatever share of glory may await us'. Jones replied in the same generous and cordial manner, and also wrote to Franklin complimenting him on his 'liberal and nobleminded instructions' which, he said, 'would make a coward brave'. The plans for the raid on Liverpool, which Jones submitted to Franklin, were within days in the hands of the British authorities, courtesy of Dr Bancroft, and Liverpool was thrown into an almighty panic. The city council pleaded with the government to rush the completion of fortifications round the Mersey estuary and begged for six thousand muskets and ample ammunition for the defence of the port. French prisoners-of-war were hurriedly transferred from camps in the vicinity. Richard Dawson, lieutenant-governor of the Isle of Man, alerted his militia on 19 May that 'Paul Jones lately sail'd from Brest with four or five sail of armed vessels with Land Forces aboard'.

It is interesting to speculate what might have been the outcome of such an ambitious and audacious project. Certainly with two young, energetic, able and resourceful commanders such as Jones and Lafayette working in harmony, anything would have been possible; mercifully for Liverpool, it never materialised. By 22 May

Lafayette was writing regretfully to Jones saying that His Majesty now had other plans for him, so that he would not now be able to witness the captain's 'Success, abilities and Glory'. Ominously he added, 'What will be further determined about your squadron is yet uncertain, and the Ministers are to consult with Doctor Franklin.' The frigate *Alliance*, built in America, had conveyed Lafayette back to France and was now, on Sartine's orders, assigned to Jones's expedition.

She was commanded by Pierre Landais, an eccentric, mentally unstable Frenchman ten years older than Jones. A native of St Malo, he had entered the French Navy as a boy, had served in the Seven Years' War (1756–63), and had commanded a small ship in Bougainville's voyage round the world. By 1775 he had attained the rank of *Capitaine de Brulôt* (literally, 'fireship captain'), a rank usually granted to masters of merchant ships or privateers in recognition of distinguished service. In that year, however, Landais refused the appointment of port-lieutenant at Brest and left the Navy. Within two years he had persuaded Silas Deane to send him to America in command of a supply ship. In his pocket he had Deane's letter of recommendation to Congress, on the strength of which the Marine Committee appointed him captain of the frigate *Alliance* then under construction at Salisbury on the Merrimac. Landais ingratiated himself with Sam Adams who prevailed upon the General Court at Boston to make him an honorary citizen of Massachusetts. The Adams-Lee faction saw in this mercurial Frenchman the ideal naval counterpart to Lafayette, as well as a worthy rival to Jones. That such a mountebank as Landais should have so readily got command of the latest American frigate did nothing to endear him to Jones.

The crossing to Lorient from New England gave ample hint of what was to come, for Landais faced a mutiny which was only narrowly averted by the intervention of his illustrious passenger, Lafayette. At Lorient, he was closely observed by John Adams who recorded in his journal that Landais

> is jealous of every Thing, jealous of every Body, of all his officers, all his Passengers; he knows not how to treat his officers, nor his passengers, nor any Body else. Silence, Reserve, and a forbidding Air will never gain the Hearts neither by Affection nor by Veneration of our Americans. There is in this man an Inactivity and an Indecisiveness that

will ruin him. He is bewildered – an absent bewildered man
– an embarrassed Mind.[10]

By contrast, John Adams left a very interesting and perceptive
description of Jones and his crew. Because Jones was at first
debarred from accepting French seamen as volunteers, his crew was
a motley assortment drawn from many nations. The few Americans
originally in the ship's complement were mainly sailors who had
escaped from English prisons, though their number was augmented
in May by some men landed at Paimboeuf from the first exchange
of prisoners. Many of these men were induced to enlist on the
assumption that *Bonhomme Richard* was bound immediately for
America, but even this blatant subterfuge did not persuade more
than thirty men to sign on. Subsequently Jones was obliged to enlist
a number of British seamen then languishing in French prison hulks.
They had no compunction about changing sides, and Jones's misgivings were allayed by Sartine's bland assurance that Lafayette's
troops would make sure that the British sailors behaved themselves.
The rest of the crew was made up of Spaniards, Portuguese, Maltese,
Swiss, Germans, Italians, Bengalis and Scandinavians as well as quite
a few Frenchmen, despite the earlier ban. A French Marine
detachment under Colonel de Chamillard and Lieutenant-Colonel
Weibert was seconded to the ship, but many of the marines were,
in fact, English, Irish or Scottish prisoners-of-war, still wearing the
red uniforms with white facings in which they had been captured.
This was a startling feature of the ship's crew that struck John Adams
– that and the captain's conceit in wearing gold epaulettes on *both*
shoulders, doubtless intended as the outward expression of his
position as commodore of the flotilla. 'Eccentricities and irregula-
rities are to be expected from him,' noted Adams. 'They are in his
character, they are visible in his eyes. His voice is soft and still and
small; his eye has keenness and wildness and softness in it.'[11]

It had originally been Sartine's plan to send Landais in *Alliance*
straight back to America with John Adams aboard, but a French
frigate being available and ready to sail sooner led to a change in
plans, much to Honest John's relief. Instead, *Alliance* was ordered to
proceed from Nantes to Lorient and join Jones's squadron. In
addition to this well-armed frigate, the French allocated three other
warships: the frigate *Pallas* of twenty-six 9-pounders, commanded by
Capitaine de Brulôt Denis-Nicolas Cottineau de Kerloguen. This
privateer, built in 1778, had distinguished itself so well in action

against HMS *La Brune* that she and her crew were promptly inducted into the French Navy. Cottineau and his men would prove to be one of Jones's best assets in the coming conflict. The brig *Vengeance*, under Lieutenant de Vaisseau Philippe-Nicolas Ricot, was lightly armed with a dozen 4-pounders, while the cutter *Le Cerf*, under Ensign Joseph Varage, carried a couple of 8-pounders and sixteen 6-pounders. All three French skippers were given captain's or lieutenant's commissions in the United States Navy, Dr Franklin filling in the details on blank commission forms. With the exception of *Alliance*, these ships were fitted out, paid for and maintained by the French Navy at no cost to the United States. Jones estimated that French expenditure in this regard amounted to over three million livres ($600,000). It was a generous gesture from the French to their poverty-stricken allies, but it would cause endless trouble for Jones later on.

Even before the expedition set sail, intrigue and double-dealing were at work. Arthur Lee started the ball rolling with a scurrilous letter to Sam Adams saying that it was a 'shameful and illegal business' to put *Alliance* under Jones's command, and alleging that the expedition was nothing more than 'a project of Chaumont and Williams to make money for themselves'. This calumny would subsequently surface in Paris, the Netherlands and the United States over the years, much to Jones's intense anger and disgust.

When the raid on Liverpool was aborted and Lafayette and his land forces assigned to other tasks, Sartine ordered Jones's squadron to carry out a diversionary operation against Scotland or northern England in order to tie up as many British troops as possible while the main French landing took place on the south coast. This ambitious plan, intended to repeat the success of William the Conqueror seven centuries earlier, was regarded as the major feat of arms planned for 1779; but in the event it was Jones's side-show that stole the limelight. An army of twenty thousand men was assembled for the invasion, transported and protected by the combined battle fleets of France and Spain. To this end d'Orvilliers left Brest on 3 June and cruised in Spanish waters off Corunna and Cape Finisterre for six weeks before the Spanish joined with them. The combined navies mustered sixty-four ships of the line against the Royal Navy's thirty-eight, but the Allied expedition was racked by indolence and inefficiency compounded by poor shipboard hygiene. By the time the armada was off Land's End on 14 August, it was ravaged by smallpox, scurvy and typhus. When d'Orvilliers' only son succumbed to disease, the sixty-nine-year-old admiral lost the will to continue, and resigned command to his chief of staff, Captain Pavillon.

The armada anchored in Plymouth roadstead on 16 August, the sea like a millpond and no sign of the British anywhere; but instead of making an unopposed landing at their leisure, the French and Spanish sat tight in the harbour while their provisions and water ran out. On the last day of August the French sighted the battle fleet of Admiral Sir Charles Hardy off the Scilly Isles and gave chase, but the wily Hardy gave them the slip. The situation aboard the French ships was now so desperate that they were forced to return to Brest, and the Spaniards promptly headed for Cadiz. Although not a shot had been fired in this campaign, several hundred men perished through disease and over seven thousand had to be hospitalised at Brest. The much-vaunted Franco-Spanish expedition was a total fiasco; it achieved nothing apart from severely denting the reputation of its commanders and generally reducing the morale of its seamen to a very low ebb.

It is against this background that the success of John Paul Jones has to be measured. As usual Jones was up against a combination of circumstances and individuals who hampered him at every turn. Promoted to principal antagonist was Chaumont who, like Colonel Langdon before him, was perceived to be meddling unduly in the outfitting and equipping of the expedition. Jones, his conscience pricking him no doubt, was convinced that *Le Commissaire* (as he sardonically referred to Chaumont) was deliberately blocking him in revenge for having been cuckolded. In truth, Jones's complaints against Chaumont were pretty groundless and betray a tendency to get upset over small matters; in place of the boatswains' pipes which Langdon had withheld, it was now manacles for the proper immobilisation of prisoners. The matter of preparing the squadron for action is put in a better perspective in the correspondence of Grandville, the port captain at Lorient, and Thévenard his successor, to Sartine, now preserved in the Marine papers in the French national archives. On 5 April Grandville reported that Commodore Jones had been to Nantes and recruited sixty French volunteers, 'wretches picked up on the street and absolutely good for nothing'. Grandville suggested that Jones ought to have enlisted volunteers from Count Walsh's regiment of Irish artillery who were itching to take a pot-shot at the ould enemy. Grandville confidently predicted that *Bonhomme Richard* would be ready for action within two weeks.

In fact, it would be four months before she was battle-ready. Grandville was not optimistic about the crew of *Alliance*, many of whom had been with d'Estaing in the West Indies and had effectively been invalided home. Nor did he or Thévenard have a high opinion of the English prisoners who had been recruited; they were regarded as unruly, unreliable and potentially mutinous.

By 12 June, however, Thévenard was able to report that the bulk of the squadron was ready to sail. A week later Jones and his ships weighed anchor and acted as escorts for merchant shipping evading the British blockade. On the first night out, the flagship collided with *Alliance* during a sudden squall. The deck officer on *Richard* was court-martialled and cashiered for negligence, but the real culprit was Landais who refused to give way to the flagship, and who went below to prime his pistols when he should have been on deck. During this preliminary cruise Jones found to his dismay that his ship was not fast enough to go 'in harm's way' as he intended, and failed to catch up with British warships which turned and fled rather than give battle. *Cerf* had a good scrap with a couple of British cutters and Varage acquitted himself so well that he received a presentation sword from King Louis and a handsome bonus of six hundred livres. When the squadron returned to Lorient on 1 July Jones was greeted on the quayside by M. Salomon, gentlemen's outfitter, dunning him for 1776 livres in respect of unpaid bills on uniforms for *Richard*'s officers.

More appetising was the fresh set of orders from Sartine, countersigned by Franklin, giving him qualified discretion in a commerce-destroying cruise round the British coasts. Specifically he was ordered to sail round the west coast of Ireland, then north round the Orkney Islands and down the North Sea to raid shipping off the Naze and the Dogger Bank, with the aim of terminating the cruise by mid-August at Texel in Holland where he was to escort a French merchant fleet bound from the Baltic with much-needed naval stores. When Jones protested about the time limit on his cruise and questioned the part about escorting merchantmen, Franklin quietly rebuked him, reminding that as the French Court were paying the piper, they had a right to call the tune. The orders still gave Jones sufficient freedom of action, though he could not resist getting in the last word to Franklin:

It appears to me to be the province of our Infant Navy to Surprise and spread Alarm, with fast sailing ships. When we

grow stronger we can meet their Fleets and dispute with
them the Sovereignty of the Ocean.[12]

Jones's policy of lightning hit-and-run raids was sound, but in this
respect he was a century and a half ahead of his time, and naval
tactics in the 1770s remained firmly wedded to large fleet actions
with ships of the line operating in stately formation.

It is significant that Jones suffered one of his first bouts of serious
illness about this time. The precise nature of the malady that laid
him low for a week is unknown, but one suspects a bad cold which
confined him to his cabin for several days. He was in low spirits,
worn out by overwork and worry and at a low ebb physically. His
ongoing problems were also exacerbated by difficulties with his
polyglot crew; the French and American volunteers fought constantly, while the English ex-prisoners were impossible to control.
In the nick of time a plot to seize the ship and take Jones prisoner
back to some English port was discovered. Following the resultant
court-martial the ring-leader, Quartermaster Towers, was given 250
lashes and consigned to a French prison. By contrast, a French volunteer with the distinguished name of Jean Rousseau was found guilty
of theft and given thirty-three lashes. The outcome of the abortive
mutiny was the discharge of the English crew, of whom seventy-
seven were former prisoners and twenty-three deserters from the
Royal Navy. Interestingly, Jones retained many of the Irish and
Scottish ex-prisoners who were regarded as trustworthy and, in fact,
proved their mettle. In place of the Englishmen Jones recruited a
contingent of Portuguese, despite Sartine's misgivings on the grounds
that no Catholic chaplain could be found to minister to their spiritual
needs.

By 28 July Jones had recovered sufficiently for the fleet to set sail,
but foul weather delayed their departure. Four days later Chaumont
returned to Lorient with orders from Sartine to get the expedition
under way immediately, but departure was again delayed for several
days while Jones waited for a contingent of American seamen newly
released from English prisons under exchange. By 6 August *Richard*
had a complement of 380 officers and men which Sartine considered
sufficient. As *Richard* was midway between a thirty-gun and a fifty-
gun ship whose respective complements were 280 and 440, the size
of the flagship's crew was about right. Jones, of course, thought
otherwise and complained loud and long that he was being ill-used
to be so deprived. Sartine remained deaf to his entreaties and

ordered the commodore to sea at the earliest possible opportunity.

On 9 August *Bonhomme Richard, Pallas, Cerf* and *Vengeance* left Lorient to join *Alliance* off the Île de Groix where they rendezvoused with two French privateers, *Monsieur* and *Granville,* who decided to join the venture. The following day the American privateer *General Mifflin* hove in sight, but her skipper refused to join the Jones expedition as he had other orders. Jones was irritated that Chaumont had come along; far from being a passenger, he had arrogated to himself the role of unofficial staff officer for Sartine and intensely annoyed the commodore by distributing the minister's orders to each captain, rather than doing so through the commodore. Matters were not improved when Chaumont insisted that a concordat be drawn up between the commodore and his captains. Jones protested that this was unprecedented and improper, although an agreement of this sort had previously been made between Esek Hopkins and the captains of the Continental Navy. The concordat provided that all the ships would be regarded as belonging to the United States Navy, would fly the Stars and Stripes and be subject to American regulations, especially in the ticklish matter of dividing prize money. All prizes were to be consigned to Chaumont and the portion of each ship in prizes taken by any vessel of the squadron was to be determined by the American minister at the Court of Versailles and the French minister of marine. These two clauses would be a source of endless trouble later on; but in view of the fact that the French were financing the expedition it was reasonable that they should have a say in the disposal of prizes. The two French privateers were excluded from this deal because Jones rightly surmised that they would leave the squadron whenever it suited them. *Monsieur,* a large, powerful vessel mounting twenty-six 12-pounders and a dozen 4-pounders, was second only to the flagship in size and firepower, but deserted a few days later and *Granville* a week after that, much to the disgust of Jones who recorded dourly that privateers were unreliable in military operations and devoid of honour or good faith.

At four o'clock on a clear, sunny morning with a light breeze blowing, the squadron weighed anchor and left the Groix roadstead. It was the beginning of a cruise which immortalised John Paul Jones and brought undying glory to the officers and men of *Bonhomme Richard*.

10. The Way to Flamborough Head
August – September 1779

A willing foe and sea room!
— OLD NAVAL TOAST

Commodore John Paul Jones, Commander-in-Chief of the American Squadron in Europe, was now at the zenith of his career. Just past his thirty-second birthday, with twenty years' sea-going experience and the most distinguished war record of all the American Navy's captains, he was in peak physical condition. A few months after the *Bonhomme Richard* expedition, Jones's bust-portrait was executed by Jean-Antoine Houdon, the most celebrated portrait sculptor of his era, and as Jones himself considered it so highly that he had a number of casts made for presentation to his friends, we may suppose that it was up to Houdon's usual standard, and is a faithful likeness. It shows a man keen and alert, fine-looking rather than handsome, with high cheekbones, a sharp aquiline nose and an expressive mouth which we can imagine giving the full play of emotions. The sensuous lips that so often charmed the ladies could also curl with disdain or anger. He possessed a strong chin and a firm jaw-line that bespoke strength of character and wilfulness. Here was a man accustomed not only to command, but to get his own way; a man who was quick to anger if thwarted in anything.

Apart from John Adams, other eye-witnesses have testified that Jones, in polite company, spoke in a soft, low, quiet voice and gave the impression of a mild manner. Others more accurately said that he was a man in full control of his emotions. His eyes could light up as he turned on the charm; but they could also blaze with anger. He had a penetrating gaze which subordinates often found disconcerting but which sent a frisson of excitement through the ladies whenever he entered a room. Jones had the kind of eyes variously described as glowing or smouldering, though an intensity of gaze was often a characteristic of seafaring men, used to scanning the horizon.

Houdon's bust betrays Jones's fastidiousness in matters of appearance: his hair is firmly brushed back from his forehead and tied severely in a queue at the back. His neck-cloth is neatly arranged and his uniform impeccable rather than elegant. The overall impression is of a strong, even stern, countenance, proud, unyielding, dour, defiant, ambitious, restless. Here is a man who was thoroughly professional in everything he tackled, but not the sort of person to suffer fools lightly. From his voluminous correspondence and the journals of those who came into close contact with him during his turbulent career, we may form the impression of a man of strong feelings about life, love and, above all, his career. Pride, honour and status were of paramount importance to him. This was a driven man, a man who was seldom at peace with himself, let alone the rest of the world. There is no hint of humour in that strong face; a sardonic streak perhaps. This is a man who was jealous of rank and extremely sensitive to slights, real or imagined, from others. This is a man who was loved by many women and who loved them in return, but only up to a point. He never had any compunction about casting them aside as occasion demanded. He was supremely egotistical and singularly ungenerous to those who were most loyal to him, while often imagining insults and injury from others whose only fault was that they did not always see eye to eye with him, or who occasionally stood their ground and did not invariably give way to him. This is a man who was driven forward by his own ambition, though he was not always clear what his ultimate goals were. This is a man who, while proclaiming himself a devotee of sense and sensibility, could often be quite insensitive to others, superiors and subordinates alike.

In personal habits Jones was invariably well dressed and he expected the same high standards in his officers. He had a healthy diet, and was ahead of his time in appreciating that good, wholesome, nourishing food was essential to the well-being of his crew. He himself ate simply and sparingly. Nathaniel Fanning, who served as a midshipman on the *Bonhomme Richard*, recorded: 'I never knew him to drink any kind of ardent spirits. On the contrary his constant drink was lemonade (lime juice and water, with a little sugar added to make it more palatable).' After dinner, at sea, in fine weather, 'he made it a custom to drink three glasses of wine', which was by no means excessive in an age when gentlemen often drank as many bottles of port or madeira at a sitting. Whereas Horatio Nelson often suffered ill-health and was prone to seasickness, Jones had an iron constitution, and exposed himself recklessly to foul weather and enemy gunfire with equal abandon. Prolonged exposure to cold, wet weather would eventually undermine his health, but in spite of his insisting on being at the forefront of every naval engagement, no bullet ever found its mark. Nelson was a walking disaster area, but the only wounds inflicted on Jones were from Cupid's darts.

In the crew of *Bonhomme Richard* Jones was infinitely more fortunate than he had been with *Ranger*. Profiting from that bad experience, he had selected his officers with great care, and in this respect he had the pick of the lieutenants who had either escaped from British prisons or who were among the first exchange of prisoners. His first-lieutenant was Richard Dale of Virginia, only twenty-two years of age but with eight years' seagoing experience. He had served under John Barry and Henry Johnson in *Lexington* and when that brig was captured he had been consigned to the infamous Mill Prison at Portsmouth. He escaped but was recaptured and put in solitary confinement in the black hole. He escaped again and eventually reached Lorient where he volunteered to serve under Jones. Significantly, Jones was unstinting in his praise of Dale for whom he had considerable affection. Dale served as a captain in the French War of 1798 and subsequently became Commodore of the Mediterranean Squadron.

The junior lieutenants were Henry Lunt and his cousin Cutting Lunt, both from Newburyport, Massachusetts. Henry had served as an able seaman under Jones in *Alfred* and *Providence*, before joining Cutting aboard a privateer which was captured in December 1776. After two years in the Mill Prison, the Lunts were released and arrived in a cartel at Nantes in March 1779. Jones had a high opnion of Henry Lunt and took him on as second-lieutenant, with Cutting as master. The ship's surgeon was Dr Lawrence Brooke of an old Virginia family. John Adams was impressed by Brooke's taste and erudition, but Fanning dismissed him unfairly as more butcher than surgeon. Matthew Mease, a Philadelphia shipowner who happened to be stranded in France, accepted the position of purser as a last resort, but during the coming battle took charge of a gun battery and behaved 'with distinguished coolness and intrepidity' as Jones later reported.

The midshipmen included 'three brave, steady officers' from South Carolina: John West Linthwaite, Robert Coram and John Mayrant (the lastnamed being later singled out for mention as 'a young gentleman of fortune, whose conduct in the engagement did him great honor'). Nathaniel Fanning, best-known of the *Richard's* midshipmen on account of his much-published account of the cruise, hailed from Stonington, Connecticut, and had been captured while serving aboard the privateer *Angelica* and later exchanged. Jones had a high opinion of Fanning, especially of his courage under fire, but regrettably these feelings were not reciprocated, and Fanning's narrative has been the source of untrue and derogatory stories about the commodore, much embellished by many later writers. Beaumont Groube, one of the American colony at Nantes, later acquired doubtful immortality as the Lieutenant Grub of the chapbooks, allegedly shot by Jones for striking the ensign. The other midshipmen were Thomas Potter, Benjamin Stubbs and Reuben Chase, the first two of whom were wounded in action.

Three officers seconded from Walsh's Irish regiment were Lieutenant Eugene Macarthy and Sub-Lieutenants James Gerard O'Kelly and Edward Stack. The lastnamed served with considerable distinction, as a result of which Jones secured his promotion and a pension. These Irishmen later settled in the United States and their commodore was instrumental in getting them elected to the Society of the Cincinnati. Paul de Chamillard de Varville and Antoine-Félix Weibert occupied the roundhouse originally intended for Lafayette, and commanded the French marines; both officers had long and distinguished careers in the French Navy and Weibert subsequently settled in America where he obtained a colonelcy in the Engineering Corps of the United States Army. Major Frazer begged Jones to give him a berth on this cruise, but the commodore had had enough of his drunkenness and took on board instead Captain Alexander Dick of the United States Army as a volunteer, with the duty of liaising with the French marines. Dick was decribed by John Adams as being 'of good family and handsome fortune in Virginia'. Although the ship's officers were drawn from diverse backgrounds and nationalities, they were all hand-picked by Jones and, in the outcome, justified his good judgment.

Conversely, Jones had considerable misgivings about the crew, yet the men turned out to be the best he ever commanded. Various rosters have been published,[1] based to a greater or lesser extent on reports by Thévenard and Jones himself, but containing discrepancies and anomalies. The consensus of opinion is that *Bonhomme Richard* had twenty officers, forty-three petty officers, sixty able seamen, forty-three ordinary seamen, forty-one boys, three cooks, thirty-three French landsmen and a hundred and thirty-seven French marines. Apart from the Frenchmen, who accounted for almost half the ship's complement, the ethnic breakdown of the crew was seventy-nine Americans, fifty-nine Englishmen, twenty-nine Portuguese, twenty-one Irishmen, four Scots (not including the commodore himself), seven Swedes, three Norwegians, two Bengalis, one Swiss and one Italian. While seventeen of the officers were Americans, the majority of the petty officers and able seamen were Englishmen who, in spite of Jones's earlier misivings, proved to be fairly dependable. Before the ship got under way the crew were left in no doubt as to the commodore's capacity for strict discipline. The crew of the commodore's barge had left the boat unattended ashore while they got drunk in a tavern. As a result Jones had had to hire a common fisherman to row him out to his flagship, an insult to his rank and dignity which he punished by having the barge crew triced up to the rigging and severely flogged before the entire ship's company.

Despite this inauspicious beginning, Jones proved to be a fair commander. Colonel Weibert later testified that:

> Commodore Paul Jones, far from commanding with haughtiness and brutality, as certain persons have endeavoured to circulate, was always (though very strict and sharp in the service) affable, genteel, and very indulgent, not only towards his officers, but likewise towards the sentries and soldiers, whom he ever treated with humanity.[2]

By contrast with the spoiled home-town boys of *Ranger* who were only interested in rich pickings and easy money, Jones now had a hard core of experienced professional seamen who, having for the most part suffered in English prisons, had a real incentive to fight. And as professionals, they recognised Jones as one of the best, and they gave him their unstinted respect and loyal support.

Jones drew up elaborate regulations for the running of the ship down to the minutest details. He also adopted the French signalling system devised by Captain Pavillon, acutely aware of the importance of good communications between ships, especially during battle. In this respect he learned a valuable lesson at others' expense, for it was poor signalling which led to the foul-up off Ushant.

The account of *Richard's* cruise is based mainly on Jones's own fourteen-page report to Benjamin Franklin, written on 3 October 1779, amplified by the personal accounts of Dale, Fanning and Gunner's Mate John Kilby,[3] as well as the lengthy contemporary reports in the British newspapers as they monitored the progress of the American raiders round the coast. The first leg of the cruise was accomplished in a rather leisurely fashion, taking eight days to reach the south-west of Ireland. A merchantman bound for Madeira from London was intercepted on 16 August; although her master and supercargo were entertained to dinner aboard the flagship, their ship was not captured as it sailed under a neutral flag. Two days later the privateer *Monsieur* took a prize but Captain Guidloup refused to allow Jones to put a prize crew aboard her, and the very next day deserted the squadron. A large vessel was pursued during the night of 19–20 August but escaped under cover of darkness. On 21 August the brigantine *Mayflower, en route* from Liverpool to London with a cargo of foodstuffs, was taken after two shots were fired. Reuben Chase and four men were put aboard as a prize crew and headed back to Lorient.

By eight o'clock on the morning of 23 August the squadron was off Mizen Head and proceeded in a north-westerly course along the rugged Kerry coast. Off Dingle Bay that afternoon Jones sent two boats out to capture the brig *Fortune*, on her way from New-foundland to Bristol with a cargo of staves and whale oil. One of *Granville*'s officers was put aboard as prizemaster and ordered to take the ship into St Malo or Nantes. That evening in a flat calm, *Richard* began to drift with the tide perilously close to the Skellig rocks, so Jones ordered out his barge with a crew of seven to tow the flagship out of danger. Unfortunately, the coxswain was the very petty officer who had been flogged for drunkenness when the barge was deserted at Lorient, and he selected a crew of Irishmen who seized the opportunity to desert to their native isle. At 10.30 p.m. these men cut the tow-rope and headed for the shore. Cutting Lunt promptly lowered the jolly-boat and gave chase. The barge disappeared into a fog bank with Lunt in hot pursuit, and both pursuer and pursued vanished, never to be seen again by the squadron.

The thick fog persisted all the following day. Jones's problems were compounded when Landais came aboard the flagship on the afternoon of 24 August in high dudgeon and proceeded to berate the commodore in the grossest language in front of the two French marine colonels. Weibert obligingly translated for Chamillard who understood no English. Landais was in a foul temper because Jones had forbidden him to chase a ship close inshore the previous day because fog was coming up. Landais now insulted the commodore, claiming that he, Landais, 'was the only American in the squadron' (on the strength of his honorary citizenship of Massachusetts) and that henceforward he would chase 'when and where he thought proper, and in every other matter', which is precisely what he did.

As the fog seemed to be thinning out, Jones ordered *Cerf* to scout out the coast and recover the missing boats, while the rest of the squadron tacked back and forth at a safe distance from the shoals. By the afternoon of 25 August the fog had abated sufficiently for the squadron to approach the coast, but of *Cerf* and the two boats there was no sign. The following day the wind got up and, acting for once on the advice of Landais, Jones gave orders for the squadron to abandon the search and set a northerly course under reduced sail. Despite masthead lights and an hourly signal gun, dawn the following day found *Bonhomme Richard* alone except for *Vengeance*. Landais had been as good as his word and slipped off on his own during the night, while *Granville* withdrew with a prize and *Pallas* was delayed by a broken tiller. Jones was chagrined to discover subsequently that, by following the advice of Landais, he had missed a golden opportunity to intercept a fleet of East Indiamen heading for Limerick.

Meanwhile, Varage in *Cerf* had sighted Lunt's boat and hoisted British colours and fired a gun. Lunt, supposing the vessel to be the British cutter HMS *Stag*, fled as fast as his crew could row, got lost in a patch of fog and landed at Ballinskelligs Bay where he and his men were promptly captured by the Kerry Rangers. *Cerf* never rejoined the squadron but eventually returned to Lorient, Varage making the excuse that he had been attacked by a British cutter and that his mainmast had broken. By this foggy fiasco Jones lost an eighteen-gun cutter, two boats and sixteen men, not to mention a gallant officer, Cutting Lunt, who sadly did not survive his second spell in British captivity. More importantly in the short term, this episode now alerted the Irish countryside and over the ensuing fortnight the British newspapers published long letters from Cork and Kerry giving the complete battle plan as revealed by the deserters. Fortunately these men could not resist embroidering a good story and claimed that Commodore Jones intended to burn Limerick or Galway. Despite this, the Admiralty reacted by despatching HMS *Ulysses* and *Boston* to the Irish Sea, wrongly assuming that Jones was planning a second raid on Whitehaven.

Jones in fact was now making good speed, spanking along before a stiff northerly breeze which took his ship to St Kilda at the rate of a hundred miles a day. By two o'clock on the afternoon of 30 August he was off the Flannan Isles west of the Outer Hebrides and by evening *Richard* and *Vengeance* had rounded the Butt of Lewis. At sunrise the following day they saw three sail to windward and two to leeward. Giving chase, *Richard* took the letter-of-marque *Union* bound for Quebec from London with a valuable cargo of clothing for the British forces in Canada. Cape Wrath, the north-westerly extremity of the Scottish mainland, had been named by Jones as a rendezvous if the ships got separated, and it was here that the flagship met up with *Alliance* which had in tow a prize ship of her own, the brig *Betsey*. Landais was still in a foul temper, and in a bid to mollify him Jones gave him the privilege of manning the prize *Union* which he sent, along with his own prize, into Bergen in Norway — contrary to Jones's wishes but at the behest of Chaumont. When Jones sent the two marine colonels, Purser Mease and Captain Cottineau aboard *Alliance* to remonstrate with Landais, the latter 'Spoke of Capt. Jones in terms highly disrespectful and insolent, and said he would see him on shore when they must kill one or t'other, etc,' according to Mease.

During the night of 1–2 September *Pallas* caught up with the squadron and the following afternoon *Vengeance* captured an Irish brigantine returning from Norway. That evening the squadron passed Foula, remotest of the Shetland group, and, having attained their most northerly point, now headed due south for North Ronaldsay and Orkney. *Alliance* took a couple of small prizes, but when Landais was ordered aboard the flagship for a conference he flatly refused and soon afterwards deserted the squadron again. On 4 September a gale blew up and for several days the squadron stood well out to sea, not sighting land again until 13 September when the ships were off the entrance to the Firth of Forth. The following day Jones seized two colliers from Leith bound for Riga and put Linthwaite aboard one as prizemaster with orders to take them to a friendly port.

On the afternoon of 14 September Jones called a council of war aboard his flagship. What he now proposed was a descent on Leith to hold the port of Edinburgh to ransom, as an alternative to sacking and burning the town. According to his own account, Jones had argued through the evening and far into the night with Cottineau and Ricot, neither of whom thought much of this hare-brained scheme, until, with strong black coffee as dawn broke, Jones suggested a payment of two hundred thousand pounds as a suitable price for not destroying Leith. The mention of money got the French captains' undivided attention, and they entered warmly into the project. That morning the wind was set fair for the attack, but while the French captains were having this marathon pow-wow with the commodore, their ships were busy chasing after prizes, and by the time the flagship got within signalling distance the wind had changed. Such were the vagaries of naval warfare in the days of sail.

Undeterred by a contrary wind, Jones decided to beat up the firth. While the ships tacked and wore, Jones organised a formidable landing party of 130 men in six boats, and also drafted an ultimatum 'To the Worshipful the Provost of Leith' which Chamillard was to present, as well as articles of surrender for the town council to sign. Half the ransom was to be paid, cash down, and the rest guaranteed by the taking of six hostages. If the money was not forthcoming then Leith would be 'laid in ashes'. The huge sum of money, Chamillard was to explain, was intended as

> a contribution towards the indemnity which Britain owes to the much Injured Citizens of America. Savages Would blush at the Unmanly Violation and rapacity that has marked the tracks of British tyranny in America, from which neither virgin innocence nor helpless age has been a plea of protection or Pity.[4]

Thanks to the contrary wind, the savages blushed in vain and the innocent virgins went unavenged. The atrocities to which Jones referred were indeed a disgrace to British arms. To be sure, the worst excesses, such as the raping and scalping of innocent women, were carried out by Indians under Burgoyne's command; but the large-scale looting and burning of coastal towns by British and Hessian troops under General Vaughan, Sir George Collier and General Tryon had even been reported in the British press, and excited considerable adverse comment in the Whig opposition papers as well as in broadsides and satirical pamphlets. Tryon's troops had only lately conducted a campaign of systematic destruction along the coast of Connecticut, burning countless dwellings, shops, mills, factories and even churches. The worst atrocity was the complete destruction of the town of Fairfield. At this juncture Congress seriously considered giving instructions to Franklin to send a commando unit to London to wage a terror campaign by means of bombs and incendiaries, with the Houses of Parliament and St James's Palace the principal targets, but fortunately had second thoughts. Interestingly, the opposition press reported the Jones raid very fairly, and placed it in the context of British atrocities in

America, comparing George Collier unfavourably to Jones who 'is a pirate indeed, a plunderer, but no Barbarian'.

After seizing the Kirkcaldy collier *Friendship* and impressing her skipper as his pilot for the firth, Jones learned that, far from being heavily defended with gun batteries as he had been led to believe, both Leith and Edinburgh were virtually unarmed. At four o'clock on the afternoon of 16 September while *Richard* was standing out from the Inchcape Rock, a boat came out from the Fife shore. It seemed that Sir John Anstruther of Elie House had heard a rumour that the dreadful pirate Paul Jones was approaching. He had a brass cannon and a quantity of cannonballs to protect his mansion, but no gunpowder. So he sent off his yacht *Royal Charlotte* with instructions to speak to the commander of HMS *Romney* and request a keg of powder. Unaware that *Romney* was many miles away over the horizon, the yacht approached the man-o'-war tacking close to the Ainster Rocks. Skipper Andrew Paton clambered aboard the warship and was confronted by the ship's captain, smartly dressed in navy blue with white facings, epaulettes and gilt buttons. Paton assumed that he was addressing Captain Johnston of *Romney* and readily answered his casual question regarding other naval vessels in the vicinity. Thus Jones learned that the naval patrol in the firth consisted of only two armed ships and two cutters. Jones readily agreed to Anstruther's request, and a hundredweight sack of powder was duly lowered into the waiting boat. The masquerade was completed by a letter addressed to Sir John Anstruther from Captain Johnston hurriedly forged by Jones. The yacht's crew were informed that Paton would remain aboard to help pilot the ship into Leith and off it went, oblivious of the true situation.[5]

Meanwhile, the unsuspecting Paton was providing the ship's captain with fuller details concerning coastal defences on both sides of the firth. After the yacht had shoved off, Jones drew Paton out, asking him for the latest news.

'Why, that rebel and pirate Paul Jones is off the coast, and he ought to be hanged.'

'Do you know whom you are addressing?'

'Are you not Captain Johnston of HMS *Romney*?'

'No, sir,' replied the deck officer with a crooked grin. '*I* am Paul Jones!'

Paton fainted at this, grovelled on the deck and begged for mercy. Jones, laughing, helped him to his feet saying, 'Get up! I won't hurt a hair on your head, but you are my prisoner.'

Later that afternoon the strange squadron was observed by telescope from the ramparts of Edinburgh Castle. By now the alarm was up and the citizens of Leith and Edinburgh were thrown into an almighty panic, hardly helped by the beating of drums and blowing of bugles and bagpipes which went on through the ensuing night as a militia of sorts was hastily armed with pikes, pitchforks and rusty old claymores as well as a few shotguns. The three companies of regular soldiers manning the castle were swiftly augmented by almost five thousand citizens. 'Jones and his myrmidons,' reported one citizen, 'frightened the people more than Charley did in the late rebellion. Everyone was for securing his effects by hiding them; the three banks had all their money packed up and ready to be sent off.'[6]

For several days the menacing squadron tacked back and forth in the firth, waiting for the squally weather to abate. During this period, the inhabitants on both sides of the firth waited with bated breath while reinforcements were hurriedly summoned from other parts of the country. By dawn on 17 September the squadron was less than a mile off Kirkcaldy on the Fife coast. Now it was the turn of the inhabitants of the Lang Toun to fear for their lives. They turned in their hour of crisis to the parish minister, the Revd Alexander Spears, who proved the man of the moment. Like King Canute he had a chair brought down to the water's edge and there he harangued the Almighty, while his congregation looked on:

> Now deer Lord, dinna ye think it a shame for Ye to send this vile piret to rob our folk o Kirkcaldy; for Ye ken they're puir enow already, and hae naething to spaire. The wey the ween blaws, he'll be here in a jiffie, and wha kens what he may do? He's nae too guid for ony thing. Meickle's the mischief he has dune already. He'll burn their hooses, tak their very claes and tirl them to the sark; and wae's me! Wha kens but the bluidy villain might take their lives? The puir weemen are maist frightened out o their wits and the bairns skirling after them. I canna thole it, I canna thole it! I hae been lang a faithfu servant to Ye, Laird; but gin ye dinna turn the ween about, and blaw the scoundrel out of our gate, I'll na staur a fit, but will just sit here till the tide comes. Sae tak Yer wull o't![7]

Strange to relate, this unorthodox prayer was apparently answered, for shortly after it ended the enemy squadron came about on the starboard tack and stood across the firth, past Inchkeith Rock. The ships were once more within cannon range of Leith, and Jones ordered out the boats to effect a landing, when suddenly 'a Very severe gale of Wind came on, and being directly Contrary obliged me to bear away after having in Vain Endeavoured for some time to Withstand its violence', as Jones subsequently reported. The severity of this gale obliged *Richard*'s topgallant masts to be housed. One of the small prize ships capsized and sank, while the other, *Friendship*, was prudently released on payment of a sum of money, and her master given a safe-conduct. Under shortened sails, the squadron beat a retreat to more open waters, but by the time the weather slackened Jones felt that the defences of Leith and Edinburgh would have been strengthened, and prudently he decided to call it a day. In fact, only one small cutter was actually stationed to defend the port, and it fled at the first approach of the Americans. A further week would elapse before the Admiralty managed to despatch the frigate *Emerald* with the armed ships *London* and *Content*. Ironically, this squadron must have passed the Americans in the night as they headed south to their date with destiny.

Jones must have been in sombre mood as his ships left the Pentland Hills astern. So far, the cruise had failed in its principal objective, a diversionary raid to tie up British forces while the main landing took place on the south coast of England. Jones was unaware that the great Franco-Spanish invasion had by this time collapsed, but his own record so far was anything but impressive. He had lost two boats and a cutter off the Skelligs, due to the treachery of a coxswain and the poor judgment of Varage. His orders had been flagrantly flouted by Landais off Cape Wrath and Shetland. He had wasted valuable time arguing with Cottineau and Ricot, and thus lost a favourable wind and the element of surprise at Leith. Ruefully he must have wondered at the quality of his captains, and wished that *Bonhomme Richard* were cruising on her own. That way, he would have achieved more spectacular results.

Aware that British warships were probably scouring the North Sea for him, Jones kept his squadron close inshore as they sailed cautiously down the reef-girt coast of Northumberland. As they sailed past Bamburgh Castle Jones loosed off a cannon as a *jeu d'esprit*; the ball missed the venerable fortress and landed in the garden of a private house whose owner and his descendants prized this souvenir of the Jones raid thereafter.

Jones now formed a bold plan to attack Newcastle upon Tyne and destroy the collier fleet in order to deprive London of its winter fuel supply. On Tuesday, 19 September, the boats were lowered, their oars muffled, and the French marines armed for the execution of this assault. The squadron anchored off Tynemouth Castle presented an awesome sight to the terrified citizenry, but once again dissension broke out among the captains. This time it was Cottineau who argued against a shore raid, on the grounds that after Leith the coastal defence would be ready and waiting for the raiders. Cottineau even informed Chamillard that if Jones did not head south immediately, both *Pallas* and *Vengeance* would abandon the expedition. Despite this, Jones and the officers of *Richard* were all for pressing on regardless, on their own; but realising the hopelessness of the situation, Jones eventually gave way. To the inhabitants of South Shields, who could clearly make out the figures on deck and count the gun-ports, it seemed that they were doomed to suffer bombardment at the very least, and they were astonished when they saw the ships turn about and sail off without firing a shot.

By way of consolation Jones seized a collier in ballast and the sloop *Speedwell* off Whitby. Both vessels were stripped of their valuables and Jones ordered that they be scuttled; but Cottineau let the sloop go on payment of ransom, a common practice among French privateers of which Jones heartily disapproved. Passing Scarborough on the evening of 21 September, the squadron pursued a merchant fleet whose sails had been silhouetted to the south at sunset, but to little purpose. A little after midnight a collier in ballast was detected and captured soon afterwards. A second ship was forced ashore between Flamborough and Spurn Head, and a third, a brigantine from Rotterdam, was later taken. The people of Scarborough, noting this flurry of activity offshore, hoisted warning signals on the coast and alerted the Yorkshire militia. The more affluent citizens packed off their womenfolk with the family silver, and urgent despatches were sent to London calling for assistance. At Hull an emergency meeting of the town council came to the sad conclusion that they could do absolutely nothing, as their fort was derelict and its cannon likely to explode if any attempt were made to fire them. The Northumberland militia was hurriedly mobilised and tramped south to Bridlington and Beverley. These warlike preparations continued for several days, long after Jones had fought his battle and sailed away.

By eight o'clock in the morning the squadron was off Spurn Head at the mouth of the Humber estuary. Wishing to pursue a merchant fleet which he had seen heading upriver, Jones hoisted the Union Jack and signalled for a pilot. Two boats came out to *Richard* and the Rotterdam collier and were promptly detained, their boats taken in tow. Jones sailed into the lower estuary opposite Grimsby in the hope of enticing naval vessels escorting the convoy to come out and fight, but this ploy failed. As the wind dropped, Jones deemed it more prudent to head out to sea again, and by evening the flagship was heading north to rejoin *Pallas* which had already altered course in pursuit of lucrative prizes. Just before midnight two sail were sighted on the horizon. All hands were called to quarters and Jones signalled the other ships of the squadron. At half past five the following morning, as dawn was breaking, Jones discovered that the two ships were *Alliance* (which had not been seen for over two weeks) and *Pallas*. As well as *Vengeance*, Jones now had four ships in his squadron once more. Together the ships sailed slowly north towards Flamborough Head in a dying wind. At two in the afternoon Lieutenant Henry Lunt was despatched in one of the captured pilot-boats to seize a brig sighted to windward, which Jones thought might have been the vessel which he had previously run ashore. While this exercise was taking place the rest of the squadron stood to.

An hour later, Jones's patience was at last rewarded when a fleet of forty-one sail appeared off Flamborough Head, bearing north-north-east from the flagship and standing in her direction. From the captured pilots, Jones gleaned the information that this was a Baltic convoy escorted by the forty-four-gun frigate *Serapis* and the twenty-gun sloop of war *Countess of Scarborough*. *Serapis*, commanded by Captain Richard Pearson, was a new copper-bottomed frigate; this technique of retarding the fouling of a ship's bottom gave such vessels greater speed and manoeuvrability and was now being extensively applied to ships of the Royal Navy and later the French Marine. The frigate, though rated a forty-four-gun ship, actually carried fifty guns: a main battery of twenty 18-pounders on a lower deck, compared with *Richard*'s six of that calibre; twenty 9-pounders on an upper covered gun-deck, compared with *Richard*'s twenty-eight 12-pounders; and ten 6-pounders on the quarterdeck (against *Richard*'s six 9-pounders). Pearson had reached Elsinore, Denmark, on 19 August with a convoy from the Nore, and was then joined by *Countess of Scarborough* commanded by Captain Thomas Piercy. They left Elsinore on 1 September, sheltered from a storm near Christiansund, set off again on 15 September and approached Whitby eight days later. *Serapis* was a fast ship, constructed to the latest specifications and completed at Deptford only four months earlier; but Pearson was less than happy with the old 18-pounders furnished by the Admiralty: their vents were too large and consequently used up too much powder, and their muzzles were so long that when the guns were drawn in there was not sufficient room to coil down the hawsers properly. Despite these drawbacks, *Serapis* was more heavily armed than *Richard* and in every other respect a far superior fighting ship.

Pearson was on the lookout for Jones after receiving warning from Scarborough that the American squadron was in the vicinity, although his primary task was to protect his convoy. To that end he ordered the merchantmen to sail as close to shore as they dared while he stood offshore to give them protection. Not surprisingly, the merchant skippers ignored this order, fearing the reefs and the capricious currents more than they did the American pirate. Just after midday on 23 September the convoy sighted the American ships and speedily headed inshore to shelter under the guns of Scarborough Castle, while *Serapis* hoisted full sail and succeeded in getting between the enemy squadron and the convoy. Pearson's report noted that:

> At one o'clock we got sight of the Enemys ships from the masthead, and about four we made them plain from the Deck to be three large ships and a brig; upon which I made the *Countess of Scarborough* signal to join me. She being in shore with the Convoy . . . I then brought too, to let the *Countess of Scarboro* come up, and cleared ship for Action; at ½ past five she joined me, the Enemy's ships then bearing down upon us with a light breeze at SSW; at six Tacked and laid our Head in shore, in order to keep our Ground the better between the Enemy's ships and the Convoy.[8]

Pearson was on his mettle and did not think twice about engaging an enemy which, at first glance, seemed far superior. When it was observed that the three smaller American ships seemed to be hanging back, this stiffened Pearson's resolve. On the other side, Jones was spurred on by his desperation not to let such a rich prize as a Baltic convoy evade him, whatever obstacles the Royal Navy might place in his path. In a light wind he must have cursed *Richard*'s comparative clumsiness, for it took three and a half hours to cover the ten miles between him and *Serapis*. As he drew closer, he realised that he would have to do battle with the naval ships and take or sink them before dealing with the convoy itself.

At three in the afternoon Jones sighted the enemy; thirty minutes later he fired a signal gun to recall Lunt and the pilot-boat, but apparently Lunt did not hear the shot. The flagship hoisted the signal General Chase, crossed royal yards and set all three topgallants. At four, studding sails were set on both sides and the gunners, seamen and officers quietly took up their positions on the gun-deck, below deck or aloft. At five, the marine drummers marched up and down beating the roll for General Quarters. At six, as the sun sank below the mainland, Jones hoisted the flags signalling 'Form Line of Battle'. Predictably, this was ignored by the rest of the squadron. *Alliance*, in the lead, sailed off, leaving *Richard* to go it alone, while *Pallas*, astern of the flagship, sheered off, though Cottineau later redeemed himself by engaging *Countess of Scarborough*. It was subsequently stated that Cottineau, seeing *Richard* suddenly change direction, assumed that her English crew had mutinied and were about to surrender to *Serapis*. Ricot, in *Vengeance*, merely sailed about at a safe distance, watching the scrap.

By six-thirty *Richard* had hauled up her lower sails for better visibility and rounded-to on the port quarter of *Serapis*. This brought both ships on a parallel course on the port tack heading west, *Richard* to the southward and windward of *Serapis*, the wind being then south-west by south. The commodore stood on the quarterdeck with Mayrant as his aide close by, Chamillard and a score of marines on the poop, Dale in charge of the gun-deck and the main battery, Stack and twenty seamen and marines manning the swivel-guns and muskets in the main top, Fanning in the foretop with fourteen sharp-shooters and Coram and nine men in the mizzen top. At moonrise the sea was like a millpond and the two great ships were only about thirty metres apart. Pearson challenged first, asking for identification. *Richard* was flying the Union Jack, and Master Stacey, on a nod from Jones, answered in his best English accent that the ship was the *Princess Royal*. When Pearson asked where she was from, the response was inaudible. The question was repeated and Pearson called out, 'Answer immediately, or I shall be under the necessity of firing into you.' Jones immediately lowered his British flag, hoisted the American ensign, and ordered the starboard battery to open fire. *Serapis* fired a broadside almost immediately. During the second salvo from *Richard* two of the 18-pounders blew up, killing many gunners and disabling the rest of the battery as well as destroying a good part of the deck overhead. 'The battle being thus begun,' noted Jones laconically, 'was Continued with Unremitting Fury.'

Both ships constantly jockeyed for position across the other's bows or stern in order to rake with gunfire. *Serapis* with her copper bottom had a decided advantage in these manoeuvres, 'in spite of my best Endeavours to prevent it', as Jones conceded. After several salvoes of this sort Jones realised that he was hopelessly outgunned, and his only chance was to close and grapple with *Serapis*. He backed his ship's fore and main topsails, dropped astern on the enemy's port quarter, both vessels firing rapidly at a range of thirty metres, 'filled again, put his helm a-weather', ran *Richard* up on the enemy's starboard quarter and attempted to board. This put *Richard* more or less at right angles to *Serapis*, the worst possible position for an assault. The British enfiladed the Americans with withering musketry and the attempt was easily repelled.

Pearson now tried to cross *Richard*'s bow in order to rake her decks, but his ship lacked the headway to achieve this. Jones, closely following his opponent's movements, ran his ship's bow into the stern of *Serapis*. It was at this point (and not towards the end of the battle as generally stated) that Pearson called across: 'Has your ship struck?'; to which Jones made his immortal answer: 'I have not yet begun to fight!' So far as Jones was concerned the battle had hardly commenced. He now backed his topsails to disengage momentarily and presently the two ships straightened course to lie parallel to each other. A fortuitous puff of wind from the south-west gave Jones the chance to pull ahead. *Serapis,* blanketed by *Richard*'s sails, lagged behind. *Richard* turned hard to port and tried to cross the enemy's bow in order to rake her decks, but the jib-boom on the British frigate fouled *Richard*'s mizzen shrouds. As the wind got up the two ships, thus locked together, began to turn clockwise with *Richard* dancing on the end of the *Serapis* bowsprit. They now closed, with *Richard* and *Serapis* lying head to tail as night fell. To make matters worse, a fluke on the frigate's starboard anchor got tangled up with the bulwarks of *Richard*'s starboard quarter and the topsides of both ships clapped together so that the muzzles of their guns were touching. Sizing up this situation Jones cried out, 'Well done, my brave lads, we have got her now! Throw on board her the grappling-irons and stand by for boarding!' Jones himself grabbed hold of an enemy forestay which had fallen across his quarterdeck and securely lashed it to his mizzenmast. At that moment Master Stacey ran up with a spare line, swearing most horribly. Jones checked him with the rebuke: 'Mr Stacey, it's no time to be swearing now – you may by the next moment be in eternity; but let us do our duty.'[9]

This accidental locking together of the ships worked to Jones's advantage. After two of his heaviest guns had exploded he had not dared use the others for fear that they would suffer the same fate. Deprived of his heaviest armament, against an enemy whose gunfire was superior anyway, Jones's only hope was to grapple and board or disable the enemy's rigging and kill her crew by musketry and hand-grenades, an exceedingly difficult task in view of the two covered gun-decks on the *Serapis*. Conversely, Pearson had to shake off *Richard*'s deadly embrace if he were to profit from his superior gunfire. Accordingly, he ordered that *Richard*'s grappling-hooks must be severed, but the American sharpshooters picked off the British sailors who tried to do this. The British captain now dropped anchor in the hope that the wind and current would drag *Richard* off. This ploy failed and the ships remained locked in their struggle to the death, pivoting through a semi-circle as *Serapis*, held fast by her anchor, faced south into the wind and tide, while *Richard* pointed north.

By eight-thirty the harvest moon, two days short of a full moon, rose over the eastern horizon and lit the battle scene in a deathly glow. With the 18-pounders on boths sides immobilised or out of action, ragged gunfire was kept up with the smaller cannon. Mease controlled the 9-pounders till he was wounded in the head. Dr Brooke bandaged his wound and Mease struggled to continue directing fire, but Jones himself lent a hand and supervised three guns loaded with grape and canister or double-headed shot with the aim of disabling the spars and rigging on *Serapis*. Now Pearson managed to blow out the lower starboard gun-ports and began a withering series of broadsides that beat in one side of *Richard* and blew out the other side close to the water-line. It would be only a matter of time before this hammering led to the American ship's defeat, but Jones had one advantage over the British vessel: the superb marksmanship of the French marines and the dogged courage of his cosmopolitan seamen and gunners in the fighting tops who lobbed grenades, incendiaries and deadly musketry against the enemy crew. This had the effect of clearing the decks of *Serapis*, as the American topmen picked off their counterparts and from their over-hanging yardarms were able to direct accurate fire into the lower deck of the British frigate.

During this furious engagement *Vengeance* kept well clear, while Henry Lunt's boat was powerless to take part, but *Pallas* slogged it out with *Countess of Scarborough*. Meanwhile Landais in *Alliance* seems to have lost his wits and in the early part of the battle came close to *Richard* and raked her from stem to stern, killing several men and forcing others to abandon their fighting stations and take cover. He then sailed off to watch *Pallas* tackle *Countess* but did nothing to help. Then he sailed upwind in a very leisurely manner and two hours later crossed the axis of the locked ships. Turning downwind, *Alliance* crossed *Richard*'s stern and 'while we were hailing her' (said Mayrant), poured a broadside into the flagship, holing her below the water-line. He then passed ahead, returned athwart *Richard*'s bows and, despite Jones's frantic hailing, 'Don't fire – you have killed several of our men already!' and Stack crying from his fighting top, 'I beg you will not sink us!', Landais gave *Richard* a third and final broadside, destroying the forecastle where several men had taken shelter from the gun-deck and killed several more, including a chief petty officer.

The actions of Landais were entirely reprehensible and inexcusable. With American colours and recognition signals, not to mention distinctive black topsides (the *Serapis* had bright yellow topsides), there could be no doubt as to the flagship's identity, and Jones concluded that, in view of the excellent moonlight and good visibility, the actions of the madman were deliberate. Later Landais confided to Weibert that it was his intention to help *Serapis* sink *Richard*, then board and capture the British ship and emerge as hero and victor of the battle. Afterwards he changed his tune and had the cheek to claim that his broadsides had forced Pearson to strike; and Pearson was not slow either in claiming that he had engaged not one but two enemy frigates. Nevertheless, the testimony collected by Jones at Texel later on was pretty damning. After that third and fatal broadside, Landais drew off to a safe distance and took no further part in the action. *Alliance* sustained not a single casualty and the ship itself was completely unscathed. She was hit only three times, by *Countess of Scarborough*, at such long range that two of the cannonballs bounced off her topsides while the third lodged harmlessly.

During a slight lull in the furious fighting Jones sat down for a moment on a hencoop. When a seaman approached and said, 'For God's sake, Captain, strike!' Jones leaped to his feet and said fiercely, 'No! I will sink. I will never strike!' and resumed his efforts with the 9-pounders. Jones's courage and indomitable spirit were sorely tested that night, but the sight of the little commodore in the thick of the fighting, regardless of his own safety, put new heart in his men. They themselves kept a cool head and systematically picked off the British gunners one by one, with the result that the gun batteries were gradually silenced and the boys who brought the powder cartridges up from the magazine dropped them on the deck. Seeing this, William Hamilton, one of the *Richard*'s four Scotsmen, crawled out along a yardarm and dropped a grenade on to the pile of cartridges left by the powder monkeys. The detonation of the explosives killed at least a score of men and badly burned many others. Pearson was on the point of striking after this explosion rocked his ship, when three of *Richard*'s petty officers (two of them wounded) decided that their own ship would sink if she did not strike. The chief gunner, an Englishman named Henry Gardner, ran aft to haul down the American ensign but finding that it had been shot away, he began crying out, 'Quarters, Quarters, for God's sake!' At this Jones drew a pistol from his belt, hurled it at Gardner, and knocked him senseless to the deck. This seems to be the origin of the myth about Jones shooting 'Lieutenant Grub'. In reality, Midshipman Groube served with distinction throughout the battle and was nowhere near the jackstaff when this incident took place.

Pearson, hearing the cry, called across to Jones, 'Sir, do you ask for quarter?'

'No sir, I haven't as yet *thought* of it, but I'm determined to make *you* strike.'

Pearson's response was to command, 'Boarders away!' but by the time the British boarding party had clambered over *Richard*'s bulwarks they found, to their dismay, a large number of Americans with pikes at the ready to repel them. The boarders thereupon beat a very hasty retreat. It is singularly odd that neither side attempted to board the other till very late in the action. Morison speculated that Pearson may have been deterred because *Richard*'s crew looked like such desperate cutthroats while Jones decided that his men could do more damage with firearms than with pikes and cutlasses at close quarters.[10] Remarkably, neither captain was wounded in the battle though both men were in full view on their respective quarterdecks throughout. Jones may have given his sharpshooters specific orders to spare Pearson so that he might have the pleasure of capturing a captain RN; and Pearson may likewise have spared Jones in the hope of taking the 'pirate' alive.

By ten o'clock, thanks to the Landais broadside earlier on, *Richard* was now taking in a considerable amount of water, impelling the ship's master at arms to release the prisoners in the hold and set them to work manning the pumps. One of the prisoners, the master of the prize ship *Union*, took advantage of the situation to escape through the gun-ports on to the deck of *Serapis* where he told Pearson that if he could only hang on a bit longer victory would be his, for there was already five feet of water in *Richard*'s hold. To be sure, the situation aboard the American flagship was now desperate: the ship was on fire and beginning to sink, and while *Serapis* still had all her 18-pounders blazing away, *Richard* could only reply with three 9-pounders. Prisoners were now running around the deck at will, officers were losing control and a chief petty officer was bawling, 'Quarters!': the situation was now hopeless – everybody could see that. Everybody, that is, except Commodore Jones, deaf to the reasonable entreaties of friend and foe alike, who continued doggedly directing the double-headed shot of his 9-pounders at the mainmast of *Serapis*. Just before ten-thirty this dour persistence paid off: the mainmast gave an ominous creak, and Pearson lost his nerve. Though four of his 18-pounders were still firing sporadically, he decided that the time had come to strike. Before engaging the enemy he had nailed the Red Ensign to its staff, letting his crew know that he would never surrender. Now he was obliged to tear the flag down with his own hands, since no one near him could move for fear of the American sharpshooters.

These are the facts as set down in several eye-witness accounts. Pearson, however, later fiddled his report in order to minimise his personal role, and the British propagandists did the rest. Contemporary engravings of the battle, executed soon after the event, imply that the Red Ensign continued to fly until the ship was dismasted. Even more glaring are the prints depicting *Alliance* firing on *Serapis* because Pearson gave out that he had been defeated by two ships acting in concert. When Pearson struck his colours, Dale took a boarding party across to *Serapis*. In this manoeuvre Midshipman Mayrant was wounded by a British pikeman who was unaware that his captain had surrendered. Similarly, John Brenton Wright, first-lieutenant of *Serapis*, kept on fighting until expressly ordered by Pearson to lay down his arms. Dale then led Pearson across to *Richard* and formally presented him to the commodore. At that precise moment the mainmast of *Serapis* gave way and toppled overboard carrying with it the mizzen topmast. Pearson handed his sword over to Jones who made a pretty little speech about Pearson's gallant fight, and then handed him back his weapon. Then, even though the ship was sinking, he invited his captive below for a much-needed glass of wine, amid the wreckage of his day-cabin.

Meanwhile, the brisk sideshow between *Pallas* and *Countess of Scarborough* had terminated some thirty minutes previously. Cottineau had conducted a textbook operation, directing gunfire against his opponent's masts, spars and rigging to such devastating effect that after two hours the British ship was disabled. Captain Piercy then surrendered and his ship, her hull intact, proved to be a valuable prize. Together with prioners taken earlier in the cruise, the victory off Flamborough Head brought the total bag to 504, including twenty-six officers of the Royal Navy and eighteen masters and mates of merchantmen. Although *Serapis* was in a terrible state after the three-and-a-half-hour battle, she was still afloat, which was more than could be said for *Bonhomme Richard*. Her rudder was hanging by one pintle, her stern frames and transoms were almost entirely shot away, the quarterdeck was about to collapse into the gunroom, the hold was rapidly filling with water and her topsides were open to the stars. The extensive damage from gunfire, both from *Serapis* and *Alliance* revealed that the ribs and timbers of the flagship were 'greatly decayed with age' as Jones drily observed in his report:

> and a person must have been an Eye Witness to form a Just idea of this tremendous scene of Carneg, Wreck and ruin that everywhere appeared. Humanity cannot but recoil from the prospect of such finished horror, and Lament that War should be capable of producing such fatal Consequences.[11]

The mythmaking began before the last whiff of gunpowder had dissipated. In the confusion just after Pearson surrendered, Thomas Berry, one of the British volunteers serving aboard *Richard*, together with half a dozen other English sailors, seized a boat and made their escape to Scarborough where they made lengthy statements to the authorities. Berry's affidavit, published in the London *Evening Post* of 30 September, states that Jones was dressed in a short jacket and long trousers, with about twelve pistols in his belt and a cutlass in his hand; that he shot seven of his own men for cowardice or desertion, including his very own nephew, 'and had the barbarity to shoot at the lad's legs who is a lieutenant in his ship'. The facts are that Jones wore regulation naval uniform, shot no one of his own crew and had no nephew aboard; but Berry's tall stories were very soon repeated, then embellished and expanded, by the legion of hacks turning out broadsides and chapbooks, with the result that these yarns persist to the present day. Among the numerous inaccuracies perpetrated by eye-witnesses at the time was one (at Leith) stating that Jones wore a Scotch bonnet edged with gold. This bystander also stated that Jones was of 'a middle stature, stern countenance and swarthy complexion' – the genesis of the hoary old chestnut that Jones glowered like a dago, the manner in which he was customarily portrayed in British prints and popular literature. Thus Commodore John Paul Jones, United States Navy, was swiftly transformed into the bloodthirsty pirate of the bloods and penny dreadfuls.

11. Alliance
1779–80

O Captain! my Captain! our fearful trip is done,
The ship has weather'd every rack, the prize we sought is
won.
— WALT WHITMAN, *O Captain! My Captain!*

For two days and a night after the battle, superhuman attempts were
made to save *Bonhomme Richard*. While the pumps were manned
continually and repairs were effected, Jones transferred the wounded
to other ships of the squadron. The fires raging below decks were
not extinguished till ten o'clock on the morning of 24 September,
and men worked under extremely dangerous conditions to transfer
barrels of gunpowder from the ship's magazine to the attendant
vessels. Despite valiant efforts with the pumps, *Bonhomme Richard* was
taking in more water. Nathaniel Fanning went below to retrieve the
officers' trunks and found them blown to smithereens. 'Such a
breach was made through our ship's quarter that one might have
driven in one side with a coach and six and out the other.'[1] Jones
himself remained aboard his flagship till seven-thirty that evening,
before formally transferring his flag to *Serapis*. At ten o'clock he gave
the order to abandon ship, but it was to be done in a systematic
fashion throughout the night, the pumps being operated as long as
possible to prevent the ship taking a sudden dive.

Fanning and those still aboard the stricken ship abandoned her at
ten the following morning in a small tender and boarded *Serapis*, but
Jones made him go back and retrieve the ship's log-book and other
vital papers from his cabin. The wind was now getting up and it was
with some trepidation that Fanning and his party reboarded the sinking ship. By now *Richard* was lying nearly head to the wind with her
topsails aback, and the water running in and out at her lower deck
ports. Fanning's boat sheltered under *Richard*'s stern and to his consternation he found that the ship was on the point of going down.
The boat's crew rowed as hard as they could and only just got clear

'when she fetched a heavy pitch into a sea and a heavy roll, and disappeared'. The resultant suction almost swamped Fanning's boat, and had it not been decked it too would have gone to the bottom off Flamborough Head. Today the flagship of Commodore John Paul Jones lies on the bed of the North Sea in seventy metres of water, close under the cliffs. Occasionally fishermen tangle their nets or lines on her and in this manner a swivel gun was brought to the surface. The wreck was located and positively identified as recently as 1980.

It was a little after half past ten on the morning of 25 September that the ship sank. Jones recorded how he saw 'with inexpressible grief, the last glimpse of the *Bonhomme Richard*' as she went down at the bows. Out of a crew of 322 at the beginning of the action, almost half were killed or wounded. Of the crew of 284 aboard HMS *Serapis*, more than 130 lay dead or dying and many more were wounded. Pearson had lost two warships, but he had foiled the American objective of seizing the Baltic convoy which made good its escape during the battle and sheltered under the guns of Scarborough. Pearson later mitigated his loss by claiming that he had been attacked by two American warships. In fact, only one seaman aboard *Serapis* was killed as a result of a stray shot from *Alliance*. The plain facts are that a brand-new, fast, much more manoeuvrable British frigate, well armed with 18-pounders, had surrendered to an old, lumbering ship whose effective armament consisted only of 12-pounders. To overcome *Serapis* under those conditions speaks volumes for Jones's superior seamsnship and tactics. Pearson, on the other hand, showed a lack of judgment in allowing himself to be grappled. Of course, to some extent, the clinch was fortuitous, but Jones's genius lay in his ability to turn this accident to his own advantage and effectively silence the enemy's main armament as well as cancelling his greater speed and mobility.

Pearson and Piercy were subsequently court-martialled but acquitted on the grounds that they had 'done infinite credit to themselves by a very obstinate defence against a superior force'. Both captains were given the freedom of Scarborough and other towns and given a tumultuous heroes' welcome in London. Pearson received a magnificent silver trophy from the Russian Company in gratitude for saving the Baltic convoy, and the accolade from King George III. Sir Richard Pearson, who lost the battle, thus gained far more from it than the victor. When Jones learned of the knighthood he commented to Maréchal le Duc de Biron, 'Let me fight him again, M. le Maréchal, and I'll make him a lord!'

On receipt of first reports of the battle, the Admiralty despatched numerous ships in all directions (except the right one) in search of the American squadron. A formidable flotilla consisting of *Prudence* (64 guns), *Amphitrite* (28), *Pegasus* (28), *Medea* (28) and *Champion* (24) was sent from Spithead; at Scarborough on 28 September they were told that Jones had gone to Norway, but other reports placed him off Inverness. This sent the British warships on a wild-goose chase to the far north. Not until mid-October did the Admiralty learn that the American ships were now at the Texel in Holland. Belatedly the fifty-gun *Jupiter* and three frigates were sent from Spithead to blockade the Texel.

For weeks the British newspapers were full of stories about the American raiders. In these reports, more imaginary than real, were sown the seeds of the Paul Jones legend. One enterprising paper even sent a reporter to Kirkbean to garner tales of Jones's boyhood. One of these told how Jones, in retaliation for a flogging from his schoolmaster, beat the man senseless with a club before running off to sea aboard a warship, for which 'we are indebted for having such a formidable and desperate pirate at sea'.[2] Even more scurrilous was the allegation which gained widespread currency that Jones, while in the Scottish merchant service, had once poured a bucket of turpentine over the head of a carpenter sleeping on deck, and then, with a train of gunpowder, set the wretched man alight. The carpenter awoke in flames, leaped overboard and was never seen again. Some sailors were alleged to have laid charges against their captain for this crime, 'but Paul being good at manoeuvring, so contrived it that on his trial no evidence appeared, and he was of course acquitted'.[3] Many newspapers used the defeat – 'a naval combat the like of which has never been fought before' – to attack the government in general and the Admiralty in particular. The First Lord, that Earl of Sandwich whom Captain Cook sought to immortalise by naming the Hawaiian archipelago after him, but who is best remembered today for his habit of eating his meat between slices of bread at the gaming-tables, was satirised in a popular ballad under his nickname of Jeremy Twitcher (hero of *The Beggars' Opera*):

> If success to our fleets be not quickly restor'd
> The leaders in office to shove from the Board,
> May they all fare alike, and the de'il pick the bones
> Of Germain, Jemmy Twitcher, Lord North and Paul Jones.

Lord Sandwich was also the butt of a humorous letter, purporting to come from Jones himself, which appeared in the London *Evening Post*. After thanking the First Lord for the opportunity given him to take prizes and raid the coast, Commodore Jones ventured to say that this singular complaisance was due to the fact that he and Sandwich had similar tastes: 'Your Lordship and I do, both of us, love a bottle and a wench.' This squib was hardly likely to endear the renegade Jones to the English establishment, particularly the Royal Navy, for he had run rings round them and made fools of them. There was a singularly unattractive anti-Scottish thread running through much of the press condemnation of Jones, together with the denunciation of him as a pirate or buccaneer, and this image of him persisted for well over a century.[4] In contrast to the extremely bitter view of Jones in official circles was the attitude of the ordinary people, as exemplified by the many popular ballads of the period in which John Paul Jones was painted as a hero. Interestingly, the earliest printed example of these was published at Pocklington, Yorkshire, soon after the battle and ran to eight stanzas.[5] Understandably, Cumbria which had felt the effects of a land raid by Jones, took a rather different view. In 'A New Song of Paul Jones, the Cumberland Militia and Scarborough Volunteers' the balladeer complains how

> It vexes my patience, I'm sure, night and day
> To think how that traitor *Paul Jones* got away.

And rakes up the Mungo Maxwell affair for good measure. By and large, however, Paul Jones, as he was usually referred to (and, incidentally, how Jones styled himself from then on), got a very good press in the popular broadsides and chapbooks that proliferated within weeks of the battle. The dash, panache and audacity of the young commodore appealed to the sporting instincts and anti-authoritarian feelings of the average Briton. Soon Paul Jones the pirate joined Robin Hood and Dick Turpin in the gallery of likeable rogues famed in song and fable. One of the most celebrated stories was the shooting of Lieutenant Grub – 'the reader is assured of the fact, which came from the most undoubted authority, that of William Grub's widow'. Why the innocent Midshipman Beaumont Groube should have been singled out for this blatant lie has never been explained. Groube not only served with distinction during the battle, but went on to serve under Jones in *Alliance* and *Ariel*, about as far from the story of the cowardly gunner as one could get.

On the other hand, Jones's humanity and generosity towards his foes was well documented at the time, and went a long way towards winning over the British public. His kindness to prisoners whom he released at Belfast Lough in April 1778 has already been mentioned; but there was also the case of John Jackson, the Humber pilot whom he had detained and who lost an arm during the battle off Flamborough Head. Jones not only had his wounds tended by Dr Brooke but, when Jackson had recuperated, Jones sent him back to England from the Texel in his own boat with a hundred ducats in gold. Furthermore, he wrote to the Mayor and Corporation of Hull that Jackson had been subjected to *force majeure*, and that if they would twice yearly certify to the American Minister at the French Court that he was still alive, he would receive half-pay for life. Sadly, this promise was repudiated by Congress, to whom Thomas Jefferson referred the matter, and Jackson, who lived on until 1836, never got more than his hundred ducats out of the Americans.

The British public derived some crumb of comfort from the outcome of the greatest sea battle fought off its coasts, in that the hero was, after all, a Scotsman, and that most of the petty officers and able seamen on *Richard* were British. The spectacle of Briton fighting Briton only underlined the pointlessness and futility of the American War, and undoubtedly this exploit was a major turning-point in forming public opinion against the prolongation of the struggle. In France, on the other hand, the impact of Jones's victory was stupendous. News of his exploit reached Paris hard on the heels of the dismal reports of the failure of the Franco-Spanish expedition on the south coast of England. France desperately needed some good news to counteract this fiasco, and consequently the naval victory was magnified beyond reality in the French newspapers. John Adams summed up the generally ecstatic feeling when the news broke by recording that 'the cry of Versailles and the Clamour of Paris became as loud in the favour of Monsieur Jones as of Monsieur Franklin, and the inclination of the Ladies to embrace him almost as fashionable and as strong'.[6] As early as 7 October the first French chapbook account of the battle was published at Rouen, rapidly followed by countless others.

In the United States the news was greeted even more rapturously, for 1779 had been a very bad year for the American cause. Coming in the wake of the British recapture of Georgia, the disastrous failure of the Penobscot expedition and increasingly severe British raids on those coastal areas still in American hands, the victory off Flamborough Head was the one positive moment of the bitter conflict. Characteristically, though, Jones's victory was rubbished by the faction led by Arthur Lee and Sam Adams. One of Lee's henchmen in Congress, James Lovell, went so far as to write disparagingly to George Washington complaining of 'the little proud Affectations of our rising Navy'. Sensibly Washington ignored these snide comments and left the Navy well alone. Much to the chagrin of the Lee-Adams clique, Jones's star was now in the ascendant and Congress actually took to heart the commodore's recommendations, for in December 1779 it scrapped the Marine Committee and replaced it with a Board of Admiralty along British lines. This body, nominally of five men, in fact consisted of only three: Francis Lewis, William Ellery and that rising young Virginian politician, James Madison. Jones learned of this sweeping change shortly after Commodore Whipple's fleet had been captured by the British at Charleston. To his friend William Carmichael he confided: 'There is a Board of Admiralty at last appointed. This ought to have been done long ago . . . as we have now lost, I may say, all our Navy'.[7]

With her sails reduced to the foremast and the stump of her mizzen, *Serapis* as the new flagship of Commodore Jones made slow progress in company of *Alliance, Countess of Scarborough, Pallas* and *Vengeance* due east across the North Sea. Jones himself directed the erection of a jury rig on 28 September and a new mainsail the following day. At two o'clock on the afternoon of 2 October *Serapis* raised the Dutch coast. A pilot came aboard two hours later and, after a delay caused by squally weather, the squadron entered the Texel roadstead by midday on 3 October. In this anchorage at the largest of the islands running along the top of the Zuider Zee, the American squadron would spend the rest of the year. Jones had wished the squadron to put into Dunkirk, but he was overruled by Chaumont and his captains who felt that the Texel, in Dutch waters, was the nearest haven. The choice of a neutral, rather than a French, port caused immense problems, especially in the matter of the 504 prisoners. The naval base at the Texel was the deep-water anchorage for ships belonging to Amsterdam, some seventy miles away. The channel from the Texel to Amsterdam was so shallow that it could only be navigated by barges and small craft, a tedious voyage that generally took three days. All provisions, even fresh water, had to be obtained from Amsterdam, and the Texel offered few facilities, either for repairs or rest and recreation.

The choice of this unsuitable base was dictated solely because Sartine wished Jones's squadron to escort the French Baltic fleet from there back to France, but neither Sartine nor Chaumont had thought out the implications of such a move. The presence of the American squadron was a source of grave embarrassment to the Dutch, who wished to remain on friendly terms with the British. Soon Jones found himself embroiled in Dutch politics, with mixed results. He was fortunate, on the one hand, in finding a staunch ally in J.D. Van der Capellen, leader of the pro-French faction in the Dutch parliament. The French ambassador to the Dutch Republic was the Duc de la Vauguyon and he, too, proved very supportive. The third man on whom Jones could rely was the Swiss philosopher and man of letters, Charles-Guillaume-Frédéric Dumas, a close friend of Franklin and a long-time sympathiser with the American cause. He and Jones were mutually attracted by their common interests in the promotion of the welfare of mankind in general, 'the advancement of human nature' as Jones liked to style it. Dumas, however, disliked the French ambassador. Jones also came across the evil genius of Stephen Sayre, quondam banker and sheriff of London but latterly an American adventurer and mischief-maker of the worst kind. He had briefly been private secretary to Arthur Lee, and although he had soon quarrelled with him he retained from that connection a bitter hatred of Franklin and everyone associated with him. Sayre was now in Amsterdam, cultivating Van der Capellen, through whom he planned to sell to the Dutch vast tracts of the American wilderness which he did not possess. Dumas, who had translated Henry Bouquet's account of his expedition to the Ohio and therefore had some knowledge of the American frontier, exposed this scheme, much to the anger of Sayre who referred to Dumas in his letters to Van der Capellen as 'that insignificant little Shoemaker'. Sayre spread a rumour that *Bonhomme Richard*, *Pallas* and *Vengeance* were Chaumont's privateers, and he even had the brass neck to recommend himself as captain of *Alliance* when Landais was relieved of his command. Thus Jones soon discovered that the situation in Holland was just as bedevilled by intrigue and petty jealousies as at Passy.

Jones and Vauguyon hoped that the Dutch would allow the squadron to carry out vital repairs, replenish provisions and offload the prisoners. The British government, however, leaned on the Dutch, insisting that Jones be treated as a rebel pirate. Even if the Dutch were to draw the line at surrendering Jones to the British, the British argued forcefully that they should have no compunction about returning his prizes *Serapis* and *Countess of Scarborough* to their rightful government. The argument that the Americans were rebels without belligerent rights had been sufficient to persuade the Danish authorities to hand back the three prizes which Jones had sent into Bergen; but the United Provinces, which had been rebels against Spanish rule, were not minded to take this line. Having thrown off the shackles of Spain in the 1570s, the Dutch had a natural sympathy for the Americans trying to gain their independence. And even in England itself, the government's attempts to extradite Jones from Holland did not go down well with the Opposition. The London *Evening Post* echoed this sentiment in its editorial on British atrocities in Virginia and Connecticut which had so far gone unpunished. Now the editor wished to know why, if steps to punish the perpetrators of these outrages had not been taken,

> with what propriety or justice does it now demand Captain Paul Jones? Is not the requisition to the last degree ridiculous and absurd? And will not the inflammatory and diabolical proceedings of the British troops in America excite retaliation, and make poor Old England (once famed for mercy and sound policy) contemptible in the eyes of every nation on earth?[8]

The Patriot Party in the Netherlands was, for the moment, in the ascendant over the pro-British Orange faction, and this reflected the feelings of the ordinary people. On his first visit to Amsterdam, to sort out the provision of a shore base for the treatment of wounded and the security of prisoners, Jones found himself fêted wherever he went. When he attended the theatre on 9 October he received a standing ovation from the audience, among them the artist Simon Fokke whose lightning sketch of the commodore on that occasion was used for the earliest authentic likeness, published soon afterwards. When he visited the Stock Exchange, business was momentarily suspended. The financial correspondent of one London newspaper reported that the commodore was 'dressed in a blue frock coat, metal buttons, white cloth waistcoat and breeches, with a broadsword under his arm. When he quitted the 'Change the Crowd followed him to his Lodgings and huzzaed him all the way home'.[9] Other correspondents of British newspapers seethed at the appearance of this 'desperado' on the streets of Amsterdam and rumoured that he was about to be placed in command of a large amphibious force for a major invasion of England or Ireland.

There was even a popular song in his honour which has since passed into the standard Dutch repertoire. Entitled *Hier Komt Paul Jones Aan* ('Here Comes Paul Jones'), it extols the exploits of Paul Jones – 'such a nice fellow!' – to this day. While Jones was a great popular hero with the Dutch, especially with the people of Amsterdam, their commercial rivals at The Hague and the faction led by the Prince of Orange intrigued with Sir Joseph Yorke, the British ambassador, but the wily Stadholder prevaricated. When Yorke tried to have Jones arrested on the street and charged with piracy, Dedel the High Bailiff of Amsterdam refused to comply with this request. The French ambassador, meanwhile, counselled the commodore to keep a very low profile, hoping that the delays while *Serapis* was made seaworthy would weary the British of their watch on the Texel.

In the matter of landing prisoners and tending to the wounded among them, Jones was hampered by Captain Pearson, aided and abetted by Yorke who wrote to London of 'the difficulties of knowing how to treat with these Piratical people without committing His Majesty's Dignity'. In other words, British pomposity and protocol overrode common decency and humanity. Yorke was eventually forced to concede that Jones had acted humanely. He had, in fact, offered to release the officers on parole, but Pearson had stuffily refused, perhaps afraid that the seamen, if left aboard ship, would desert to a man and enlist in the United States Navy as so many of their compatriots had already done. Consequently it was not until the end of October that Jones was allowed to land the wounded prisoners where they could be tended in a fort on Texel island, under French marine guard. It has to be said that Pearson's conduct throughout this episode was boorish in the extreme. When Pearson was paroled and found lodgings ashore, Jones sent him his mess furniture and plate from *Serapis*. Although Pearson had requested this favour, he showed his ingratitude by sending the commodore a silly note saying that he could receive nothing from the hands of a rebel, although he had already accepted the return of his sword. Jones indulged Pearson by letting him think that his personal effects had been returned to him by courtesy of Captain Cottineau, and they were accepted without a word of acknowledgment.

Jones would readily have released all the British prisoners, had an equal number of American seamen been liberated from English prisons. In the case of Richard Pearson, he wished to make an exception; the latter was far too valuable a prize to be let go so easily, and Jones planned to exchange him for Gustavus Conyngham, America's most successful commerce raider who, in the fourteen-gun cutter aptly named *Revenge,* took over sixty prizes in eighteen months. When Congress sold this ship to a merchant syndicate for fitting out as a privateer, Conyngham resigned his naval commission and became her master. On his first cruise under letter of marque, however, he was captured and placed in solitary confinement in the Mill Prison's infamous black hole. While Jones was actually trying to negotiate his release, Conyngham tunnelled his way out of the prison and escaped to Holland where Jones, who had never met him before, greeted him like a long-lost brother and welcomed him aboard *Alliance* until he could obtain a ship of his own.

Jones himself took up quarters aboard *Alliance* while *Serapis* was being extensively refurbished. Landais had either been despatched to Paris, or more probably went of his own accord in order to argue his case against Jones. The commodore, however, had sent a bulky packet of reports and depositions on the conduct of the lunatic Frenchman. Many of these affidavits were sworn by officers of *Alliance* as well as by the commodore and officers of *Bonhomme Richard*, and altogether they provided a pretty damning indictment of the Frenchman's conduct before, during and after the battle. Franklin took one look at the papers and suspended Landais on the spot. Unfortunately, he had not reckoned with the influence of Landais, especially with Arthur Lee. Between them, this malevolent pair would later cook up a scheme to thwart Franklin and get the better of Jones.

While his squadron was being refitted at the Texel, Jones spent a great deal of time in Amsterdam and The Hague. Van der Capellen prevailed on him to write an account of his life to append to his report of the battle, with the aim of countering the slanders being put about by the Orange party. The result was one of those long autobiographical letters which, with Jones's earlier letter to Franklin and his later *Memoire* to King Louis XVI, form the basis of the authentic biographies of Jones. He also gave Van der Capellen a copy of his letter to the Countess of Selkirk, which, more than anything else, convinced the Dutch statesman that he was dealing with no 'rough, unpolished sailor' but a gentleman of sensibility. Jones was all for publishing the text of this letter at Van der Capellen's suggestion, but Dumas advised him to be 'more reserved' and Jones demurred on the grounds that he could not publish the letter without the Countess's permission.

Amid all the business of getting his ships ready for action again and disposing of the prisoners, Jones still found time for amatory dalliance. In Passy he had been told that Dumas had a beautiful daughter and Franklin had jocularly suggested that Jones might like to try his luck with her. This he obeyed with alacrity, as a letter to Edward Bancroft from the Texel on 26 October testifies:

> I have seen the *fine lady* of this country which I came to Europe to espouse. She is really a fine Woman yet I have seen also a second sister equally a Belle who will soon be fit for a Man; and I should prefer this younger because one might prevent some little Errors from taking root in her mind which the other seems to have contracted. It is a great pity that two such lovely lasses should be watched with so much Jealousy; for they are not so come-at-able here as they might be in France. I have left to me only Doctr. Franklins remedy, Patience.[10]

Coarse and coldly calculating: that was Gentleman John's way with the ladies. Anna Jacoba Dumas, the younger daughter to whom he took such a fancy, had only just turned thirteen. Despite being closely watched by her chaperone, Jones managed to flirt with the girl on several occasions in November and early December. His interest was apparently reciprocated, for Anna composed a song in his honour under the pseudonym of the Virgin Muse. Jones was far too preoccupied with his first passion, getting a ship ready for sea, to respond immediately; but later on, when he was cruising in *Alliance*, he wrote her a verse epistle:

> Were I, Paul Jones, dear maid, 'the king of sea',
> I find such merit in thy virgin song,
> A coral crown with bays I'd give to thee,
> A car which on the waves should smoothly glide along.
> The nereids all about thy side should wait,
> And gladly sing in triumph of thy state
> 'Vivat, vivat, the happy virgin muse!
> Of Liberty the friend, who tyrant power pursues!'

Or happier lot! were fair Columbia free
From British tyranny – and youth still mine,
I'd tell a tender tale to one like thee
With artless looks and breast as pure as thine.
If she approved my flame, distrust apart,
Like faithful turtles we'd have but one heart;
Together then we'd tune the silver lyre,
As love or sacred freedom should our lays inspire.

But since, alas! the rage of war prevails,
And cruel Britons desolate our land,
For freedom still I spread my willing sails,
My unsheathed sword my injured country shall command.
Go on, bright maid! the muses all attend
Genius like thine, and wish to be its friend.
Trust me, although conveyed through this poor gift,
My New Year's thoughts are grateful for thy gift.[11]

Jones was mightily pleased with this poetic effusion, for he kept a copy and this was preserved among the papers collected by his niece Janette Taylor, although Morison ungenerously suggests that he saved it as ammunition on a future target. There is no record that Jones ever ran into Anna Jacoba again. Little more than a year later she married Abraham Senserff and eventually bore him three children. This poem at least gives a flavour of Jones's skill as a versifier. Shorter snatches of verse appropriate to the moment pepper his private correspondence, notably his letters to Lafayette. Virtually none of the other naval officers of the American Revolution wrote prose with the accuracy, far less with the impassioned grace of which Jones was capable; while his metrical talent likewise set him apart.

For the officers and men of the American squadron who spent the winter in the Texel, there would have been little or no opportunities for such pleasantries. Jones kept his crews as busy as possible with repairs and refitting but, with little prize money and even less to spend it on, the sailors suffered from boredom. Whenever they grumbled about their lot, however, they needed only to look out to sea where British sails ominously filled the horizon. Then they would be sharply reminded that although life at the Texel was extremely dull, it was infinitely more comfortable than a cell in Fortin Prison. The repair work was delayed by periods of bad weather, icy rain and thick fogs which did little to restore the sailors' equanimity.

Meanwhile frenzied diplomatic activity was going on, as the British were determined to get possession of *Serapis* and *Countess of Scarborough*. When pressure was put on the Dutch and they, in turn, leant on Vauguyon, the latter claimed that the squadron was part of the French Navy. A Dutch official was sent down from Amsterdam to examine Jones's French commission, and Vauguyon tried to persuade the commodore to sign an affidavit that he had lost it when *Bonhomme Richard* had gone down, but Jones would not stoop to such subterfuge. At this juncture, however, he decided that it might be more prudent to transfer his flag to *Alliance*. To that end he moved a quantity of furnishings and equipment to *Alliance*, but he did so with the utmost regret, for *Serapis* was not only the finest frigate he had seen but 'a proud trophy of his Valour'. To his disgust, he found that Landais had left his cabin like a pig-sty. The slobbishness of the skipper had infected the entire ship's crew; the officers were habitually drunk, while the men, wallowing in their own excrement, were riddled with disease. For someone as fastidious as Jones, *Alliance* was anything but the tight ship to which he was accustomed.

Vauguyon had warned Jones on 12 November to delay his departure from the Texel, but later the same day Vice-Admiral Pieter Hendrik Reynst of the Dutch Navy arrived at the island and replaced the easy-going Captain Riemersma with whom Jones had struck up a friendship. The pro-British Reynst was a man of a very different stamp and, acting under the direct orders of Prince William, he constantly hectored and nagged Jones into clearing off forthwith. Jones got so annoyed with Reynst's haughty, insultingly peremptory notes that he challenged him to a naval duel, offering to fight any three Dutch ships with his own squadron if they would sail out of the harbour. Reynst ignored this challenge but five days later delivered an ultimatum from the Dutch government which had now narrowly voted in favour of expelling the Americans. Vauguyon tried to salvage something from the situation by ordering *Pallas* and *Vengeance* to show French colours, and even persuaded Jones to hoist the lilies of France on *Serapis* and *Countess of Scarborough* with a view to their being used to convey the prisoners to England under cartel. In the end *Scarborough*, accompanied by *Vengeance* and two French cutters, did take 191 prisoners to Portsmouth, where they were exchanged for Frenchmen and not Americans – much to Jones's disgust.

As part of the French subterfuge, Sartine now offered him a letter of marque as commander of privateers. At that Jones exploded in indignation. He was intensely irritated at the way the British condemned him as a pirate while the French often dismissed him as a corsair. Sartine's offer, though well meant, was the last straw. Jones's response was a veritable flood of letters to friends at home and abroad, complaining of 'a most impertinent proposal' and of 'so unworthy a proposition' as to be offered 'a dirty piece of Parchment'. To Robert Morris he wrote on 5 December that he proposed to sail back to America, blockade or no blockade. To Samuel Huntington, President of Congress, he sent a sixteen-page document, the Texel Memorial, reciting his services to his adopted country since 1775, and concluding with the hope that he would be employed under 'the immediate direction' of Congress, without diplomatic or other foreign intermediaries.

To make matters worse, and unbeknown to Jones, Alexander Gillon, the self-styled commodore of the *South Carolina*, was in Paris at this time, trying to persuade Chaumont to purchase *L'Indien* for six hundred thousand livres and, with Jones's ships, to give Gillon command of a squadron in order to 'do something clever'. Fortunately Gillon's preposterous proposal came to nothing, but when Jones got an inkling of it he realised that the time had come to make a move. He might have been heartened had he known what consternation his continued presence at the Texel was causing the British Admiralty. On 23 November Sandwich wrote to Captain Francis Reynolds: 'For God's sake, get to Sea instantly, in consequence of the orders you have received. If you can take Paul Jones, you will be as high in the estimation of the public as if you had beat the Combined [French and Spanish] Fleets.'[12] Jones took advantage of foul weather in December to have *Alliance* careened and thoroughly cleaned. A couple of days later he had the ship fully provisioned. The British blockade had been temporarily lifted during the December gales, but two days after Christmas the weather abated and Jones seized the opportunity to break out. Rigging a springline on a second anchor in order to let the wind fill the sails promptly and gain headway in the crowded roadstead, Jones slipped that cable. *Alliance* bounded forward like an uncoiled spring, and with the Stars and Stripes fluttering in a stiff breeze, Jones took his ship to sea.

He gambled that the British ships, forced back to Portsmouth by the severe easterlies, would not be back on station for at least twenty-four hours, and consequently decided to set a course through the Channel rather than take the safer but longer route back round the north of Scotland and the west of Ireland. By early afternoon the frigate passed Camperdown, the Flemish village which would give fellow Scot Admiral Adam Duncan his greatest victory eighteen years later. By four o'clock *Alliance* was scudding along at ten knots under shortened sail before a galeforce wind, reaching the estuary of the Maas by six o'clock. During the night the wind moderated and *Alliance* under full sail passed the British fleet riding at anchor in the Downs. At nine the following morning the frigate passed through the Dover Straits; at ten Calais slipped astern; and by midday Cap Gris Nez bore south-east by south, six miles distant. *Alliance* had slipped through the enemy net unscathed.

Patches of fog and generally poor visibility protected *Alliance* from the vigilance of the Royal Navy during the following day, but as the ship passed the Isle of Wight Jones took the precaution of calling the crew to general quarters, clearing decks for action and exercising the cannon. By noon on 30 December, when immediate danger was past, he felt confident enough to chase a ship and a brig as potential prizes, but these proved to be neutral vessels from Stockholm and Danzig and so were allowed to continue on their way. The weather worsened again as the ship headed south but by midnight *Alliance* was off Ushant. We do not know whether Jones brought in the New Year in the time-honoured fashion. Probably not, though his journal records his elation at getting back to sea again. The prospects for 1780 seemed excellent, and he looked forward to repeating his exploits at the expense of the enemy. Little could he have realised that the period of greatest achievement was at an end.

Chaumont sold *Countess of Scarborough* at Dunkirk for conversion to a merchantman. *Serapis* originally suffered the same rather ignominious fate, but when later repurchased by the French Navy her bottom was recoppered and she was fitted out as a warship for service in the Indian Ocean. Off Ste Marie de Madagascar one night in July 1781, a lantern was accidentally dropped into a vat of brandy and the ship entirely destroyed. The other prize ships brought only moderate sums; the National Archives in Washington preserve the schedule of prize money for the *Bonhomme Richard* cruise, indicating that the sale of the captured vessels netted 132,915 livres 12 sols and 8 deniers. Jones's share was 10 per cent, or about $2,658 in gold. Richard Dale, Stacey and the two Lunts each got about a third of that sum, although Cutting Lunt, who died in captivity, never saw a penny of it, the practice then being that if a sailor died in action or from his wounds his heirs got nothing. Jones also had to settle with the tailor at Lorient and advance money out of his pocket to seamen, and recouped very little of this. All in all, the cruise can hardly be regarded as profitable in terms of hard cash. The money was soon spent, but the glory lingers on.

Contrary to Jones's high expectations, 1780 got off to an inauspicious start. To begin with, the ship's company was deeply divided between the original crew which had served under Landais and the veterans of *Bonhomme Richard*. The behaviour of *Alliance* during the recent battle was endlessly argued in the wardroom and below decks, and the two factions frequently came to blows. To counter this animosity, Jones had orders published that expressly forbade 'loud speaking except in Case of Necessity'. He preferred the ship to be worked silently and efficiently. Between Ushant and Finisterre *Alliance* cruised in search of prizes, but all but one of the ships intercepted turned out to be neutral or friendly. A small English brig, bound for Liverpool from Leghorn (Livorno), was seized and a prize crew installed. One of the neutral vessels was the Dutch brigantine *Berkenbosch*. Although Jones let her pass he insisted on swapping ship's cooks, since the cook on *Alliance* was worse than useless. Although the brigantine was subsequently captured by the British in the West Indies after war broke out between Holland and Britain, the Dutch skipper lodged a complaint against Jones over the high-handed manner in which he had shanghaied the cook. The owner of the vessel turned out to be a close relative of the Grand Pensionaris (Dutch prime minister). The skipper of *Berkenbosch* maintained that the useless cook he had acquired was really an American prizemaster in disguise and he blamed him for the loss of the ship. Although this was ludicrous, it caused considerable embarrassment to the American government, and required the intervention of Chancellor Robert Livingston to placate the Dutch authorities in 1782.

At Corunna on 16 January Jones put in for repairs and provisions, but the crew, who claimed that he had promised to take them direct to Lorient, downed tools in protest. The following day he had talked them round and the log duly noted that 'the People were satisfied by the Captain, so as to appear chearfully to Duty'. On 27 January Jones entertained the Governor of Corunna and other local dignitaries aboard ship, fired a thirteen-gun salute, and weighed anchor at midday in company of the French frigate *Sensible*. Fanning states that Jones informed the officers that he planned to cruise in search of prizes for three weeks before heading for Lorient, but that the officers dissuaded him, largely on the grounds that they lacked proper cold-weather clothing. The ship's log contains ominous entries concerning Boatswain's Mate Darling, confined to his cabin for drunkenness, and an unseemly brawl between Lieutenant Degge and Master Carpenter James Bragg, the latter being knocked to the deck and kicked in the stomach – because he had sent his mate to batten down hatchways in a gale instead of doing it himself.

The ship made slow progress across the Bay of Biscay in heavy seas, liberating a French barque that been taken by a Guernsey privateer. This vessel proved to be so badly waterlogged that she had to be scuttled, after her valuable cargo of wine was transferred to *Alliance*. Then the ship fell in with the American merchantman *Livingston*, bound for France with a cargo of Virginia tobacco, which was escorted into Groix roadstead on 10 February. The ship tarried there a week carrying out necessary repairs before heading for Lorient and anchoring there on 19 February. From Lorient Jones wrote straightaway to Franklin, complaining that he was 'about blind with sore eyes'. Ashore, he found congenial lodgings with his friend James Moylan who, since Jones had seen him last, had acquired a lively seventeen-year-old French bride.

By contrast with the *Bonhomme Richard* cruise, this outing in *Alliance* was fraught with numerous problems of man-management and morale. The saddest aspect of it was that Henry Lunt, who served as first-lieutenant and whom Jones had always regarded very highly, now demanded his discharge. In a simple, dignified note to Jones he wrote:

> Sir, you have treated me with disrespect all the Late Cruze which Makes My Life Very unhappy when I think of it & that almost all the Time. I have often Said it & will say it still, I would Sooner Go in a Warlik Ship with Capt. Jones than any Man Ever I Saw if I Could be treated with Respect, But I Never Have Been; wich Makes me Very uneasy & Discontent.[13]

Morison rightly holds this up as a perfect example of the fault-finding, nagging and perfectionism on Jones's part which, coupled with his unpredictable temper, made him disliked by so many ship-mates. Fortunately, Jones could also turn on the charm when it suited him; at all events, he managed to mollify Lunt who stayed on with him till the war ended.

Jones's niggling extended from the crew to the ship itself. On past performance we know that he was never satisfied with any ship unless he personally had a hand in her rigging and fitting-out. By the time he got to Lorient he was only too well aware of *Alliance*'s shortcomings. Some of these, such as the distribution of the ballast, were the result of some daft notion of Landais; but others were more fundamental and could only be rectified with the greatest difficulty and at considerable expense. When Jones sent a detailed list to Franklin, he held up his hands in horror, but in the end he sanctioned most of Jones's recommendations, apart from copper-sheathing for the ship's bottom.

At the same time, Franklin was now under great pressure from the new Board of Admiralty to send Jones back to America in *Alliance* with 16,000 stands of muskets procured by Lafayette, together with 120 bales of uniform cloth purchased at Nantes by John Ross for Washington's army. Jones was also to take on board some very important passengers, including Samuel Wharton, a Philadelphia businessman, and two troublesome diplomats, Arthur Lee and Ralph Izard of South Carolina. Jones was aware that Lee was anything but well disposed towards him, but he was determined to be charm personified. When Lee turned up at Lorient with a huge carriage and an even larger baggage train, complete with furniture and servants, all of which he insisted should be loaded aboard ship, Jones quietly pointed out that *Alliance* was a man-o'-war with very little cargo space, and what little there was was already crammed with much-needed arms and supplies for the Continental Army. If Arthur Lee had not been his enemy before this incident, he certainly was from then onwards.

To make matters worse, there were fresh grumblings among the crew who had received neither pay nor prize money for upwards of a year. Franklin eventually scraped together enough cash to give everyone a month's pay. The inordinate delay over prize money was entirely due to Chaumont, who had the money and promised to deposit a hundred thousand livres with his banker at Lorient, but when Jones called there for the cash he was appalled to find that no money had been sent. The truth is that Chaumont was using the money to finance his own rather questionable business deals. The delay also arose partly over the disposal of the two British warships by auction, as the men demanded, rather than an outright sale to the French Navy as was customary. The men were distrustful of this arrangement, and as a consequence not only had to wait for their money but actually received far less than the royal agent had originally offered. By 15 April Bancroft was writing to Jones saying that the month's pay scraped together by Franklin ought to keep the men quiet for the time being, and urged him to put to sea as soon as possible. Jones, however, felt that this was very unsatisfactory, so he set off for Paris to deal with the matter in question.

As a consequence of this decision, *Alliance* did not sail the following week, nor indeed for three months; and then only after a great deal more trouble that was as unpleasant as it was unexpected. Paradoxically, Jones would also have the time of his life.

12. Heights of Glory
1780–81

Not in the clamour of the crowded street,
Not in the shouts and plaudits of the throng,
But in ourselves, are triumph and defeat.
— HENRY WADSWORTH LONGFELLOW, *The Poets*

The six weeks that John Paul Jones spent in Paris were the happiest of his entire life. From the moment he arrived in the French capital and lodged as Bancroft's guest at Passy, he was fêted, lionised and petted by the cream of French society, from King Louis downward. Benjamin Franklin personally conducted the American naval hero to the royal levee at Versailles and the following day Commodore Jones was presented to King Louis by the Prince de Beauveau, captain of the palace guard. Jones has left no record of any conversation with the King and it is likely that Louis merely smiled in his pleasant but rather vacuous manner. Later the King expressed 'his satisfaction at the zeal and courage' which Jones had shown in support of the common cause, and hinted that he intended conferring on him certain tokens of distinction.[1] Marie Antoinette, whom Jones described naïvely in one of his letters as 'a sweet girl', presented him with a seal showing Neptune with the arms of France surmounted by an American eagle, flanked by the French and American flags draping naval guns. According to Fanning, the Queen invited Jones to join her in the royal box at the opera, but as Jones is silent on the matter it may be supposed that this never happened. He was an avid theatregoer and on several successive evenings he was as big an attraction as anything on stage. He had to endure being crowned with victor's laurels amid the plaudits of thousands and he savoured every delicious moment of it. Only when one impresario intended that a crown should descend from the ceiling on to his head, did Jones draw the line. Unabashed, the same theatrical director, dressed in the costume of Comte d'Estaing in *The Siege of Granada*, conducted Jones to his coach. On the streets

205

and boulevards, people stood and cheered as he passed by.

Jones had kept up his masonic connections in America, but now he was invited to join the Lodge of the Nine Sisters, a lodge which, as its name suggests, was the haunt of artists, writers, composers and other devotees of the muses, Voltaire and Franklin being among the members. Jones was formally inducted on 1 May 1780 with a eulogy from Frère de la Dixmerie, its leading orator. Dixmerie was well primed, for as well as extolling Jones's merits as 'pilot, gunner, sailor and captain', he dwelt at length on his literary skills, from his rhythmic prose to his aspiring verse. Even his early experiences as a Shakespearean actor in Jamaica were alluded to – 'You courted Apollo before you enrolled yourself under the flags of Mars' – and he compared Jones with Alexander the Great who 'possessed all the learning of Aristotle and carried the *Iliad* constantly with him'. By way of light relief Dixmerie recited verses which likened Jones's naval exploits to that of a coquette whom one thinks to capture, but instead is captured by her, but he ended on an extravagantly high note: 'We will by no means forget that you combine with your native genius to sing of great deeds a quality indeed even still more rare – that of doing them.'[2] Indeed, not since the time of Raleigh in Elizabethan times had there been such a sailor-poet; and if Sir Walter were the better poet, there can be no doubt that Jones was by far the greater naval genius.

At this lodge meeting Jones was introduced to a fellow-mason, Houdon, who, having previously sculpted the busts of Franklin and Voltaire, now begged the opportunity to execute the commodore's portrait which was exhibited to wide acclaim at the Salon the following year. Jones had originally intended only a flying visit to Paris, and having concluded all that was strictly necessary in the way of business, he planned to return to Lorient on 20 April; but by that time the invitations to balls, levees and banquets were showering upon him. He dined with the Baron de Castille, Count Sarsfield and the Duc de Biron, and made the friendship of Baron Grimm, the German diplomat who described the intrepid Jones in his memoirs:

> This brave corsair who has given so many proofs of the strongest heart and the most distinguished courage is none the less a man of the world, of great intelligence and sweetness. It is a curious thing that he makes many verses characterised by delicate sensibility and grace.[3]

Sensibility may have cut no ice with the Selkirks but it opened many doors – and a great deal more besides – in the easy-going Paris of the early 1780s.

Though now estranged from Madame de Chaumont, Jones found many other ladies only too willing to take her place. He was a welcome, and frequent, guest at the town house of François Genet, deputy to Vergennes at the French foreign office. One of Genet's daughters was Madame de Campan, lady-in-waiting to Marie Antoinette, while his son Edmond-Charles would later become better known as that Citizen Genet which the Girondin ministry sent as their envoy to America in 1792. Commodore Jones, at thirty-two, was just what France desperately needed at that moment, a dashing young hero who had trounced the invincible Royal Navy, something that the combined might of France and Spain had failed to achieve. He was handsome, personable, genteel and refined. In his splendid new uniform, he was a singularly striking figure despite his lack of stature but this was more than balanced by his magnetic personality, his ready wit and good conversation. Although M. Bachaumont, who encountered Jones at a dinner in his honour on 20 May, commented that he had to use an interpreter because he was 'completely incapable' of expressing himself in French, he must have been a quick learner, for others testified to his fluency later on. Perhaps, in such exalted company at that early stage he was not yet confident of his ability to converse with the same articulateness he had in English. In an era when Englishmen spoke French execrably if they spoke it at all, Jones's linguistic accomplishments were regarded as extraordinary. Clearly he took to heart Franklin's sound advice about sleeping with his dictionary. Now, in that heady springtime in Paris, he would have ample opportunity for polishing his *bon mots*. When Commodore, soon to be Chevalier, Jones entered a salon, conversation ceased and the ladies experienced a frisson of excitement. Abigail Adams, wife of the American plenipotentiary and future president, described her first meeting with Jones, in a letter to her sister written some years later:

> From the intrepid character he justly supported in the American Navy, I expected to have seen a rough, stout, warlike Roman – instead of that I should sooner think of wrapping him up in cotton wool, and putting him in my pocket, than sending him to contend with cannon-balls. He is small of stature, well proportioned, soft in his speech, easy

in his address, polite in his manners, vastly civil, understands all the etiquette of a lady's toilette as perfectly as he does the mast, sails and rigging of his ship. Under all this appearance of softness he is bold, enterprising, ambitious and active. He has been here often and dined with us several times; he is said to be a man of gallantry and a favorite amongst the French ladies, whom he is frequently commending for the neatness of their persons, their easy manners and their taste in dress. He knows how often the ladies used the baths, what color best suits a lady's complexion, what cosmetics are most favorable to the skin.[4]

This was a sharp observation. Jones was the ladies' man *par excellence* who made it his business to know everything about them; the conduct of any campaign depended on having the best intelligence of one's objective.

That louche adventurer, the Prince de Nassau-Siegen who had botched the purchase of *L'Indien*, wrote to Jones inviting him to make free with his mistress, Mademoiselle Guimard. At the other extreme, he dined with Madame la Présidente d'Ormoy, France's leading female intellectual, a prolific author of romantic fiction and a prolix correspondent with Rousseau among others. She was wont to hold entertainments at her salon where matrons of her acquaintance dressed in diaphanous white and sang choruses to Madame's own words and music. Jones was invited, with Franklin, to one of these soirées on 18 May at which the ladies, who were neither young nor pretty, sang verses praising his exploits. An embarrassed Jones did not preserve these paeans of praise. As a parting gift he presented Madame d'Ormoy with an inkstand and hoped that she would use it 'to instruct Mankind and support the Dignity and Rights of Human Nature'. She subsequently wrote one of her long letters to another of her pen-friends, Frederick the Great, recommending Jones to the Prussian monarch in fulsome terms. Another of the intelligent ladies who lionised him was Madame de Saint-Julien who fussed over Voltaire like a broody hen. In conversation with this blue-stocking, Jones manfully tried to keep his end up, but that he left something to be desired is evident in her note of 28 May in which she remarked that it was a pity that Jones could not command words as he did action 'since the two go as well together as promises and performances'. Jones was also patronised by Madame Thilorié and her sister Madame de Bonneuil. The fashionable painter Elisabeth

Vigée Lebrun was a frequent visitor at their salons and recorded that she often dined there

> with that celebrated sailor who rendered so many services to the American cause and did so much harm to the English. His reputation had preceded him to Paris, where everyone knew the number of battles in which he had triumphed with his little squadron over the ten-times superior forces of England. Nevertheless I have never met so modest a man. It was impossible to get him to talk about his great deeds, but on all other subjects he willingly talked with a great amount of sense and wit.[5]

More congenial, one suspects, were the aristocratic contacts. Jones renewed his acquaintance with the Duc de Chartres, now the Duc d'Orléans, and his charming Duchesse at the Palais Royal. Above all, there were the royal honours. As protocol demanded that any foreigner on whom a decoration was conferred had to obtain permission from his own government before accepting the honour, and because this permission could not be granted in the short term, Jones did not receive the insignia of the Order of Military Merit direct from the hand of Louis himself at Versailles, but through the post from the minister of marine, Sartine, who wrote to Congress on 30 May on Jones's behalf requesting permission for him to wear it. Due to the exigencies of war, this request was long-delayed and did not come before Congress for consideration until February 1781. Congress obligingly held up the ratification of the Articles of Confederation till 1 March in order to permit Jones to accept the decoration on 27 February, which was expressly forbidden under the terms of these very Articles. Thus the honour, which was uniquely awarded, was uniquely received.

The case containing the breast star and sash of the order arrived at Lorient at the beginning of July 1780 along with a box containing a magnificent gold-hilted sword, a personal gift from King Louis. The handle of the sword was decorated with medallions of Mars and Hercules, and had figures of Neptune on the pommel and Mars and Minerva on the guard plate, the whole extravagantly ornamented with dophins, flags and fleurs-de-lis. Jones, whose classical education was rudimentary, got Genet to identify the figures. This sumptuous presentation weapon, with its Latin inscription from King Louis to the Victor of the Seas, was to become Jones's proudest possession.

After his death his niece, Janette Taylor, sent it to Robert Morris who presented it to Commodore Barry as the ranking officer of the United States Navy at the time and he, in turn, bequeathed it to Richard Dale, one of whose descendants, Edward C. Dale, granted it on permanent loan to the United States Naval Academy where it may be seen to this day in the chapel crypt beside the tomb of its original recipient.

The Order of Military Merit was created by Louis XV as a means of decorating Swiss and other foreign officers in the French service who, being Protestants, were debarred from the orders of Saint-Louis, Saint-Esprit, Saint-Michel and Saint-Lazare. There were three grades, of which Chevalier, to be conferred on Jones, was the lowest though it was on a par with the knighthood of the Bath in Britain. The breast star of the order appears prematurely on Houdon's bust as well as in a miniature which one of Jones's many lady admirers, the Comtesse de Lowendahl, painted before the decoration was actually conferred. Shortly after receiving this order, Jones commissioned a new heraldic seal in which the shield was surmounted by the coronet of a chevalier with a screaming eagle as the crest. The cross of the French decoration was superimposed on the Paul and Jones quarterings, while Neptune as a cherub appeared as supporter.

At the home of the Genet family Jones met the Comtesse de Lowendahl. Charlotte-Marguerite de Bourbon, daughter of Prince Charles de Bourbon Condé, was the wife of General de Brigade le Comte François-Xavier de Lowendahl, son of the Maréchal de Lowendahl. She was twenty-six, beautiful, bewitching and gifted. She captivated Jones by her singing and demonstrated her versatility by painting his miniature portrait. The course of the ensuing flirtation was faithfully charted by Caroline Edes-Herbert, an English-woman whose stepfather was then employed on the delicate task of arranging the exchange of prisoners-of-war, a matter in which Jones took a very close interest. Miss Edes sent gossipy despatches, via Holland, to the London newspapers. One of these columns described

> the famous Paul Jones who sups here often. He is a smart man of thirty-six, speaks but little French, appears to be an extraordinary genius, a poet as well as a hero; a few days ago he wrote some verses extempore, of which I send you a copy. He is greatly admired here, especially by the ladies, who are all wildly in love with him, as he for them, but he

adores Lady —— who has honored him with every mark of politeness and attention.[6]

Aside from the error over Jones's age, this is a pretty fair description of the impression which he made on Parisian society. The eleven lines of verse which Miss Edes reproduced were actually addressed to one of the Genet girls and concluded significantly:

Grateful for praise, spontaneous and unbought,
A generous people's love not meanly sought;
To merit this, and bend the knee to beauty,
Shall be my earliest and latest duty.

Caroline's next despatch to London titillated her British readers still further:

Since my last, Paul Jones drank tea and supped here. If I am in love with him, for love I must die; I have as many rivals as there are ladies, but the most formidable is still Lady —— who possess all his heart. This lady is of high rank and virtue, very sensible, good natured and affable. Besides this, she is possessed of youth, beauty and wit, and every other female accomplishment. He is gone, I suppose, for America. They correspond, and his letters are replete with elegance, sentiment and delicacy. She drew his picture (a striking likeness) and wrote some lines under it, which are much admired, and presented it to him, who, since he received it, is, he says, like a second Narcissus, in love with his own resemblance; to be sure he is the most agreeable sea-wolf one could wish to meet.

When these titbits inevitably bounced back to Paris everyone knew that Lady —— was the Comtesse de Lowendahl, and she was definitely not amused. She had, in fact, been leading on the gallant commodore in the hope of securing an American commission for her husband who was then on half-pay. Her ardour for Jones evaporated abruptly after the Edes revelations. To be sure, as Caroline reported, there had been an exchange of letters, and if she had been privy to the commodore's 'elegance, sentiment and delicacy' we now have only the other side of the correspondence by which to judge the course of the affair. The first note from the Comtesse declared that what had passed between them the previous day was 'nothing but badinage' and she could not respond to his sentiments, flattered as she was by them, *'sans tromper un galant homme avec lequel je vis'* – in other words, without deceiving her husband. We may surmise the nature of the proposition that Jones had made her the day before and her immediate reply; but Jones was not the man to take no for an answer.

On his last day in Paris he spent the evening at Versailles with the Comtesse. What transpired on that occasion one can only speculate, but from Nantes on 7 June he wrote glowingly that he was full of Gratitude and Sensibility towards her. She had made him in love with his own picture because she had 'condescended to draw it' (Edes was right on that score). He sent her a cipher so that they could correspond freely in secret, together with a lock of his hair, and would gladly send his heart. Her next letter to him was delivered by her husband the brigadier who came not to demand satisfaction at dawn but to ask Jones's help in finding him a job. In this letter the Comtesse guardedly referred to the cipher which she claimed she had not received, and that the letter must surely have been intended for somebody else. Perhaps Jones's carelessness in addressing it to La Vendahl instead of Lowendahl had some bearing on this. When he replied on 14 July Jones said how honoured he had been by the brigadier's visit, adding that he would be happy to share with him the command of a Franco-American expedition. He told her about the sword from King Louis and begged her to look after it for him till his return to France from America. If she declined a friendly correspondence with him by secret cipher, 'as Friendship has nothing to do with Sex' (a recent discovery by Jones), 'if you please to write me in French I shall be able to Read it'.[7]

The next letter from the Comtesse, dated 5 August, has not survived but some inkling of its tone and content may be gained from Jones's reply, dated 21 September aboard *Ariel*. It is a very cold and stiff performance; he acknowledges her 'very polite' letter but regrets her refusal to be the 'deposite' of his sword, so will keep it himself. He hopes that they may continue to be friends, and to correspond, but the tone of the letter is final. Jones had no illusions: the Comtesse had merely strung him along in the hope of advancing her husband's career. Now that that prospect had receded, she had given Jones the brush-off, no matter how elegantly it might have been worded.

If she had not been so coldly calculating, or indeed so obviously in love with the dashing brigadier, Charlotte-Marguerite might have been to Jones what Lady Hamilton was to Nelson. She had blue blood, charm, elegance and beauty, and if any man deserved a mistress like her it was the gallant John Paul Jones. Sadly, though he had many mistresses, none ever equalled, far less surpassed, the Comtesse de Lowendahl.

Although Jones had more luck with the ladies than his compatriot Robert Burns, he would occasionally suffer the same disappointments and rebuffs when he set his sights too high. During this Paris interlude Jones seems to have been more content with intimate friendships of a more cerebral nature. As well as Mesdames d'Ormoy, Thilorié, Bonneuil and Saint-Julien, Jones corresponded with a Madame Tellisson, a friend of Franklin, to whom he wrote an interesting account of his 'late expedition' from Lorient on 24 July. There was also an exchange of letters with Aglaé de Hunolstein, lady-in-waiting to the Duchesse d'Orléans and a dear friend of Lafayette. This was more in the nature of a business correspondence, Madame being anxious to advance the career of her brother-in-law, the Comte de Vauban, who wished to join Rochambeau's French troops in America. Jones, on the other hand, sought her influence at court in getting a better ship than the one he was then being offered.

The brisk, matter-of-fact tone of Jones's letters to these high-born ladies is markedly at variance with the warmth and passion expressed in a series of letters to a lady who is best known to posterity as Delia, the poetic name which he adopted for the purpose of this postal courtship. She was aristocratic and she was a married woman, qualities that tended to attract rather than repel Jones, and she had the added advantage of being of Scottish Jacobite descent. Born of a family called Nicolson which had settled in the Netherlands in 1693, she had married a Scottish Jacobite expatriate named Count William Murray who added his wife's maiden name to his own. The Murray-Nicolsons had been so long in exile that they wrote English with difficulty, and Delia, Comtesse de Nicolson, habitually addressed her lover in broken and highly idiosyncratic French.

The affair seems to have begun in May 1780 when Jones received an invitation to spend a day and night with the Murray-Nicolsons at their château in Sennonville near Pontoise. If he was unable to make this visit, then they looked forward to seeing him at their town house in the Chaussée d'Antin, the most fashionable residential street in Paris at the time. Jones visited the Comtesse at that house and fell in love with her at first sight. The attraction was mutual, and the affair rapidly progressed with hothouse intensity. Jones endeavoured to find employment for her brother, the Chevalier William Nicolson, who came with her to Lorient that summer when she and Jones spent five days and nights of the tenderest passion in each other's arms at Hennebont on the Blavet, six miles from the naval base. Delia's letters to 'My angel, my adorable Jones' bubble over with passion, to the extent that she was willing to sacrifice everything – position, wealth, even her children – to elope with her lover. She even offered him eighty thousand livres, her personal fortune, to get him out of his problems about paying his crew. The generous Delia told him in one letter: 'I have diamonds and effects of various kinds; I could easily find a sum; command your mistress, it would make her happy. Twenty times in your arms I wished to speak to you of this, but I feared to displease you.'[8] Jones was suitably touched, but would not hear of the Comtesse disposing of her jewels to help him out of his embarrassing predicament.

Delia loved Jones with all her heart, but he was corresponding with the Comtesse de Lowendahl simultaneously and did not give poor Delia his undivided attention. Another undated letter from her complains of having received no letter from him, and she threatens to terminate the correspondence if she does not hear from him by Tuesday. She was about to take Jones's latest heraldic seal, along with a sword-belt she had embroidered for him, to Dr Bancroft to forward to Lorient, but she relented, and wrote again, pouring out her heart to him, declaring that her love was unworthy of his glory. The next letter is even more impassioned and angst-ridden:

> Six posts and no news . . . what am I to think of such cruel forgetfulness; could you be sick, would you have ceased to love me? God! This idea makes me shudder! No, I cannot think you so barbarous, you do not wish my death. I am too sensitive and fearful; the amiable and tender Jones is as faithful lover as valiant warrior and zealous patriot.

The only letter which can be dated accurately is one written 'on the 22nd' in response to one from him on Sunday the 20th, which places them in August 1780. She remarks that his letter to her was spotted with traces of tears, and the sight of these splotches moves her to a torrent of weeping. This was a technique employed by Robert Burns too in his impassioned correspondence with Clarinda (Mrs McLehose); clearly it was the mark of the Man of Feeling to weep

copiously while writing to his lady-love.⁹ In this passionate letter
Delia fervently wishes that 'she would willingly be the lowest
member of your crew'. The nearest thing that Jones got to recipro-
cating the lady's fervour was in a long poem of four eight-line
stanzas which he addressed to her soon after those five days and
nights at Hennebont, as he was on the point of departure for
America. The verses have a more passionate beat and a bolder
imagery, a greater melodic rhythm than his previous performances.
The last verse gives the flavour of the whole:

> Thus when thy warrior, though no god,
> Brings *Freedom's* standard o'er the main;
> Long absent from thy blest abode,
> Casts anchor in *dear France* again;
> O, thou more heavenly, far more kind,
> Than Juno, as thy swain than Jove,
> With what heart's transport, raptured mind,
> Shall *we* approach on wings of love!¹⁰

Among Jones's papers is the draft of an affectionate letter to Delia,
written at Portsmouth, New Hampshire, on Christmas Day 1781;
but his love did not survive an absence of two years. When he
returned to Paris late in 1783 she was still there, more loving and
receptive than ever, living in a modest apartment and apparently a
widow. Her 'adorable Jones' gave her a wide berth, however, no
doubt fearing entrapment by the lively young widow. The last we
hear from her is a poignant, sorrowful note in which she begs him,
'O most amiable and most ungrateful of men, come to your best
friend, who burns with the desire of seeing you. Come, in the name
of Heaven!,¹¹ Finally she appears briefly in the official register of
those who fled from France at the Revolution where she was listed
as *Comtesse de Murray et ses trois enfants, originaires de l'Escaut, et
émigrés*.¹² Her family had, indeed, settled in the region of the Scheldt
estuary. It is comforting to think that this spirited lady who gave her
love so unreservedly that she would have been content to live with
Jones in a cabin, escaped the guillotine.

The Paris interlude came to an abrupt end on 1 June 1780 when
Jones received a brief note from Franklin enclosing a copy of a
despatch from the Congressional Board of Admiralty. This directed
Jones to take *Alliance* to sea immediately, as Washington's army was
desperately short of arms and equipment. He left Paris that very

evening, but tarried at Nantes for over a week, attending masonic functions and a series of balls and dinners in his honour. It seems that the week was one long fête, giving him ample opportunity to direct the complete arsenal of his charm on the ladies. Anecdotes regarding his wit and gallantry in this hectic week are legion. When Mademoiselle de Menou asked him if he had ever been wounded, he replied, 'Never at sea, but I have been hit by arrows that were never discharged by the English!' She thought this so *charmant* that she presented him with a cockade which he vowed he would wear in every battle thereafter. But all good things must come to an end, and by 9 June he was back at Lorient where he was confronted with a mountain of problems.

One of the reasons Jones tarried so long in Paris was that he endlessly importuned Chaumont and Sartine over pay and prize money. Having declined Delia's generous offer of help, he was compelled to return to Lorient empty-handed, much to the anger and disappointment of the ships' crews. Furthermore, he had tried to persuade Franklin, Sartine and Vergennes, the foreign minister, to adopt a more aggressive naval policy. His aim was to repeat the *Bonhomme Richard* expedition on a grander scale, using as his flagship either *Alliance* or the ship-of-the-line *America* which was then under construction in New Hampshire. With a squadron of French frigates under his command and a well-equipped landing force under Brigadier Lowendahl (if the Comtesse repaid the favour), Jones was confident that he could achieve something worth while. When he broached the subject with Sartine, however, he was told that the French Navy was still recovering from its abortive south-coast expedition and, although several ships were available, no men could be spared for this venture. Jones seriously considered crossing to America in *Alliance*, getting command of *America* and returning to France with double crews to man the French frigates lying idle at Brest for want of manpower. Sartine readily assented to this scheme, cynically confident that Jones would get neither *America* nor the necessary crews.

By this time Jones realised the impracticality of shipping the vital arms and stores for Washington aboard *Alliance* and was anxious to take advantage of Moylan's offer of his brig *Luke* as a storeship, but Franklin lacked the cash for the charter, and Jones had to look elsewhere. On 3 June Sartine informed Franklin that he had assigned the corvette *Ariel* to Jones for this purpose. Subsequently Jones acquired *Luke* and a second brig, *Duke of Leinster*, but even they were inadequate for the vast quantity of war *matériel* which was now piling up on the quayside at Lorient, destined for America. Franklin hoped to kill two birds with one stone, easing Jones's desperate situation by assigning to him the fleet of American privateers then in French ports and which were giving him endless headaches; but inevitably the mere mention of the word 'privateer' provoked a storm of protest from the commodore.

One of Jones's earlier proposals was to capture the strategically positioned island of St Helena in the South Atlantic. Now this plan was revived by an anonymous French supporter. For over a century the island had been an important staging post for ships of the East India Company and it would have made an ideal base for American and French privateers in disrupting Britain's lucrative trade with India and the Far East. Foreign Minister Vergennes, on whose desk this proposal landed, regarded it as too preposterous for words, and after a good laugh he filed it away for posterity. The proposal called for a squad of handsome young Americans to be disguised as the wives and daughters of British officials returning from the Indies, together with a number of New England Negroes disguised as Moslem servants. The ship was to anchor in the roadstead at Jamestown with the crew concealed. An officer with a passable English accent was to inform the port officer that the crew had succumbed to an epidemic, but that the ladies were mirculously immune. Now the ladies and their black servants wished to come ashore and set up a temporary hospital. On this pretext the 'women' would disembark with pistols and grenades concealed about their petticoats, while boats containing sick sailors were also lowered and sent ashore. Jones, in the leading boat, would then announce himself in a loud voice and declare: 'You are prisoners of your Anglo-American brothers!' At the dread name of Jones, the English garrison, it was confidently predicted, would lay down their arms. The pretty Yankee boys would meanwhile enter the fort and seize the governor. 'Thus St Helena will be conquered without shedding a drop of blood!' concluded the proposal. Jones never mentions this plan in his papers, so it may be assumed that Vergennes did not bother to tell him about this tribute to his reputation. He would have loved such a quixotic adventure, and was just the man to have pulled it off. Sadly he never got the chance.

The chief problem confronting Jones on his return to Lorient was Landais. When Franklin had refused to reinstate him, the madman had planned to return to America and demand a court-martial. He had gone back to Lorient with the intention of taking a berth on the privateer *Luzerne* owned by Robert Morris, but there he had run into Arthur Lee, chafing at the delay and seething with anger at what he regarded as Jones's intransigence. Now Lee and Landais put their heads together, with the impudent aim of restoring Landais to command of *Alliance*. Lee devised a quasi-legal document asserting that Landais, by virtue of his Congressional commission, was the rightful captain of *Alliance*, and that neither Jones nor Franklin had any right to remove him. This document was backed up by letters from Lee to various cronies in and out of Congress, aimed at discrediting Franklin and Jones whom he detested. During Jones's absence, Lee and Landais got to work on the crew who, having completed the necessary repairs, were now idle. Anxious to return to sea and take valuable prizes, they grumbled while the commodore had a high old time to himself in Paris. While Jones was making love to countesses and sleeping with perfumed courtesans, they had scarcely two sous to rub together for a pint or a quick tumble with the trulls and strumpets who frequented the dockside bistros. When they saw *Serapis* stripped down and dismantled instead of being sold, they suspected a conspiracy between Jones and Chaumont to cheat them out of their rightful prize money. When Landais approached them, with promises to secure their back pay and prize money with the help of Lee, they readily fell in with his plans. Besides, under Landais they knew that they would get home without a scratch; whereas Jones only went in harm's way, deliberately seeking out the enemy. The original *Alliance* crew were hometown boys from the Merrimac valley, with the same outlook and attitudes as *Ranger's* crew. The survivors of *Bonhomme Richard* despised these men, messed separately and had as little to do with them as possible.

On 29 May, the very day that Jones was at Versailles taking a fond farewell of the Comtesse de Lowendahl, Landais sent a petition to Franklin which he himself had drafted, and which was signed by 115 officers and men of *Alliance*. This mutinous document declared that the crew would not sail from Lorient until six months' back pay had been paid, along with all their prize money (including the value of the ships sent into Bergen and subsequently returned to the British), and 'until their legal captain, P. Landais, was restored to them'. Fourteen officers of the ship who had previously deponed that Landais had fired more on *Bonhomme Richard* than on the enemy *Serapis*, now perjured themselves by signing a statement that their captain's conduct during the battle had been irreproachable. Franklin replied robustly to these treacherous missives, advising officers and men to do their duty under Jones and warning them that if they did otherwise they would be condemned as cowards. Franklin wrote separately to Landais advising him not to meddle with the command, and to Jones he sent a warning: 'You are likely to have great trouble. I wish you well through it.'

Unfortunately this warning did not reach Jones until it was too late. Instead of immediately going on board ship and remaining there, Jones lodged ashore at Hennebont (where he and Delia spent their delicious five days together), and on his own admission, only visited *Alliance* once during this period, when he addressed the ship's company, set the record straight regarding pay and prize money and asked for complaints. No one spoke up, and Jones returned to his mistress, convinced that all was well. A couple of days later Landais pulled the stroke which he and Lee had planned so meticulously. The ship's log for 13 June indicates that:

> Capt. Landy came on board, and took command, he said by Order of Congress, his Orders were read to the Officers & People. Capt. Landy Ordered all the Officers that belonged to the Late *Bon Homme Richard*, Capt. Jones, on Shore, and any other Officers that would not Acknowledge him Capt. of the *Alliance*. Capt. Jones' Officers came on Shore. Capt. Jones set out for Paris.[13]

Jones showed a singular lack of judgment, and one can only assume that he was so besotted with Delia that he did not act with his usual promptness in dealing with this matter. Had he gone aboard *Alliance* he would have faced down Landais easily. Even if it had come to blows, Jones was more than a match for the craven braggart and, as we have already seen, was not slow in drawing his blade when the occasion demanded. But instead of forcibly ejecting the imposter from the quarterdeck, Jones set off for Paris to take up the matter with Franklin and Sartine. Both of them completely backed him, but Landais, with Lee at his back, successfully defied them. Lee's travelling carriage and mountain of baggage were stowed away in the hold while Washington's badly needed stores were dumped on the quay.

Jones returned to Lorient on 20 June, only to discover that a few hours earlier *Alliance* had slipped her moorings and moved to the neighbouring harbour of Port Louis. Jones thought that he had Landais in a trap, for the only way the Frenchman could take *Alliance* to sea was by passing through a narrow strait at the entrance to the harbour defended by two forts. Through his friend Thévenard, Jones had orders issued to the port authorities at Port Louis to lay a boom across the mouth of the harbour, with the batteries of both forts trained on *Alliance*. Similar orders were given to three French frigates then in port, and their armed boats manned by over a hundred marines were made ready to board the mutinous vessel. Finally a French gunboat was on hand to protect the boom lest Landais attempt to cut it. At this juncture, Jones – to the astonishment of his French allies and the glee of Landais and Lee – changed his mind, and countermanded the orders to detain *Alliance*. Justifying this *volte face*, Jones wrote to Franklin that he was concerned to avoid bloodshed and the loss of such a fine ship. Besides, if word of such an incident had leaked out, the British would have made immense capital out of it, to the embarrassment of America and France. 'Had I remained silent an hour longer the dreadful work would have been done,' he wrote. 'Your Humanity will I know Justify the part I acted in preventing a scene that would have rendered me miserable for the rest of my life.' Given Landais's previous track-record and the readiness with which his crew had gone along with him in avoiding action, it is extremely unlikely that they would have been foolhardy enough to attempt to break out of such a tight trap. A couple of shots across *Alliance*'s bows from the gunboat guarding the boom ought to have sufficed, while there would have been no difficulty in putting out a cutter in order to serve the arrest warrant issued by Sartine in the name of King Louis which was then on its way from Paris. The truth of the matter is that Jones had no great desire to retake *Alliance* and was glad to see the back of Landais and such a troublesome crew. This is borne out by his next letter to Franklin in which he suggested that he should take over *Serapis* (which King Louis had just purchased) and have her fitted out as an armed transport to take Washington's supplies to America, escorted by *Ariel* under Jones's command. In America *Serapis* could be converted for amphibious operations in the raid he proposed making on Britain.

On 27 June he wrote to Robert Morris, now his chief ally in Congress: 'My humanity would not suffer me to remain a silent witness of Bloodshed between Allied Subjects of France and America.' He maintained that Arthur Lee's deplorable behaviour was motivated by his hatred of 'the Venerable the Wise and Good Franklin . . . Envy itself is Dumb when the Name of Franklin is but mentioned'. On the very same day, however, he wrote in cipher to

Bancroft that the port officers had 'acted rather like Women than Men' and he suspected 'a secret understanding between them and Lee. If Franklin sits still in this matter I shall pronounce him and Bancroft philosophers indeed! I am no Philosopher here but am stung to the core to find that my honest endeavours are not supported.'

Franklin was not at all enthusiastic about the proposal to convert *Serapis* for use as a transport and he added tetchily, 'I am perfectly bewildered by the different schemes to get the goods across. Now you have *Ariel*, for Heaven's sake load her as heavily as she can bear, and sail! I will see to moving the rest.' On 5 July, having studied Jones's reports and read the petulant letter sent in code to Bancroft, the sage and philosopher wrote a studied reproof to the commodore:

> If you had stayed on board where your duty lay, instead of coming to Paris, you would not have lost your ship. Now you blame them [the port officers] as having deserted you in recovering her, though relinquishing to prevent mischief was a voluntary act of your own, for which you have credit

and he added the advice (previously quoted) about giving his officers and friends a little more praise from time to time and a little less criticism.

The boom was removed and Landais took the ship out into the comparative safety of Groix roadstead. Here his near-mutinous crew refused to weigh anchor until they were paid, but fortunately Arthur Lee's agent Schweighauser was promptly summoned and coughed up almost 32,000 livres for 'supplies' but which was used to pay wages and mollify the crew. Franklin later refused to honour Schweighauser's bill so the wily Swiss clapped a lien on the Washington stores still lying on the quay. The arms were eventually seized by the French Revolutionary authorities who purchased the muskets for about 8,000 livres. Schweighauser's heirs, after incurring bills amounting to $12,500 for storage and interest, tried to recover the whole from the American government in 1807, but without success.

Landais eventually set sail with impunity, but his voyage to America was anything but trouble-free. On the first day out he quarrelled violently with Captain Matthew Parke of the Marine Corps who was thrown into the brig for refusing to swear an oath of loyalty to the skipper. Seamen who had formerly served on *Bonhomme Richard* were similarly put in irons and imprisoned in the rat-infested hold when they, too, refused the loyalty oath demanded by their demented captain. Landais gave orders and just as rapidly countermanded them, so that the crew were at sixes and sevens and did not know what they were doing half the time. There were ferocious arguments about fishing on the Grand Banks and slaughtering livestock which had been put aboard for the use of the passengers. Even the Honourable Arthur Lee soon found himself on the wrong side of the mercurial Landais. When Lee complained about the drinking water, Landais told him in no uncertain terms that he could drink from the common scuttlebutt like the sailors, and when Lee helped himself first to roast pig at the wardroom table, Landais threatened him with a carving knife. In the end, on 11 August, the officers and passengers led by Lee ganged up on the captain who was sulking in his cabin and forced him to give up the command to his first-lieutenant, Degge, who was languishing in the brig at the time. Degge, released from close confinement, set a course for Boston, not Philadelphia as ordered, and made landfall on 19 August. On receipt of Landais's unintelligible and incoherent report, the Board of Admiralty ordered John Barry to relieve him. When Landais refused, Barry had to summon three burly marines to drag him, kicking and screaming, out of his cabin and put him ashore. At the subsequent court-martial even Arthur Lee was compelled to testify that Landais was insane. The court found Landais guilty of resuming command of the ship without Franklin's permission and of allowing private goods to be shipped in place of public stores. He was deemed to be incapable of handling a ship and his dismissal was accordingly recommended. Congress ratified this decision immediately.

Landais published at Boston an extraordinary pamphlet defending his actions but anyone who took the trouble to read this gibberish would have concurred with the findings of the court-martial. Landais was now ridiculed and deserted by all his former friends – all, that is, except Sam Adams who wrote to Richard Henry Lee stoutly defending the demented Frenchman as 'a martyr to Republican Virtue, victim of a Faction on the other side of the Atlantick' and urged Congress to vote back pay and prize money to this unfortunate fellow, rather than to 'this Jones' or other officers who had served the country so well. Landais eventually returned to France where he obtained admiral's command in the Revolutionary Navy. On retiring in 1793 he went back to the United States and, with the help of Congressman Joseph B. Varnum, last survivor of the Adams-Lee faction, in 1810 he obtained a Congressional grant of $4,000 for the prize money he might have had from *Betsey* and *Union* had the Danish authorities not sent these ships back to Britain. Though disgruntled that the award was so paltry, Landais used it to purchase a modest annuity on which he lived in New York until his death in June 1818 at the age of eighty-seven.

Meanwhile, back at Lorient, Jones had to be content with the 435-ton corvette *Ariel*, built for the Royal Navy in 1777 and captured by the French frigate *Amazone* off the Carolinas. Sartine lent the ship to Franklin expressly for the purpose of getting Washington's long-delayed stores across, and the good doctor hoped that she would be loaded up and away as soon as possible; but four months elapsed before she eventually weighed anchor. The nucleus of her crew were those officers and men from *Bonhomme Richard* whom Landais had so peremptorily put ashore. The rest were Americans whom Jones recruited or poached away from Alexander Gillon, as well as the usual complement of Englishmen enticed out of their prison camp. A detachment of French marines also came aboard. Henry Lunt was first-lieutenant and Master Stacey next in command. Jones arrived from Paris on 20 June and assumed command. The vast quantity of stores, which included 11,000 muskets, 10,000 uniforms, 120 bales of cloth and 800 barrels of gunpowder, weighed three hundred tons, and stowing away that quantity in a ship the size of *Ariel* meant that she had to be completely rerigged and her armament drastically reduced. Ten of her twenty-six 9-pounders were removed and her crew, normally 150, scaled down to eighty. More seriously, she carried provisions for only two months, but even when essential stores were pared down to such a risky level it was found that she could take only two-thirds of the cargo. To minimise further delays Franklin eventually chartered the merchant brigs *Luke* and *Duke of Leinster*, but even so, a considerable quantity of much-needed muskets had to be left behind.

By 18 July the ship was rerigged to Jones's satisfaction and the loading of stores began. Ten days later Franklin, assuming that the ship was on the point of departure, sent his reports for Congress to Lorient in the care of the Comte de Vauban who was to take passage to America. According to the logbook the weather was set fair for weeks on end, but August came and went, and still *Ariel* remained at Lorient. Jones blamed the further delay on contrary winds, though the log reveals that the wind was from the east for much of the time, ideal conditions for a transatlantic crossing. It seems probable that Jones delayed as long as he dared because he did not wish to leave

France until the great amphibious operation had been set in train, as his impassioned pleas to Vergennes and Prime Minister Maurepas on 2 August reveal. A week later he wrote to Genet saying that he was ready to sail, but would not depart until he knew which Parisian bankers he could draw upon in America for the prize money which Chaumont was still holding back. He also expressed uneasiness at not hearing from 'my fair Friend Lady Lowendahl', though on 22 August Delia sent him the passionate letter in which she told him that she wished she could come along as a crew-member. By 25 August the ship was ready, but still Jones tarried at Lorient. A week later the log records that the crew were busy decorating the quarterdeck for 'a Grand Entertainment' and sixteen cases of wine were brought on board. The following evening the festivities commenced with a salute from 'Great Guns and small arms'.

This entry was followed by the intriguing statement: 'The Capt. Kicked Mr. Fanning, Midshipman, and Ordered him below'. This was the incident to which Fanning referred at great length in his *Narrative*. Fanning took his revenge by inventing a number of untruths and anecdotes which are either contrary to the known facts or otherwise unsupportable. For example, according to Fanning, Jones abused a marine officer named Sullivan, both ashore and afloat. As this fine officer was the nephew of General John Sullivan who remained on the most cordial terms with Jones, and as the incident is mentioned by no other contemporary, it must be concluded that, like many of Fanning's other allegations, this never happened. Fanning described the farewell entertainment at Lorient as an extravagant affair, with expensive silk awnings, 'indecent' French paintings, hired plate worth £2,200, a dinner of several courses prepared by a French chef, a lavish outlay on wines and a French lady 'gallanted aboard by Captain Jones the evening before' to supervise the decorations. According to Fanning the occasion was graced by a prince of the royal house, three admirals and 'more ladies of the first quality'. The banquet began at three-thirty in the afternoon and continued till sunset, when fireworks and gunfire commenced. At midnight the guests were put ashore and Jones and his officers gallantly convoyed them home. Fanning does not explain at which point in the jollifications he was kicked, or why Jones had to take such extreme measures.

Fanning is probably more credible when he gossips about his captain's extracurricular activities ashore. In particular he describes how Jones flirted with Moylan's pretty young bride and was caught 'in a very loving position' by her husband. Later on, Jones gave strict orders that after Moylan came out to the ship on business with the purser, no boat was to leave the ship till he, the captain, returned. By eight in the evening Moylan was getting restless but the officer on deck punctiliously obeyed Jones's orders while the other officers plied him so liberally with wine that he had to be put to bed on board ship for the night. In this manner Jones managed to have an uninterrupted night of bliss with young Mrs Moylan. Fanning also relished the story of a jape played by himself and two other midshipmen. One evening Jones escorted 'a lady of pleasure' to the theatre and retired with her during the interval to 'a house of assignation' where he left behind his gold watch. A midshipman assigned to the same room later on discovered and recognised the watch and then, in concert with two other young devils, pawned it at a coffeehouse for a dozen bottles of the best vintage claret, and sent the pawn-ticket anonymously to their bemused captain.

Ariel weighed anchor on 5 September and moved to Groix roadstead where she stayed for more than a month, until a succession of westerly gales abated. On Saturday, 7 October, she finally put to sea in 'fine pleasant weather', wind north-north-west, in company of the brigs *Luke* and *Duke of Leinster*. The following day, before *Ariel* was clear of the coast, the wind backed to west-south-west, then south by west and gathered momentum at a terrifying rate. This provoked Jones's solitary description of 'the awful Majesty of Tempest', which speaks volumes for the frightful spectacle. 'The tremendous scene that Nature then presented . . . surpassed the reach even of Poetic fancy and the pencil'. Under close-reefed sails and with gunports and hatches battened down tightly, Jones attempted to round the dreaded Penmarch peninsula. When *Ariel* was only three miles off the rocks the storm rose with such violence that all sail was taken down, except a double-reefed foresail. Jones tried desperately to keep his ship from being blown on to the reef, but the overloaded ship was taking in water badly and one of the chain-pumps seized up. He tried to bring the ship head on to the wind by dropping the bower anchor, but to no avail. At 2 a.m. on 10 October, in a bid to reduce the amount of sail to minimise the effects of the gale, he took the drastic decision of ordering the foremast cut away, and as the step of the mainmast had twisted off in the violent motion of the ship, he ordered the mainmast to be cut away as well. During this tricky operation the chain plates securing the lee shrouds gave way and the mast toppled over the weather bulwarks, bringing down the mizzenmast and a quarter gallery with it.

The ship, now totally dismasted, came head to wind off the reef. Had she struck, *Ariel* would have gone down with all hands. The next two days were the longest of Jones's life, as officers and men alike strove to keep the pumps going while the ship's carpenter rigged a jury mizzenmast. When the wind began to slacken around midnight on 11–12 October the cable was cut and *Ariel* under jury rig limped back to Groix. She reached the roadstead at ten o'clock in the morning, took aboard a pilot and was guided back to Lorient. Fanning says that the French volunteers behaved badly during the crisis, and they now drew up a petition to Sartine alleging that Jones had deceived them 'in the most horrible manner', by refusing to pay them until they had signed on 'for the duration'. They now begged Sartine to free them 'from slavery to the government of a nation which shows no consideration for Frenchmen except when it has absolute need of their help'.[14] Sartine very properly ordered them to toe the line. Putting this episode in perspective, it should be noted that the great storm of October 1780 left scenes of carnage all along the Breton coast, many ships having foundered in these savage gales, with immense loss of life. That Jones succeeded in saving his ship without losing a single man testifies to his skill and courage under immense pressure. Thévenard, in fact, wrote to Sartine, 'The Commodore showed in this gale the same strength that he had exhibited in battle . . . The crew and passengers all credit him with saving the ship.'[15] Even Fanning, not Jones's most ardent fan, was unstinting in his praise for the manner in which the skipper kept the ship off the 'Pin Marks'.

Inevitably the damage sustained during the storm caused further delays spread over two months, during which Jones tried to obtain a better ship, the French frigate *Terpsichore*. He even sent Vauban to Paris to use his influence with the Duc d'Orléans to intercede on his behalf, but Vauban found that the duke was now out of favour with the Court. Jones wrote to Silas Deane, now back in Paris, as well as the Maréchal de Castries, who had superseded Sartine as minister of marine. Even Chevalier William Nicolson, whom Jones had appointed captain of marines aboard *Ariel*, used what influence he had on Jones's behalf but urged him to go to Paris in person. After his experience with Landais, however, Jones decided to stay put. It is doubtful whether his presence in Paris would have had any effect.

Eventually, after prolonged delays and postponements, *Ariel* got under way on 18 December – more than seven months after Franklin had ordered Jones to sea at the earliest opportunity. The brig *Luke* which, being a faster vessel, had got well clear of the coast before the storm struck, had returned to Lorient unscathed, then set sail again without an escort and was promptly captured by the British. Moylan got no compensation from the Congressional Board of Admiralty on the grounds that the loss of the ship was his own fault for not waiting for *Ariel*. That ship, heavily laden with gunpowder and carrying important despatches from Franklin to Congress, could not afford to take any risks, so Jones set a course which took him far to the south in order to avoid the Royal Navy.

The passage across the Atlantic was uneventful until *Ariel* was several hundred miles north-east of the West Indies, when a large sail was sighted. The stranger gave chase and though Jones took evasive action and tried to escape under cover of darkness, dawn found the enemy vessel almost on top of him. As the British ship was obviously faster, Jones had no alternative but to turn and fight. *Ariel* cleared for action but the gunports were kept shut, and Jones hoisted the Union Jack to pass off the ship as a corvette of the Royal Navy (which, indeed, she originally was). When the strange ship ranged up on *Ariel*'s beam and to leeward Jones in his best English accent and quarterdeck manner hailed the vessel and demanded that her captain identify himself and his ship. He replied that he was John Pindar and his ship *Triumph* was a British privateer of twenty guns. Ironically, she had once been the American privateer *Tracy*, owned by Nathaniel Tracy of Newburyport and commanded by John B. Hopkins, son of the erstwhile commodore of the Continental Navy. She had been seized by HMS *Intrepid* and *Cyclops* off Bermuda in September 1780 and fitted out under the Red Ensign by a syndicate of United Empire Loyalists at New York. Jones tried to bluff Pindar into coming aboard *Ariel* so that the ship's papers could be checked, but Pindar demurred. After a few minutes, Jones hoisted the Stars and Stripes, opened his gunports, wore ship across *Triumph*'s stern and engaged the enemy at close range. Pindar was taken completely by surprise and after a ten-minute bombardment struck his colours and called for quarter. Jones ceased fire and his crew gave three cheers, which proved premature for Pindar suddenly clapped on sail and bounded away. Jones pursued *Triumph* but the privateer showed a clean pair of heels. Jones was disgusted at Pindar's 'base and cowardly' trick, but considering that he himself had been pretending to be friendly right up to the moment he opened fire, Pindar cannot be blamed for adopting a similar ploy to make his escape.

This inconclusive action was Jones's last battle under the Stars and Stripes. There was some consolation in knowing that, had he not handled the situation as coolly as he did, the privateer which was faster and more heavily armed would almost certainly have got the better of the action. Not long after this incident Jones was apprised of a plot by a score of *Ariel*'s English volunteers to seize the ship. The would-be mutineers were clapped in irons under marine guard and there was no further trouble. On 18 February 1781 *Ariel* dropped anchor in the harbour of Philadelphia.

Three years and three months had elapsed since John Paul Jones had last seen his adopted country.

13. America Again
1781–83

Home is the sailor, home from the sea.
— ROBERT LOUIS STEVENSON, *Requiem*

In one sense Jones's delay in returning to America was regrettable, because the court-martial of Landais, presided over by John Barry, could only deal with matters arising after Landais retook command of *Alliance*. On the other hand, by the time Jones went ashore at Philadelphia on 18 February 1781, Landais had been disgraced and the Lee-Adams faction which had protected and backed him was discredited. Nevertheless, the day after Jones's arrival, Thomas Bee of South Carolina and Joseph Varnum of Rhode Island proposed and seconded a motion to summon Jones before Congress so that his relationship with Landais could be thoroughly examined. Interestingly, after some debate, Sam Adams moved to postpone further consideration of the motion. Shrewdly, he realised that his friends Lee and Landais were skating on thin ice, and that their assertions would not stand up to such a sharp-tongued eye-witness as Jones. Instead of a public hearing, Congress ordered the Board of Admiralty to interrogate the commodore in private. John Brown, secretary of the Board and an old friend of Jones, gave him a list of forty-seven questions which he was asked to answer in writing.[1] In the meantime, Jones submitted to Congress the decoration and sword awarded by King Louis together with commendations from Franklin, Lafayette, Sartine and others. Congress was suitably impressed and on 27 February, without waiting for his written answers, passed a resolution entertaining 'a high sense of the distinguished bravery and military conduct of John Paul Jones, esq. captain in the navy of the United States, particularly in his victory which was attended with circumstances so brilliant as to excite general applause and admiration'. And Franklin was ordered to 'communicate to His Most Christian Majesty their high satisfaction at Captain Jones having merited the attention and approbation of the King whose offer of adorning Captain Jones with the cross of military merit is highly acceptable to Congress'. A few days later the Chevalier de la Luzerne, the French minister plenipotentiary, invested Jones with the sash and breast badge of the order at a reception attended by members of Congress and the leading citizens of Philadelphia. Jones was extremely proud of this distinction and thereafter liked to be addressed as Chevalier Paul Jones, and got into the habit of signing his name in this manner. The only other officer in the American forces who wore this decoration was General Johan de Kalb, but he had won it for services with the French Army long before he came to America.

Chevalier Jones delivered his written answers to the Board of Admiralty on 21 March; but though this document was supported by numerous affidavits, depositions, letters and other papers, Jones's replies were not always as straight as they might have been. The questions were framed in such a way that he was given immense scope to show off his narrative skills to perfection, and he lost no opportunity to give himself full credit for his successes. Where he was obliged to explain delays or other problems he blamed everything fairly and squarely on Landais or Chaumont. A few rather embarrassing questions, drafted by the Lee faction, were skilfully parried. For example, when asked why *Alliance* did not take advantage of the security of Admiral de Ternay's convoy which left Brest in May 1780, Jones replied that 'the reason already assigned' would suffice, that is to say, the rerigging of the ship and the settlement of the prize money. The real reason, of course, is that Jones was absent in Paris.

In reply to the question 'what induced Landais to sail contrary to Franklin's orders, what passengers did he take and what private property?', Jones stated 'Mr Lee and the rest of his council can best answer why he sailed contrary to *my* orders, as well as the orders of Mr Franklin'. As to the passengers, he began with 'Mr Lee and his two nephews', but he declined to reply as to the private property, knowing full well that this vexed matter had been thoroughly exposed during the Landais court-martial. In answer to the question regarding private property conveyed on *Ariel,* Jones did not hesitate to respond with 'eight or ten small trunks and boxes containing presents to congressmen or purchases made at their request'. Lee's mutterings about jobbery and corruption were effectively silenced when *Ariel* unloaded her stores, including 437 barrels of gunpowder, 146 chests of small arms, and a large quantity of shot, sheet-lead and much-needed medical supplies.

While there was some disappointment that no clothing was carried, it was generally conceded that Jones had done very well in bringing over such a heavy load. Congress was favourably disposed to Jones and Franklin, and even if his answers to the searching questions were not always as candid as they might have been, in the current climate they were more than enough to rebut his enemies' allegations and, indeed, to increase his reputation still further. On 28 March the Board of Admiralty formally reported to Congress that Jones and Franklin had 'made every application and used every effort' to transport the wanted articles promptly, and that the delay was caused wholly by 'the mal conduct of Landais', by bad weather and by lack of cash to charter suitable merchant vessels. Furthermore, it paid tribute to Jones's 'unremitted attention in planning & executing Enterprizes calculated to promote the essential interest of our Glorious Cause', and it recommended that Congress give some 'distinguishing mark of approbation to Captain Jones. On 14 April Congress passed a complimentary resolve praising his 'zeal, prudence and intrepidity . . . bold and successful enterprizes' and his work on behalf of prisoners-of-war, not forgetting 'the officers and men who have faithfully served under him'.

This should have been praise enough, but Jones wrote to Washington, ostensibly to explain the non-arrival of the army clothing, but in effect to canvass the commander-in-chief for his support in securing a suitable command. Jones wished 'to be instrumental to put the naval force that remains on a more useful and honorable footing' – in other words, that Jones be appointed admiral with the task of reorganising the United States Navy and putting new life into it. Washington wrote from his headquarters at Windsor, Connecticut, on 19 May, a warm and friendly letter which must have considerably boosted Jones's ego. Washington said that he had never suspected him of having been responsible for the delay in transport; and if he had, Jones's answers to the Board of Admiralty would have satisfied him completely. And he alluded to Jones's exploits, especially off Flamborough Head and to the honours from King Louis 'which can only be obtained by a long and honorable service, or by the performance of some brilliant action'. Jones meticulously filed this commendation along with the resolve of Congress and other letters; some day they might come in useful in promoting him and, in fact, the more outstanding documents would eventually find themselves appended to the *Mémoire* which he compiled for Louis XVI in 1786.

While his ship lay at anchor in the harbour, Jones and the personal servant he had hired in France lodged at the Indian Queen Tavern, where the bill for them both came to $76.87. Chevalier Jones spent most of his time meeting old friends and cultivating new ones, especially congressmen who might be influential in getting him the command he desired. Hitherto Jones had been punctilious about seeing that his men were paid, even to the extent of advancing them cash from his own pocket; but on this occasion the crew of *Ariel* were badly let down. On 19 May the Board itself drew his attention to the fact that the officers were demanding their pay which the Board could not settle without the official payroll. When no response to this was forthcoming, the Board wrote again to Jones two weeks later demanding that he 'exhibit a complete Pay Roll of the *Ariel*'s Crew with all possible dispatch'. Eventually Jones tore himself away from more congenial matters and provided the necessary roll. Subsequently he handed over the ship to the Chevalier de la Luzerne, as she was only on loan from the French Navy. Under the Chevalier de Capellis, and with a French crew, *Ariel* sailed back to France. Her marines, however, were seconded to the squadron of Admiral de la Touche at Newport.

Meanwhile the war was now rapidly reaching its climax. Washington and Rochambeau were preparing for the final offensive against the Marquis Cornwallis who was about to make his last stand at Yorktown in Virginia. At the same time, the French fleet under Admiral de Grasse would shortly gain complete control over the Atlantic seaboard. While the land campaign enabled American forces to play a vital role, the naval operations in the closing phase of the war were entirely conducted by the French. Neither Jones nor what was left of the United States Navy played any part in this campaign. The frigate *Confederacy* surrendered to the Royal Navy on 15 April 1781, the frigate *Deane* under Samuel Nicholson only briefly sallied out of her home port and achieved nothing, while John Barry, in *Alliance*, was employed in the passive role of despatch boat between America and France. A few vessels were on the stocks in various stages of construction, and among them was the ship of the line *America* which had been built in a leisurely fashion over the past four years. Jones cast covetous eyes on this fine vessel which would have made an admirable flagship to go with his grand designs.

When the Board of Admiralty was abolished in June 1781 and replaced by Robert Morris in his role as finance minister, Jones felt increasingly confident of realising his ambition. Morris, officially appointed Agent of the Marine on 7 September, was now the equivalent of the First Lord of the Admiralty in London. He had a formidable and well-deserved reputation as the foremost administrator in the United States, but he was also the owner of a merchant fleet and several privateers and was fully conversant with all aspects of naval matters. Furthermore, since the death of Joseph Hewes in 1779, he was Jones's chief backer in Congress. The appointment of Morris revitalised the Navy, and Congress responded by ordering him to complete *America*, get her launched and fitted out for sea as soon as possible. On 26 June 1781 Congress formally appointed Jones as her commanding officer.

As commander of the largest ship in the Navy he was entitled to flag rank, and would have got it had it not been for the spiteful intervention of James Nicholson. It will be remembered that he was the senior captain in the list of 10 October 1776 and not unreasonably he felt that if Congress were about to appoint a rear-admiral he was the obvious choice on grounds of seniority. But Nicholson had lost the frigate *Virginia* on her maiden voyage and soon afterwards lost *Trumbull* as well. Having discovered that Congress had recommended Jones for promotion to rear-admiral, Nicholson and Captain Thomas Read (who was eighth on the list) joined forces to slander Jones to any congressmen who would give them an ear. As a result, Congress reconsidered the matter and ordered a promotion committee to let Read and Nicholson air their views. Nicholson pleaded eloquently that to promote Jones over the heads of all those captains senior to him would be a grave injustice. In a letter to John Barry, moreover, Nicholson admitted that he had said 'many things pretty severe of the Chevalier's private as well as Public Carrector too odious to mention'.[2] Not content with scuppering Jones's chances of promotion, Nicholson tried to prevent him getting command of *America* by urging the Agent of Marine (whom he referred to disparagingly as 'Bob Morris the Financier') to offer it to each of the five captains now senior to Jones, but Morris rejected this notion. When Morris recommended Jones to Congress the vote of the Congressional committee was unanimous. Nicholson ended his letter to Barry on a petulant note: 'I am convinced he will never get her to sea. It will suit his Vanity & only tend to expose himself and his friends to Congress.' Barry ignored this nasty letter and remained, as he had always been, a true friend to Jones. One of Jones's early biographers drily noted that 'The same cause which defeated the creation of the grade of Admiral in the service at that time has operated ever since – namely, jealousy among the older officers as to whom the rank should first be conferred on.'³ It would not be until 1861, at the commencement of the American Civil War, that David Farragut became America's first rear-admiral.

Jones had to be content with an increase in salary, as the captain of a ship of the line was entitled to $75 a month. Now he concentrated on getting *America* ready for sea, with a view to realising his cherished ambition of a large-scale attack on Britain. On the day of his appointment as captain of *America,* he submitted his accounts to Congress which promptly approved them and sent them to the Treasury for payment. Up to this point Jones had never received a penny of his salary, but now he applied for the money owing to him right back to his appointment as lieutenant in 1775 and as captain from 10 May 1776 to 26 June 1781. The entire sum amounted to £1,400 5s in Pennsylvania currency, equivalent to $3,734. On top of that, however, Congress owed him about $4,000 for expenses incurred in *Alfred* and *Providence*, $5,900 advance pay, bounties and other expenses on behalf of *Ranger*'s crew at Portsmouth, $734.40 paid to the same crew at Nantes, $2,891.33 'sundry disbursements incurred on the *Ranger*', $720.88 spent at the Texel and $3,802.80 in France for Jones's later commands. Against this total of $17,800 he credited Congress with $4,028 advanced by John Langdon and $2,004 in cash received from Jonathan Williams at Nantes. On top of this, he tried to extract an unspecified sum in respect of rations for himself and servants from 7 December 1775, 'having been Considered in Europe as an American Flag officer' – though it is hard to imagine how Jones could claim admiral's privileges when only a lieutenant in the Continental Navy. The impoverished Treasury was unable to settle Jones's accounts but strung him along for several weeks while he hung about Philadelphia hoping to get at least part of his back-pay. It would be eighteen months before the Treasury could pay him and during the interim he was reduced to borrowing four hundred pounds in Philadelphia currency from Robert Morris to settle his tavern bills and travelling expenses. On 9 December 1782 he collected $20,705.27 in respect of his wages and expenses since the inception of the war. Cannily, he handed over most of this to John Ross, one of the Americans he had met in Paris, to invest on his behalf.

Jones must have been immensely bucked by reading in the Philadelphia *Freeman's Journal* of 8 August an epic poem by Philip Freneau, 'On the Memorable Victory obtained by the Gallant

Captain Paul Jones', recounting the battle off Flamborough Head. Among the twenty-one verses there were the ringing lines:

'Twas Jones, brave Jones, to battle led
As bold a crew as ever bled
Upon the sky-surrounded main.

Four days later Jones left Philadelphia with his manservant in a hired phaeton and headed for Portsmouth. As the British were still in control of New York he had to make a wide detour which took him as far as White Plains, New Jersey, on 17 August. On this first leg of his journey he had the congenial company of Robert Morris and a Richard Peters, escorted by a troop of dragoons. At White Plains, then the field headquarters of Washington and Rochambeau, Jones was cordially received by the two generals, although he was somewhat crestfallen when one of Washington's aides drew him aside and suggested that it might be more politic not to wear his French decoration as the New Englanders had a puritan prejudice against crosses and a republican apathy towards royalty. After resting at White Plains for several days Jones and his steward continued on their way, reaching their destination on 31 August. Portsmouth, unlike White Plains, was a town of Anglican and royalist traditions without prejudice against cross or crown, so Chevalier Jones resumed wearing the sash and breast star of his order.

He was still settling in at Portsmouth when news came of the surrender of Cornwallis at Yorktown on 18 October. This virtually brought the war to a close although it was not until 30 November 1782 that preliminary articles of peace were signed, followed by a definitive treaty concluded at Paris in September 1783. Land operations ceased soon after the surrender of Cornwallis, though it was not until November 1783 that the last British troops left New York. Jones himself recorded the jubilation at Porstmouth on news of the British surrender, and how the people of that town began to spend money more liberally. Portsmouth had a hectic social life, with dances that went on till after two in the morning, and Jones, after a brief fling with 'the fair Miss Xxxx' at Philadelphia, soon embarked on fresh affairs. There were fashionable balls every month and weekly dances in between, together with soirées and Sunday services where the ladies vied with each other in the parade of their elegant clothes.

After lodging at the Marquis of Rockingham Tavern for five

weeks, Jones and his servant moved to a fashionable boarding-house kept by the widow of Captain Gregory Purcell. Jones paid ten dollars a week for board and lodging for himself and his steward, his bill for fifty-five weeks coming to $550. Today, this house is the home of the Portsmouth Historical Society, and Jones's bedroom, with his signature scratched on a window-pane, is now a little museum to the naval hero. He resumed his intimate friendship with Colonel John Wendell and General William Whipple and even Colonel John Langdon put aside past differences and welcomed him with open arms. Soon Jones was paying court to the young ladies whom he had met in 1777; every door was open to the dashing Chevalier with his polished European manners and racy descriptions of Paris and Amsterdam. Karl Tornqvist, a Swedish officer in the French fleet which visited Portsmouth in 1782, has left an interesting description of 'Pohl Jones'; Jones had now put on weight from good living and lack of exercise. Characteristically, Tornqvist was surprised to find that Jones was 'far from brutal as report has spread about him', but in fact quiet and mild-mannered in society. 'He has much knowledge of naval affairs, and speaks, contrary to the custom of Englishmen, tolerably good French'. Interestingly, the Swede concluded with the remark that Jones 'does not seem to have been in as great favour with the Americans as has perhaps been supposed'.[4] It seems likely that Tornqvist had heard disparaging remarks about Jones from some of the former officers of *Ranger*, such as Elijah Hall and David Cullam, and perhaps even from Colonel Langdon who was, by that time, discovering what an awkward cuss Jones was to deal with, even if he had forgotten past differences.

The animosity rekindled between them arose over the vexed question of completing the construction of *America* and getting her to sea. Jones railed against Langdon's seeming indifference, but in fairness to the colonel, the chief problem was Congress which, perennially hard up, starved the project of hard cash. Jones was so dismayed when he saw how little progress had been made in four years that he considered applying for leave of absence in order to serve on Lafayette's staff during the closing phase of the Yorktown campaign. Lafayette wrote a charming letter of invitation to Chevalier Jones, but by the time he responded in the affirmative, the British resistance had unexpectedly collapsed. Robert Morris scraped together sufficient money from the Treasury to enable work on *America* to go ahead. While waiting for timber, spars and cordage for the rigging, Jones kept the wrights and carpenters gainfully occupied in carving the elaborate figurehead and the allegorical figures and groups that adorned the quarter galleries and the stern under the windows of the admiral's cabin.

Jones kept himself busy during this period by reading everything he could lay his hands on regarding naval tactics and organisation, all part of his preparations for the day when he would be admiral in fact if not yet in name. Nevertheless, seeing how little progress was being made in the construction of his flagship, he was plunged into despair. In a very revealing letter to his old friend Hector McNeill, he gloomily reviewed the situation:

> In the course of near seven years' service I have continually suggested what has occurred to me as most likely to promote the honor of our marine and render it serviceable to our cause; but my voice has been like a cry in the desert . . . but were I used ever so ill I determine to persevere till my country is free.[5]

And a few months earlier, in a letter requesting his friend to procure for him a guinea's worth of hair powder in Boston, Jones reflected on how little the United States Navy had accomplished since its inception:

> It has upon the whole done nothing for the Cause and less for the Flag. The Public has been put to a great expense, yet the poor Seamen have, almost in every instance, been *Cheated*, while the public has reaped neither honor nor profit; And the whole result . . . only appears to have augmented the purses of the Agents, besides enabling a few of the Actors, perhaps not the first in merit or abilities, to purchase Farms &c.[6]

The Christmas and the New Year festivities lifted Jones out of his sombre mood. To this period belongs his affectionate letter to 'his most lovely Delia' whose concluding paragraph showed that the gallant Chevalier was still the Man of Feeling:

> Providence all good and just has given thee a Soul worthy in all respects to animate nature's fairest Work. I rest therefore sure that *absence* will not diminish but *refine* the pure and spotless Friendship that binds our souls together; and will ever impress each to merit the Affection of the other.[7]

Twenty years later Horatio Nelson was writing to Emma Hamilton in much the same vein.

At this period Jones was carrying on a correspondence with a young lady in Philadelphia, with whom he had been intimate that summer. With commendable economy, he revised his ode to Delia, substituting the line 'In fair Columbia's moors again' for 'Casts anchor in *dear France* again' and making other subtle alterations to suit the present circumstances. After he left Philadelphia he apparently relied on John Brown, Morris's secretary, to keep on the courtship 'by proxy' on his behalf. Unfortunately Jones gives us no clue as to the identity of 'Miss Xxxx' as he habitually refers to her, but he was still discussing his amatory prospects with Brown as late as September 1782. His correspondence is silent on the matter of affairs of the heart in Portsmouth, but given the fact that he spent over a year in that seaport it is probable that he found pleasant diversions there too, even if his first love, the outfitting of a ship, was receiving most of his attention.

For Jones, getting *America* to sea was now a race against time. Although the land campaign was at an end, the war was still in progress at sea. After Grasse had defeated the British in Chesapeake Bay on 13 September 1781, sealing the fate of Cornwallis, the French admiral had returned to the West Indies where he captured St Christopher the following February. He then planned to join forces with the Spanish battle fleet for an attack on Jamaica, but this was foiled by Sir George Rodney in a brilliant action on 12 April 1782. This setback, together with the failure of the Franco-Spanish forces to dislodge the British from Gibraltar, took the heart out of the alliance, and the naval campaign gradually ran out of steam. Nevertheless, British and French squadrons continued to spar with each other in the West Indies until June 1783. To Jones, this closing phase of the naval war seemed ineffectual, and he fretted at having to be a helpless bystander. How he longed to take the fine battleship to sea for one last crack at the British before it was too late.

Even Morris was now aware that the delays in completing the ship were due to Langdon and he wrote repeatedly to the contractor to try and get things moving. Morris also sent Brown to Boston to be nearer to the construction site, but his efforts were continually foiled by James Warren, the dominant personality on the Eastern Navy Board there, a crony of Samuel Adams and Arthur Lee and a bitter enemy of Jones. From time to time Jones and Brown met at Ipswich, away from the suspicious eyes of Langdon. By now work on *America* was nearing completion and Jones set about procuring guns. The nucleus of her armament was the battery of 18-pounders which had been cast for *Bonhomme Richard* and which *Alliance* had brought back from Lorient as ballast. Through Brown's good offices, Jones also acquired a number of 12-pounders and swivel guns. Second-hand cables were scrounged from captured British ships, but even the procurement of something as basic as oil and paint, needed to preserve the newly planed green timbers from rotting, gave Jones endless headaches. In April the timber for the quarterdeck and the forecastle deck and beams was brought down the Piscataqua River. As the job neared completion, however, Jones was beset by a severe cash-flow problem. Thomas Russell, one of Boston's wealthiest businessmen, wrote to him on 1 April saying that he could not cash his cheques drawn on a Philadelphia bank but though 'greatly distressed' he managed to send Jones two hundred Spanish dollars to pay the men. Langdon was then threatening to withdraw the carpenters, and had already diverted many of them to work on his own privateers. At a crucial moment when Jones was gearing himself up to cajole, browbeat or otherwise persuade Langdon to relent, a remittance of $10,000 reached the contractor from Robert Morris. Langdon did not honour his end of the deal, as Jones wrote bitterly to Morris on 15 April saying that Langdon had refused to reinstate the workforce which he had taken off the job. By 8 May only eight men were at work on *America* and Jones in desperation wrote a 'most confidential' letter to Brown, partly in code, denouncing Langdon in measured terms. Apart from wilfully diverting manpower, Langdon was alleged to be charging an exorbitant sum for the 'little barren Clod' where his shipyard was sited on the least convenient part of the river. Furthermore, Jones charged that Langdon had diverted not only workmen but the finest timbers for his own projects. That last charge seems true enough, for *America* lasted only three years.

To compound his difficulties, Jones also got wind of a British plot to raid the Piscataqua and burn *America* on the stocks. To protect the battleship he asked for a guard from New Hampshire but that state refused. In the end he was reduced to paying the few carpenters still at work on the ship overtime to stand guard duty at night. Every third night he himself stood on guard, armed with musket and pistols. The British threat was no idle one, for although land warfare was at a standstill the Royal Navy continued to blockade the coast, and there were numerous reports of unidentified boats with muffled oars operating in the Piscataqua estuary. The only light relief during this anxious period was the gala celebration on board the half-finished *America* on 20 June 1782, the official birthday of the Dauphin, the only son born to Marie Antoinette. Congress decided to make this day a public holiday and directed state governors and field commanders to mark the occasion with universal rejoicing. In Portsmouth, therefore, the jollifications centred on the great ship on the stocks. At dawn on the appointed day the Bourbon lilies were hoisted on the jackstaff and a twenty-one-gun salute was fired from the main battery, to which the cannon of the nearby forts responded. This gunfire was repeated at midday as the signal for the official banquet to start in the town hall. Thirteen toasts were drunk in madeira wine and, at a signal from the cupola of the town hall, *America* fired a salute each time the glasses were raised. As if these repeated salutes from the great guns were not sufficient, Jones kept up a rolling fire from the swivel guns and the ship's musketry. At sunset the ship was gaily decorated with lanterns, and there was a magnificent fireworks display. This went down so well with the townspeople that Jones laid on a similar display of pyrotechnics and gunfire two weeks later for the Fourth of July. His thirty-fifth birthday, two days later, passed unnoticed.

As Langdon continued to drag his heels, and as rumours began to circulate that the project was to be abandoned altogether, Jones made his first approach to a man who would play a major role in the closing phase of his life. Gouverneur Morris was then serving as personal assistant to Robert Morris (no relation) and, as such, had the general superintendence of finance and was effectively deputy head of the Navy Board. On 15 July 1782 Jones wrote to him, begging him to organise a subscription among the patriotic ladies of Philadelphia for the completion of *America*. In return for this favour Jones promised to organise a banquet and ball aboard ship the first time she sailed into Philadelphia. Gouverneur Morris seems to have ignored this plea; doubtless he was too preoccupied at that moment in devising the common currency for the United States, on a decimal system using the terms 'dollar' and 'cent'.

Fate intervened a month later when a French fleet under the Marquis de Vaudreuil put in at Boston and suffered a serious accident. Due to pilot error three ships ran aground in a strong head wind. The flagship *Magnifique* struck a reef near high water and, as the tide ebbed, listed so badly that her back broke. The admiral had plenty of time to evacuate his ship and remove most of her arms and stores. Blame for this mishap fell on the Boston pilot who was dismissed on the spot. Later he obtained shore employment as sexton of a Boston church where boys used to taunt him with the couplet: 'Don't you run *this* ship ashore, like you done the Seventy-four!' The loss of *Magnifique* is recalled to this day in the name of Man-of-War Bar, and in recent years divers have recovered coins and various artefacts from the wreck. But the foundering of *Magnifique* was also the wreck of Jones's ambitions. As the negligence of an American pilot had been responsible for the loss of the French ship of the line, Congress voted on 3 September 1782 to present *America* to His Most Christian Majesty as recompense. Robert Morris broke the news to Jones the following day, and tried to soften the blow by urging him to remain in command of *America* until she was launched and fit to be handed over to Vaudreuil. Ironically, when Jones heard of the sinking of *Magnifique*, he had written immediately to Robert Morris urging him to procure her heavy guns for *America*.

A lesser man would have reacted violently to this crushing disappointment; but Jones was a pragmatist. Bowing to the inevitable, he accepted Morris's dictate as manfully as possible and got on with the task of fitting out the ship for sea. For two more months he redoubled his efforts to get her ready, but it must have been extremely galling to know that, at the end of the day, he would have to hand her over to Vaudreuil. The Marquis detached three ships of the line and a frigate and sent this squadron under his brother, the Comte Rigaud de Vaudreuil, to obtain new spars at Portsmouth. On the way north the French ships ran into the British frigate *Albemarle* commanded by a twenty-three-year-old captain named Horatio Nelson whose star was beginning to rise, just as Paul Jones's was setting. Nelson led the Frenchmen a merry dance over Georges Bank and, by superior seamanship, gave them the slip.

After this diversion the squadron continued on its way to Portsmouth where *America* was about to be launched. Even this operation was not without incident, for a ship of this size had never been constructed on the Rising Castle site before. A ledge of rock ran out into the river, and even allowing for a launching at high tide *America* was in danger of being drawn by the current on to this reef as soon as she hit the water. Jones got over this problem by securing anchors in the river bed and attaching them by cables to the ship's stern and quarters, with a large number of men aboard to take up the slack promptly and warp her clear of the ledge. The first attempt to launch the ship, on 23 October, failed when *America* stuck fast on the slipway. Jones tried again on 5 November and, with the aid of the boats from the French ships and an elaborate arrangement of cables and anchors, he managed to get *America* safely afloat. At the precise moment when high water was reached, Jones from the ship's bow gave the signal to the gang of shipwrights to drive in the wedges that lifted the keel into her cradle. The blocks on which she was built were knocked away from under her keel and the great ship began to slide slowly and majestically down the ways. The intricate network of cables to anchors and bollards controlled her momentum and Jones supervised the entire operation which was carried out with incredible precision. When the mighty battleship came to a halt and was securely moored in the channel, Chevalier Jones formally handed over his would-be flagship to Capitaine de Vaisseau de Macarty-Macteigne, formerly captain of *Magnifique*. A further eight months elapsed, however, before *America* was completely fitted out and ready for sea, but by that time the war was over. Though suitably grateful for this present, the French Navy did not like *America* which, being broader in the beam and shallower than her French counterparts, was not as manoeuvrable. In 1786, at Brest, she was condemned when it was found that her timbers were riddled with dry rot. The report to the ministry of marine concluded that American timber was useless for the construction of warships. In fact, it is obvious that Langdon was culpable in supplying unseasoned timber. *America*, neglected by the French, served no useful purpose. Had she remained as the flagship of the United States Navy, she could have been used by Jones for a goodwill cruise to Europe after the war. Had he got his way, she would also have been employed on an expedition against the Barbary pirates and in his skilful hands would have proved her worth many times over.

Even at this late stage Jones had not given up hope of getting back to sea. Shortly before the preliminary articles of peace were signed, he wrote to Gouverneur Morris: 'An honorable Peace is and always was my first wish. I can take no delight in the effusion of human Blood, but if this war should continue, I wish to have the most active part in it.'[8] And to Robert Morris he later wrote confidentially, 'When the *America* was taken from me I was deprived of my tenth command. Will posterity believe that out of this number the sloop of war *Ranger* was the best I was ever enabled *by my country* to bring into actual service?'[9]

On 7 November 1782 Jones and his manservant hired a phaeton and returned to Philadelphia, a circuitous journey that lasted twenty days and cost him $120 for horses and $102 for board and lodgings along the way. With renewed vigour he canvassed congressmen and friends in search of a new command, and actually came close to securing *L'Indien*. This ship, metamorphosed into *South Carolina* as the flagship of that state's navy under 'Commodore' Alexander Gillon, had gone from Amsterdam to the West Indies, but after an ineffectual cruise had been berthed in Philadelphia and ever since had lain idle at her moorings. Her owner, the Duc de Montmorency, having never seen a penny piece of the money promised by Gillon, had now applied to the French minister at Philadelphia to repossess her. Robert Morris gave serious thought to getting his hands on this fast frigate and placing her, along with the remnant of the Navy, under Jones's command with a view to sending an expeditionary force to Bermuda. The wily Gillon, however, foiled these plans and got the ship to sea under a South Carolina colleague. No sooner was the ship clear of the Delaware Capes than she was intercepted by three British frigates and captured. This was the third time *L'Indien* had been snatched under his nose, and Jones was understandably aggrieved. Almost as long as *America* and with a gross tonnage of 1,430, she was bigger and faster than the American frigates of 1776. Her time in Philadelphia was not entirely wasted, though, for Joshua Humphreys seems to have based his design for *Constitution* and *Constellation* on her.

Now more determined than ever to get back to sea at all costs, Jones offered his services as a volunteer with Vaudreuil's fleet. He was genuinely interested in gaining more experience of big ship action and the opportunity to study fleet evolutions and battle tactics. Some day, he dreamed, the United States would create a navy that was truly worthy of the country, and then it would need the services of an admiral who had not only read everything on the theory of naval tactics and strategy but who also had first-hand experience. His proposal met with the approval of Robert Morris and on 4 December Congress voted that, 'having a high sense of the merit and services of Captain J.P. Jones, and being disposed to favour the zeal manifested by him to acquire improvement in the line of his profession', they recommend him to the favour of the Marquis de Vaudreuil. A few days later Jones left Philadelphia for Boston in fine style, having purchased a sleigh and a team of horses to expedite his journey. Vaudreuil welcomed Jones aboard his eighty-gun flagship *Triomphant* and the Chevalier found a gallant band of like-minded officers in the wardroom. Many of them were senior officers from the recent Yorktown campaign who expected to lead the taskforce invading Jamaica. Jones hoped to be used as a pilot, for he had extensive knowledge of Jamaican waters.

The fleet left Boston on Christmas Eve and after encountering foul weather in the Gulf of Maine squared away for San Juan. To Jones's immense delight, the fleet spent a week off Puerto Rico practising the intricate naval manoeuvres of ships of the line in formation. Vaudreuil successfully evaded the British fleet under Lord Hood and headed south for Puerto Cabello and a rendezvous with another French fleet under d'Estaing and the Spanish Navy under Don Solano. Vaudreuil's fleet, however, failed to take account of the strong westerly current in the Caribbean and ended up on the Spanish Main far to the leeward of the rendezvous. During the three weeks wasted in rectifying this error, the fleet's *Bourgogne* foundered on a reef with the loss of two hundred men. By the time Vaudreuil and several of his ships reached Puerto Cabello in mid-February 1783 neither Solano nor d'Estaing was there, and as no one knew their whereabouts, Vaudreuil decided to wait there. Weeks went by in this unhealthiest of Caribbean ports, during which many officers and men succumbed to putrid fever and the black vomit. Jones himself went down with what he called an intermittent fever, probably an attack of malaria. This illness, however, did not lessen his enjoyment of the cruise, helped by the relative comfort and commodiousness of the cabin which he shared with Lieutenant-General Baron de Vioménil, and the excellent table which the French officers kept. Along with fine wines and good food (which included varied salads cultivated on board) Jones passed the time agreeably with music, card games and above all stimulating conversation. This cruise, in more ways than one, was his finishing school; rubbing shoulders with upwards of a hundred French aristocrats, many of them the élite of His Most Christian Majesty's armed forces, Chevalier Jones studied the fleet and polished his French.

Before Jones had an opportunity to see the big ships in action, however, word reached Puerto Cabello that the definitive treaty of peace had just been signed at Paris. Hostilities in American waters were scheduled to cease on 7 April, and the following day Vaudreuil's fleet sailed for Cap Haitien where Jones was invited to tarry at the governor's palace. After a few days' rest and recuperation, he took passage on a merchantman for Philadelphia, armed with glowing testimonials from Vaudreuil and Vioménil as to 'the wisdom, prudence and courage' he had shown in the course of the five-month cruise.

By the middle of May 1783 Jones was back in Philadelphia where he was ordered to Boston for a task that must have been extremely congenial, presiding over the court-martial of Nicholson and Manley for having lost their ships during the war. Regretfully, his health broke at this juncture and on the advice of Robert Morris and other friends he spent the rest of the summer convalescing at a sanatorium run by the Moravians at Bethlehem, Pennsylvania. After the rigours of daily cold baths he left Bethlehem, fully recovered and ready for a change of direction. After years of delay and disappointment he had no illusions about furthering his naval career in the service of his adopted country. At this point he was ready to leave the sea and buy himself a small estate. The money he had already received from Congress was sufficient for that purpose, and he could look forward to a substantial sum from the prize money arising out of the cruise of *Bonhomme Richard*. These thoughts were already in his mind when he wrote from Puerto Cabello to John Ross on 16 March, proposing to liquidate sufficient of his investments in order to purchase a confiscated Tory estate near Newark, New Jersey, a mere ten miles from New York. To Ross he confided that he now wanted a place of his own, where he could offer his hand 'to some fair daughter of liberty'. This deal fell through, like the one for Fox's Ferry in 1777, but not for want of cash.

About the same time, Jones wrote to a friend in Paris saying that he wished to invest three or four thousand pounds sterling in France. This indicates that, even at this early stage, Jones had a hankering to return to the world's most glittering capital. There the Chevalier, who had acquired a taste for the French high life, might truly feel at home. The more he thought about it, the less appealing was the notion of a New Jersey farm with a Yankee wife, when he could have a fashionable apartment on one of the great boulevards of Paris and court a high-born lady. If Delia had grown impatient and taken another lover, there were plenty of other delectable countesses to choose from.

The immediate problem was how to get to France. To this end he put a proposal to Robert Morris of 'sending a proper person' (himself, of course) 'to Europe in a handsome frigate to display our flag' and study the naval organisation of different countries. It could even be done without a frigate 'though perhaps not with the same dignity'. As an American ambassador of goodwill and professional purpose, Jones was uniquely qualified. This remarkable document seems to have been drafted at Puerto Cabello and reworked over the ensuing months. It is particularly revealing of Jones's personal vanity and ambitions, interwoven with his far-sighted plans for the creation of a United States Navy on a proper footing. This lengthy memorandum was inspired by the fact that Vaudreuil and other senior French officers were in the course of receiving promotion and high honours at the conclusion of the war. Thus the memorandum began:

> It is the custom of nations on the return of peace to honor, promote, and reward such officers as have served through the war with the greatest zeal, prudence, and intrepidity. And since my country has, after an eight years' war, attained the inestimable blessing of peace and the sovereignty of an extensive empire, I presume that (as I have constantly and faithfully served through the Revolution, and at the same time supported it, in a degree, with my purse) I may be allowed to lay my grievances before you, as the head of the marine. I will hope, sir, through you, to meet with redress from Congress. But as any personal honor occupies only a part of my thoughts, I shall introduce in this letter such ideas as occur at present and regard the establishment of our future marine.[10]

He then went on to set out his vision for a future United States Navy. Among his numerous recommendations were the establishment of naval academies aboard ships and at shore stations for the training of officers. He advocated the thorough study of foreign naval systems. Each navy yard should have a school where junior officers could be taught the principles of mathematics and mechanics. While he appreciated that these measures could not be achieved overnight, he drew the attention of Morris and Congress to the sorry state of Holland which had allowed its navy to decline. 'In time of Peace it is necessary to prepare, and be *always prepared* for War by Sea,' he advised. He commented unfavourably on the British system of naval signals which had proved lamentable during the recent conflict, and recommended the adoption of the French system devised by Pavillon, whereby permutations and combinations of flag hoists could produce upwards of sixteen hundred different commands, questions or answers. Jones shrewdly commented on the major shortcoming of the French Navy being its paucity of experienced junior officers. Indeed, the French defeat at the battle of the Saints in April 1782 had begun with the collision of *Zélé* and *Ville de Paris* which arose from an inexperienced ensign having the deck.

This long memorandum was the most clearly thought-out survey of naval matters ever devised by Jones and it shows him at his most perceptive and prophetic. His own advancement may have been the immediate inspiration of the document, but it rapidly moved from the personal and immediate to the general and more philosophic. His recommendations regarding efficient signalling and the establishment of a naval academy would in the long run be proved beneficial; but sixty years would elapse before the Naval Academy at Annapolis was established.

For the moment, Congress was unable or unwilling to fit out a frigate for the goodwill cruise Jones proposed. Nothing daunted, he next proposed to Morris that he be sent to Europe on full pay plus expenses with the intention of recovering the prize money due to officers and men of *Bonhomme Richard*, *Ranger* and *Alliance*. Incredibly, a congressional committee acceded to this proposal on 1 November 1783 when Jones was given the authority to proceed to France to receive all prize money and to take the usual commission allowed to agents. As a safeguard, however, he was required to put up bonds amounting to two hundred thousand dollars for the faithful discharge of this mission. This was done with alacrity by John Ross and his partner James Wilson. Jones also requested flag rank to enhance his prestige but this was refused. He had to be content with his election to the Society of the Cincinnati, the élite body of officers who had served with distinction through the war, and this gave him another decoration to wear alongside his French order.

On 10 November 1783 he boarded the little packet ship *General Washington* bound for Hâvre de Grace. All things considered, everything seemed to be going in his favour. Who but John Paul Jones, Captain United State Navy, could have parleyed a packet of unpaid prize money into a free trip to Paris?

14. Twilight of the Ancien Régime
1783–88

Fair stood the wind for France
When we our sails advance,
Nor now to prove our chance
Longer will tarry.
— MICHAEL DRAYTON, *To the Cambro-Britons*

The ship that bore Jones across the Atlantic was a leaky old tub commanded by Joshua Barney, a comrade-in-arms from the Providence expedition. Later, as captain of the privateer *Hyder Ally*, Barney had retaken *General Washington* from the British who had captured her earlier. Ironically, this ship was one of the few vessels retained by the Navy now that the war was at an end, the more serviceable ships being promptly sold off. What the ship may have lacked in comfort was amply compensated for in the congenial company of an old friend. Every evening, Barney and Jones would pace the quarterdeck together or sit on a hencoop, yarning about the good old days. Barney noted, however, that his friend was 'reserved, and not entirely free from moroseness'.[1] Jones was clearly suffering a depressive reaction as he took stock of his situation. At thirty-six he was in the prime of life and should have had a brilliant future; but the prospects of serving his adopted country seemed dismal, and after the current mission he would probably be on the beach for good.

His long-term frustration as he looked back on what might have been was compounded by his present relative idleness. He did not make a good passenger, and though he never interfered in the running of the ship he was anxious to disembark at the earliest opportunity. As the lumbering ship began to beat up the Channel for the coast of France against a strong headwind, Jones persuaded Barney to put him ashore at the first convenient spot in England. Barney tried to dissuade him, warning him that British opinion was still unfavourable towards a man widely regarded as a traitor and a pirate; but Jones decided to take the risk. He was carrying important papers for John Adams, now the American minister in London, and felt that it was better to get them to Adams as soon as possible, rather than entrust them to a courier from Paris. Assuring his friend that he knew what he was doing and that it was not 'the first time if I have to traverse all England with the bloodhounds upon my track',² Jones went ashore at Cawsand in Plymouth Sound on 1 December 1783. At Plymouth he boarded a post-chaise and arrived at London at nine in the evening on 5 December, departing for Dover at three the following morning. He thus spent under six hours in the metropolis.³ It was not fear of arrest that determined the brevity of this visit, nor was it a sudden desire to see Delia again, as speculated by Lorenz,⁴ but a wish to deal as speedily as possible with the vexed question of the prize money. In fact he was in Paris for several days before Delia learned of his arrival and wrote him a very reproachful note: 'Is it possible that you are then so near me and that I am deprived of the sight of a mortal who has constituted the misery of my life for four years?'⁵ Jones merely endorsed this *cri de coeur* with 'From her apartments in the boulevard' and filed it away in his private papers.

Jones took lodgings with a M. la Chapelle on the Boulevard Montmartre, and here he resided for upwards of three years. At first he had his mail from America directed to him at the Hôtel Valentinois in Passy where Franklin was living; but he never actually stayed there, as Franklin habitually wrote to Jones at Paris. It appears that relations between the two men had now cooled. Although Franklin did what he could to expedite the matter of the prize money Jones nurtured a resentment that Franklin had not done as much as he might in the Landais affair. On 17 December Franklin gave Jones a document granting him authority to solicit and receive money due to the officers and men of any American ships formerly under his command. Armed with this, Jones called upon the Comte de Vergennes and the Maréchal de Castries, respectively foreign minister and minister of marine, and they in turn presented the Chevalier to King Louis on 20 December. Louis conveyed to Jones through Castries a few days later that he would always be ready to promote his interests – a promise of which Jones gently reminded the King when he submitted his *Mémoire* two years later.

Before the year was out, Jones launched into negotiations over the unpaid prize money, but the matter dragged on for two years. The chief bugbear was Chaumont who had collected all the money from the *Bonhomme Richard* cruise but had not released a single sou of it, arguing that the Crown was heavily indebted to him for expenses in fitting out these ships. Round one went to Jones when Castries admitted that whatever Chaumont did was irrelevant to the liability of the French government for seeing that Jones's people got their money. Castries then compelled the reluctant prize agent to hand over all the paperwork connected with the prizes and deposit it with Chardon, the Maître des Requêtes under the Duc de Penthièvre, Grand Admiral of France. By February 1784 Chardon reported to Castries that Chaumont had disposed of the prizes for 456,787 livres (about $91,358), but after deducting his expenses this left only 283,631 livres ($56,726) for distribution among all the officers and men of the squadron, not only belonging to *Richard* and *Alliance* but *Pallas* and *Vengeance* and also, to a certain extent, *Cerf* and the two privateers. Jones objected to this account under two heads. The first was a deduction of four deniers per livre (1.66 per cent) for the Hôtel des Invalides, on the grounds that he could not imagine why any American seaman would ever wish to enter this French home for retired soldiers and sailors. Castries accordingly gave way on that score.

The other objection Jones raised regarded Chaumont's deduction for repairs to *Countess of Scarborough* and *Serapis* at the Texel, and for feeding the British prisoners there. Jones averred that, had he been aware of such likely charges he would have effected temporary repairs and taken the ships into Lorient under jury rig, for he had ample time to do so before the Royal Navy got around to blockading the Dutch coast. As for the British prisoners, he repudiated any charge for their sustenance in view of the fact that they were traded for French, not American, prisoners. Franklin stoutly supported Jones in this matter, and once more Castries gave way after appealing to Vergennes and dragging his heels for several months. In May 1784 Castries told Jones that King Louis had agreed to waive the deduction for repairs and other expenses incurred at the Texel, but a further five months elapsed before Castries, on 23 October, signed the necessary papers on the disposal of the prize money to Jones's satisfaction.

Getting clearance for payment was one thing; getting his hands on the actual cash proved to be another matter altogether. Jones was compelled to spend a second winter in Paris while the business dragged on, and by June 1785 his patience was running out. The official excuse for non-payment was that some assurance be given that Jones would, in fact, pay the money over to the claimants, and as security Castries demanded a bond from the banker Ferdinand Grand. By this time Thomas Jefferson had taken over from Franklin as American minister and he showed his customary energy in grappling with the slippery minister of marine on this score. By the time a warrant for payment had been extracted from Castries, however, the French Treasury was on the verge of bankruptcy. Instead the order for payment was issued to Clonet, Ordonnateur de la Marine at Lorient, so Jones had to retrace his steps to the place where he had had all his troubles with Landais.

If Jones had any premonition about going back to Lorient, this was fully justified when he ran up against a slimy character named Puchilberg, a partner of Arthur Lee's old crony Schweighauser, who produced a letter of attorney from the crew of *Alliance* empowering him to collect their prize money. Until this dispute could be settled, Clonet refused to give a sou to Jones. From Lorient Jones wrote to Jefferson urging him to persuade Castries to issue an order that the whole amount be paid over to him. Castries, however, jumped at the opportunity so readily provided by Puchilberg to stall payment still further. Jones refused to accept this and stuck it out at Lorient until he got satisfaction. In the end Castries gave way, on condition that Jones furnish him with the muster roll of *Alliance*. On 5 September 1785 the Commissaire de la Marine certified that Clonet had paid the whole amount for the *Alliance* crew to Jones in addition to the sum due in respect of *Bonhomme Richard*, which had already been remitted to him the previous month.

Jones returned to Paris in late September, but remained there for ten months before 'this lingering and disagreeable business' as he called it was finally wound up. On 7 July 1786 he submitted his accounts to Jefferson. He had received from the French government 181,039 livres 1s 10d, about $36,208, in gold. From that he deducted his 'ordinary expenses' since his arrival in France in December 1783 amounting to 47,972 livres (about $9,600), together with advances out of his own pocket to members of *Richard*'s crew (about $1,300), a pilot's fee which he had disbursed, together with his own share as commodore of the squadron and captain of *Richard* (about $2,660). The balance of 112,172 livres 2s 4d (about $22,435) he paid into Jefferson's hands. On 5 August Jefferson accepted this as correct, although he disclaimed the authority to make a final settlement, because Congress had not paid his salary since his arrival in France. So Jefferson got out of his own financial embarrassment by sending Congress his IOU instead. Jones's naval biographer Alexander Slidell Mackenzie considered Jones's expenses exorbitant, pointing out that George Washington's expenses throughout the war were less than Jones's for his two years in Paris. But this ignores the fact that Washington lived a spartan life in the field, whereas Jones had to maintain proper standards in the world's most expensive capital. The only grounds for exception in Jones's accounts were the way he deducted his own share of the prize money and his expenses simultaneously, which meant that his share was exempted from a proportion of the expenses. On the other hand, no amount of expenses could compensate Jones for all the trouble which he had to endure in getting the money, as he hinted to John Jay (now minister for foreign affairs) when he reported to him in May 1786.

Very little is known regarding those ten frustrating months when Jones kicked his heels in Paris waiting for the final settlement of his accounts, although it appears that he found ample time to combine business with pleasure. Seeing an opportunity for business, he invested some of his money in luxury goods which he shipped across the Atlantic to his friend John Ross. It will be remembered that Jones had invested the cash received from Congress in 1783 with Ross, but from Paris he wrote to his business partner on 25 August 1785 chiding him:

> I have no favors of yours to acknowledge since that dated in March 1784 inclosing a bill for half a year's dividend on my bank stock. You then promised to send me immediately the remainder of the goods of mine in your hands that were unsold, but you have not performed that promise, although many opportunities have offered directly from Philadelphia to the ports of France. You knew that I was under great embarrassment here for want of those goods . . . Your profession of attachment and friendship for me led me to expect a more delicate attention from you than is commonly to be looked for from one merchant to another. But you are silent, and have not given me the least account of the situation of my bank stock, notwithstanding the important and alarming alteration of that institution by the loss of the charter . . . You may believe that it is my situation alone (and the circumstances of your long and unaccountable silence) that extort from me this letter. My feelings are hurt, and I have been reduced to great difficulties; therefore you must excuse the plain dealing.[6]

Jones entrusted this letter to another friend, Jonathan Nesbitt, who was about to depart from France for Philadelphia. Nesbitt was instructed only to deliver the letter if his preliminary investigation of the situation warranted it, as Jones had no wish to fall out with Ross if it could be avoided. In the end Ross continued to handle Jones's investments, but this was one of the salutary experiences that deterred Jones from embarking on a full-time business career. In this respect he was also advised against it by Robert Morris. It appears that Jones contemplated going to India where it was rumoured vast fortunes were being made. Instead, Morris promised him a share in the lucrative tobacco trade now developing between Virginia and France where the government had a monopoly of retail distribution. All that was required of Jones was that he should purchase a suitable ship.

At this juncture he ran into John Ledyard from Connecticut who had sailed round the world with Captain Cook on his third voyage. Ledyard concocted a scheme for purchasing sea-otter pelts in North America, selling them in China and putting the proceeds into tea, lacquerware, porcelain and silks to be imported into Europe. Ledyard proposed to purchase a vessel of 250 tons, provide a crew of forty-five French seamen with Jones as captain, for a cruise departing about 10 October 1785 and sailing round the Horn to Vancouver and Alaska, thence across the Pacific to China. Jones got the bit between his teeth and argued that two vessels would be better than one. He was confident that he could persuade King Louis to finance at least one, if not both, of the ships. Jones also figured out that the scheme would be more successful if they established a factory on the north-west coast of America where the pelts could be collected and processed prior to shipment. Ledyard, with one of the ships, would spend the summer there, trading beads to the Indians for pelts, while Jones, in the other ship, would try to sell the pelts in China or Japan. He would then return to Alaska for more furs and both ships would proceed to the Far East, trade the furs for Chinese luxury goods and return to France via the Cape of Good Hope. Ledyard calculated that a profit of 1,000 per cent could be made on an operation lasting three or four years.

This scheme was not as quixotic as it sounds, for many traders did exactly as Ledyard suggested, but he and Jones were too late in starting their venture. When Edward Bancroft, Franklin's former secretary, whom they had decided to cut in on the deal, discovered that two English merchantmen had got a head start, their enthusiasm waned; and an inability to secure a suitable ship for anything less than three times what they had budgeted eventually put paid to their plans. Neither King Louis nor the French Navy showed any interest in a co-partnership. In the end Jones delayed further action until he had got the approval of Robert Morris, but that was not forthcoming. As a last resort, he contacted his friend William Carmichael, now American chargé d'affaires at Madrid, to see whether the Spanish government might be interested, but Carmichael's response was very pessimistic. The King of Spain, it seems, regarded the entire western seaboard of America as his territory, and King Louis, as a staunch ally of His Most Catholic Majesty, would not allow any French ship to infringe Spanish rights. Jones came out of the venture with nothing; in fact he was out of pocket for he kept Ledyard for the five months he spent in Paris. In the end he preferred to entrust his money to others and invested heavily in the Bank of North America and a variety of land development companies. He also staked Bancroft to the tune of £1,800 in a hopeless venture to import quercitron bark from America and sell the yellow dye it produced to English textile manufacturers. Likewise he burned his fingers on 'an unfortunate adventure' by importing American goods into Lorient. When he found no takers he instructed M. Lamoureux of that port to sell the unspecified goods at public auction and cut his losses. Whatever his skills as a seaman and naval tactician, Jones seemed to be singularly lacking in business acumen.

Although he gave poor Delia (now a widow) a wide berth, Jones renewed many of his former friendships. The Genet family welcomed him with open arms, and he was an enthusiastic attender of meetings at the Lodge of the Nine Sisters. He was punctilious about attending royal levees and balls, where he never missed the opportunity to remind sundry ministers and high officials of his existence. When Dr John Jeffries crossed the Channel by balloon in January 1785 and was fêted in Paris for his sensational exploit, he recorded that he met 'the celebrated and brave Commodore Paul Jones, from whom I received many compliments on my enterprise, and returned them, he deserving them much more than I'.[7] A month later Jeffries dined with Franklin at Passy and again met 'Commodore Paul Jones who was very attentive, candid, and complimentary to me, and who brought me to Paris in his chariot'.[8]

Although Jones widened the circle of his friends during this period he steered well clear of the Lowendahls; he had no attractive proposition to dangle before the brigadier, and without that he knew full well that Madame la Comtesse would not bestow her favours. But having avoided entanglement with one widow, Jones now become involved with another. The lady to whom he referred habitually as Madame T has been identified as Thérèse Townsend, the widow of an Englishman of whom absolutely nothing is known. Until Julian Boyd edited the papers of Thomas Jefferson[9] even that slender amount of information was unknown, and previous biographers speculated endlessly as to the lady's identity. A fairly obvious choice was Madame Thilorié whom Jones had met during his previous sojourn, but other candidates included Mesdames Tessan, Trusson, Turgot, de la Trémouille and Tellisson. The lastnamed was, in fact, the recipient of a plain, no-nonsense letter in July 1780 but was in no way romantically connected with the Chevalier. Nevertheless this was enough for one biographer, Augustus Buell, to concoct a pretty name for her: Aimée Adèle de Telisson [*sic*] and this was blindly followed by many writers from 1900 onwards, notably Mrs De Koven (1913) and Valentine Thomson (1939).[10]

Where and when precisely this torrid affair began is anyone's guess, but it was well established by the end of 1785. Jones seems to have been attracted to Madame Townsend on hearing it rumoured that she was the illegitimate daughter of Louis XV by a royal lady-in-waiting. Thérèse claimed that her mother had abandoned her at an early age, and that she had been brought up by the Marquise de Marsan who arranged for her to be presented to her alleged cousin Louis XVI after the death of her husband, in the hope that His Majesty would be generous enough to provide her with a pension. In fact, the presentation never took place, and the pension was therefore never forthcoming. This much about the lady is set out in a letter which Jones wrote to Jefferson on 4 September 1787 when Jones was temporarily in New York. He relayed the information that the Marquise de Marsan had recently died, leaving her fair ward utterly destitute. Jones described the lady's royal pedigree and urged Jefferson to have her presented at Court so that an injustice could be put right.

To his credit, Jefferson did his best to fulfil Jones's requests. On immediate receipt of the Chevalier's letter on 14 October 1787 he wrote to the lady herself and enclosed a rather pathetic effusion from Jones which he had sent under cover to Jefferson. Madame replied promptly, saying that she wanted to meet Jefferson as she had a project in which she hoped he would share. Jefferson responded in some alarm, anxious to avoid becoming involved in whatever scheme she had in mind; but the following day she hastened to set his mind at rest. She only wished to travel to London in order to sell some Bank of England stock. As she had no money she wondered whether Jefferson would lend her twenty-five or thirty louis d'or for a month. Jefferson wrote back the same day saying that he was 'infinitely distressed' that he was unable to comply because he, too, was short of funds, and Thérèse replied gracefully with her apologies for having troubled him.

From Jones's correspondence it appears that the affair with Thérèse was intensely passionate while it lasted, and only his precipitate departure for New York in the summer of 1787 interrupted what was rapidly developing into the great love of his life. Interestingly, Jones kept the affair secret, and none of his Parisian friends were aware of it at the time. To all intents and purposes, he moved in the same circle as the Genets, Madame de Bonneuil and her sister Madame de Thilorié. Madame de Bonneuil was the wife of Cyrille de Bonneuil, principal *valet de chambre* to the King's brother, the Comte d'Artois, while her sister was married to Jacques Thilorié, one of the capital's foremost lawyers. Several letters from these couples were preserved among Jones's papers, but they also included an illiterate note from one Angélique, Madame de Bonneuil's maid, which conveys the impression that Jones was either using the girl as an intermediary to get at her mistress or, more probably, was having an affair with Angélique on the side. This much seems clear from the note in which the girl thanks the Chevalier for the nice things he has said about her and begs his portrait, a gift which would complete her happiness. The Bonneuils survived the Revolution, but after the death of her first husband, Madame Thilorié married Jacques Duval d'Esprémenil, and the two of them went to the guillotine during the Terror.

The celebrated painter, Elisabeth Vigée Lebrun, who was intimate with both sisters, often met Jones at their salons and formed the shrewd opinion that the Chevalier was angling to become an admiral in the French Navy. Indeed, he even broached the subject with King Louis himself, and to this end he compiled the memoir which he had translated into excellent French and copied out by a hack named Benoit André. Jones had two copies made and bound in red morocco emblazoned with the royal arms. In each volume copies of his various commendations were included as appendices. One copy was presented to Louis early in 1786 while Jones kept the other, along with the original English draft which has unfortunately vanished as it apparently contained many details which he decided, on reflection, were not worth bringing to the king's attention. Jones even composed a dedicatory poem to his royal patron which, in light of Louis's subsequent fate, now reads ironically:

> Protector of fair Freedom's Rights
> Louis, thy virtues suit a God!
> The good Man in thy praise delights
> And Tyrants Tremble at thy nod!
>
> Thy people's Father, lov'd so well,
> May Time respect! – when thou art gone,
> May each New-Year of Hist'ry tell,
> Thy Sons, with lustre, fill thy Throne.

Although the *Mémoire* purported to be a series of extracts from Jones's journals, it was a well-constructed account of his life from 1775 to 1784. The text reaches its climax when the Chevalier recalls that the King had expressed the highest confidence in him using his presentation sword for the glory of America and the House of Bourbon. He then suggested that the time might soon approach when he might prove himself deserving of this compliment. He was, in effect, offering his services to Louis. The timing seemed propitious, for there was the threat of a renewal of war with Britain; but the scare passed, a fresh treaty was signed by the two powers, and Louis began reducing his Navy instead of expanding it. Once more, Jones was to be denied his hopes of attaining flag rank.

Shortly after he presented this autobiographical work, Jones received settlement in full from Jefferson and there was no good reason for him to tarry in Paris any longer. There was, however, still the matter of the prizes sent into Bergen, and which the Danish government had turned over to the British contrary to the rules of naval warfare. At first Jones tried to negotiate with the Danish minister in Paris but, getting nowhere, he persuaded Jefferson to let him go to Copenhagen to deal direct with the Danish authorities. In the spring of 1787 he set off in that direction but on arrival in Brussels he suddenly changed his mind and decided to return to the United States.

The chief reason for this decision was alleged to be that a bank draft which he was expecting to collect in Brussels had not materialised, leaving him short of funds. The draft was from Bancroft, now back in London, and was supposed to be a dividend on Jones's investment in the dyewood venture. As a trip to New York was much more expensive than an overland journey to Copenhagen, the non-appearance of the bank draft does not seem the likeliest of explanations. The only clue Jones gave for his *volte face* came in a letter to John Jay on 18 July 1787, shortly after he landed in New York, saying that he had returned to America as a result of 'unforeseen circumstances in my private affairs'. He added that as soon as he had sorted out this problem he would take the next ship to Europe and then proceed to Denmark. The only rational explanation for this trip, which took seven weeks going westward and five on the return, is that Jones was concerned about congressional approval of his prize-money account. Certainly this matter, which in fact dragged on through the winter of 1787–88, was the reason for his remaining in New York for several months longer than he had anticipated.

The chief problem was that America was in a transitional state. The constitution of the United States was then in course of being drafted and Congress, sitting at New York since the departure of the British, was about to be replaced by the Federal Convention then meeting at Philadelphia. The several departments of the old Congress, including the Treasury Board, were gradually being wound up, and as a consequence Jones could get no satisfaction. He sweltered through the hot summer of 1787 and shivered in the cold winter that followed, lodging all the while in the humble home of a friend of his family, Robert Hyslop, formerly of Dumfries, who kept a shop at the foot of Dey Street on the East River and lived over his shop. At this time Pierre Landais was living in straitened circumstances over in Brooklyn. One day the disgraced officer happened to see Jones, with his back turned to him, conversing on the sidewalk with a friend. Jones ignored his approach and did not hear Landais cry out, 'I spit in your face' as he spat in the gutter. Landais seized the occasion to circulate reports that his enemy was a coward, but Jones retaliated with a statement, signed by his witness, to contradict the arrogant remarks, and added that he would not lower himself by taking notice of any future words or deeds of Landais.

On 28 September 1787 the Treasury Board, of which Arthur Lee was a member, reported unfavourably to Congress on Jones's accounts. This report was shown to Jones who produced a lengthy response on 4 October, defending the size of his expenses and asserting that he was the only man who could get money out of the French government. What upset him in particular, however, was the Board's 'over-zealous' espousal of Landais – 'that broken and disgraced officer'. The Board's report accused Jones of not preventing deductions from being made in respect of the Texel expenses, when in fact Jones had succeeded in having these deductions waived. The Board's report also made gratuitously insulting comments on Jones's old accounts of 1781, but he dealt with these nasty insinuations one by one and successfully rebutted them. On receipt of Jones's reply a congressional committee, under the chairmanship of Edward Carrington of Virginia, reported favourably on his accounts and Congress accepted them on 11 October 1787. An attempt by Henry Lee Junior, a new scion of that malevolent family, aided and abetted by William Grayson, likewise of Virginia, to have Carrington's motion set aside was rejected.

It has been alleged that Jefferson and Congress treated the officers and men of Bonhomme Richard and Alliance very shabbily and never paid them the money that was owing to them. This is untrue on both counts. Jefferson, to be sure, retained the money collected by Jones and used it to pay his own salary and those of other American officials overseas; but he rendered exact accounts of the money to Congress, and the Treasury Board remitted the full sum of $20,772.55 to its New York paymaster William Edgar, along with the ships' muster rolls showing the exact amount due to each officer and seaman. Edgar duly paid out three-quarters of the cash to those who applied to him for their shares, and on 26 February 1789 returned the balance of $5,274.57 to the Treasury of the new Federal Government. The United States Treasury subsequently disbursed a further $1,374.89 to late applicants, leaving an unclaimed balance of $3,899.68. Half a century later Congress ordered that this sum, with interest, be distributed among the survivors and the heirs of those now dead. The account was finally closed in 1861, eighty-two years after the battle off Flamborough Head.[11]

Although another attempt to have himself promoted to rear-admiral proved abortive, Jones did not go back to Europe empty-handed. Congress, sitting in New York on 16 October 1787, 'resolved unanimously that a medal of gold be struck and presented to the Chevalier John Paul Jones in commemoration of the valor and brilliant services of that officer in command of a squadron of American and French ships under the flag and commission of the United States'. Jefferson was instructed to have it engraved and struck at the Paris Mint, as well as to write a letter to King Louis begging that the Chevalier be allowed 'to embark with one of his fleets of evolution; convinced that he can nowhere else so well acquire that knowledge which may hereafter render him more extensively useful'. No doubt Jones himself had a hand in drafting this instruction, having persuaded Congress that he only wanted to improve his professional knowledge the better to serve his adopted country at some future date.

Just where the idea of the gold medal originated, an honour which was not conferred on any other veteran of the American Revolution (Washington included), no one can say; but it seems very odd, indeed, that Chevalier Jones, before leaving Paris, had actually commissioned a French medallist, Jean-Martin Renaud, to produce preliminary sketches for just such an award. Benoit André is the source of the amusing anecdote that Jones ran up such an enormous bill for this artwork that when he saw Renaud coming along the street he darted up an alley to avoid him. Renaud spotted him ducking out of sight, and when they met the following day he twitted the Chevalier with the question: 'Can you imagine what happened to me yesterday? I frightened the man to whom all England has never given a moment of fear!'[12] Jefferson, however, entrusted the final commission to Augustin Dupré, the foremost medallist of his era, who had previously sculpted medallic portraits of Washington and other leading figures of the American Revolution. Dupré based his profile on the Houdon bust executed seven years previously, whereas Renaud's profile (reproduced in André's volume of 1798) reveals the heavier jowls of the *bon viveur* of 1786–87 as well as the dramatic change in hairstyles since 1780. Both medallists attempted to depict the encounter between *Bonhomme Richard* and *Serapis*; Renaud's version is regarded as technically more accurate and Dupré's as more artistic. Renaud's sketches were engraved for reproduction in André's book of 1798 and also formed the basis for a wax medallion commissioned by Mrs Belches, a Scotswoman, in 1786.

Both sides of the Dupré medal bore Latin texts, the obverse being inscribed JOANNI PAVLO JONES CLASSIS PRAEFECTO. COMITIA AMERICANA (to John Paul Jones, Commander of the Fleet. The American Congress), and the reverse HOSTIVM NAVIBVS CAPTIS AVT FVGATIS. AD ORAM SCOTIAE XXIII. SEPT. M.DCCLXXVIIII. DUPRÉ. F. (the enemy's ships captured or put to flight. At Scotland's shore 23 September 1779. Dupré fecit).

The design was finalised and the medal struck during Jones's absence in Russia, otherwise he would surely have rectified that glaring error that placed Flamborough Head on the coast of Scotland. The original gold medal presented to Jones disappeared after his death, but fortunately numerous copies were struck in silver, copper and Wedgwood stoneware. The original dies were retained by the Paris Mint and were employed for a gold restrike which is now to be seen in the chapel crypt at Annapolis close to Jones's body.

On 25 October 1787 Congress authorised Jefferson to settle with King Christian VII of Denmark the claims for prize ships returned by his government and 'to dispatch the Chevalier J.P. Jones or any other Agent' to Copenhagen to negotiate. The following day Congress instructed its Secretary to communicate this to 'the Chevalier John Paul Jones'. Two days earlier, Jones himself had written to Jefferson saying that he would have embarked on the French packet leaving the following day but for a rumour 'that the English fleet . . . was seen steering to the westward, and that a British squadron is cruising in the North Sea'. As a result, he proposed delaying his departure from New York until he could get a passage aboard an American ship. At this point it seemed as if hostilities were about to break out again between Britain and France. Jefferson had issued warnings to American merchants in France as early as mid-September that war between the two leading naval powers was imminent. In this conflict it was probable that America would remain neutral and therefore its ships would not be prone to seizure by the belligerents. On 11 November Jones took ship, arriving at Dover whence he took the coach to London and conferred with John Adams before setting off for Paris where he arrived on 19 December. His visit to London on this occasion was much more leisurely than it had been four years previously, for he records that he 'passed some days with my friends there and went to Covent Garden Theatre'.

As soon as he was ensconced in his bedroom at the Hôtel de Beauvais in the rue des Vieux Augustins, Jones wrote a peculiar letter to Jefferson, saying that he had important despatches and private letters for the minister; and that he had 'several *strong reasons* for desiring that no person should know' that he was in Paris until he had seen Jefferson and secured his advice on 'the steps I ought to pursue'. He would not leave the hotel, where he had registered incognito, until he had seen Jefferson who, when he called, was 'to ask for the Gentleman just arrived, who is lodged in No. 1'. The 'strong reasons' were of an amatory type, of course. Jones wished to hear from Jefferson how the land lay regarding Thérèse Townsend before venturing out on to the streets where he might be recognised by her, or any other lady of his acquaintance. Jefferson's visit to 'the Gentleman in No. 1' obviously set his mind at rest, for soon he was taking up his passionate affair where he had left off. The other piece of good news which Jefferson imparted was that the Russian ambassador at Versailles wished to know whether the Chevalier Jones would be interested in a commission in the Imperial Russian Navy. Jones was elated at the prospect, but first of all he had to settle the Danish business.

It was on 12 September 1779 that the prize ships taken by Jones's squadron, the letters-of-marque *Betsey* of twenty-two guns and eighty-four men, and *Union* of about the same strength, laden with uniforms and supplies for the British Army in Canada, were sent across the North Sea to Bergen in Norway, then under the Danish crown. Subsequently a smaller prize, *Charming Polly*, taken off the English coast, was also sent into Bergen and suffered the same fate. Jones blamed Landais for this decision, although responsibility actually rested with Chaumont who thought that he had sufficient pull with the French consul there to have the ships disposed off as prizes. At that point in time, however, the Danish authorities were anxious to avoid trouble with Britain and as part of their policy of appeasement promptly surrendered the ships to the British consul, so that the American prize crews were left 'on the beach' to fend for themselves. On being apprised of this high-handed action, Franklin lodged a strong protest with the Danish government. The Danes were keen to settle the matter and offered a lump sum of ten thousand pounds, but the French consul at Bergen reckoned the prizes were worth five times as much, and Franklin, then on the point of departure for America, did not wish to be seen as hastily settling for much less.

This resulted in a stalemate, and it was in order to get the matter settled amicably that Jones was now despatched to Copenhagen via Hamburg, arriving in the Danish capital on 4 March 1788. He travelled in his own comfortable coach, hiring horses and postilions at each stage of the journey. Despite journeying in relative style, however, Jones was frozen stiff and extremely fatigued when he reached his destination, and took to his bed for several days until he had recovered sufficiently to do battle with the Danes. First of all the Chevalier paid his respects to Baron de la Houze, the French minister plenipotentiary, who in turn presented him to Count Bernstorff, the Danish foreign minister. In his report to Jefferson, Jones said that Bernstorff had received him amicably and together they had conversed about the new Federal Constitution of the United States. Bernstorff considered it unwise to make the president commander-in-chief of the Army and Navy, and Jones heartily agreed. A week later Bernstorff presented the Chevalier to King Christian and the royal family who invited him to dine with them at their palace. Later Jones reported to Jefferson that he found the king 'complaisant', the crown prince affable, the princess royal charming and the dowager queen 'civil and attentive'. He was flattered by their attention and had high hopes of settling the question of the prize money at an early date. He had not reckoned on the canny Danes who succeeded in dragging out the dispute with America for eighty years!

He soon discovered that he could not pin down the slippery Bernstorff who smoothly assured him, on 4 April, that the matter would have to be settled in Paris where Jefferson had full powers. To soften the blow King Christian even offered Jones a pension of 1,500 kroner (about $200) per annum, ostensibly to show his esteem for the respect which Jones had shown to the Danish flag during the late war. Jones reluctantly declined since the acceptance of such a pension was expressly forbidden by the Articles of Confederation as well as the new Federal Constitution. At Christmas 1789, however, when he was short of funds, he proposed to draw for the arrears of this pension, presumably by a bill of exchange on King Christian. Before taking this highly questionable step he ascertained that his draft would almost certainly be dishonoured and therefore did nothing further about it. Royal largesse had no value if it were declined at the time it was offered, yet Jones subsequently listed 'arrears of my pension from the King of Denmark' as one of his assets when making his will.

Jones achieved nothing by his month's sojourn in Copenhagen; but then neither did Jefferson back in Paris, or anyone else later on. The United States continued to press its claim periodically, and Denmark to reject it equally emphatically, on the specious grounds that the ships had been seized in the course of a civil war. After Denmark relinquished Norway to Sweden in 1814, the American claim fell between the stools of Danish intransigence and Swedish indifference, yet it was sporadically revived until the outbreak of the Civil War gave the American government far more serious problems to contend with.

After Congress voted $4,000 to Landais in 1810 in respect of the hypothetical value of his share of the Bergen prizes, Jones's heirs decided to follow suit. In 1837 his redoubtable niece Janette Taylor (who had more than her share of her uncle's tenacity) joined forces with a son of Captain Matthew Parke to enter a claim, and eleven years later their persistence was rewarded when Congress generously assumed that the three prizes of 1779 had been worth £50,000 and voted $165,598.37 to be distributed among the officers and men of *Bonhomme Richard* and *Alliance* or to their heirs. Thus the American taxpayer paid for Chaumont's mistake and the Danish disregard for international law. Jones's share amounted to $24,421.78, which was distributed among his ten nephews and nieces; this sum was substantially more than he ever got for his share of *Serapis*, *Countess of Scarborough* and the prizes sent into France.

15. Pavel Ivanovich Jones
1788–89

Valour and Innocence
Have latterly gone hence
To certain death by certain shame attended.
— RUDYARD KIPLING, *The Queen's Men*

If there was now peace in the Atlantic, there were other seas where trouble was brewing and which might offer scope to a naval officer of Jones's considerable talents. One such was the Black Sea, where the tottering Ottoman Empire was in retreat before a rapacious Russia under its dynamic Czarina Catherine II. Born in 1729 the Princess Sophia of Anhalt-Zerbst (an insignificant German principality), she was taken to Russia in 1744 to be affianced to the Grand Duke Peter, the nephew and designated heir of the Empress Elizabeth II. The following year she was accepted into the Orthodox faith and then took the name of Catherine Alexeyevna before marrying the Czarina's nephew at St Petersburg. Feeble-minded and physically sub-normal, Peter was no match for the headstrong girl. Their seventeen-year marriage was a sham, though it did produce a son, Paul (1754). Catherine bided her time, consoling herself with numerous love affairs, but when her husband succeeded his aunt in 1762 she plotted his overthrow and had him strangled. The long reign of Catherine the Great (1762–96) was a turning point in Russian history, especially in her aggressively expansionist foreign policy. In the space of three decades she virtually doubled the size of her European territory, recovering from Poland the western provinces (modern Belarus and Ukraine) and later taking part in the dismemberment of Poland itself. In the Baltic region she annexed Courland, but it was in her drive towards Constantinople that Catherine really made her mark. By the time of her death Russia extended from the Niemen and Dniester in the west to the Black Sea in the south.

In her first Turkish war (1768–74), Rumiantsev's brilliant victories gave Catherine a protectorate over the Tartar khanate of the Crimea and a tenuous toehold on the Black Sea, the ultimate gateway to Constantinople. More importantly, the Treaty of Kuchuk-Kainardji started the Eastern Question by giving Catherine the right to protect the Christian minorities in the Ottoman Empire, a position which she and her successors later exploited shamelessly. In her second Turkish war (1787–91), Catherine absorbed the Crimea as well as the steppe between the Dniester and the Bug. Among her numerous lovers, Grigori Orlov flattered the imperial ambitions of her early years (1762–75), but he was supplanted by Grigori Potemkin whom she later created field-marshal and Prince of Tauride with virtually vice-regal powers over southern Russia. In 1787 Catherine made a triumphal progress down the Dnieper, brilliantly stage-managed by her former lover who erected mock villages on the deserted riverbanks, dressed his servants as khans and princes to offer homage and despatched troupes of jubilant peasants in fancy dress from place to place along the river to sing and dance for their empress. The brilliance of this imperial progress was marred by the fact that when Catherine was within sight of the open sea she found her way barred by the Turks who had clung on to the mouth of the river.

This was an intolerable situation and the removal of the Turks became the principal objective of the war which broke out later that year. This proved to be no easy matter, for the Turks in recent years had strongly fortified Ochakov at the Liman, as the mouth of the estuary was known. Since 1776 Russia had countered this by developing Kherson at the head of the Liman as a military arsenal, with Sevastopol in the Crimea as a naval base and Ekaterinoslav (later Dniepropetrovsk) as a supply depot. All of this owed much to the organising ability of Potemkin who also constructed two formidable fleets based on Kherson and Sevastopol with a combined strength of fifteen ships of the line and twenty-five frigates and smaller vessels. Like everything else that Potemkin tackled, however, the Russian army was ill-equipped and unprepared while the power of the Black Sea fleet was greatly exaggerated. Potemkin, promoted to commander-in-chief on the outbreak of war, would have resigned in a fit of deep depression had Catherine not stiffened his resolve and used her diplomatic network to recruit foreign military advisers, experts and field-commanders. In the war which broke out in August 1787 the Turks had two objectives: the destruction of the Russian battle fleet in the Black Sea and the land operations to recover the southern provinces. The Russian objective was more specific: the capture of Ochakov and the removal of the Turkish naval blockade in the Liman. Naval operations were thus crucial to both sides.

As far back as 1785 Jones had been recommended to Catherine for the role of admiral in the proposed Liman campaign. In Paris he had been befriended by David, Comte de Wemyss. A fellow Scot whose earldom had been forfeited on account of his father's complicity in the Jacobite rebellion of 1745–46, Wemyss had written to a contact at St Petersburg close to the Czarina on 18 February 1785 in glowing terms:

> Since coming to Paris I have made the acquaintance of my compatriot, the celebrated Commodore Paul Jones. Your highness knows that he is a brave and great sailor. More than that, my lord, he is an agreeable man, full of all sorts of attainments. I can see that he does not love the inactive life and, without having actually spoken to him of service, I feel that he would not be averse to it, although he is very well off. If your highness finds it advisable to write of him to the Court of Russia, if there is occasion, I undertake to discuss it with him.[1]

A month later Wemyss wrote to St Petersburg again. By now he had sounded out Jones who, predictably, was extremely enthusiastic at the prospect. In this letter Wemyss commented that 'when America forms her Navy he is sure to be Commander-in-Chief; he is regarded as one of the best of sailors'.[2] Wemyss was sure that if the Czarina offered him 'advantageous terms' Jones 'would prefer the service of Her Imperial Majesty to every other'. But Russia was far from ready for her longed-for showdown with the Turks at that time, so the matter was allowed to lapse.

Two years later, when war broke out, the Russian Navy was in a chaotic state, despite Potemkin's efforts. The Baltic fleet, under the command of the able Scottish admiral Samuel Greig, was gradually being knocked into shape. By contrast, the Black Sea fleet looked good on paper but was in fact a motley assortment of vessels old and new, manned by conscripted serfs, Volga boatmen, Levantine pirates and a ragbag of newly subject nationalities including Poles, Ukrainians, Tartars and Cossacks. The officers were an even odder assortment and, while a few were competent professionals, the majority were adventurers and unscrupulous mercenaries. Having observed the marked improvements being wrought by Greig in the Baltic, backed up by a cadre of senior officers of the Royal Navy who had been laid off since the end of the American war, it was then that the notion of having another Scottish admiral to lick the Black Sea fleet into shape came under active consideration. The Russian minister in Paris, Simolin, was instructed to negotiate for the services of Commodore Jones. Simolin contacted Jefferson at the time when Jones was temporarily back in America. On the very day that Jefferson visited the gentleman in room No. 1 at the Hôtel de Beauvais, he delivered a lecture on the contemporary monarchs of Europe as 'all body and no mind' but reserved judgment in the case of Catherine who had not yet lost her common sense. Though Russia was an unknown quantity, and highly suspect on account of her autocratic régime, Jefferson felt that a spell in the Russian service would give Jones excellent experience for high command, so he gave the proposal his blessing.

His recommendation was endorsed by Baron Grimm, as well as Lewis Littlepage, a Virginian vagabond, quondam aide to John Jay and soldier of fortune in the French and Polish service (the latter earning him the Order of St Stanislas). On 1 February 1788 Simolin himself had a meeting with Jones and immediately informed Catherine that he was interested. The Czarina is said to have greeted the good news with the cry 'Jones will get us to Constantinople!'. Potemkin was less enthusiastic but ordered Simolin to make the necessary arrangements while Jones was on his trip to Copenhagen. When Simolin reported to Potemkin that Jones was 'one of those geniuses whom nature rarely produces', Catherine herself offered the Chevalier the title of 'Captain of the Fleet with the rank of Major-General'. This was, indeed, a step up for Jones and the equivalent of rear-admiral in the navy, but it sounded too military and at his request Catherine subsequently acceded to his wishes. On 4 April (15 April in the western calendar) she ordered Potemkin to change the rank accordingly. Thus it was that Kontradmiral Pavel Ivanovich Jones entered the Imperial Russian service.

Swallowing those much-vaunted principles of liberty and the advancement of human nature for which he had unsheathed his sword in 1775–76, Jones eagerly embraced his new appointment. Even at this late hour he made one last attempt to secure the flag rank which had so far eluded him, and persuaded Jefferson to write to Congress with a view to having him promoted to rear-admiral, retroactive to the battle off Flamborough Head, as a gesture 'to gratify the Empress', but as the United States now had no navy, Congress rejected the proposal. As a Russian rear-admiral his pay was 150 roubles a month (about $145, double what he had received as commander of *America*) but the money was the least of his considerations. Far more important was the opportunity to command a battle fleet in action, even if the scope of operations in a land-locked sea were bound to be rather limited. Long term, of course, he cherished the dream of being the first admiral in the American service, if and when Congress heeded his warning that even in peacetime a strong navy was essential.

Jones's appointment was not greeted with universal approval. Some twenty British officers in the Baltic fleet signed a petition to the Czarina, protesting against the appointment of an illegitimate smuggling, piratical murderer; everything from his supposed illegitimacy to the death of Mungo Maxwell was thrown into this remonstrance, which closed with a threat to resign their commissions *en masse*. Common sense prevailed when Admiral Greig talked the protesters out of sending the document as highly offensive to the Empress. Besides, Jones would be far away in the Black Sea so that there need not arise any grounds for personal conflict.

In mid-April, having received the Czarina's offer through Baron Krudener, the Russian minister to Denmark, Jones set out from Copenhagen for Stockholm and the following day went to Grissle-hamn where he hoped to take the packet-boat across the Gulf of Bothnia; finding it still icebound, he chartered an undecked thirty-foot boat attended by a smaller craft which could be dragged across the ice if need be. Thus he sailed southwards along the Swedish shore, probing the ice floes for a channel across to Finland. By nightfall, however, the boats were back in the latitude of Stockholm and the crewmen were getting restive. Jones drew his pistols and forced them to steer due east and then north-east through the night, he himself navigating by means of a pocket compass by the light of the lantern from his travelling carriage. At dawn they were rewarded by the sight of the Finnish coast, some miles distant across the ice. All that day they sailed up the Gulf of Finland searching for an opening in the ice, but on the following night the smaller boat sank though her crew were saved. After four days and nights in sub-zero temperatures, the boat managed to reach land at Reval (now Tallinn) in Estonia, 'which was regarded as a kind of miracle' as Jones noted laconically.[3]

Here Jones handsomely rewarded the boatmen, purchased provisions for them and hired a pilot for their homeward passage, then he bought horses for his carriage and travelled overland to St Petersburg, arriving on 23 April (4 May in the western calendar). On the same day Catherine wrote jubilantly to Baron Grimm, 'Paul Jones has just arrived here; he has entered my service.' Two days later she wrote to the same correspondent that she had seen Jones that day, adding, 'I think he will suit our purpose admirably.' Jones presented her with a copy of the new American Constitution, Catherine having the reputation (in western Europe and America if not elsewhere) of being something of an enlightened liberal, the correspondent of Voltaire, Diderot and the Encyclopedists. Catherine accepted the gift graciously but probably never gave it a second glance, though she commented that 'the American Revolution cannot fail to bring about others and to influence every other government'. Prophetic words indeed. Jones was flattered and delighted with his reception, later admitting:

> I was entirely captivated and put myself into her hands without making any stipulation for my personal advantage. I demanded but one favour, 'that she would never condemn without hearing me'.[4]

The last seems a rather strange request, especially as it was made at their first meeting, but Jones may have had some premonition. In an empire where freedom of speech was a luxury, it was a bold request to make of the Autocrat of All the Russias. A Russian eye-witness to this interview recorded that Jones had 'made a good impression on the Empress, has entrée to the Hermitage, is welcomed everywhere, except among the English who cannot bear him'.[5] The temptation to link the Messalina of the North with the Lothario of the High Seas was far too great for the chapbook writers, who later concocted a great romance between them, thereby – so the scenario went – rousing the jealousy and implacable enmity of Potemkin who thereafter engineered the gallant admiral's downfall and disgrace. Potemkin, who was Catherine's lover from 1771 to 1775, had subsequently seen a steady stream of paramours come and go while he remained her closest confidant. Although the latest of these lovers was the Guards officer Zubov, Catherine was now in her sixtieth year, grossly overweight, with swollen legs and false teeth. To be sure, she still possessed that magnetic charm which had dazzled courtiers for three decades, but Jones sought nothing more than her support and confidence in securing him his Black Sea command at the earliest opportunity.

Admiral Jones remained at St Petersburg only long enough to have some splendid Russian uniforms made, for which Catherine gave him an allowance of two thousand ducats (about $1,000). After a formal leave-taking at Tsarskoe-Selo on 7/18 May, Pavel Ivanovich boarded his travelling carriage and, accompanied by Pavel Dimitrevski, an interpreter supplied by the Grand Chamberlain, he set off on the long journey south. In his luggage Jones carried the Czarina's order to Prince Potemkin appointing him to the rank of rear-admiral and enjoining that he be employed 'in accordance with your best judgment in the Black Sea Fleet'. On 19/30 May Jones reached Ekaterinoslav and was presented to Potemkin who greeted him cordially. The following day Potemkin wrote to Catherine, 'Rear-Admiral Jones has arrived and I sent him to the fleet. He now has his chance to show his experience and courage. I have given him every chance and facility.'

The correspondence of Catherine and Potemkin, it will be noted, was couched in broad terms. Jones, on the other hand, was convinced that he was being despatched to the Black Sea with over-all command, blissfully ignorant of the fact that there were already three rear-admirals there. Therein lay the roots of considerable trouble over the coming months. Accompanied by one of Potemkin's aides, the Chevalier Don José de Ribas, as liaison officer, Jones sailed down the Dnieper to Kherson where he met Rear-Admiral Mordvinov, in charge of the naval arsenal. Here Jones encountered the first unpleasantness, all the more shocking as it was unexpected.

> He did not affect to disguise his displeasure; and though he had orders from the Prince Marshal to communicate to me all the details concerning the force in the Liman, and to put me in command of the silk flag belonging to my rank as rear-admiral, he gave himself not the least trouble to comply therewith.[6]

After this inhospitable reception Jones continued along the north shore of the Liman to the roadstead of Shirokaya where he found his squadron at anchor and presently went aboard his flagship *Vladimir*. More unpleasantness arose when he ran into Brigadier Panaiotti Alexiano whom Jones described as 'a Greek by birth, as ignorant of seamanship as of military affairs, who under an exterior and manners the most gross, concealed infinite cunning'. Alexiano stormed and raved at being superseded by this newcomer, and threatened to resign and take the rest of the officers with him. Jones coolly faced him down and settled in as best he could. The next surprise was that the Flotilla, as the small craft accompanying the Squadron was designated, was under the command of Rear-Admiral the Prince de Nassau-Siegen. Prince Pierre, who last figured in Jones's story when he generously offered Jones the use of his kept woman, at first greeted the newcomer cordially and entertained him for several nights aboard his yacht, but in the end he, too, bared his fangs. Nassau-Siegen had an abysmally poor record afloat. He had sailed round the world with Bougainville, yet never learned how to box the compass. He had directed a French expedition against Jersey but failed to capture his objective and lost his ships in the process. Later he had commanded the floating batteries at the siege of Gibraltar but failed to dent that stronghold's defences. Along the way he had seduced Queen Pomare of Tahiti and married a Polish heiress with a vast fortune which enabled him to campaign in lavish style. Because of his connections with Austria, Holland and France by birth he was regarded highly by Catherine and her ministers, but as a naval commander he was a total liability. Ironically, Nassau-Siegen had come to Russia to enter military service, but no general would have him, which was why he was now relegated to the Flotilla, as yet another of the rear-admirals milling around. All too soon, Jones would discover that he had another Landais on his hands, but infinitely more dangerous because of the immense fire-power at his disposal.

Remembering his disappointing connection with Nassau-Siegen ten years previously, Jones gritted his teeth and determined to make the best of a bad job. With the Spaniard de Ribas, the one officer on whom he could rely, in tow, Jones set out in a small vessel to reconnoitre the Liman and inspect the ships under his command. The estuary was about eight miles wide at its broadest point, but the channel, between mudbanks, was seldom more than two miles across. The average depth was three fathoms, but nowadays it is even less, due to the estuary silting up. The entrance, between Ochakov Point and the narrow spit of Kinburn, was barely two miles wide. On one side sat the Turks, heavily fortified; on the other was Fort Kinburn where the Russian General Suvorov had his headquarters. Suvorov's aim was to keep the channel open, and do everything he could to foil the Turkish attempts to close it. Suvorov, then at the outset of his brilliant career, impressed Jones immensely. The rear-admiral suggested to the young general that a gun battery on the very tip of the Kinburn Peninsula would be most effective in engaging the Turks opposite, and Suvorov had the good sense to defer to him in this. By the time Jones and Don José had returned to the roadstead, the fuss with Alexiano had died down. The Greek himself reported to Potemkin on 29 May/9 June that 'the Squadron has this day been transferred to the command of Rear-Admiral and Chevalier Paul Jones'.

Under Jones's direct command was the Squadron, including the ship of the line *Vladimir*, designed to mount sixty-six guns but in fact carrying only twenty-four 24-pounders and two mortars for lobbing fireballs. The lesser vessels comprised eight frigates and four smaller armed ships. Under Nassau-Siegen, the Flotilla consisted of twenty-five galleys, floating batteries, barges and shallow-draft boats, accompanied by a large number of small craft each mounting a single gun and known locally as Zaporozhye boats, because they were manned by Cossacks from that district on the Dnieper. In the right hands, the Flotilla would have been a formidable weapon, able to manoeuvre in the shallow estuarial waters and, being mainly powered by oars, not so dependent on the vagaries of wind and tide as the larger vessels. As Nassau-Siegen was of the same rank as Jones and took his orders direct from Potemkin, working relations between the Squadron and the Flotilla were not as close as they might have been. With a hostile Greek commodore aboard his flagship and a shore admiral who detested him, Jones already had more than enough to contend with, let alone the rival fleet of Rear-Admiral Voinovich at Sevastopol – and, of course, the Turks.

The enemy had a Black Sea fleet comparable to the Russians' in size and strength, under the able command of Hassan el Ghazi, known as the Capudan Pasha (Lord Captain). Jones had a healthy respect for Hassan whom he considered a brave man and a very professional seaman. On one occasion he got close enough in action to observe that the Pasha sported an enormous moustache. Hassan's battle fleet was larger than Jones's Squadron, but the Flotilla was more numerous and better armed than the small craft accompanying the Turkish fleet.

The Russian strategy was very simple. The Navy was expected to keep the Turkish fleet at bay long enough for the Army to come up on the landward side of Ochakov. In view of the relative size, draft and armaments of the Russian and Turkish ships, Jones devised the sound plan of deploying both the Squadron and the Flotilla in a line across the Liman about halfway between its entrance and the mouth of the River Bug, thus giving cover to the Army in its advance from Kherson. Jones held a council of war and got the consent of both Nassau-Siegen and Alexiano to this disposition of their ships. On the night of 5/16 June the vessels moved out to take up their positions accordingly, with the Russian fleet drawn up on a NNE-SSW line across the Liman about four miles east of Ochakov. Hassan countered by sending a detachment of his flotilla inside the entrance. The first shots in the First Battle of the Liman were fired around two o'clock the following morning when Nassau-Siegen tried to cut off the Turkish retreat but met with such stiff resistance that he was chased back to the Squadron. Jones, turning this to his advantage and anticipating that the Turks would take the offensive, got Nassau's and Alexiano's consent to form two reserves, one of eleven craft at the right of the line and the other of six craft in the centre, with fifteen Zaporozhye boats in the rear, ready to support whichever group needed help.

The Capudan Pasha fell into the trap and committed virtually the whole of his flotilla as well as part of his battle squadron. During the night of 6/17 June he drew up his small craft in two formations close to the north shore and, with a north-westerly breeze at his back, attacked Jones's right flank the following morning. As the Russian fleet had no signals, Jones personally rowed along his front line giving verbal orders to each vessel in turn. He even detailed ships' boats to tow the craft of the Flotilla into position because they were having difficulty in making headway against the wind. Hassan, in his flagship (actually a lateen-rigged galley mounting fourteen guns), led his flotilla reserve and began pounding Nassau-Siegen's vessels. When the wind changed suddenly Jones seized the opportunity to move up the five ships of his left wing to form a wide angle and bring the enemy ships under crossfire. Realising that he was about to be caught in a trap, Hassan prudently withdrew his flotilla, but lost several craft as a result of 'brandcougles', hollow cannon-balls filled with combustible material. These incendiary devices were fired with deadly effect from the mortars and created more havoc and destruction than conventional gunfire.

Jones later wrote up a narrative of the battle in which he took all the credit, not sparing Nassau-Siegen's stupidity and idiotic behaviour in the course of the day. At the time when he drew up his report to the Prince Marshal, however, he formed a more balanced view of events, and actually went out of his way to single out the Prince's coolness and intelligence under fire, and admitted that in this engagement he was little more than Nassau-Siegen's aide. The following day he wrote to Potemkin saying, 'We sang a *Te Deum* in honor of the victory that the Prince de Nassau won yesterday over the Capudan Pasha's Flotilla.'[7] In reply, Potemkin praised Jones for his 'zeal and intrepidity in aiding the Prince de Nassau'; but on 11/22 June Jones wrote to Ribas at Kherson:

> I wish I could tell you that the Prince de Nassau is now as he was before you left; but he has the air of wishing me *au Diable*, for no other reason so far as I know than that I extracted him out of his foul-up and peril in the affair of the 7/18th.[8]

Clearly there is some discrepancy between the tone of Jones's report to Potemkin and his letter to Ribas, not to mention the later narrative. The last may be discounted, because it was written after Nassau-Siegen had got the better of Jones, but it is still difficult to reconcile the other two. The truth is that Jones was less decisive than he might have been during the action. Nassau wrote to his wife on 14/25 June declaring that Jones 'has changed. Good luck has robbed him of that intrepidity which people said he had'. The consensus is that, in writing to Potemkin as he did, Jones was trying to ingratiate himself with his commander-in-chief and as Nassau-Siegen was one of Potemkin's protégés he probably felt that he should be unstinting in his praise, even if privately he considered the Prince a bit of a poltroon. Too late he was heeding the advice given him by Benjamin Franklin; and in this case fulsome praise for an officer who did not really merit it would lead to Jones's undoing.

Jones may not have been fully aware of the Byzantine politicking going on behind the scenes, the network of intrigue, conspiracies and antipathies that surrounded him. He was far from well at this time, having suffered exposure during his epic boat trip from Sweden to Estonia. From his flagship he wrote to his friend Ribas on 13/24 June. Interestingly, it is one of the few partly French documents in Jones's own hand:

> My Dear Friend,
> I am unwell in my turn. Since I wrote you last I have been much indisposed; and from the within Papers, you will see

that I have room enough for vexation. You will doubtless find it necessary to send these Papers to his Altess the prince de Potemkin, to obtain positive Orders to preventing any too hasty Step. Je vous prie de faire mes excuses à son Altesse, de n'avoir pas ecrit depuis l'Onze. Je n'avais rien de nouveau à lui mander, excepte q'on vient de me dire q'on a vu sortir d'Ochacoff un fort detachement de Troupes, qui paraissait monter au Nord. Je vous envoye ce ci par exprès et suis avec un vrai attachement, votre très Obeissant Serviteur et Ami,

Paul Jones

N.B. be so good as to forward my Letter to Little-Page.[9]

The 'too hasty Step' referred to the fact that Nassau-Siegen was now hellbent on advancing from the Liman to engage the Turkish fleet off Ochakov and the mouth of the Beresan. By this time the Prince had augmented the Flotilla to seventy-one vessels, mostly small craft but well armed and manoeuvrable. Such boats were ideal in amphibious assaults and small-boat actions but would have been no match for heavily armed frigates and line battleships. Jones, alarmed at Nassau-Siegen's suicidal impetuosity, wrote him a tactful letter on 14/25 June, delicately asking what he, Jones, had done to upset him, and suggesting joint tactics in the coming battle. Jones could easily have given way, and followed Nassau-Siegen in his foolish venture, for it was his dearest wish to fight a full-scale classic line-to-line battle with the Turks in deep water; prudently he realised that to do so would throw away the superiority of the Russian Flotilla over its Turkish counterpart and risk the destruction of the Russian Squadron at the hands of the more heavily armed and numerically superior Turkish battle-fleet.

Nassau-Siegen, on the other hand, had nothing to lose. If he were beaten, he could always blame someone else. Jones had an international reputation to uphold and he was mindful of the fact that his main task at the Liman was to provide naval cover for Potemkin's land forces. If he gambled and lost his fleet, the way would be open not only for the Turks to reinforce Ochakov but to blockade the Bug and Dnieper. For these reasons, therefore, Jones insisted that the Russian fleet remain inside the Liman and invite rather than offer attack. This strategy was very sound; the Capudan Pasha had withdrawn into the Black Sea after the battle but was anxious to get to grips with the Russians again, and his impetuosity resulted in the Second Battle of the Liman.

On 16/27 June the entire Turkish fleet, with a south-westerly breeze filling their sails, proceeded into the estuary. The Turkish plan was to destroy the Flotilla by gunfire and then burn the Squadron with fireships and incendiary missiles. Jones drew his ships up in much the same position as he had done before. In addition to the battleship *Vladimir*, Jones had the frigates *Aleksandr Nevskii*, *Skoryi*, *Kherson*, *Boristen*, *Taganrog*, *Ptchela*, *Sveti Nikolai* and *Malyi Aleksandr* together with the smaller vessels *Grigori Potemkin*, *Sveti Anna*, *Mailet* and *Bogomater Turlenu*. At midday the Turks were sighted approaching under full sail, an impressive sight. Jones summoned a council of war and addressed his captains in French, concluding with the ringing words: 'I see in your eyes the souls of heroes; and we shall all learn together to conquer or die for the country!' There is something endearingly incongruous about this Scottish-American exhorting in French the patriotism of his Russian subordinates; but the situation was grim enough. The Russian fleet was bottled up with little room for manoeuvre, and opposed by a fleet of twice the size. The sight of all those tall square-riggers and lateen sails bearing down on them must have been bad enough, but the defending ships also had the psychological disadvantage of being on the receiving end of a hideous cacophony of clashing cymbals, shrill trumpets and the cries of the mullahs exhorting the Turks to slaughter the infidels.

Tension was rising among the Russian ships, when suddenly the situation changed. The Pasha's flagship, a sixty-four-gun battleship, ran aground about two in the afternoon little more than a mile from Jones's flagship, and the rest of the Turkish fleet then pulled up short and anchored in disarray. Nassau-Siegen wanted to attack immediately, but Jones held him back, which was fortuitous because the wind veered strongly to the north-west, putting the enemy directly to windward, so that no Russian vessels, under sail or by oars, could have made any headway. With the two fleets at a standstill, Jones took the opportunity that evening to make a close reconnaissance. A fascinating eye-witness account was provided by a Cossack named Ivak who lived to a very old age. When he was a hundred (in 1844) he was interviewed by a senior officer of the Russian Navy who took down the following reminiscence verbatim. 'Pavel', as the Russian sailors called their admiral, was dressed in a Russian uniform and armed with excellent weapons:

> He looked very impressive and brave, had some grey hair but
> remained decidedly strong, and it was obvious at once that

he was an expert in what concerned him. As soon as he stepped into the vessel, he began to arrange everything in the way he thought best. He examined the sails, the guns, the ammunition, having help from the interpreter only to the extent of his ability to translate. He then had a small boat hoisted aboard, attached a little rudder to it, chose a pair of good oars, wrapped about them some pieces of cloth, and after various other minor preparations sat down for a rest.

It had grown dark, supper was served, and Pavel seated himself with us around the table. He ate and made jokes through his interpreter just as if he were one of us. After our meal he gave us a double ration of spirits; we became really good-humoured and started to sing, but the song proved to be a very sad one . . . Our Pavel listened very attentively as though he were trying to understand the meaning of the song; yet it seemed that clouds of sadness passed over his face, although he tried hard to conceal his mood. Well, it is no shame to shed a tear when one is in a strange land.

'It is time,' cried Pavel, jumping to his feet suddenly.

Jones chose me among his fellow sailors after he examined us as if he wished to pierce through our characters; and we two entered the little boat, Pavel at the rudder and I at the oars. We made for the Turkish lines, brazenly met some enemy boats, and subtly drew from the Turks their password. Never in all my life have I seen a man such as he was. When he wished, he was like honey, and when necessary like stone. I wonder . . . how I entrusted myself to a man, not a Christian at that, to be led directly into the hands of the enemy . . . And how one trusted him! One movement of his hand you obey like a commanding voice. It seems that some people are created to command.

We soon reached the enemy's fleet. It looked like an entire town as it lay at anchor, a whole forest of masts. We were asked for the password and Pavel himself gave it. We kept moving among the ships like a seagull. Some threatened us, others paid no attention – we crawled along silently in some places, in others we swooped boldly. When finally beyond range of the enemy's fire we removed the cloths from the oars and rowed quietly to the galley of Prince Nassau with our information. Not one of the Turks had suspected us.[10]

This simple Cossack came nearer to the heart and soul of Paul Jones than did most of his sophisticated friends. And the admiral appreciated stout fellows like Ivak, to whom he presented a dagger inscribed 'From Pavel Jones to his friend the Zaporozhye Ivak, 1788'.

As a last piece of bravado, Jones ordered Ivak to row under the stern of one the largest battleships and hold on to her. While Ivak chatted in Turkish with one of the seamen on deck, Jones worked quickly and silently with a piece of chalk, inscribing over the gilded Turkish insignia across the stern: TO BE BURNED. PAUL JONES. The following day, the Turks did not notice this graffito but the sight of it put heart in the Russian Flotilla and this very ship was attacked and burned by *Vladimir*.

Jones spent some time jotting down the dispositions of the Turkish ships and drawing up his plan of attack, then he gave orders for the movement of all the ships on the right flank (north side) of his line towards the centre so that they formed an obtuse angle with the left flank toward which the Turks were advancing, in the hope of gripping them in a pincer movement as he had done during the first battle. This manoeuvre was silently accomplished just after midnight. With the rising tide the Turkish flagship floated off her mudbank, weighed anchor at 2 a.m. on 17/28 June and began to form line of battle. Within two hours the Capudan Pasha's entire fleet was advancing to the attack. Now the wind veered to the northeast, giving the Russians a slight advantage.

The ensuing battle was a confusing dogfight; Jones found that what looked fine on paper was virtually impossible to control in action. Soon friend and foe were milling around and shots were fired indiscriminately. Such signals as Jones could give were invariably ignored. Fortunately the Turks were even more disorganised. The Turkish deputy commander's ship ran aground, and then the Capudan Pasha's flagship was grounded on the north shore. Up to this point Nassau-Siegen had hung back, rather as Landais had done off Flamborough Head; but now he darted forward with his entire Flotilla to attack the helpless battleships which were listing so heavily that they could not use their big guns. Instead of grappling and boarding, Nassau-Siegen and his ships kept their distance and contented themselves with lobbing brandcougles into the two great ships until they were blazing from stem to stern. Jones was dismayed and disgusted at this wanton destruction.

While the Flotilla concentrated on the stranded battleships, they left Jones's battle line unprotected from the Turkish small craft. *Malyi Aleksandr* was sunk by Turkish incendiaries, and the other frigates were so hard pressed that Jones in desperation rowed across to Nassau-Siegen's yacht and begged him to concentrate on helping the Squadron. Nassau-Siegen refused point blank, but one of his Russian subordinates, Korsakov, rounded up as many of the small craft as he could and rowed across to support the big ships. This reinforcement was sufficient to tip the scales in Jones's favour and by mid-morning the Squadron had driven the entire Turkish fleet back to the mouth of the Liman. That evening the gun battery which Jones had suggested be placed at the tip of Kinburn Point opened up on the Turkish fleet as it rode at anchor and tried to sort itself out. This well-directed gunfire had such deadly effect that the Turks panicked, weighed anchor and in the darkness sailed off in every direction. When dawn came up on 18/29 June no fewer than nine warships had run aground. Suvorov suggested that they should be destroyed before they could be refloated and Jones reluctantly agreed. Now Nassau-Siegen proposed to use the entire Flotilla for this task, though Jones maintained that it could be accomplished with only a few craft.

Nassau-Siegen flew into a rage and cried, 'I know how to capture ships as well as you!'

'I have proved my ability to capture ships which are not Turkish,' riposted Jones.

In the end Jones persuaded him to leave five units behind to support the Squadron. Nassau-Siegen burned seven of the stranded Turkish ships and captured the other two. When Jones reported to Potemkin he made a point of praising the courage of the Russians 'which is the more glorious because it is without show-off'. As far as Jones was concerned, the Russians won the battle despite the flamboyant antics of Nassau-Siegen. In two days of fighting, the Turks lost ten large and five smaller ships, 1,673 prisoners and sixty-seven wounded, but over three thousand were killed. Nassau-Siegen claimed – and got – all the glory. 'I am master of the Liman!' he boasted to his wife. 'Poor Paul Jones!' he gloated in the same letter. 'No place for him on this great day!' And Potemkin, reporting to Catherine, echoed these cries: 'Prince Nassau was tireless in his efforts. It was all his work.'[11] Jones was entirely ignored, although it was his strategy that defeated the enemy attack and the execution of it would have been more perfect had Nassau-Siegen obeyed orders.

A few days later Potemkin, accompanied by the Chevalier Littlepage (as an observer for the King of Poland) and the Prince de Ligne, a prominent Austrian diplomat, dined with Jones aboard *Vladimir*. By that time relations between Jones and Nassau-Siegen were so strained that nothing short of pistols at dawn would resolve the matter; but the distinguished visitors persuaded Nassau-Siegen to apologise to Jones for his bad behaviour on the second day of battle. Jones accepted this gracefully and embraced Prince Pierre 'in the presence of this honorable company, and I believed him as sincere as myself'.[12] In light of Potemkin's report to Catherine it is hardly surprising that while Nassau-Siegen was awarded Russia's highest decoration, the Cross of St George, and Alexiano was promoted to rear-admiral, Jones had to be content with the Order of St Anne, which was also conferred on Mordvinov, the deskbound admiral who had taken no part in the action. The decoration was not a Russian Imperial order at all, but a gong awarded by the duchy of Holstein whence the Empress Elizabeth II and her sister Anne (mother of the ill-fated Peter III) had originated. It was about equivalent to the British Empire Medal or the American Bronze Star and, in the circumstances and in view of Jones's rank, a derisory award. Later there was a distribution of bejewelled and gold-hilted presentation swords, but again Jones was left out.

Adding injury to insult, he had to endure the high-handed behaviour of Nassau-Siegen and Rear-Admiral Alexiano which made his position increasingly untenable. These two conspired to rob Jones of a rich prize during operations on 1/12 July when Potemkin brought his army across the Bug and launched the attack on Ochakov. Jones refused to commit his big ships to an artillery duel with the Turkish shore batteries, but sent in the Flotilla, directing them in person from the deck of a small chaloupe. At six in the morning he took this craft out ahead of the Flotilla to seize five galleys within case-shot of the fortress. He boarded the nearest galley himself and got a Russian lieutenant to tow it out of danger. Then he boarded the Capudan Pasha's own galley, but the task of taking her in tow was bungled by a junior officer and while cables and anchors were being brought from *Vladimir*, Alexiano and Nassau-Siegen (who were in the latter's yacht), sent in a small craft manned by a Greek officer to set fire to the galley. Jones was disgusted and horrified at this, especially as the Greek left the wretched galley slaves, chained to the thwarts, to burn to death before his eyes. The remaining three galleys were attacked by brandcougles and likewise burned out.

The Russian Army settled down to besiege Ochakov, and during this period Potemkin sent Nassau-Siegen to inspect the base at Sevastopol. Command of the Flotilla now passed to Ribas, and Littlepage was given a squadron under Don José. When Nassau-Siegen returned to the Liman on 1/12 August, Jones noted to his chagrin that Prince Pierre was now sporting a vice-admiral's flag which Jones refused to salute. Incredibly, Nassau-Siegen had just been promoted by Potemkin, a situation which would be analogous nowadays to promoting the commander of a special boat squadron to a rank higher than the taskforce admiral. To be sure, there was a way out of this impasse, when Potemkin, angered at the inactivity of Rear-Admiral Voinovich at Sevastopol, considered replacing him by Jones. Potemkin's secretary wrote to the latter on 8/19 August asking if he would care for it. Jones replied that while he would always obey the orders of the Prince Marshal, he did not fancy the idea for several reasons. The Sevastopol fleet was in poor shape and would take time to bring up to scratch. More importantly, Jones had just been ordered to attack Fort Hassan Pasha on the tip of the Ochakov Peninsula, and jumped at this chance to show his mettle.

An assault of this sort was only feasible if complete surprise were maintained. Jones's carefully laid plans were upset by a Greek lieutenant in Littlepage's squadron who opened fire prematurely and alerted the Turks. The only sensible course was to abort the attack, but Nassau-Siegen claimed that Jones's cowardice had robbed the Prince of yet another important victory. Littlepage, who witnessed this tantrum, resigned on the spot and returned to Warsaw forthwith. His parting shot was a letter to Jones which concluded, 'Adieu, my dear admiral, take care of yourself, and be cautious in whom you trust. Remember you have to sustain here a political as well as a military character, and that your part is now rather that of a courtier than a soldier.' To this realistic warning Jones appended a note typical of his inflexible principles: 'I never was made to play that part.'[13]

Having declined the offer of the command at Sevastopol, Jones was sidelined by Potemkin, though he continued to maintain an effective blockade of Ochakov throughout September and early October. When the Capudan Pasha returned with a reinforced fleet on 8/19 October, Potemkin withdrew the Flotilla to save it from possible capture. Jones obeyed this order under great protest and as a result the Turks broke through and relieved the hard-pressed fortress. The following day the Flotilla attacked the Turks and lost a ship, for which Jones was conveniently blamed. This led to an unseemly exchange of increasingly hot-tempered notes between Jones and Potemkin, exacerbated by the Prince Marshal's fears that his headquarters, in a villa on the water's edge, would be overrun by the Turks. Potemkin treated his rear-admiral like an errand boy every time a Turkish galley or gunboat showed up, and Jones, infuriated with chasing after every small craft that came close, eventually rounded on his commander-in-chief. Someone with a more equable temperament would have curbed his tongue, but Jones was incapable of knuckling under. In the end, even Nassau-Siegen fell out with Potemkin. When the Prince Marshal felt that the Flotilla's gunfire was having little effect on the walls of the fortress, despite Nassau-Siegen's repeated boasts that he would soon breach them, Potemkin rounded on him nastily and asked how many walls he had breached during the siege of Gibraltar. Prince Pierre resigned on the spot and immediately set off in high dudgeon for St Petersburg. This should have left the way open for Jones, but the last straw came when Potemkin ordered him 'to receive the enemy courageously' or he would be accused of negligence. At that affront to his honour Jones lost his temper altogether and penned a vitriolic note back:

> If you find me any use to the Imperial Navy, it is for you to keep me in Russia. But, as I did not come here as an adventurer or charlatan or to repair a ruined fortune [a dig at Nassau-Siegen] I hope to be subjected to no more humiliation and to find myself soon in the situation that was promised me when I was invited to enter Her Imperial Majesty's Navy.[14]

Such blunt words got Jones nowhere. From 18/29 October 1788 he was effectively on the beach. On immediate receipt of this letter, Potemkin ordered Mordvinov to relieve him.

With the benefit of hindsight it is obvious that the situation in the Black Sea campaign was intolerable from the start. Jones, who usually did not suffer fools lightly, in fact showed remarkable patience, tact and forbearance in dealing with blackguards like Potemkin, Nassau-Siegen and Alexiano, who were out for themselves and whose jealousy impelled them to drag down the one capable commander. Potemkin took delight in playing off one commander against another, and because his own grasp of strategy was weak he would always tend to favour someone like Nassau-Siegen who attacked the enemy with furious panache but with little method, whereas the dour Scotsman with his careful planning merely irritated him. Jones's verdict was sombre: 'In my whole life I have never suffered so much vexation as in this one Campaign of the Liman, which was nearly the death of me.'

Interestingly, when Jones collected his *pièces justificatives* to append to his narrative of the Liman campaign, many Russian officers risked their own careers, if not their lives, to provide him with testimonials or affidavits which proved beyond a shadow of a doubt that the Scotsman had won the loyalty, respect and admiration of his Russian subordinates. And it is an incontrovertible fact that amid the Byzantine chicanery and double-dealing on the Liman, not one Russian officer intrigued against him.

Jones left *Vladimir* on 29 October/9 November and proceeded by open galley to Kherson. The journey took three days and nights and in extremely cold, damp weather Jones succumbed to pneumonia which confined him to his bed at Kherson till the end of November. He was at Ekaterinoslav on 6/17 December when Ochakov was stormed and its hapless garrison slaughtered in an orgy of blood-letting without parallel in modern times. On arrival at St Petersburg on 17/28 December Jones was graciously received by the Empress at the Hermitage and this smoothed his ruffled feathers somewhat. Admiral Greig having died recently, Jones hoped that the Empress would appoint him to the command of the Baltic fleet in the campaign now raging with Sweden, and in order to be close at hand when pressing his claim he rented an apartment in a house called Pokhodyashina near the magnificent Admiralty Building. Here he installed his own household which included his interpreter Pavel Dimitrevski, a German manservant named Johann Bahl, his Russian orderly Yakovlev from the Black Sea fleet and a peasant coachman named Ivan Vasiliev to take care of his stable of horses, sleighs and carriages. The French ambassador, Comte de Ségur (who had fought in America under Rochambeau), and his first secretary, Edmond-Charles Genet (son of Jones's old friend), were among his closest friends during this period and did their best to ensure that he met everyone who had influence at Court. One of these was the Princess Naryshkina with whom Jones embarked on a short-lived affair.

Soirées and levees were not enough to keep such a restless spirit as Jones fully occupied. He drew up an elaborate plan for a political and commercial alliance between Russia and the United States. He urged Catherine to place herself at the head of a coalition to suppress the Barbary pirates, some of whom, he averred, had served with the Turks in the recent Black Sea campaign. He also prepared a proposal for the complete restructuring of the Black Sea fleet 'built on false principles, unable to sustain its enormous artillery or to manoeuvre properly'. Jones's plan was, indeed, adopted and implemented by Rear-Admiral Ushakov in 1790 with the result that the Turks were decisively defeated. In addition he laboured long and hard on his *Narrative of the Liman Campaign* which, with the aid of Dimitrevski, he composed in French for Catherine's edification, though it is extremely doubtful whether she ever glanced at it. The tone is that of injured virtue and misunderstood integrity and sadly reeks of self-pity. Like the letter to Lady Selkirk, Jones thought that he had pitched this curious document at the right level to tug at the lady's heart-strings. It contains such wonderful phrases as 'I was formed for love and friendship, and not to be a seaman or a soldier' and 'since I am found too frank and too sincere to make my way at the court of Russia without creating powerful enemies, I have philosophy enough to withdraw into the peaceful bosom of friendship'.[15]

Friendship was something Jones would soon be sorely in need of. For several months he tarried in St Petersburg, always hoping that his abilities would be rewarded with a senior appointment. He learned some Russian and German, and now spoke excellent French, but for months he never heard a word spoken in his own language. The United States was not recognised by Russia and therefore had no diplomatic representation in St Petersburg, while the British community shunned him. Catherine's secret police intercepted or impounded his mail, so that he communicated with Jefferson in Paris with the greatest difficulty. Jones, being Jones, sought solace not in the bottle but in bed. He appears to have had an affair with Princess Anna Kourakina, a lady-in-waiting to the Empress, and it is alleged that she bore him a son. In 1926 a woman calling herself the Baroness Weissereich turned up at the American consulate in Riga, Latvia, hoping to obtain an American passport by claiming that she was a descendant of the son of Jones and the princess. Her claims were based on forged documents, and no hard evidence has ever been forthcoming to substantiate her story.

Early in April 1789 the whole of St Petersburg was astonished, scandalised, outraged or amused by a report from the chief of police, Major-General Nikita Ivanovich Ryleyev, that Admiral Jones had raped a nine-year-old girl named Katerina Stepanova Koltzwarthen, daughter of a German immigrant who had a dairy near by. According to the official report, the little girl was hawking butter on 30 March when a 'lackey' (Jones's German manservant) told her that his master wanted some and led her to the admiral's apartment. The girl testified that the master was wearing a white uniform with a gold star and a red ribbon. He purchased fifteen kopeks' worth, then locked the door, knocked her out with a blow to the chin, carried her to his bedroom and raped her. She ran home, told her mother who went to the apartment, identified the assailant as Rear-Admiral Jones and reported the incident to the police. She was supported by a statement from Bahl, who said that he had witnessed the assault through the keyhole, and affidavits from an army surgeon and a midwife that the girl had been raped.

Once this news broke Jones was shunned by virtually all his friends and acquaintances. One of the few people who stood by him was the Comte de Ségur who gave Jones's version of the affair in his memoirs.[16] When the ambassador called on his friend he found him extremely distraught and suicidal, his pistols, primed, on the table. Jones was reduced to tears by the kindness of Ségur. When he had recovered his composure Jones told him that the girl had called to ask if he had any lace or linen that required mending, but he had none. 'She then indulged in some rather lively and indecent gestures,' said Jones. 'I advised her not to enter upon so vile a career, gave her some money, and dismissed her.' As soon as she left the apartment she tore her sleeves and fichu, began screaming 'Rape!' and threw herself into the arms of her mother who just happened to be loitering outside. Ségur made his own enquiries and soon ascertained that the admiral had been set up. Jones himself, through his lawyer, Crimpin, discovered that Mamma Koltzwarthen had been put up to the sting by a gentleman who wore the star of some order and that she had conspired with her daughter solely for money. She confessed that her little daughter, far from being an innocent virgin, had been seduced by Bahl three months previously. Crimpin also discovered that the girl had still been peddling butter after the assault instead of rushing home to her mother as had been alleged. Papa Koltzwarthen later deponed that his daughter was twelve and that his wife had left him to live with a young lover and had taken Katerina with her. It also transpired that the mother had been pimping for her daughter and other young girls. Finally Katerina later admitted to the police that she had once sold butter to Jones when he had briefly lodged at the London Tavern when he arrived at St Petersburg the previous December.

Suddenly pressure was put on Crimpin by the Governor of St Petersburg no less and forced to desert the case. Jones, as a last resort, appealed to Potemkin himself for justice. In a letter to the Prince Marshal dated 13 April, he concluded:

> The charge against me is an unworthy imposture. I love woman, I confess, and the pleasures that one only obtains from that sex; but to get such things by force is horrible to me. I cannot even contemplate gratifying my passions without their consent, and I give you my word as a soldier and an honest man that, if the girl in question has not passed through hands other than mine, she is still a virgin.[17]

This letter was forwarded to Potemkin on 25 April by Ségur with a covering letter appealing to the Prince Marshal 'In the name of friendship of which you have given me such frequent proofs, come to the aid of this brave officer and free him from a trial whose publicity and continuance discredit a reputation won by the most brilliant valour.'[18]

Jones's appeal to Potemkin was written two weeks after the alleged rape, and until the early 1950s was the only version believed to have been given by him of what took place. Then a letter in French from Jones to Major-General Ryleyev, the chief of police, dated 2 April 1789 was discovered, putting the affair in a rather different light:

> The accusation against me is an imposture invented by the mother of a depraved girl who came several times to my house and with whom I often frolicked, always giving her money, but whose virginity I have positively not taken. I have never been capable of doing the least violence to this girl or to any person of her sex. I thought her to be several years older than Your Excellency says she is, and each time she came to my home she lent herself with the best grace to do all that a man would want of her. The last time passed off like the rest, and she went out appearing content and calm, and having in no way been abused. If one checked on her having been deflowered, I declare that I am not the author of it, and I shall as easily prove the falseness of this

assertion as of several other points included in the deposition
which you have sent to me.[19]

This letter, written so soon after the event, is as close to the truth
as we will ever get, and was supported by affidavits from Yakovlev,
Vasiliev and Dimitrevski who all deponed that the girl left Jones's
apartment quietly, without blood, bruises or tears. The nature of the
frolics (*badinage*) in which Jones engaged with this girl – 'all that a
man would want of her' short of deflowering her – can be imagined.
Jones had obviously behaved foolishly, but this was a far cry from
the serious felony with which he was now accused.

By indulging in sexual activity with this girl Jones laid himself
open to blackmail or worse. It is clear that the situation was
exploited by someone at a very high level (the 'decorated gentleman'
of Mamma's confession), and the involvement of people in St Petersburg's German colony seemed to point to a German or Austrian
connection. A suggestion that the British community were behind the
frame-up was immediately dismissed by Jones himself; the British
naval officers might give him the cold shoulder but they were
incapable of anything so devious or nasty. Jones eventually concluded
that the culprit was Nassau-Siegen who was well connected with the
Austro-German community. The matter did not come to trial but
although Jones was never formally charged, the allegation was
allowed to hang over him like an ugly question-mark. The accusation
itself was sufficiently scandalous for almost everyone to drop the
admiral. By contrast, the conduct of Ségur stands out like a shining
light. He wrote to Potemkin and the Empress on Jones's behalf,
even hinting that Louis XVI would take offence at the way his
Chevalier had been treated. Ségur later claimed that it was due to
his efforts that the threatened trial never materialised, but it is more
probable that Catherine and Potemkin realised that matters might
then come to light which would reflect badly on them, so the matter
was quietly dropped. Ségur even published his heavily sanitised
version of the incident in the official *Gazette de France*, from which
the leading newspapers of Europe reprinted it. Jones planned to sue
the Koltzwarthen family, but was dissuaded in the end, and little
Katerina went on peddling butter and *badinage*.

Jones continued to wait in St Petersburg, hoping in vain that he
would be restored to favour and get the Baltic command for which
he so desperately yearned, but in June it was announced that the
appointment had been given instead to Vice-Admiral the Prince de

Nassau-Siegen. A few weeks later Jones was granted two years' leave of absence by Catherine, effectively his dismissal from her service. On 26 June/7 July 1789 he was allowed to kiss her hand at a public audience and received a curt *bon voyage*. Whatever the profligacy and debauchery of her own life, the Empress could be extremely puritanical where other people were concerned. It took Jones a further two months to get his clearance papers to leave the country, but at the end of August he boarded his travelling carriage and headed for Warsaw. After his departure, his friend Genet obtained 1,800 roubles (a year's pay) and sent on a draft for that amount.

Jones never saw Russia again, but till the day he died he could never get that strange land out of his mind, and pathetically hoped that his Empress would some day relent and recall him. All his mishaps and disastrous experiences in Russia had been caused by foreign adventurers and mountebanks. Of the Russians themselves, especially the officers and naval ratings under his command, he had nothing but the highest regard, and this feeling was mutual.

16. Last Years

1789–92

Good Americans, when they die, go to Paris.
— OLIVER WENDELL HOLMES, *Autocrat of the Breakfast Table*

John Paul Jones reached Warsaw some time in September 1789. Significantly, one of his first acts was to write to Catherine, enclosing the *pièces justicatives* which were to form the appendix to his *Narrative of the Liman Campaign*, and in the same packet he sent her a copy of the *Mémoire* he had prepared for Louis XVI. This was only the first in a string of increasingly grovelling letters which he addressed to the Empress over the next three years. Getting back into her good graces became almost an obsession, but she steeled her heart against him and never condescended to reply.

In Warsaw, Jones found ample evidence that his trust in the Czarina was misplaced. Poland had suffered the first of its three partitions in 1772, and on that occasion Catherine had taken as her share the territory east of the Dvina and the Dnieper. Now, almost two decades on, the elective King of Poland was Stanislas Poniatowski who had actually been one of Catherine's lovers, a matter of common knowledge all over Europe and the butt of numerous jokes even coarser than these lines of Burns:

> Auld Kate laid her claws on poor Stanislaus,
> And Poland has bent like a bow;
> May the deil in her ass ram a huge prick o brass!
> And damn her in hell with a mowe*![1]   [fuck*]

Stanislas was Catherine's puppet and within three years he would meekly acquiesce in the second partition which would lose him Volhynia, Podolia and a large part of Lithuania. Littlepage secured Jones an audience with Stanislas, and the admiral also became friends with Thaddeus Kosciuszko, the great Polish hero who had fought in the American Revolution. Kosciuszko had some connections with the

Swedish government and offered to intercede on Jones's behalf to procure him an admiral's commission in the Swedish Navy. The notion of getting his revenge on Nassau-Siegen was extremely tempting, but Jones's sense of honour prevented him from taking this course. Technically he was still an admiral in the Russian service and he could not actively solicit such a commission from a country then at war with Russia. On the other hand, were the offer to come from Sweden, he might then consider it.

Without waiting for a response from Stockholm, Jones set off on his travels once more. Leaving Warsaw on 2 November he journeyed to Montbéliard in Alsace where he stayed for several days with the Duke of Württemberg, a friend of his late compatriot David Wemyss. By 23 November Jones was in Vienna, a considerable detour which leads one to suppose that he had gone there, perhaps at the Duke's suggestion, in the hope of an audience with the Emperor Joseph II and securing high command in the Austrian Navy, still a potent force in the Adriatic and Mediterranean. From Vienna he wrote on that date to a mother and daughter whom he had met in Warsaw, saying that he had visited their youthful kinswomen at a convent and left for them a copy of the poems of James Thomson, his favourite poet.[2]

By 9 December Jones was in Amsterdam and here he remained until May 1790. Very little is known of this period, though it may be supposed that he renewed the friendship of the Dumas family and may even have met his former 'virgin Muse' Anna Jacoba, now a wife and mother. In Amsterdam, there was a further development in the Swedish matter, Kosciuszko writing to him to call upon the Swedish ambassador and await an offer. Gouverneur Morris happened to be in Amsterdam at the time and discussed the matter with Jones, though there is no evidence that the offer was actually forthcoming. Morris discovered that Jones had concocted a wild scheme for 'going around the Cape of Good Hope and laying under contribution the places subject to the Turk', but this would have been to the benefit of Russia, not Sweden. Jones subsequently elaborated the idea in a letter to Baron de Krudener, the Russian minister in Paris. If the Empress were to supply him with a small taskforce, under the American flag if need be, he would execute this plan, though what he expected to extract by way of tribute from the barren wastes of Arabia in the pre-oil era is hard to imagine. He also kept up an extensive correspondence with Washington (now President of the United States) and the aged Franklin (who died soon afterwards), as well as other powerful and influential friends, not seeking any favours in particular but merely reminding them of his existence. John Ross sent him a bill of exchange in respect of his Bank of North America dividends, but the Dutch bankers refused to cash it. To John Parish, an American businessman in Hamburg, Jones wrote jocularly that he 'might make a visit in the spring, and pay my court to some of your kind, rich old ladies'. But he 'must stay in Europe till it is seen what changes the present policies will produce'.³ By that he meant the French Revolution which had erupted the previous July. Strangely enough, this was the first reference to that earth-shattering event anywhere in Jones's voluminous correspondence. Gouverneur Morris observed that Jones showed not the slightest interest in that almighty upheaval. His only concern was that the Revolution might trigger off another European war and thereby give him the opportunity to distinguish himself.

Instead of heading for Hamburg to woo some rich old lady, Jones crossed the North Sea with a view to going to London in order to salvage something from his investment in Bancroft's dyewood project. Gouverneur Morris, who also happened to be in London at the time, agreed rather reluctantly to act as arbitrator in the dispute between the admiral and the one-time spy. Jones, however, encountered a hostile mob at Harwich: 'I escaped being murdered on landing,' he wrote to a lady friend a few months later.⁴ Further details were given two decades later, from a contemporary manuscript. This confirmed that Jones, in the white-and-blue uniform of a Russian admiral, had been recognised at the customs house in Harwich 'in such manner that he thought proper to retreat to the inn, with the utmost precipitation'. The mob 'surrounded the inn, and were not sparing in denouncing their intention of exercising vengeance upon him if they laid hold of him; in consequence of which he privately escaped out of town the same day'.⁵ The reason for this hostility was probably the lurid accounts of the alleged rape of Katerina Koltzwarthen which had appeared in some of the English newspapers. The English might have forgiven Jones for his daring exploits round the coasts, but a brutal sexual assault on a little girl was unforgivable. He proceeded to London without further mishap and probably lodged at the Freemasons' Tavern where room and board cost a pound a week. His mission was partially successful, though even at the time of Jones's death Bancroft was still trying to pay off the balance, amounting to £1,050, with scrip for Mohawk Valley lands.

At the conclusion of this business Jones took ship from Dover to Boulogne and then travelled on to Paris where he would remain for the rest of his life. His dreadful experiences in Russia had taken their toll and Jones was now ill and prematurely aged. In reduced circumstances he could no longer afford to maintain a household in grand style, but had sufficient income to rent a fine apartment at 52 rue de Tournon, a broad, attractive thoroughfare on the approach to the Palais de Luxembourg. The house is still standing, though renumbered 19. Jones's landlord was a M. d'Arbergue (whom the admiral, remembering his Shakespeare, instantly dubbed 'Dogberry'), *huissier* or marshal of a court of justice. The house had only recently been erected and was conveniently located for the Lodge of the Nine Sisters and the Jardin du Luxembourg, where Jones took his daily stroll.

In a few short years Paris had changed utterly. To be sure, the streets and buildings were much the same, but the atmosphere was very different. Many of Jones's former friends were now émigrés while others had withdrawn to remote country estates from where they anxiously watched political developments in the capital. Louis and Marie Antoinette, evicted from Versailles by the Paris mob, were now virtually under house arrest in the Tuileries. The balls and levees of yesteryear had vanished, and the salons of the revolutionary hostesses were not to Jones's taste. In one of the purple passages in his *French Revolution*, Thomas Carlyle paints a fanciful picture of our hero in his decline:

> In faded naval uniform, Paul Jones lingers here; like a wine-skin from which the wine is drawn. Like the ghost of himself! Low is his once loud bruit; scarcely audible, save with extreme tedium, in ministerial ante-chambers; in this or the other charitable drawing-room, mindful of the past. What changes, culminatings and declinings! . . . Poor Paul! hunger and dispiritment track thy sinking footsteps; once or at most twice, in this Revolution-tumult the figure of thee emerges, mute, ghost-like, as 'with stars' dim-twinkling through.[6]

His stars dim-twinkled for the last time on 10 July 1790 when he was chosen to head the delegation of the American colony in Paris to congratulate the National Assembly on the new Constitution, though the reponsibility for making an appropriate speech fell to another man, William Henry Vernon.[7] A few days later the same

delegation had special seats reserved for them at the great celebrations on the Champ de Mars marking the first anniversary of the
storming of the Bastille. Jones is silent on both occasions; one
suspects that, despite his profession of Liberty and Universal
Brotherhood, he regarded the progress of the French Revolution
with mounting anxiety. He loved the pomp and circumstance of the
Court, the rigid hierarchy of the Crown and the grades of the
nobility, just like a well-run ship with its officers, petty officers and
seamen. He had had his fill of democracy aboard *Ranger* and recoiled
at the memory. His former friend Lafayette, now commander of the
National Guard, was at the height of power and popularity but far
too busy to bother with him. Jones had brought back from Russia
some furs, probably sables, which he sent to Lafayette together with
a second set which he wished the general to give to King Louis. On
7 December 1790 Jones wrote to Lafayette regarding these gifts and
making some very peculiar requests:

> When my health shall be re-established M. Simolin will do
> me the honour to present me to His Majesty as a Russian
> Admiral; afterwards it will be my duty as an American officer
> to wait on His Majesty with the letter which I am directed
> to present to him from the United States.[8]

Lafayette, no doubt too embarrassed for words, never replied. The
letter, incidentally, was one entrusted to Jones by Congress in 1787
but which he had never got around to delivering.

The extensive journal kept by Gouverneur Morris during this
period contains numerous references to Jones which indicate that the
naval hero was becoming a bit of a bore. He was in poor shape
physically and, as the letter quoted above indicates, seems also to
have been going a bit soft in the head. One can sense the mounting
exasperation of Morris as he records the visits of Jones to the
American legation, at least once a week, sometimes more often. The
entry for 14 November 1790 is not untypical: 'Paul Jones calls on
me. He has nothing to say but is so kind as to bestow on me all the
Hours which hang heavy in his Hands.'[9] Sometimes Morris felt
remorse at his impatience with Jones. In June 1792, a few weeks
before the admiral died, Morris invited him to dine but only because
he had earlier that day sent him packing and now felt sorry for him.
Morris's diary also affords a few tantalising glimpses of Jones's
threadbare existence. On one occasion he and Morris were guests,

with Bancroft and his mistress, at a dinner given by William Bosville, an eccentric Scot related to the Macdonald of the Isles, and at another dinner, given by William Short of the American legation, Jones met Basil, Lord Daer, and discussed the raid on St Mary's Isle.

Edmond-Charles Genet had given Jones a letter of introduction to his sister, Madame Campan, lady-in-waiting to Marie Antoinette, but there is no record that he ever followed this up. Madame d'Altigny, whom he had met in Warsaw, invited him to visit her at Avignon, but his health was too poor to permit him to travel. Madame Clément admitted him to her circle in Paris and subsequently he carried on a desultory correspondence with three of her friends who had retired to Trevoux near Lyons. They, too, begged him to come and share their 'frugal meals, freedom, and appreciative hearts' but he could not face the journey. Much of Jones's time, in fact, was taken up in letter-writing. In the spring of 1791, when war between Russia and Britain seemed imminent, Jones wrote to the Empress Catherine through her intermediary Baron Grimm, outlining a plan for an attack on India. Catherine's response to Grimm was that if war did break out the quickest and cheapest solution would be to issue letters-of-marque and let privateers play merry hell with English shipping. Catherine considered India so remote that the war would be over before her ships could get there. In case Jones had not already taken the hint, she added a nasty postscript reminding him that he knew very well why she had given him leave of absence. When Jones tried another tack and recommended to the Empress a new kind of warship without ballast which some crank had invented, Catherine wrote to Grimm: 'I have no more to say to Paul Jones. Tell him to go and mind his business in America.' After that rebuff Jones never attempted to communicate with her again.

Perhaps he also had some premonition that he was not long for the world, for his thoughts began to return to the land of his boyhood. By now his mother was dead, but there were still his two sisters and their numerous offspring. Unfortunately the two women were not on speaking terms. Previously he had written to his sister Janet in March 1787 and March 1790, expressing a wish to see her again and writing at considerable length concerning the education of his nephews and nieces.[10] He was particularly anxious that Janet's son William should be sent to St Paul's School in London before going on to Oxford or Cambridge. He also felt particularly drawn to Janet's daughter Janette of whom he had heard good things. Indeed, his impression of his niece was amply fulfilled when, over the years,

Janette became the most faithful custodian of her uncle's memory.

In December 1790 he tried to get his sisters to kiss and make up and wrote to them both individually, quoting Pope's 'Universal Prayer':

> Teach me to *feel* another's woe,
> *To hide the fault I see*;
> That mercy I to others show,
> *Such mercy show to me!*

And he commented, 'You will find more morality in that little piece than in many volumes that have been written by great divines.' Carlyle thought that Jones was nostalgic for the land of his birth and regretted the day when, 'young fool', he looked 'wistful over the Solway brine, by the foot of native Criffel, with blue mountainous Cumberland, into blue Infinitude, environed with thrift, with humble friendliness'. Not so. Jones never made any enquiries about old friends or former haunts in any of these family letters. His fond reveries concerned his sea-going exploits or those rapturous days at Hennebont with Delia. If he had any regrets about the course his life had taken, he kept them to himself.

By 1791, however, he was in straitened circumstances, exacerbated by the fact that Ross was extremely tardy about remitting his bank dividends. Jones petitioned William Short about finding him an American consulate somewhere in Europe and he even approached the French minister of marine regarding arrears of wages still outstanding for the officers and men of *Bonhomme Richard* but without any luck on either score. Jones seems to have been quite oblivious to the tumultuous events going on all around him. In one respect alone, he was still in touch with the real world and that was in his correspondence with Thomas Jefferson, now Secretary of State under George Washington. A common interest had been their concern for the plight of the American sailors who had been captured by the Barbary pirates of North Africa. While these corsairs were careful not to molest the shipping of countries with powerful navies, they were quick to realise that the United States was not in that category and consequently preyed especially on vessels flying the Stars and Stripes. Jones had run up against these 'Algerines', as he called them, in the Liman campaign and therefore had a double interest in getting to grips with them. He petitioned Jefferson with a plan to deal with this scourge of Atlantic and Mediterranean shipping. If he could be appointed to command a taskforce, he promised to sail to Algiers, destroy the pirate base and liberate the American crews, some of whom had been in durance vile for many years. Congress, seeking reparation on the cheap, got a Portuguese consul to offer $10,000 to the Dey of Algiers as ransom for the American prisoners, but the Dey scornfully rejected this sum. The only diplomatic crumb salvaged from this episode was a commercial treaty with the least disreputable of the Barbary princes, the Sultan of Morocco.

Concern for the American prisoners rotting in Barbary gaols had been a recurring theme with Jones for several years. In 1787 he had even proposed to John Jay a tax of a shilling a month on all American seamen, the accumulated fund being used specifically for redeeming captives. Jefferson, when American minister in Paris, discovered to his disgust that all of the European powers paid regular tribute to the Barbary states rather than fight them. He and Jones were as one in their loathing of this blackmail system and often discussed ways of destroying it. In 1789 Jones wrote to Jefferson proposing a treaty allowing Russia to recruit American seamen to punish Algiers, in exchange for the right of American ships to trade freely in the Black Sea. The situation became intolerable by the end of 1790 when the Dey of Algiers raised the price of releasing prisoners to $3,000 a head. Washington and Jefferson conveyed this alarming fact to Congress in January 1791, giving Congress the choice 'between war, tribute and ransom, as a means of re-establishing our Mediterranean commerce'. Although the Senate passed a resolution saying that the Mediterranean trade could not be protected without a navy, nothing was done to implement this. Lamely, the Senate authorised the President to redeem the prisoners so long as the total cost did not exceed $40,000. The only resistance to the pirates came from Portugal which was then at war with Algiers. Even the pathetic petition of thirteen Americans, the survivors of twenty-one taken prisoner seven years previously, had little effect in moving Congress out of its lethargy.

When Washington heard that the American prisoners were faced with the prospect of converting to Islam and abandoning their families and country, the President was galvanised into action. On 1 June 1792 he signed, and Jefferson countersigned, a commission appointing 'John Paul Jones, a citizen of the United States, commissioner with full powers to negotiate with the Dey of Algiers concerning the ransom of American citizens in captivity, and to conclude and sign a Convention thereupon'. The following day

Washington signed a second commission appointing Jones American consul for Algeria. Simultaneously Jefferson drafted detailed instructions with a summary of this sorry business, and authorising him to pay $27,000 to ransom the thirteen captives still alive, plus $25,000 for a treaty, $1,000 to clothe the released prisoners and $2,000 per annum to cover his own salary and expenses.

Had these documents testifying to Washington's and Jefferson's 'special trust and confidence in the integrity, prudence and abilities of John Paul Jones' reached him expeditiously his last days would have been infinitely happier. But instead of entrusting the packet to the first ship bound for France, Jefferson gave it to Thomas Pinckney, American minister designate in London, and Pinckney did not depart till mid-July, by which time Jones was dying.

The admiral had been suffering from jaundice since early May and by the first week of July he was also affected by a swelling of the legs which gradually spread upwards into his abdomen. An autopsy performed on Jones's body in 1905 revealed that he had suffered from glomerulo-nephritis with indurated masses in the lungs, some having the appearance of broncho-pneumonic lesions. It appears that on top of jaundice and nephritis Jones contracted bronchial pneumonia which was the immediate cause of death.

He was virtually alone, with no Delia or other mistress to give him the tender loving care he needed. His forty-fifth birthdy on 6 July passed unnoticed by anyone. By that time his only friends were Jean-Baptiste Beaupoil, a former aide-de-camp of Lafayette, and Samuel Blackden, a retired colonel of dragoons from North Carolina. It seems singularly appropriate that someone from that state, whose congressional delegate Joseph Hewes had procured Jones his first naval appointment, should be the last to see him alive.

Blackden's concern contrasts with the relative indifference of Gouverneur Morris. On the afternoon of 18 July the American minister got 'a message from Paul Jones that he is dying'. Morris with a couple of notaries public in tow, scurried over to the rue de Tournon and found Jones in his sitting-room 'in an easy chair, sick in body but of sound mind, memory, judgment and understanding'. Jones dictated his will to Morris, leaving all his property to his sisters Janet Taylor and Mary Ann Lowden of Dumfries and appointing Robert Morris his executor. To this he appended a list of his property: $6,000 worth of stock in the Bank of North America together with accumulated dividends; a loan office certificate for $2,000 with about twelve years' accumulated interest in the hands of John Ross; lands in Vermont; five shares in the Ohio Company; three hundred shares in the Indiana Company; the balance of Bancroft's debt; claims for the Danish pension; and arrears of pay from Russia and the United States. Having attended to this matter, Morris rushed off to a dinner engagement with the future Duke and Duchess of Sutherland. All through the meal he had the sorry spectacle of Jones in his mind, so afterwards, about eight in the evening, he returned to Jones's apartment, accompanied by his mistress, Madame Flahaut, and an eminent physician, Dr Vicq d'Azyr of the Académie Française, who happened to live near by.

By the time Morris and his friends got there, Jones was already dead. Blackden had left him seated in his easy chair soon after the will had been executed. A few minutes later Jones got up, staggered through to his bedroom and laid himself face down on the bed with his feet on the floor. There the visitors found him; after such a turbulent life he presented a picture of calm and ease. Morris immediately gave instructions to the landlord d'Arbergue that Jones should be buried privately and as cheaply as possible, afraid that he might be saddled with the expense. Luckily, Blackden intervened and contacted Pierre-François Simonneau, *commissaire* for the *arrondissement* in which Jones had died. Simonneau promptly reported the death to the Legislative Assembly then in session and protested at the decision of the American minister to dump the great hero in a pauper's grave. Simonneau offered to foot the bill himself for a funeral worthy of such a great man. It is due to Simonneau's presence of mind that the body was placed in a lead cylinder filled with alcohol, in the hope that some day it would be repatriated to America for proper interment. Something similar happened to Nelson after Trafalgar, his corpse being placed in a hogshead of brandy for shipment back to England.

All Jones's uniforms and decorations were sold off by public auction on 20 October and thus dispersed to the four winds, purely because Gouverneur Morris did not wish to be burdened with the admiral's debts, although they only amounted to a modest sum for board and lodging. Morris bid on Jones's French decoration and his Cincinnati Eagle but both have long since vanished, along with the special gold medal of Congress. The sword presented by King Louis was reserved by Morris for the family but apart from that and his papers, the only possessions of Paul Jones that have survived are the coat-of-arms painted in America in 1777, a small pistol, two miniature portraits, his captain's commission and his certificate of membership in the Society of the Cincinnati – not much to show for the career of the most brilliant seaman of his age.

Jones's funeral took place on 20 July 1792. In religion he was something of a deist, adhering to no particular faith but respecting them all. But as he had been born a Protestant, the Legislative Assembly appointed the Revd Paul-Henri Marron, a French Presbyterian minister, to conduct the service. According to French law the only place where he could be buried was the Protestant cemetery outside the city walls. The cortège formed up in the rue de Tournon late in the afternoon and wound its way slowly across the city. Contrary to the niggardly intentions of Morris, the Assembly decided that Chevalier Jones should be properly buried with full military honours, and accordingly a detachment of grenadiers of the gendarmerie was detailed to escort the coffin, in full dress uniform with loaded muskets and drums beating a mournful cadence. They were followed by the hearse and then came the carriages for the committee of the Assembly men, looking suitably solemn in their official black costume with white lace jabot and ruffled cuffs, silver buckles and tricorne hats bearing the tricolour cockade. The Protestants of Paris were represented by four of their faith together with the minister. Next came the brethren of the Lodge of the Nine Sisters, followed by Colonel Blackden and the few friends of Jones who were still in Paris. Morris did not have the decency to attend, on the specious ground that the funeral conflicted with yet another of those dinner parties he was forever attending. Instead, he was represented by Major J.C. Mountflorence of the American legation and Thomas Waters Griffith, an American traveller who had met Jones at Morris's residence and who signed the burial certificate.

Behind the carriages of the quality tramped a score or so of the ordinary Parisians, including Jones's valet and chambermaid, the shopkeepers whom he had patronised or with whom he had exchanged greetings as they passed in the street, boys whom he had tipped to run errands, girls he had complimented and from whom he had stolen the occasional kiss, even a few old sailors who had come to pay their last respects to a gallant comrade-in-arms. It was a hot, sultry evening with rumbles of thunder and the odd flash of lightning across the lowering sky, and the mood of the Parisians matched the weather. The revolutionary war which had recently broken out with Austria and Prussia was going badly, and only the previous week the Assembly had declared a state of emergency when the Prussians crossed the eastern frontier. News of the admiral's funeral spread like wildfire, and along the route to the cemetery thousands of people turned out to clap respectfully and doff their caps as the hearse passed them by. The route extended about four miles and must have taken upwards of an hour and a half to pass from the rue St Sulpice, via the rue des Fossés St Germain (now the rue l'Ancienne Comédie), to the Carrefour de Buci. The mourners would have crossed the Seine by the Pont-Neuf, not forgetting to salute the statue of Henri IV as they passed. A huge banner had been slung across the bridge proclaiming in strident lettering LA PATRIE EN DANGER, and the mourners probably felt that France had need of valiant men like Jones at that critical moment. From the river the route ran uphill all the way to the cemetery, past the great church of St Eustache (which was partially demolished by a shell from Big Bertha on Good Friday 1918), and then through a warren of tiny alleys and across the rue Quincampoix to rue St Martin, the ancient Roman road from Paris to the Channel. Eventually they crossed the Grand Boulevard marking the outer limits of the city and passed under the Porte St Martin, one of the monumental gateways erected by Louis XIV. Here they would have paused for a customs inspection, giving the drivers and mourners a chance to quench their thirst.

Beyond the gate the road became a quiet country lane. Farther on, they turned right into the rue de Récollets, named after the missionaries who first evangelised Canada. The sombre journey ended on the rue Granges aux Belles beside the great hospital of St Louis. On the south-western corner, where this road now intersects with the rue des Écluses St Martin, lay the tiny cemetery set aside for the interment of foreign Protestants. There was no religious service, Marron merely preaching a *discours* in which he urged those present to emulate the illustrious foreigner in his contempt for danger, devotion to country and 'his noble heroism which, after having astonished the present age, will continue to be the object of veneration of future generations'.[11] The scene was tranquil; no one present that evening could have imagined that, only three weeks later, the tiny cemetery would be heaped with the corpses of the Swiss Guard who perished to the last man in their heroic defence of the Tuileries against the Paris mob. Soon the king and queen whom Jones revered and d'Estaing whom he admired would go to the guillotine, and even the great popular hero Lafayette would be subjected to a long period of barbaric imprisonment.

Gouverneur Morris noted in his diary how amusing it was that Jones, who detested the French Revolution, should be accorded by it a public funeral. Catherine the Great went further; to Baron Grimm she commented nastily about the admiral who had served her so faithfully: 'This Paul Jones was a wrongheaded fellow; very worthy to be celebrated by a rabble of detestable creatures.'[12]

That may be so, but for John Paul Jones death was not the end it is for lesser mortals; in many senses it would be a beginning.

Soon after the burial of the Swiss Guard in a mass grave, the little Protestant cemetery was closed. In time it was built over as the city burst forth from its ancient walls and spread out into the suburbs. Simonneau's pious hopes that Jones's body would soon be claimed by a grateful United States were never realised in his lifetime. More than thirty years elapsed before anything was done about retrieving the admiral's remains when John H. Sherburne, Jones's first serious biographer, tried to locate the burial site. Despite opposition from Jones's family (notably F.E. Lowden in 1851) who felt that the admiral's remains should be left undisturbed, several other attempts to find the cemetery were made in the course of the nineteenth century, but after the great redevelopment of Baron Haussmann and the wholesale destruction of the Siege and Commune, followed by further building, the quest seemed hopeless. Then in 1899 General Horace Porter, the American ambassador to France, began an obsessive search which involved the needless expenditure of considerable sums in payment to researchers. The cemetery was clearly marked on maps of 1775 and 1789 and it should have been a fairly easy task to pinpoint the location from landmarks still surviving, but six years passed before Porter identified the site and obtained permission to start excavation. Shafts were sunk and gangs of miners were recruited to dig galleries. The diggers knew they were on the right track when they uncovered the layer upon layer of bones of the unfortunate Swiss Guard, then there was great excitement as two lead coffins were unearthed, followed by disappointment when they were found to contain civilians.

On 7 April 1905, a third lead coffin was discovered and when this was opened the searchers were rewarded by confronting the well-preserved head of John Paul Jones, complete in every detail and bearing an uncanny resemblance to the Houdon bust portrait. A few hours later the body was removed to the École de Médecine for examination by two leading anthropologists. Jones was positively identified by a peculiarity of the ear lobe which was also a feature of the Houdon bust. The body was in such an excellent state of preservation, thanks to the lead seal and the alcohol, that a full autopsy could be carried out and the exact nature of the admiral's terminal illnesses determined.

The progress of the excavation and subsequent autopsy was closely followed by President Theodore Roosevelt, who quickly perceived the immense propaganda value for the United States Navy which he was then in the process of building up into the most powerful in the world, as John Paul Jones had once predicted it would become. Consequently Roosevelt despatched the four cruisers *Brooklyn*, *Tacoma*, *Chattanooga* and *Galveston* to bring Jones home. On 6 July 1905, the admiral's 158th birthday, an elaborate service was held over his body, replaced in its original lead cylinder and now encased in a splendid mahogany casket which was placed on a bier inside the American Church on the Avenue de l'Alma. After the service the coffin, borne on a gun carriage, escorted by French cavalry and infantry as well as five hundred American bluejackets, followed by dignitaries of the French Republic, was taken to the Gare du Nord where it boarded a special train to Cherbourg. There, following another ceremony, a French torpedo-boat transferred the coffin to the cruiser *Brooklyn* which had distinguished itself during the recent Spanish-American War. The squadron formed up and steamed slowly out of the harbour and thence across the ocean that Jones had crossed so often under sail. Thirteen days later the squadron under the command of Rear-Admiral Charles D. Sigsbee was joined off Nantucket Shoals by the new battleship *Maine* flying the flag of Rear-Admiral Robley Evans, Commander-in-Chief North Atlantic Fleet, and, in succession, by the battleships *Missouri*, *Kentucky*, *Kearsarge*, *Alabama*, *Illinois* and *Massachusetts*. Forming a single column, these great ships passed the Capes into Chesapeake Bay on 22 July. The ships then peeled off, firing fifteen-gun salutes as they passed *Brooklyn* which continued to steam on to the roadstead off Annapolis. Here the coffin was taken ashore by the torpedo-boat *Standish* and with due ceremony placed in a temporary brick vault, until such times as Congress could decide on its final disposition. Commemorative exercises, addressed by Roosevelt and others, took place on 24 April the following year. All in all, it was a magnificent reception for the great national hero, in contrast to the muted funeral of 1792.

Fredericksburg, Virginia and Washington, DC, were among the places that clamoured for the honour of giving Jones his final resting place, but in the end Congress decided that the most appropriate place would be the crypt of the chapel in the Naval Academy which Jones had envisaged and campaigned so ardently to bring about. As in life, so in death, Jones suffered from the dilatoriness and prevarication of Congress, but after years of dithering, the funds were finally voted to provide Commodore Jones with a final resting place appropriate to his rank and position. Sylvain Salières designed the splendid Pyrenean marble sarcophagus consciously modelled on that of Napoleon in Les Invalides. Here, on 26 January 1913, John Paul Jones finally came to rest. A few months earlier, a life-sized bronze statue by Charles Henry Nienhaus was unveiled in West Potomac Park, Washington, near the Tidal Basin where the Navy Day celebrations take place each 27 October.

Posterity, on the whole, judged John Paul Jones harshly and the article on him in the ninth edition of the *Encyclopaedia Britannica* (1875) was not untypical, speaking of the time he spent in America after the war 'when he was much chagrined by the neglect that met his boastful requests for further employment' and making the snide comment that in the service of Catherine he 'became as enthusiastic a Russian as he had been an American'. The verdict of the anonymous writer reflects prejudices that survived throughout the nineteenth century and even beyond:

> Naval skill and bravery he certainly had, but his letters prove him to have been boastful and quarrelsome. He writhed under the suspicion of being an 'adventurer'; once and again he eagerly repels the charge. English contemporary accounts generally speak of him as a pirate; and, though he certainly ranked as an officer of the United States, the independent manner in which he cruised might well suggest letters of marque rather than a Government commission.[13]

The facts of his life and exploits were magnified, distorted and fictionalised in over forty chapbooks and almost as many biographies, at least two of which, by Augustus Buell (1900) and Valentine Thomson (1939), are virtually works of fiction with little bearing on the truth. As early as 1820–25, however, a serious biography was attempted by John Henry Sherburne. Though he relied heavily on Jones's correspondence which was reproduced with little order or sense, he deserves the credit for preserving in print many letters which have since been lost. Five years later Janette Taylor, Jones's favourite niece, either commissioned or extensively collaborated with two writers to produce the *Memoirs of Rear-Admiral Paul Jones*, which may have been ghosted for her by Sir John Malcolm, and *Life and Correspondence of John Paul Jones* by Robert C. Sands. Both works used a considerable amount of material in Janette's possession, much of which has since been lost.[14] Sands, in fact, has formed the basis for all serious biography of Jones in the past century and a half. Janette died in 1843 during a visit to the United States and her vast collection of her uncle's papers was dispersed through sale to collectors. Today the Jones papers are to be found in the Library of Congress and the National Archives in Washington as well as the Naval Academy Museum in Annapolis, but many more are scattered in smaller collections, or in private hands, or have vanished without trace.

Sufficient of Jones's prodigious correspondence has survived to reveal a man who was irascible, fiercely defensive of his honour and integrity, hypersensitive to snubs and insults real or imagined, prone to self-pity in his later years but justly proud of his achievements. Because so many of his letters were written in the white heat of the moment they reveal much that a calmer personality would have taken care to conceal. Jones could be very charming when occasion demanded, but on the whole he was not a likeable person. He made very few friends, though it has to be said that those with whom he was most intimate – Thomas Bell, Hector McNeill, John Barry, Richard Dale and Joshua Barney – remained loyal and steadfast to him as long as he lived, and cherished his memory ever afterwards. Outside the close circle of old comrades, Jones's best friends were John Brown and Dr John Read. On a rather different level there were Robert Morris, Benjamin Franklin and Thomas Jefferson who appreciated his sterling qualities and overlooked his faults; but these great men were patrons rather than friends in the true sense.

Jones was essentially a loner; even his string of mistresses never got very close to him. The man of independent mind, who worked best when given a free hand and left to his own devices, suffered early in his naval career because he was a foreigner, a newcomer, an outsider; but so too was John Barry with whom he is often compared and who shares with him the honour as co-founder of the modern United States Navy. Barry lacked Jones's overweening pride and prickly self-assertiveness, and in the long run was the more successful man, and lived long enough to see the Navy reborn and placed in good hands.

Jones died at a relatively young age. It is idle to speculate on what might have been achieved had he lived. He would still have been in the prime of life when war broke out in 1798 between the United States and France, and there can be no doubt that none would have been better qualified than Jones to conduct that naval campaign. As America's first admiral, he would have wielded tremendous influence over the reborn Navy. Significantly its earliest major operations were directed against the Barbary pirates and nothing would have given him more satisfaction in seeing that scourge of the seas eradicated; but the credit for achieving Jones's dream would go instead to Stephen Decatur, one of Barry's protégés. Jones might still have been in overall command when war broke out between the United States and the United Kingdom in 1812 – he would have been sixty-five at the time – and could have directed naval operations even if he were too old for seagoing service.

It was unfortunate for Jones that, unlike Nelson, he never had the opportunity to develop his talents to the full. What makes him so outstanding among the captains of the infant United States Navy was his foresight in preparing himself for a fleet command. Some of his contemporaries might have been his equal in single-ship action but none of them, with the possible exception of Barry, had his grasp of naval strategy. Jones alone perceived that the Navy was wasted in commerce-raiding when it should have been deployed much more effectively in amphibious operations against the coasts of Britain and its overseas possessions. Had he obtained the command of a Franco-American expedition with Lafayette the course of the American War might have been radically altered and shortened. As it was, Jones's only opportunity to command a fleet was limited to the Liman campaign, in such intolerably maddening conditions that it is a wonder he remained so loyal to Russia thereafter. Incidentally, he must have indulged in *Schadenfreude* when he learned that Nassau-Siegen suffered a catastrophic defeat at Svenskund on 12 July 1790 at the hands of Gustavus III of Sweden, losing fifty-three ships, fourteen hundred cannon and six thousand men as prisoners. Nassau-Siegen himself fled from the battle in the most cowardly fashion, yet Catherine forgave him.

Although Jones might have been as great a naval strategist as Nelson, he only had the opportunity to prove his abilities at the tactical level, but there he was brilliant. Time and time again, he made the right split-second decisions in rapidly changing circumstances, turning the tables on foes who were often faster and more heavily armed. Consider his conduct during those early spectacular cruises in *Providence* and *Alfred* and those engagements between *Ranger* and *Drake*, *Ariel* and *Triumph* and, above all, between *Bonhomme Richard* and *Serapis*. The last named is the all-time classic example of how a commander, by indomitable spirit, guts, superb seamanship and cool nerve, managed to overcome a larger, faster and much better-armed enemy against all the odds. It has been a shining example ever since, and not just for the United States Navy by any means. In the dark days of 1940, in the aftermath of the withdrawal of the remnants of the British Expeditionary Force from Dunkirk, Albert Alexander, then First Lord of the Admiralty, made a broadcast to the American people in which he said that Jones's defiant answer to Richard Pearson expressed exactly what Britain was feeling at that moment. The passage of time has mellowed the British view of 'Jones the pirate' and nowhere is his memory cherished more these days than in Whitehaven, the scene of his first raid on British soil, while in recent years the humble cottage where he was born has been wonderfully transformed into a museum, and appropriately the training ship of the Scottish Sea Cadets bears his name.

But it is in his adopted country, which he served so well, yet in which he spent only a relatively short time, that his memory is undimmed. In the days, weeks and months that followed 7 December 1941, that day that will live for ever in infamy, there was not a single American who was not stirred and uplifted by the immortal words of John Paul Jones: 'I have not yet begun to fight!'

His indomitable fighting spirit is his greatest legacy.

Bibliography

MANUSCRIPT MATERIAL

Public Record Office, London (PRO):
Admiralty Records
Naval Office Lists

Bodleian Library, Oxford:
Firth Collection

Archives Nationales, Paris (AN):
Marine Papers

Library of Congress, Washington, DC (LC):
Benjamin Franklin Papers
Gouverneur Morris Papers
Marine Committee Letter Book
Papers of the Continental Congress, 1777–89, especially vols. 54, 58, 147, 168, 193 and 639
Peter Force Collection of John Paul Jones Letters and Documents, nine volumes

Library of the Navy Department, Washington, DC:
Court Martial Testimony at the Trial of Captain Pierre Landais
Files of Letters and Records pertaining to John Paul Jones
Logs of *Ranger* and *Bonhomme Richard*
Pièces Justicatives

Library of the Naval Academy Museum, Annapolis, Maryland:
Janette Taylor Notes
Robert Morris Letter Book
John Paul Jones Letter Book (March 1778 to July 1779)
John L. Senior Moscow Papers

Library of the American Philosophical Society, Philadelphia (APS):
Bache Papers of Benjamin Franklin
Papers of Benjamin Franklin

Library of the University of Pennsylvania, Philadelphia:
Papers of Benjamin Franklin

Pierpont Morgan Library, New York:
Correspondence of JPJ with the Earl and Countess of Selkirk, George Washington and Captain Hector McNeill
Filkin Collection (mainly contemporary newspaper accounts)
Letters and Reports relating to the *Ranger* and *Bonhomme Richard*, from the records of the Admiralty, Board of Customs and Foreign Office, London

Public Library, New York:
Letters of Samuel Adams
Letters and autobiographical journal of Arthur Lee
Letters of JPJ to Hector McNeill
Letter Book of the United States Navy Board, Eastern District, Boston, 1778–79

Harvard University Library:
Arthur Lee Collections

Library of the Massachusetts Grand Lodge, Boston:
Correspondence of JPJ with Edward Bancroft, Gouverneur Morris, Robert Morris and John Ross

Bibliography

PRINTED BOOKS

Adams, Charles F. (ed.), *The Works of John Adams* (Boston, 1851)

Allen, Gardner W., *Captain Hector McNeill of the Continental Navy* (Boston, 1922)

André, Benoit, *Mémoires de Paul Jones* (Paris, 1798)

Barnes, John S. (ed.), *Fanning's Narrative* (New York, 1912)

Buell, Augustus C., *Paul Jones Founder of the American Navy: A History* (New York, 1900)

Chase, Thomas, *Sketches of the Life, Character and Times of Paul Jones* (Richmond, Virginia, 1859)

De Koven, Mrs Reginald, *The Life and Letters of John Paul Jones* (New York, 1913)

Golder, F.A., *John Paul Jones in Russia* (New York, 1927)

Lockwood, David (ed.), *The Battle of Flamborough Head* (Dumfries, 1997)

Lorenz, Lincoln, *John Paul Jones* (New York, 1943)

Lorenz, Lincoln, *The Admiral and the Empress* (New York, 1954)

Mackenzie, Alexander S., *The Life of Paul Jones* (New York, 1841–46)

Morison, Samuel E., *John Paul Jones: A Sailor's Biography* (Boston, 1959)

Paullin, Charles O., *Outletters of the Continental Marine Committee and Board of Admiralty* (New York, 1914)

Rogers, Ernest C., *Connecticut's Naval Office at New London During the American Revolution* (New London, 1933)

Russell, Phillips, *John Paul Jones: Man of Action* (New York, 1927)

Sands, Robert C., *The Life and Correspondence of John Paul Jones* (New York, 1830)

Seitz, Don C., *Paul Jones: His Exploits in English Seas* (New York, 1917)

Sherburne, John H., *The Life and Character of Paul Jones* (London, 1825)

Taylor, Janette, *Memoirs of Rear-Admiral Paul Jones* (Edinburgh, 1830)

Thomson, Valentine, *Knight of the Seas* (New York, 1939)

Urquhart, James, *John Paul Jones* (Dumfries, 1982)

Notes

1. Arbigland, 1747–61

1. Every biography of JPJ, right down to Urquhart (1982) and Lockwood (1997), gives his mother's maiden name as MacDuff or McDuff. Lorenz (1943) even went so far as to make much of JPJ's Highland ancestry. Several bogus entries appear in the International Genealogical Index relating to John Paul Senior and Jean MacDuff, apparently entered by Joshua H. Paul, an amateur genealogist, although they appear alongside the genuine entries of John Paul and Jean Duff

2. Augustus C. Buell, *Paul Jones: Founder of the American Navy* (New York, 1900), hereafter referred to as Buell, vol. I, p.3

3. An inaccurate family tree showing the descendants of John Paul appears in James Urquhart, *John Paul Jones* (1982). The details given by Lorenz are based on Sands, who presumably got them from Janette Taylor, but they are completely untrue and show the fallacy of believing family oral tradition. John Paul senior was born at Leith on 27 January 1700, the son of John Paul and Elizabeth Wright. George Paul, on the other hand, was born at Edinburgh on 16 August 1690, the son of William Paul and Joannett Reid

4. This was first asserted in 'Letter of a Fellow Lodger', published in an anonymous review of Sherburne's biography in *US Literary Magazine*, 15 October 1825

5. JPJ to Baron Van der Capellen, 29 November 1779. See W.H. de Beaufort, *Brieven van en aan J.D. Van der Capellen*

Van de Poll (Utrecht, 1879), pp.151–2

6. James Craik (1730–1814) of Arbigland emigrated to Virginia where he practised medicine at Norfolk and Winchester and then served with Washington

7. Robert Burns, autobiographical letter to Dr John Moore, 2 August 1787

8. Buell, vol. I., p.5

9. Robert C. Sands, *The Life and Correspondence of John Paul Jones* (New York, 1830), hereafter referred to as Sands, p.22

2. Ship's Boy to Sailing Master, 1761–73

1. Samuel E. Morison, *John Paul Jones: A Sailor's Biography* (Boston, 1959), hereafter referred to as Morison, p.11. JPJ's biographers antedated his departure from Whitehaven by a year, in the spring of 1760. This date is impossible as the *Friendship*, according to the British Naval Office lists, arrived at the Rappahannock from Whitehaven in January or February 1760, cleared thence for Whitehaven on 12 May and arrived back in Virginia on 7 May 1761 from Whitehaven via Barbados

2. There is absolutely no truth in this assertion by Buell (vol. I, p.6)

3. Franklin Papers in APS, memorandum dated 6 March 1779

4. The Naval Academy Museum has a fragment from the ledger of Thomas Riche, merchant, for '£40 on account', signed Jno Paul 6 June 1764, for slaves delivered in some West Indian port

5. Lincoln Lorenz, *John Paul Jones* (New York, 1943), hereafter referred to as

Lorenz, p.13

6. JPJ to Robert Morris, 4 September 1776, in Peter Force Collection, vol. I

7. Ibid., vol. IX, JPS to 'US Minister of Marine at the Close of the War, 1782'

8. Morison, p.419

9. Lorenz, pp.13–14

10. Naval Office lists, in PRO London

11. Mrs Reginald De Koven, *The Life and Letters of John Paul Jones* (New York, 1913), hereafter referred to as De Koven, vol. I, pp.12–13

12. Phillips Russell, *John Paul Jones: Man of Action* (New York, 1927), where a facsimile is reproduced

13. Nathaniel Fanning, *Fanning's Narrative* (New York, 1806). Reprinted 1912 and, in an edited version by David Lockwood, entitled *The Battle of Flamborough Head* (Dumfries, 1997), p.3

14. Morison, p.13

15. Joseph Robinson, in *Transactions of the Dumfries and Galloway Natural History and Antiquarian Society*, NS Vol. XX (1907–8), pp.179–80

16. JPS to Benjamin Franklin, 6 March 1779, in Franklin Papers, APS

3. Virginia, 1773–75

1. Sands, p.30

2. Lorenz, pp.29–31

3. Thomas Chase, *Sketches of the Life, Character and Times of Paul Jones* (Richmond, Virginia, 1859)

4. Samuel E. Morison, in *William and Mary Quarterly*, 3rd series, XVI, No. 2 (April 1959) and *American Neptune* (October 1955) for a discussion of the Willie Jones myth and the heraldry of JPJ

5. Morison, p.413

4. Lieutenant John Paul Jones, 1776

1. G.O. Trevelyan, *The American Revolution* (London, 1899), p.365

2. Peter Force Collection, vol. IV

3. Papers of the Continental Congress, August-September 1775

4. Robert Beatson, *Naval and Military Memoirs of Great Britain*, vol. VI

5. *US Navy Regulations*, reprinted by the

Naval History Foundation

6. JPJ to US Minister of Marine, 1782, in Peter Force Collection, vol. IX

7. Ernest C. Rogers, *Connecticut's Naval Office at New London during the American Revolution* (New London Historical Society, 1933), pp.130–1

8. Biddle correspondence, in *Pennsylvania Magazine of History*, vol. LXXIV (1950), p.348

9. JPJ to Joseph Hewes, 17 August 1777, in Peter Force Collection, vol. II

10. JPJ to Hewes, 19 May 1776, in Peter Force Collection, vol. I

11. Edward Field, *Esek Hopkins* (Providence, 1898), p.95

12. Letter of Montford Browne to Lord George Germain, 5 November 1776, cited by Lorenz, p.66

13. JPJ to Joseph Hewes, 14 April 1776, in Peter Force Collection, vol. I

14. The full text, from the Hayes MSS, Edenton, is reproduced in Morison, pp.55–7

15. JPJ to Captain Abraham Whipple, 31 October 1776 in Naval Academy Museum Library

5. Captain Jones, 1776

1. Marine Committee to JPJ, Philadelphia 6 August 1776, reproduced in full in Morison, pp.59–60

2. Sands, pp.48–9

3. Ibid., p.51

4. *Boston Independent Chronicle*, 17 October 1776

5. JPJ to Robert Morris, 17 October 1776. Peter Force Collection, vol. V

6. Morison, pp.68–9

7. JPJ to Joseph Hewes, 1 September 1777, Peter Force Collection, vol. II

8. Hopkins to Marine Committee, 2 November 1776, Peter Force Collection, vol. V

9. See, for example, Lorenz pp.89–90, 97–101 and 105–7. Morison (p.79) was the first biographer to ascertain the truth and set the record straight

10. JPJ to the Marine Committee, 12 November 1776, in Papers of the

Continental Congress in Library of
Congress, No. 58
11. Sands p.57

6. Boston and Portsmouth, 1777
1. Morison, p.92
2. Benjamin Franklin to JPJ, 21 June 1780,
reprinted in De Koven, vol. II, p.131
3. John Hancock to Robert Morris, 17
January 1777; no. 1183 in Stan V.
Henkel's Catalogue (1907)
4. Robert Morris to Esek Hopkins, 5
February 1777, in *Outletters of the Marine
Committee* (ed. Charles O. Paullin, 1914)
5. Robert Morris to JPJ, 1 February 1777,
Marine Committee Letter Book
6. Esek Hopkins to JPJ, 1 March 1777, in
Papers of the Continental Congress, LC
7. Esek Hopkins to Robert Morris, 28
January 1777, in *The Letter Book of Esek
Hopkins* (ed. William D. Miller), Rhode
Island Historical Society (1932)
8. Morison, p.97
9. Sands, pp.67–8
10. Facsimile in Morison, p.108
11. Text of poem accompanied by an undated letter to Captain Hector McNeill,
in the McNeill MSS, Morgan Library
12. Buell, vol. II, p.341; Roster of the
Ranger
13. Paullin, op. cit., vol. I, p.71, William
Whipple to Josiah Bartlett
14. Ibid., p.65, JPJ to John Brown, 31
October 1777

7. Paimboeuf to Whitehaven, 1777–78
1. Reproduced in full by Morison,
pp.115–16, the original being still in the
possession of the Wendell family
2. JPJ to Robert Morris, 11 December
1777, Peter Force Collection, vol. II
3. Morison, p.118
4. Lorenz, p.129
5. De Koven vol. I, pp.256–7; Archives
Nationales, Marine B7, 459
6. Orders reproduced in B.F. Stevens,
Facsimiles, XI, no. 1062
7. Gurley's report in Admiralty 1–3972,
PRO
8. Morison, p.137

9. Quoted by Morison, p.142; see Hugh
Walpole, *Journal of the Reign of King
George III, 1771–1783*, vol. I. Buell, vol.
II, p.280, asserted that JPJ spent several
days at Walpole's home at Strawberry
Hill, Twickenham, in 1791, but this is
quite without foundation

8. St Mary's Isle and After, 1778
1. Countess of Selkirk to Earl of Selkirk,
24 April 1778; full text reproduced in
Lorenz, p.155
2. Mary Elliot to a cousin in Roxburgh, 24
April 1778, quoted by Morison, p.146
3. Newspaper cutting headed 'Extract of a
Letter from Holland', from an
unidentified London newspaper, 1
December 1779, in the Jones scrapbook,
Naval Academy Museum, Annapolis
4. Sands, p.355
5. Lord Daer to Earl of Selkrik, quoted by
Lorenz, p.531
6. Jones letterbook for 1778, Admiralty
1–3972, PRO
7. Ezra Green, *The Diary of Ezra Green*, 25
April 1778, in The Historical and
Genealogical Register (January and April
1879)
8. Lorenz, p.173
9. JPJ to the Commissioners, 27 May
1778, reproduced in John H. Sherburne,
The Life of Paul Jones (London, 1825),
hereafter referred to as Sherburne, p.83
10. Morison, p.169

9. Bonhomme Richard, 1778–79
1. On the death of his father in 1785 he
became Duc d'Orléans and was later
known as Philippe Egalité for his
espousal of the revolution, but went to
the guillotine in November 1793. His
son was Louis Philippe, King of France,
1830–48
2. JPJ to Sartine, Archives Nationales,
Marine B7, 459
3. Sands, p.135
4. Ibid., p.136
5. Ibid.
6. Ibid., p.137
7. Sherburne, pp.86–7

8. Lorenz, pp.241–2
9. The full text appears in Morison, pp.185–6
10. Diary of John Adams, entries of 12 and 15 May 1779, in *The Works of John Adams* (ed. Charles F. Adams, Boston, 1851)
11. Ibid., vol. III, p.201
12. JPJ to Benjamin Franklin, 4 July 1779, in Franklin Papers, Library of the American Philosophical Society, Philadelphia

10. The Way to Flamborough Head, August-September 1779

1. Sherburne, p.141; Buell, vol. II, pp.345–51; Morison, p.205
2. Deposition by Colonel Weibert in Thévenard's reports, Archives Nationales, Marine B4, 138f.158
3. Richard Dale, *The Life of Commodore Dale*, in The Port Folio, June 1814; Nathaniel Fanning, *Fanning's Narrative* (New York, 1806, 1912), a portion being reprinted as *The Battle of Flamborough Head* (ed. David Lockwood), Dumfries, 1997; Kilby's narrative in *Scribner's Magazine*, XXXVIII (1905), pp.24–41
4. Jones's ultimatum in *Proceedings of the Society of Antiquaries of Scotland*, 4th series, vol. IV (1906), pp.89–90 (ed. F.C. Inglis)
5. Ibid., report by an unnamed member of the yacht's crew to Captain Napier, RN, in Admiralty 1–2221, Captains' Letters N, PRO
6. *St James Chronicle*, 30 September 1790
7. Text of the prayer as reprinted in the *Edinburgh Evening Dispatch*, September 1779, from an undated cutting in the JPJ file of records and letters in the Navy Department Library, Washington, DC
8. Pearson's report in Admiralty Papers 1–3972
9. Fanning, op. cit.
10. Morison, p.237n
11. JPJ's report in his MSS, vol. V, 7286, 7289

11. Alliance, 1779–80

1. Fanning, *Narrative* (1997 edition), p.17
2. *London Gazetteer and New General Advertizer*, 19 October 1779
3. Don C. Seitz, *Paul Jones: His Exploits in English Seas* (New York, 1917), p.61
4. Statistical Account of Scotland, Kirkbean parish (1791) by Revd Edward Neilson. This negative view lingered on for more than a century, cf. *Encyclopaedia Britannica*, 9th edition (1876) and other popular reference works
5. Paul Jones MS in the Firth Collection, Bodleian Library, Oxford; text in Morison, pp.247–8
6. John Adams manuscript autobiography, Adams MSS reel 180, Boston Public Library
7. JPJ to William Carmichael, December 1779, Papers of the Pennsylvania Historical Society, Philadelphia
8. *London Evening Post*, 28 October 1779
9. Seitz, p.55
10. JPJ to Dr Edward Bancroft, from The Texel, 26 October 1779
11. Sands, pp.317–18
12. Earl of Sandwich to Captain Francis Reynolds, RN, 23 November 1779, in *Proceedings of the Massachusetts Historical Society*, vol. VIII, p.77
13. Henry Lunt to JPJ, quoted in Morison, pp.271–2

12. Heights of Glory, 1780–81

1. *Facsimiles of Manuscripts in European Archives Relating to America, 1773–83* (ed. B.F. Stevens, London, 1889–93), no. 727
2. F. de la Dixmerie, *Discours addressé par le premier orateur . . . à l'illustré F.: Paul Jones, La Loge des Neuf Soeurs, Paris* (Geneva, 1780)
3. Edward E. Hale, *Franklin in France* (Boston, 1887), vol. II, p.367
4. *Letters of Abigail Adams* (Boston, 1848), p.208
5. Elisabeth Vigée Lebrun, *Souvenirs* (Paris, 1882)
6. Sands, p.288; Morison, p.280; and Lorenz, p.403, the last-named also reproducing the verses

7. Jones MSS, Peter Force Collection, Library of Congress

8. Ibid. The text of the originals in French, with English translations appear in Morison, pp.285–7

9. Cf. Robert Burns to Agnes McLehose. JPJ, like Burns, read Henry Mackenzie's novel, *The Man of Feeling*, first published in 1771, and subsequently modelled himself on the eponymous hero Harley

10. Full text in Sherburne, pp.324–5 and Lorenz, pp.444–5

11. Sands, p.278

12. Register officiel des Emigrés, 1793, in Archives Nationales, Paris

13. Transcript in Naval Academy Museum, Annapolis

14. Archives Nationales, Paris, Marine B3, 683

15. Ibid.

13. In America Again, 1781–83

1. Queries to JPJ, his answers, and Board of Admiralty recommendations in Papers of the Continental Congress, 1777–89, vol. 37; answers reprinted in full in Sherburne, pp.224–34

2. Logs of *Serapis*, *Alliance* and *Ariel* (ed. John S. Barnes), Naval History Society, New York, 1911, Appendix B, pp.125–27

3. Alexander S. Mackenzie, *The Life of Paul Jones* (New York, 1841–46)

4. Karl G. Tornqvist, *The Naval Campaigns of Count de Grasse* (trans. Amandus Johnson), Swedish Colonial Society, 1942

5. JPJ to Hector McNeill, 25 May 1782, in McNeill MSS, Morgan Library

6. Ibid. JPJ to McNeill, 15 November 1781

7. JPJ to the Comtesse de Nicolson from Portsmouth, New Hampshire, 25 December 1781, Peter Force Collection, vol. VII; full text in Lorenz, pp.490–1

8. JPJ to Gouverneur Morris, 2 September 1782, Gouverneur Morris Papers, Library of Congress

9. JPJ to Robert Morris, quoted in Sands, p.309

10. JPJ undated memo to the US Minister of Marine, Peter Force Collection, vol. IX

14. Twilight of the Ancien Régime, 1783–88

1. Mary Barney (ed.), *Joshua Barney: A Biographical Memoir* (Boston, 1832), p.143

2. Ibid., p.144

3. *London Chronicle*, 8 December 1783, recording JPJ's exact times of arrival and departure and remarking on his extremely short stay

4. Lorenz, p.515

5. Sherburne, p.234

6. JPJ to John Ross, 25 August 1785, in Massachusetts Grand Lodge, Boston

7. John Jeffries' diary entry for 11 January 1785, in *Magazine of History* (1910)

8. Ibid. Entry for 11 February 1785

9. Julian Boyd (ed.), *Correspondence of Thomas Jefferson* (New York, 1955), vols. XII and XIII

10. Lorenz, Appendix III, Madame Tellison and Madame T, pp.778–9

11. Statement of accounts in Proceedings of Congress: 24th Congress, 2nd Session, House Documents 19 and 115; 30th Congress, 1st Session, House Report No. 9; 37th Congress, 2nd Session, Senate Executive Document No. 11

12. Benoit André, *Mémoire de Paul Jones* (Paris, 1798)

15. Pavel Ivanovich Jones, 1788–89

1. Letter of Comte de Wemyss, 18 February 1785, reproduced by F.A. Golder, *John Paul Jones in Russia* (New York, 1927), a collection of letters concerning JPJ in relation to Prince Potemkin and the Empress Catherine II, hereafter referred to as Golder

2. Ibid., 20 March 1785

3. Sands, p.403

4. Ibid. p.404

5. Morison, p.364, without identifying his source

6. Sands, p.406

7. Golder, JPJ to Potemkin, 7 June 1788
8. Golder, JPJ to Ribas, 11/22 June 1788
9. Text in Morison, p.373
10. *Biblioteka dlia Tchenia* (St Petersburg, 1844), vol. LCV, Sec. 3, pp.1–46
11. *Russkaya Starina*, vol. XVI (1876), p.473
12. Sands, p.457
13. Ibid., p.444
14. Ibid., p.453
15. The original French version of the Narrative has never been found; perhaps some day it may surface among the vast archives in St Petersburg. Fortunately JPJ kept a draft and this was used by Sands for his edition of 1830. A complete MS copy of the *pièces justicatives* in French is in the Library of the Grand Lodge of Masons of Massachusetts, Boston
16. L.P. de Ségur, *Tableau Historique et Politique de l'Europe*, (Paris, 1803), vol. III, p.499
17. Golder, p.141
18. Ibid.
19. Facsimile of the letter reproduced in Lorenz, *The Admiral and the Empress* (New York, 1954), p.188, with a translation opposite. The original MS is now in the Naval Academy Museum, Annapolis. A more accurate translation is given in Morison, p.388

16. Last Years, 1789–92

1. James Mackay (ed.), *The Complete Poetical Works of Robert Burns* (Ayr, 1993), p.477. This ballad, sung to the tune 'The Campbells are Comin'', was written by Burns in December 1792. The stanza quoted refers to the second partition of Poland which took place earlier that year
2. Sands, pp.501–2. JPJ's letter to Madame de Tornatie de Valery quotes extensively from Thomson's *Seasons*
3. Morison, p.393
4. JPJ to Madame Le Mair d'Altigny, in Sands, pp.512–13
5. *The Naval Chronicle* (Washington, 1906–10)
6. Thomas Carlyle, *The French Revolution* (London, 1826), vol. II, p.38
7. Sands, p.496
8. JPJ to Lafayette, 7 December 1790, reproduced in Sands, p.505
9. Gouverneur Morris, *A Diary of the French Revolution, 1778–93* (ed. Beatrice Davenport, Boston, 1939)
10. JPJ to Janet Taylor from Amsterdam, March 1790, in Sands, pp.513–14
11. Sands, pp.565–6
12. Golder, Catherine II to Baron Grimm, 15 August 1792
13. *Encyclopaedia Britannica*, vol. XIII (1876), pp.738–9
14. Janette Taylor was tricked by an unscrupulous American publisher, Sherman Converse, hence *The Life and Correspondence of John Paul Jones* by Robert Sands. This explains the curious situation whereby two different books based on the Taylor collection of Jones papers appeared more or less simultaneously

Glossary of Nautical Terms

boom horizontal spar at the foot of the mainsail

bowsprit spar projecting forward from the bow

box the compass to name the 32 points of the compass in sequence

brig two-masted, square-rigged sailing vessel

brigantine similar but lacking a square mainsail

cathead projecting piece of timber near the bow, to which the anchor is secured

flag rank rank above captain (e.g. commodore or admiral), entitled to display a flag with one or more stars denoting rank

flagship ship carrying the fleet commander

frigate three-masted warship, smaller than a ship of the line (qv)

gaff spar on which the head of a fore-and-aft sail is extended

general quarters action stations

grape(shot) cluster of small iron balls

heave to bring ship to a halt with head to wind

helm wheel controlling the ship's steering

hull down ship viewed end on

jury rig rig for temporary use

lateen-rigged rigged with triangular sails

letter of marque commission by a belligerent nation to a merchant ship authorising it to attack and seize enemy ships, hence letter-of-marque, a synonym for privateer (qv)

man-o'-war a warship

port left side of a ship, facing forward

privateer armed private ship authorised to cruise against enemy shipping

reef to reduce a sail by rolling up all or part of it

sail expanse of fabric to catch or deflect the wind, hence the collective noun 'sail' denoting a number of ships

schooner two-masted, fore-and-aft rigged vessel

seventy-four colloquial term for a first-rate ship of the line, from the number of guns normally carried

shallop (French *chaloupe*) small, open boat

ship square-rigged vessel with a bowsprit and three masts

ship of the line the largest ship of war, with three masts and three gundecks as well as a main deck, also known as a liner or battleship, so-called because they formed the line of battle in the forefront of a naval engagement

shrouds pairs of ropes from the masthead giving lateral support to the mast

sloop fore-and-aft rigged vessel with one mast and a single foresail

sloop of war small warship with guns on one deck only

square-rig rig in which the principal sails are square

starboard right side of a ship, facing forward

stern-chasers guns mounted on the stern to ward off attack from the rear

strike (colours) lower the flag as a signal of surrender

tack the direction of a ship in regard to the trim of her sails; e.g. the port tack, when she has the wind on her portside. To tack means to pursue a zigzag course against the wind

tiller lever used to turn the rudder from side to side

truck small wooden cap at the top of the flagstaff

wear ship go about by turning the bow away from the wind

Index